IRISH ECOMEDIA

Under the Sign of Nature: Explorations in
Environmental Humanities

SARAH DIMICK, ALISON GLASSIE, AND JESSE OAK TAYLOR, EDITORS

IRISH ECOMEDIA
Empire and Environmental Justice in the
Modernization of Postcolonial Ireland

Katherine M. Huber

University of Virginia Press • *Charlottesville and London*

The University of Virginia Press is situated on the traditional lands of the Monacan Nation, and the Commonwealth of Virginia was and is home to many other Indigenous people. We pay our respect to all of them, past and present. We also honor the enslaved African and African American people who built the University of Virginia, and we recognize their descendants. We commit to fostering voices from these communities through our publications and to deepening our collective understanding of their histories and contributions.

University of Virginia Press
© 2026 by the Rector and Visitors of the University of Virginia
All rights reserved
Printed in the United States of America on acid-free paper

First published 2026

9 8 7 6 5 4 3 2 1

LIBRARY OF CONGRESS CATALOGING-IN-PUBLICATION DATA

Names: Huber, Katherine M., author
Title: Irish ecomedia : empire and environmental justice in the modernization of postcolonial Ireland / Katherine M. Huber.
Description: Charlottesville : University of Virginia Press, 2025. | Series: Under the sign of nature : explorations in environmental humanities | Includes bibliographical references and index.
Identifiers: LCCN 2025018446 (print) | LCCN 2025018447 (ebook) | ISBN 9780813954387 hardback | ISBN 9780813954394 paperback | ISBN 9780813954400 ebook
Subjects: LCSH: Ecocriticism—Ireland | Environmentalism in mass media | BISAC: LITERARY CRITICISM / European / English, Irish, Scottish, Welsh | MUSIC / History & Criticism
Classification: LCC PN98.E36 H83 2025 (print) | LCC PN98.E36 (ebook)
LC record available at https://lccn.loc.gov/2025018446
LC ebook record available at https://lccn.loc.gov/2025018447

Cover art: Downings pier, Co. Donegal, CDB47 (courtesy of the National Library of Ireland); letter background: ivstiv/istock.com
Cover design: Michael Kellner

To my mother, Sheila Malloy Huber, who has always generously and patiently provided me with a smooth path in life to pursue all my persistent questions

CONTENTS

List of Illustrations		ix
Acknowledgments		xi
Introduction		1
1	1891–1922: Photography and the Vision for Modernized Relationships to Land	25
2	1922–1950: A Critique of Picturesque Poverty as Progress in Flann O'Brien's *The Third Policeman*	66
3	1950–1970: Oral Traditions on Radio as Alternative Forms of Development in Seán Ó Riada's *Our Musical Heritage*	102
4	1970–1995: Ecomedia Embedded in Earth's Archive in Éilís Ní Dhuibhne's *The Bray House*	152
5	1995–2010: Reading Multispecies Modernities in Postcolonial Cinema Through Risteard Ó Domhnaill's *The Pipe*	188
	Conclusion: New Directions for Multiple Modernities	219
	Notes	229
	Bibliography	267
	Index	285

ILLUSTRATIONS

1. Robert John Welch, *View of Cappagh Village, Castlerea District, Co. Galway*, ca. 1906–1914   26
2. Robert John Welch, *House on Cloonmore Grass Farm near Tuam, Co. Galway*, ca. 1906–1914   32–33
3. Congested Districts Board, *Lord and Lady Aberdeen with Nurse, Outside House at Geesala, Ballina, Co. Mayo*, ca. 1906–1914   34
4. Congested Districts Board, *Frame for a New Concrete House on a Grass Farm in the Castlerea District, Co. Galway*, ca. 1906–1914   42
5. Robert John Welch, *View of Congested Village of Graigue, Co. Galway, from Where Migrants Were Taken to Holdings in Graigueachuillaire*, ca. 1906–1914   44
6. Robert John Welch, *A Grass Farm in Graigueachuillaire, Seven Miles North of Tuam, Co. Galway*, ca. 1906–1914   46
7. Robert John Welch, *A Grass Farm in Graigueachuillaire, Seven Miles North of Tuam, Co. Galway*, ca. 1906–1914   47
8. Robert John Welch, *View from the New Dwelling House of Mrs Bridget Kelly, Lisvalley Vesey, near Tuam, Co. Galway*, ca. 1906–1914   51
9. Robert John Welch, *House of Mrs Bridget Kelly, Lisvalley Vesey, near Tuam, Co. Galway*, ca. 1906–1914   54
10. Congested Districts Board, *Group of Cottages Beside the Sea*, ca. 1906–1914   59
11. Congested Districts Board, *Curing Fish, Downings Pier, Co. Donegal*, ca. 1906–1914   61
12. Congested Districts Board, *Downings Pier, Co. Donegal*, ca. 1906–1914   62
13. Paul Henry (1876–1958), *Connemara Cottages*, ca. 1936–1937   84
14. Aerial shots of the rural landscape in *The Pipe*   194
15. The Gardaí throw protesters off the road in *The Pipe*   197
16. Partial views foreground the spectral presence of Shell in *The Pipe*   200

17. Monica Müller walks along a turf-lined road in *The Pipe*   210
18. Officers laugh as the tide permeates Shell's boundary in *The Pipe*   213
19. Partial views register the limits of visual representations in *The Pipe*   217

ACKNOWLEDGMENTS

Despite the solitary work writing a book requires, the end result would not have been possible without the countless people and places that have contributed to my thinking and writing over the years. The interests that eventually led to this book began a long time ago and far from a university campus, when I worked on traditional sailing ships after graduating high school instead of going to college. At the time, I believed that I could learn more by living in a shipboard community and visiting new places than I could in a classroom. But I remember the exact moment I knew I needed to go to college: I had been working on sailing ships as a deckhand and medical officer for three years, and I was sitting at sunset on a two-masted schooner anchored off the island of Mayreau in the Northern Grenadines. This sounds idyllic, but at the time, I felt very conflicted. The people of Mayreau had recently bought "their" half of the island from a wealthy man who lived on St. Vincent. He had built a chain-link fence down the middle of the island. The islanders were limited to one side of the island because the owner of the other half rented the beach out to cruise ship companies. How could people who had lived on this island for generations be literally fenced in by property laws? I started asking questions like this, and I am grateful to my friend and shipmate, Beth Doxsee, who jokingly pointed out at the time that I was probably "doomed to academia." My experiences living in shipboard communities provided me with so much guidance and friendship during this formative period of my life that eventually led me into higher education.

In my quest to understand relationships between land and power, I earned my bachelor's and master's degrees at Leiden University in the Netherlands in literary studies. During my studies, I had many mentors who helped frame my thinking and ideas about postcolonial studies and the environment. I am especially grateful to Isabel Hoving, Frans-Willem Korsten, Madeleine Kasten, and Yasco Horsman, all of whom never gave up on me as I struggled to keep up with my classmates while earning a bachelor's degree in Dutch. My friends in literary studies Petra Opbroek, Janny Ramakers, Isabelle Bartholomey, Sharon Hagenbeek, and Tamara Kool, my many housemates in college, especially Koos Knijnenburg and

Ruud van den Hooff, and my good friends Caroline Olijve, Xiomara Sánchez, Nafiss Nia, Henrik Söderholm, and the Schokkenbroeks all gave me tremendous support as I navigated Dutch academia and acquired the skills and knowledge that I needed to answer the pressing questions I had encountered in the Caribbean. *Ik ben zo ontzettend dankbaar voor al je steun en vriendschap over de jaren!* I am also very grateful to Peter Burger and Willem Koetsenruijter in the journalism and new media minor at Leiden University, without whose support and permission to pursue this Dutch-language minor, I may never have landed the jobs in journalism and communications in the Netherlands that enabled me to regularly travel to Ireland with Irish friends to play music.

With Dublin singer-songwriter Paul O'Brien I arranged flute accompaniment for an album of songs about ports around the Netherlands and Ireland. This project on ports, spaces typically at the intersections of cultures, metaphorically and literally, brought me to places that had been affected by the same colonial and neocolonial systems of land reform and development that I had encountered during my time as a deckhand in the Caribbean. As I learned from Irish people like Paul, but also my good friend Greg Tuohy, and as I encountered the Irish language and oral cultures, like Irish traditional music, I began to see how Ireland both fit and challenged the theoretical frameworks of postcolonial ecocriticism about which I had written my master's thesis, a project that examined postcolonial writing in South Africa. These observations led me to feel the needling pressure of questions from outside academic discourse insisting that I reenter scholarly conversations about how we make sense of power and the material impacts of empire. For this, I am grateful to all who inspired and supported me on my journey back to the university after six years working in communications, especially Daný van Dam, Mary Malloy, Peggy Malloy, and Frank Power, who read floundering drafts of my graduate school applications as I tried twice to return to the Pacific Northwest and pursue a PhD.

This book would not have been possible without my graduate studies at the University of Oregon (UO). I am so utterly grateful to Mark Quigley and Sarah Wald, my dissertation advisors, whose comments on countless drafts shaped me as a writer and thinker when I had, to use one of my favorite professor's words, "the seeds of a few good ideas." Mark and Sarah have remained inspiring mentors to me as I completed my PhD and began teaching high school in rural Oregon, and they encouraged me as I returned to academia in the Netherlands at Tilburg University. Throughout my graduate studies, I had the generous support of the UO English Department, which introduced me to the incredible intellectual mentors I have had in Paul Peppis, Sharon Luk, Stacy Alaimo, Lara Bovilsky, Sangita Gopal, Elizabeth Bohls, Gordon Sayre, David Vázquez, Brent Dawson, Heidi Kaufman, Stephanie LeMenager, Betsy Wheeler, Mark Whalan, Mary Wood, Kirby Brown, Erin Beck, Jamie Bufalino, Miriam Gershow, Carolyn Bergquist, and Emily Simnitt. I am so grateful for the numerous conversations I had with Paul Peppis that have made me a more articulate and detailed thinker and close reader. Sharon Luk always challenged my thinking, and I return again and again to what I learned in her graduate seminar to examine the uneven power relations that shape the material world. I am also extremely grateful to the UO Center for the Study of Women in Society, which generously supported my research in the difficult 2020–21 academic year. Additionally, I want to thank the UO Center for Environmental Futures for introducing me to Mark Carey and Marsha Weisiger. I am grateful to them both for offering me numerous opportunities to expand the interdisciplinary scope of my work by inviting me to the Cascadia environmental history retreats in 2019 and 2020, as well as to the 2018 environmental history excursion to the Oregon Institute of Marine Biology, where I had the opportunity to present a few of my chapters in their very early stages. I am also exceedingly grateful to my friends from graduate school, including Nate Otjen, Sarah Preston, Hayley Brazier, Carmel Ohman, and Liz Curry, with whom I have shared so many ups and downs over the years while we all finished our PhDs during the COVID pandemic.

I have also found incredible support from scholars in Irish studies. I am very thankful to Lucy Collins, whom I met at the Association for the Study of Literature and Environment UK and Ireland (ASLE UKI) conference in Surrey in 2013 as I prepared graduate school applications for the second year in a row. Even though I was not presenting a paper and had no institutional affiliation whatsoever, Lucy generously discussed ecocritical ideas and projects with me, and I am very grateful for Lucy's ongoing mentorship and friendship over the years. I am also so grateful to Marguérite Corporaal, whose lectures I attended as a bachelor's student at Leiden University and who has remained a generous and insightful mentor. Attending Notre Dame's IRISH Seminar in 2018 shaped my project, and I am so grateful to Chris Fox and Catherine Wilsdon for that opportunity. The focus of my third chapter came out of conversations I had with Aileen Dillane at that seminar, and much of the archival research for my first chapter was completed during the seminar's lunch breaks. I also would not have been able to complete my archival research in Ireland without the support of the International Association for Study of Irish Literatures (IASIL), which sponsored my participation in the 2019 IASIL conference at Trinity College Dublin. I am also exceedingly thankful for the mentorship Eóin Flannery, David Lloyd, and Kelly Sullivan have given me as I have sought to learn from their experience and expertise.

I would like to thank all the archivists who made my work possible at the National Library of Ireland, National Photographic Archive, RTÉ Archives, University College Cork (UCC) special collections, and the Irish Traditional Music Archive. I am very grateful to Peadar Ó Riada for granting me permission to view and use archival materials from the Seán Ó Riada Collection/Bailiúchán Sheáin Uí Riada collection at UCC. I am thankful as well to those who answered questions I had about various aspects of the project, including Ciara Breathnach, Risteard Ó Domhnaill, and Orla McCague. I am also very grateful to Risteard Ó Domhnaill for providing permission to use images of *The Pipe* in my fifth chapter.

As I revised my book, I have had an incredible amount of support from my wonderful colleagues in the Department of Culture Studies at Tilburg University. I am especially grateful to Odile Heynders, Inge van de Ven, Inge Beekmans, Jenny Slatman, Élodie Malanda, and Sean Smith for all their mentorship and friendship at this early stage in my academic career. I am also extremely grateful to the research support and funding provided by Tilburg University for this book.

The generosity of so many scholars in the ASLE community has greatly informed my work. I have learned so much from working with ASLE on the executive council as the independent and contingent advocacy officer from 2023 to 2025 and from attending conferences as a graduate student. ASLE scholars founded the field of ecocriticism, and the knowledge and mentorship this organization has provided over the years has been essential to my work on this book. I am sincerely honored to have received the 2024 ASLE Subvention Grant, which provided the funds for licensing the archival materials included in this book.

Additionally, I am extremely grateful to the University of Virginia Press, especially Angie Hogan, the Under the Sign of Nature series editors, the press's faculty board, and the valuable feedback from the anonymous reviewers. Their support was essential to this book.

I would also like to thank the Irish American Cultural Institute (IACI), the *ISLE: Interdisciplinary Studies in Literature and Environment* editors, and Oxford University Press for their permission to reproduce published materials in my first and fifth chapters. My first chapter originally appeared as an article in 2020 in *Éire-Ireland*. My fifth chapter is an extended version of the original article appearing in *ISLE* in 2024.[1]

This book would also not have been possible without my friends and family. A big, warm *go raibh míle maith agaibh* to Bríd Ní Chumhaill and Martin Maguire of the Cloughjordan Ecovillage for generously offering me a room to write in as I met and learned from environmental activists in Ireland in the summer of 2019. The connections I drew through experiences in the world and engaging with academic discourse showed me how studying Ireland's cultural history would contribute to broader understandings of migration amid environmental change, even in my family's history. My great-grandparents emigrated from Lettermullen, Connemara, in County Galway, while the Congested Districts Board, a late imperial land reform agency, worked extensively to modernize fisheries and agriculture in the west of Ireland. These modernization projects and Ireland's later integration into the European Economic Community illuminate how representations of modernization and progress construct understandings of place and nature in changing environmental conditions. Environmental justice movements in Irish communities today harken back to the same history of land relations and cultural representations that brought my great-grandparents to a life in the copper smelter town of Anaconda, Montana. These entangled histories of colonialism, migration, and extraction inform my thinking and research, and I am exceedingly grateful for the support and stories my family has shared with me over the years. I am especially grateful to Sheila, John, and Rebecca Huber, Orlando Velazquez, all the Malloys, and Kathy and John Morefield. I also cannot thank Seho Chon enough for all the love and support throughout the final years of this project, particularly as I revised this book during our international move to the Netherlands.

Finally, I want to thank the environments and communities that have supported me as I wrote this book. The colonization and modernization of Ireland contributed to the conditions through which I became a settler-scholar on the unceded lands of the Kalapuya peoples where I completed my graduate studies and began this book. As an uninvited occupant of Kalapuya Ilihi, the traditional homeland of Kalapuya descendants, who are primarily citizens of the Confederated Tribes of Grand Ronde and the

Confederated Tribes of Siletz Indians, I would like to humbly say *hayu masi*. Indigenous scholarship and colleagues have played a formative role in my thinking about this project and why I needed to write it. I am also grateful to the Confederated Tribes of Coos, Lower Umpqua and Siuslaw Indians and in particular to tribal linguist and council member Enna Helms, from whom I learned so much and with whom I had the honor to work on a project to amplify *sha'yuushtl'a* in the Mapleton School District as I was revising this book. This language project contributed to my understanding of how sleeping languages violently oppressed by colonial powers hold so much power to decolonize and reawaken more enduring relationships to material and cultural environments.

During the research and writing of this book, I wanted to better understand the ways power strategically adapts to occlude modes of resistance and consolidate racialized and gendered forms of power in postcolonial nations like the Republic of Ireland and settler-colonial states like the United States. Ireland offers an important case study for understanding mechanisms of colonial and neocolonial power, and I hope my work supports scholarship and activism that contests colonialism and its ongoing environmental impacts on people and places around the world. Although I may be the sole author of this book, the writing process was not a solitary act. Countless people and places have contributed to this work. To all who helped me, I hope you know how grateful I am for all the encouragement, inspiration, and insight you have given me along the way.

IRISH ECOMEDIA

INTRODUCTION

> If many scholarly historians today no longer take progress as their guiding assumption, the development goal is a legacy of liberal empire so deeply embedded in political and institutional structures and practices that it is difficult for postcolonial societies to shake off; indeed, it is what makes postcolonial societies *postcolonial*. They struggle to "move on" from, even forget, the colonial past to "catch up" and arrive at a long-deferred future marked by freedom and prosperity. But to move only forward in time, to lose the *fullness* of time, the way the past lives in the present and shapes the future, is itself an inhuman and impossible expectation, given how intimately such societies have been shaped by the colonial past—including the historical imagination envisioning progress towards some developmental end.
>
> —Priya Satia, *Time's Monster: How History Makes History*

WHEN SHELL built a ninety-kilometer liquified natural gas (LNG) pipeline through an Irish-language region in northwest Ireland, locals established the Shell-to-Sea environmental justice movement. Shell-to-Sea fought to protect local ways of life and human and more-than-human relationships with surrounding ecosystems established over generations.[1] The movement gained international attention after five men were jailed in 2005 for ninety-four days for refusing government orders to cede land to Shell, and postcolonial solidarities began to emerge. Shell-to-Sea and Ogoni activists from the Niger Delta recognized similarities in how modernization projects in postcolonial nations were reproducing colonial forms of development in their regions even decades after independence.[2] These solidarities led Dr. Owens Wiwa (Ken Saro Wiwa's brother) to march with the Shell-to-Sea activists to the Irish parliament (the Dáil) in Dublin in 2005 to protest the pipeline and the imprisonment of the five local men.[3] Despite more than a decade of struggle to protect the community's ways of life and human and more-than-human relationships with surrounding ecosystems, the pipeline was fully operational by 2015. This struggle and the postcolonial solidarities that arose out of it evoke questions about the ongoing impacts that Ireland's long history as a British colony have on human and more-than-human environments.

Irish Ecomedia: Empire and Environmental Justice in the Modernization of Postcolonial Ireland demonstrates how the foundational connections between European colonialism and the environment formed historically and how they rearticulate themselves through emerging media in the twentieth and twenty-first centuries. Energy extraction projects after Ireland's partial independence in 1922 have imperial-era counterparts that reflect modernization projects implemented in other colonized regions that have since gained national independence. While national independence implies sovereignty and autonomy for a people and a place, postcolonial nations inherit the environmental changes imperial powers imposed on colonies to facilitate ongoing extraction economies. Imperial-era land reforms in Ireland during the nineteenth century broke up the commons and modernized agriculture for beef production through dislocating and relocating indigenous and first-language communities, which formed a precursor to the Gaeltacht (or Irish-speaking region) targeted by Shell's LNG pipeline in the early twenty-first century. Late nineteenth- and early twentieth-century land reform projects established neocolonial economic channels that made the pipeline project possible.

Colonial-era economic channels and forms of development persist in a neocolonial modernity because they have irrevocably altered human and more-than-human communities and their relationships to surrounding environments. These conditions are what I am calling the environmental impacts of empire, which refer to the ways in which colonial histories inscribe themselves on land and human and more-than-human relationships with each other and with their material surroundings. Environmental impacts of empire facilitate neocolonialism, or the globalized economic regimes that maintain geopolitical and social hierarchies carved out during the era of colonialism. Neocolonial economic regimes promote the ongoing transition of ecosystems into natural resources for a globalized economy that continues to marginalize and eradicate first-language oral traditions and traditional ways of life in Ireland, the Global South, and Indigenous, Native, and First-Nations communities in settler-colonial states.[4] Neocolonialism flies under the radar of a globalized neoliberal economy in which, as James Ferguson explains in the context of many African nations, "the movements of capital cross national borders, but they jump from point to point, and huge regions are simply bypassed. Capital does not 'flow' from New York to Angola's oil fields or from London to Ghana's gold mines; it hops, neatly skipping over most of what lies in between."[5] Within and between national borders, neocolonial economies perpetuate marginalization and exclusion through increasingly racist and xenophobic immigration policies in the West that maintain socioeconomic hierarchies and environmental injustices across categories of difference within postcolonial nations.

Tracing the environmental impacts of empire in Ireland revises and expands how postcolonial ecocritical and ecomedia studies scholars understand colonialism in Europe and its impact on media technologies and extraction economies. The artists, writers, musicians, and filmmakers whose work I examine in *Irish Ecomedia* engage with Irish-language oralities and lifeways that demonstrate multiple modernities emerging alongside and in ongoing interactions with the more singular conceptions of modernity envisioned in and resulting from colonial and neocolonial forms of development. My analyses show communities impacted by colonial and neocolonial forms of modernization to co-opt and rework established and emerging media to express forms of self-determination that challenge underlying colonial logics of modernization and assert more environmentally enduring relationships with their material surroundings. The Shell-to-Sea campaign arose during the digitalization of film, as well as the expansion of the Internet.[6] Through these emerging media, environmental justice movements like the Movement for the Survival of the Ogoni People (MOSOP) and Shell-to-Sea could each assert alternative understandings for what development could and should look like in postcolonial nations. They could also form transnational solidarities in protest actions and cultural expression, such as the production of music, albums, and literature that articulate their struggle.

Tracking forms of development in Ireland over the past century exposes connections between colonialism and environment that foreclose the possibility of decolonization and environmental justice, in Ireland and elsewhere. Decolonization requires structural and material shifts away from the colonial systems that have dominated Ireland in historically specific ways since 1169. While national and international media representations of the Shell-to-Sea campaign told a story of development versus a community resistant to change, the community recognized a more complex narrative unfolding. A closer inspection of self-determined narratives during postcolonial development projects gives insight into the resources upon which communities draw to rework media to form coalitions, assert agency, and represent their struggle amid tenacious colonial and neocolonial relationships with material environments. My analyses of photography, novels, poetry, radio, music, and film reveal how communities reclaim media and narrative forms to assert multiple alternative modernities that promise more enduring, just, and decolonized futures.

Why Ireland? Expanding the Geographical and Historical Scope of the Environmental Humanities

The Republic of Ireland's position on the geographic and, at least historically, the economic periphery of Europe, as well as its perceived racial, ethnic, and cultural homogeneity, enable misunderstandings that Ireland fits squarely within theories of the Global North. Globalized systems of environmental exploitation benefit populations in the Global North as they exacerbate the climate crisis and environmental injustices and fortify national borders and inequalities with the Global South. This divided and unequal world raises important questions for postcolonial ecocritics and ecomedia scholars about what cultural and representational trends led to the current planetary and humanitarian crises. While postcolonial ecocritical scholars have rightly examined the impacts of colonialism on postcolonial nations in the Global South, they have yet to engage with how colonialism in Europe shaped and continues to shape the imperial logics that endure in development projects and understandings of progress today. These colonial logics continue to marginalize ethnic and minority populations in Europe and to impact postcolonial nations that reproduce Western forms of development globally. Ecomedia studies scholars often position Ireland within broader histories of film and audio technologies in Europe that overlook the inflections of colonialism and postcolonialism in Irish media histories. By examining the entanglement of colonialism, environment, and media in postcolonial Ireland, my analyses critically assess the Republic of Ireland's position as a kind of model postcolonial nation through which it seems to have transcended its colonial past by developing into the Global North and benefiting from globalized racial and environmental injustices to which it was once historically subordinate.

As Britain's oldest colonial testing ground and as a postcolonial nation within the European Union (EU), Ireland has much to teach postcolonial ecocritics and ecomedia scholars about the relationship among colonialism, media, identity and state formation, and the environment in the era of climate crisis, mass extinction, and persistent pollutants. Settler colonialism and plantation systems in the United States, and forms of partition used in India and Pakistan and Israel and Palestine, were first implemented in Ireland. Additionally, policing systems tested in Ireland were later deployed across the British Empire to coerce native populations into the mechanisms of imperial control. The dehumanizing racist tropes upon which colonial strategies rely have a long history in English laws and media representations of Irish peoples, and these histories continue to inform contemporary racial hierarchies. Scholars such as Jane Ohlmeyer, Joseph Lennon, and Edward Said, among others, have examined how manuscript and print texts like *Topographia Hibernica* (1188) by Gerald of Wales and *A View of the Present State of Irelande* (1596) by Edmund Spenser were written, produced, and reproduced to cultivate the rhetoric of colonialism. Such texts delineated the boundaries between the supposed inhumanity of indigenous Irish people and the rich lands of Ireland that the English deemed theirs to occupy and cultivate.[7] These discursive and colonial histories materially persist in modernization projects that have had irreversible impacts on communities and their environments in Ireland and in former British colonies around the world. Modernization projects to develop Ireland's economy and natural resources over the past century thus provide an opportunity to study the environmental impacts of empire in Ireland and in postcolonial nations that have emulated Ireland's forms of development.

Depictions of Irish modernization in film, photography, radio, literature, and music expose the insidious interconnections among the environmental impacts of empire, emerging media, and modernization projects that extend back to the earliest days of colonial occupation in Ireland in the twelfth century. Through following interactions among media, culture, and environments across the twentieth and twenty-first centuries, *Irish Ecomedia* bears witness to modernization projects that have shaped constructions of Europe and Europeanness and the imperial center and periphery, as well as materially realized the uneven distribution of wealth across the Global North and South. Postcolonial ecocriticism attends to uneven histories of development and power imposed by colonialism, in the words of Graham Huggan and Helen Tiffin, "to contest—also to provide viable alternatives to—western ideologies of development."[8] My analyses show that what is dismissed as seemingly outdated traditions actually imagine alternative possibilities for development and relations to the environment. Irish cultural representations of existent oral traditions and ways of life attend to the deep time implicit in emerging media in the twentieth century as they co-opt these media and media aesthetics to assert multiple alternative modernities. These alternative modernities challenge colonial understandings of progress and demonstrate more enduring relationships among humans, more-than-humans, and material environments. *Irish Ecomedia* unearths these overlooked modernities to reveal the multiple ways in which environments change and modernize through traditional yet innovative relationships to place.

The multiple lived modernities this book reveals in an array of media and their representations of modernization rework binary understandings of the Global North and South, as well as colonial constructions of Europe, Europeanness, and center-periphery frameworks, to provide more multivalent and network-based theoretical frameworks in postcolonial ecocriticism and ecomedia studies. European colonialism is not a single or unified project but, rather, as David Lambert and Alan Lester write, "constellations of multiple trajectories. These trajectories may be those of people, objects, texts and ideas. They may also consist of the movements of rock, sediment, water, ice and air."[9] When scholars map binaries onto colonial-colonized regions, they must attend to the ways such categories obscure ongoing colonial relations and reinforce spatial and temporal divides. To again use the words of Lambert and Lester, "The unquestioning use of categories such as 'centre' and 'periphery' in particular serves not so much to describe, as to reify and perpetuate some of the many spatial distinctions enacted through colonial (and other) unequal relations. At its most damaging, when played out in broader public debates, this reproduction of a language of spatial primacy helps to bolster attitudes and practices of social/racial superiority."[10] My methodological and regional focus disrupts implicit binaries and demonstrates the complex and transnational ways colonialism and neocolonialism continually inform and build on each other. Relationships between colonial and neocolonial regimes expand through spatial networks spanning the entire planet and over the *longue durée* of both human historical and deep time. These networks and relationships shape and reshape environments throughout human and more-than-human communities. Building on postcolonial ecocriticism, ecomedia studies, and Irish studies scholarship, the historical arc and multiple modernities in *Irish Ecomedia* demonstrate interconnections between the environmental impacts of empire in Ireland and the possibilities for how scholars theorize colonial constructions of whiteness, anti-Black immigration policies in the EU, and pervasive forms of antiblackness that segregate the globe geographically and materially.[11]

Despite the environmental impacts that the long history of British colonialism has had on the island of Ireland and on postcolonial nation formation in the Republic, Irish cultural production is conspicuously absent from postcolonial ecocriticism outside of Irish studies. This lacuna implicitly perpetuates misperceptions that Ireland's position in the Global North transcends its colonial past, thereby positioning Ireland as a kind of model postcolonial nation for others (again) to emulate. Such misperceptions further marginalize ongoing histories through which colonial understandings of development continue to perpetuate uneven development while justifying racist immigration policies and nationalisms that actively promote the eradication and erasure of ethnic diversity and indigeneity in Europe. As I will show, economic integration with Europe and modernization projects to develop Ireland's environments reinforce racial and gendered social hierarchies emerging from the history of colonialism, which, in turn, propagate the ongoing environmental impacts of empire. Yet the photographs, film, radio, music, and literature I examine rework and revise implicit assumptions in postcolonial ecocriticism, ecomedia studies, and Irish studies to reveal overlooked pathways for decolonization in Ireland, Europe, and the West. These avenues of decolonization promise more just futures for intersectionally oppressed groups across the Global North and South.

My interpretive and historical approach to reading narrative forms across media offers methods for scholars to recognize the environmental impacts of empire in diverse and sometimes unexpectedly interconnected postcolonial and historical contexts. *Irish Ecomedia* contributes to postcolonial ecocriticism by building on the important scholarship of Elizabeth DeLoughrey, Rob Nixon, and Jennifer Wenzel, who all examine multiple media and narrative forms across postcolonial cultural contexts to explore how human and more-than-human communities respond to and resist colonial forms of development. In *Allegories of the Anthropocene* (2019), DeLoughrey analyzes a broad range of postcolonial texts from the Caribbean and Pacific islands to "allegoriz[e] the Anthropocene, arguing that it is vital to bring the theoretical discourse of the global north into dialogue with communities that both are at the forefront of present climate change and its historical survivors."[12] Drawing the theories of Walter Benjamin into conversation with Indigenous epistemologies of island communities, DeLoughrey reframes Western understandings of modernity and modernization. In keeping with DeLoughrey's overarching project, I draw on the complex position of the island of Ireland as both a postcolonial nation and a settler-colonial statelet situated in the Global North to expand readings of how empire and the ongoing innovation of traditional practices shape and challenge understandings of colonial histories and their effects on contemporary environmental crises.

Like DeLoughrey, Nixon, and Wenzel, I examine local case studies to theorize processes that marginalize and render disposable particular people and places within broader geopolitical hierarchies. My readings draw on concepts like Nixon's idea of the "writer activist" and Wenzel's theory of "reading for the planet" to trace the effects of modernization projects.[13] These projects operate in neocolonial processes of globalization that unevenly distribute the benefits and burdens of extraction economies, as Wenzel describes: "Globalization often works through *localizing* risk, harm, or profit—a spatial corollary of neoliberalism's tendency to socialize risk while privatizing profit."[14] Globalizing understandings of progress insidiously justify altering local lifeways and environments through emerging and established media, which rely on the extraction economies they often critically depict. My chapters demonstrate how different media shape and contribute to perceptions of tradition, modernity, and modernization amid changing environments, even as these media also materially impact environments and play a fundamental role in development projects globally. My study of modernization and media exposes the ongoing environmental impacts of empire embedded in ideas of progress and development in projects altering material environments. In doing so, it also reveals relationships with the environment and modes of resistance to changing environments and environmental injustices.

By analyzing cultural representations resisting development that harms material environments and human and more-than-human communities, this book positions environmental justice in postcolonial contexts. I use the term "environmental justice" to indicate how communities and media in Ireland address the uneven distribution of the benefits and burdens of colonial and neocolonial extraction economies across human and more-than-human environments. While environmental justice theory emerges from North American case studies and contexts, particularly those associated with the US civil rights movement, postcolonial ecocriticism emphasizes geopolitical hierarchies and uneven developments emerging in the wake of empire, often resulting in environment injustices. The theoretical focus of environmental justice scholarship in North American settler-colonial contexts historically contrasts with postcolonial ecocriticism's emphasis on geopolitical hierarchies established during the era of colonialism and continuing in neocolonial modernity. Indeed, Byron Caminero-Santangelo notes that environmental justice "suggests a focus on race and the distribution of waste and industrial sites and with who gets what within the cities and regions of the 'developed' nation-state. . . . This kind of environmental justice frame can fail to account for the ways colonial legacies and neocolonialism result in differences between the sociopolitical conditions in postcolonial nations and the conditions in the United States."[15] In Ireland, the social hierarchies established during the colonial era and the 1922 partition of the industrialized north and colonially underdeveloped south combine after World War II in the transfer of control over natural resources from Britain to the United States, in part through the Marshall Plan, as Denis O'Hearn writes: "Decolonisation simultaneously removed British colonial restrictions . . . *and* removed the most effective barrier to US economic penetration."[16] These conditions led to polluting chemical, pharmaceutical, and technology industries moving to Ireland in the late twentieth century.[17] Attending to these intersections between environmental justice and postcolonialism in Ireland allows scholars to heed the call of US environmental justice scholars Luke W. Cole and Sheila R. Foster for more coalitions between environmental justice movements and "broader political and economic struggles" to effect structural change across (settler-)colonial and postcolonial contexts.[18]

Reconsidering Ireland's wide-ranging cultural representations of land since its partial independence in 1922 establishes context-specific but interdisciplinary and historical methods for positioning environmental justice theory within a postcolonial ecocritical frame. This builds on discussions like those of Robert Allen about local resistance movements to multinational corporations and industrial pollution in rural Ireland.[19] Additionally, it expands environmental justice theory to Europe, a region where environmental justice remains largely understudied despite the potential of the Aarhus Convention for addressing interconnected human and environmental rights.[20] Legal scholars and sociologists are certainly advancing studies of environmental justice in diverse communities in Europe, from access to green spaces in urban environments to the oppression of Roma communities in eastern Europe, but environmental humanities scholars have yet to connect local environmental injustices in Europe with the ongoing environmental impacts of empire globally.[21] Such connections complicate understandings of Europe as a simultaneously unified and fractured geography of modern nation states. In doing so, these connections expand understandings of historical and contemporary relationships between former and current colonies and colonizers. By positioning environmental justice theory within a postcolonial ecocritical frame in Europe, my examination of modernization, media, and environment in Ireland across the twentieth and twenty-first centuries improves the possibilities for interdisciplinary scholarship and for forging coalitions across seemingly disconnected histories of power and extraction.

While postcolonial ecocriticism collectively seeks to analyze and foreground viable and just alternatives to uneven forms of development perpetuated by ongoing histories of colonialism, ecomedia studies scholarship uncovers the environmental impacts of media production on environments in human historical and geologic time. Tracing different media at distinct moments in Ireland's modernization across the twentieth century develops ecomedia strategies for analyzing environments and human and more-than-human relationships depicted in and materially impacted by emerging media. Media production, consumption, distribution, and waste management are part of modernization projects to extract natural resources, and they contribute to the insatiable growth of the global economy. Integration into the globalizing economy through developing the environment and expanding media technologies is often a goal of postcolonial nations, a goal much mainstream media shows the Republic of Ireland to have achieved. Indeed, the Republic's tax incentives to draw big tech companies to Irish shores has certainly boosted numbers in the Irish economy, even as socioeconomic hierarchies and social issues around housing and immigration intensify. Scholars such as Patrick Brodie demonstrate the precarity of Irish dependence on data center industries, however, and particularly where these blur the lines between private enterprise and public utilities.[22]

Media and media infrastructure in Ireland inflect ongoing power relations that echo the colonial past and materially entrench neocolonial power relations in environmental and cultural landscapes globally. They also expose alternative modernities that rework how we conceptualize race, class, ethnicity, and gender in ongoing histories of colonialism and neocolonial economic regimes. Each chapter shows interconnections among media, narrative forms, and environmental development historically to attend to how, to use Cajetan Iheka's words, "newness enters the world through the past."[23] My analyses draw on Nadia Bozak's definition of Fourth-World cinema, Iheka's conceptualization of "imperfect media," and what Jussi Parikka calls "psychogeophysics" to elucidate how colonial histories permeate understandings of identity, belonging, and place in interactions among media and environment in deep time.[24] These ecomedia theories show material connections between media and narrative forms as they shape land and relationships to place in colonial and postcolonial contexts, including in Ireland. Consequently, my analyses in *Irish Ecomedia* challenge teleological narratives of development to show how shifting media landscapes and their impact on material environments reveal constellations of power. Heeding these relationships between media and environment in Ireland expands how ecomedia studies scholars theorize relationships between narrative forms and material extraction in emerging media in postcolonial contexts. Modern media have lasting impacts on the planet across vast scales of geologic time, and these impacts perpetuate the erasure of marginalized and Indigenous communities. My analyses reveal an ongoing engagement with the complex position of various media as new to challenge understandings of advancement and progress.

Irish Ecomedia presents tools for expanding the methodological, geographical, and historical scope of postcolonial ecocriticism and ecomedia studies as it also contributes to a growing body of environmental humanities scholarship within Irish studies. In doing so, this book provides a more ecocritical perspective on the mature but often anthropocentric discussions of land and environment that play a prominent role in Irish studies scholarship more generally. By attending to more-than-human agencies in media and media depictions, my methodological approaches draw on the animal studies scholarship of Maureen O'Connor and Kathryn Kirkpatrick and chronologically extend the work of Colleen Taylor's *Irish Materialisms: The Nonhuman and the Making of Colonial Ireland, 1690–1830* (2024) to the twentieth century. Taylor uses biosemiotics and theories of new materialism to examine objects across the long eighteenth century, showing ongoing human and more-than-human collaborations. Taylor's research thus establishes a historical precedent to forms of Irish-language environmental consciousness and multispecies modernities that I discuss in the work of Flann O'Brien, Seán Ó Riada, Éilís Ní Dhuibhne, and Risteard Ó Domhnaill. My examination of social and environmental protest and assertions of resilience in ongoing relationships among humans, more-than-humans, and material environments also builds on the work of Donna Potts, whose 2018 book *Contemporary Irish Writing and Environmentalism: The Wearing of the Deep Green* offers a multimodal analysis to environmentalism in Ireland in the late twentieth century.

Through addressing important questions about Ireland's uneven forms of development and the media through which such development was documented and resisted in the wake of empire, my book draws on the print-media analyses and narrative approaches of Eóin Flannery and the historical scope of Derek Gladwin. In *Ireland and Ecocriticism: Literature, History, and Environmental Justice* (2016), Flannery builds on the idea that colonial hierarchies persist materially today in how perceptions of land and systems of value have been integrally interwoven throughout Irish history. He analyzes poetry, essays, and memoir to establish the utility and potential of ecocriticism as a theoretical framework for Irish studies. Gladwin's *Contentious Terrains: Boglands, Ireland, Postcolonial Gothic* (2016) examines cultural representations of bogs in Irish prose, poetry, and drama of the late nineteenth century to the present. Expanding the foundational work of Flannery and Gladwin, *Irish Ecomedia* examines multiple temporalities, materialities, and media at distinct moments of land reform, economic integration, and natural resource extraction in Ireland across the twentieth and twenty-first centuries. My analyses show how colonial power relations continue to constrain and erase Irish ways of knowing and forms of self-determination even as the Republic of Ireland embraces its European identity in a post-Brexit world.

By examining the narrative forms and media that shape representations and material environments in Ireland, this book draws on the rich Irish cultural and literary studies of land and power, which I bring into conversation with broader understandings of belonging, place, indigeneity, and migration in postcolonial ecocriticism and ecomedia studies. Despite the important work Irish studies ecocriticism already does to nuance understandings of Europe, Europeanness, and the ongoing environmental impacts of empire, it has yet to garner a more general and interdisciplinary audience among postcolonial ecocritics and ecomedia studies scholars outside of Irish studies. *Irish Ecomedia* seeks to make the relevance of postcolonial cultural and historical studies of Ireland legible and useful to broader fields within the environmental humanities. Studying Irish cultural production through postcolonial ecocritical and ecomedia studies lenses that account for connections across empire revises theoretical frameworks that scholars typically use to understand both Ireland and postcolonial nations globally, as well as the transnational environmental injustices emerging through the environmental impacts of empire.

Irish Ecomedia shows how people and communities rework and reclaim media and material environments in modernizing regions to demonstrate alternative ways in which Ireland might decolonize to embrace more socially and environmentally just futures. This book thus expands analyses of power and more-than-human agencies in postcolonial ecocriticism, ecomedia studies, and Irish studies by identifying and theorizing multiple alternative and often multispecies modernities across diverse narrative forms and media in the twentieth century. These multiple, multispecies modernities expose the ongoing environmental impacts of empire. Through developing historical and material frameworks for challenging the environmental impacts of empire on Ireland, *Irish Ecomedia* opens future research to connections among environment, media, and empire in postcolonial nations across enduring and expanding formations of empire.

Remediating Modernity: Developing Theories of Multiple Modernities and Remediation

Ireland's uneven forms of development in the twentieth and twenty-first centuries raise important questions about how postcolonial nations internalize the logics of empire, as well as how Ireland's position in Europe and the EU reworks scholarly understandings of race, migration, and environment. Colonial logics rely on gendered binary structures in which tradition and modernity inform one another in old and new narrative forms and media. On the one hand, understandings of outdated feminized traditions and cutting-edge masculinized technologies justify environmental development projects and natural resource extraction in Ireland from the late Victorian era through the period of unprecedented economic growth in the Republic of Ireland from 1995 to 2008, often referred to as the Celtic Tiger. On the other hand, my research reveals how entrenched gendered understandings of tradition and modernity occlude modes of resistance through which artists, writers, and performers innovate traditional narrative and cultural forms in emerging media. These innovative traditions defy modernization initiatives that would marginalize the Irish language and indigenous cultural practices. Inflections of gender across masculine modernities and feminized traditions help to elucidate what I am calling multiple modernities.

Multiple modernities splinter binary frameworks to reveal multimodal relationships among humans, more-than-humans, and material agencies that interact with the environmental impacts of empire and colonial conceptions of modernity and progress. At the same time, multiple modernities provide alternatives to colonial logics, racial formations, and forms of development. The materiality of media in each of my chapters refracts gendered representations of tradition and modernity across myriad spatial and temporal realities to demonstrate multiple modernities. Media materially and representationally embody colonial pasts through the extraction economies that enable them. Media thus haunt the postcolonial present and future through the myth of progress embedded in understandings of national sovereignty and independence expressed by certain media, such as national radio, television, and broadcast networks. Yet the different ways people rework emerging and established media at distinct moments in Ireland's modernization indicate longer histories of media in which human historical and geological temporalities intermingle. My analyses extend the historical scope of ecomedia studies into a precolonial past that reframes understandings of persistent environmental pollutants inherent in the colonial underpinnings of modern media and technology. The multimodal cultural objects I examine indicate the presence of multiple, and often multispecies, modernities that promise more just futures.

My examination of multiple modernities in emerging and established media disrupts how Irish traditions and postcolonial modernity seem to emerge in opposition. Rather, my analyses of multiple modernities challenge colonial and gendered conceptions of modernity and linear temporality to reveal alternative forms of development based on traditional relationships with the land and more-than-human communities and agencies. In the twentieth century, modernity became a process of producing borders that delineate systems of value and devaluation on people and places in the legacy of colonialism. Citing Zygmunt Bauman, De-Loughrey writes that "modernity is constituted by the boundaries erected between normative and disposable subjects, resulting in an enormous surveillance industry dedicated to policing borders between disposable and enduring objects, citizens and refugees."[25] Such understandings of modernity certainly inform EU and Irish immigration policies and the Republic of Ireland's attempts to modernize through European integration. Yet privileging this conception of modernity subscribes to US-modernization theory and narratives in which the nation-state progresses toward globalization in a US-dominated petroeconomy. In doing so, it occludes forms of modernity and modernization that materially redress the environmental impacts of empire and work toward more decolonized futures.

To examine these alternative forms of modernization and modernity, *Irish Ecomedia* builds on existing conceptions of multiple modernities. The concept of multiple modernities shows that, to quote Sandra Harding, "modernization is not the same as Westernization. . . . Many other societies around the world have developed their own forms of modernity."[26] Different conceptions of modernity and modernization, as Joe Cleary, Mark Quigley, Conor McCarthy, Michael Rubenstein, and Sorcha O'Brien separately show, become more prominently in tension with imperial, national, and postcolonial cultural frameworks and infrastructural projects at different moments in Irish history. Multiple modernities in twentieth-century Irish cultural expression counter seemingly fixed, inevitable, or singular notions of progress, tradition, and modernity in a decolonizing and modernizing Ireland. The multiple modernities my analyses demonstrate disrupt reductive understandings of a perceived racial and ethnic homogeneity in Ireland to challenge gendered and binary colonial logics that flatten complex histories of power and difference in Europe and continue to negatively affect the planet.[27]

The concept of multiple modernities in *Irish Ecomedia* revises postcolonial ecocriticism and ecomedia studies in ways that introduce a second key term: remediation. Interactions between narrative forms and media help to shape understandings of progress and development across conceptions of tradition and modernity through multiple processes of remediation. These processes indicate a threefold definition of remediation. First, Irish cultural production reworks narrative forms across media to correct modernization narratives that would divide seemingly outdated traditions from future developed environments. These instances of remediation correct dominant progress narratives evinced in imperial-era records like the Congested Districts Board (CDB) photographic archive, which I examine in chapter 1.

Second, remediation indicates how older narrative forms emerge in new media and conceptions of modernity unfolding across material environments. Clifford Siskin theorizes this process of remediation as how "in moments of change the older *form* of reality becomes the *content* of the new one."[28] As cultural and social relations changed through development projects, Irish communities remediated representational conventions across diverse media, a process I analyze in Flann O'Brien's *The Third Policeman* in chapter 2. In this understanding of remediation, imperial-era progress narratives emerge in new media to establish a continuity between colonial expectations for modern Ireland and modernization projects in the postcolonial nation. Yet, as my analysis shows, O'Brien remediates Irish-language forms into his novel to critically depict a postmodern disintegration of the separations between material environments and their representations in idealized, picturesque forms.

Finally, interactions between old and new media give rise to a third process of remediation. The shifting cultural understandings of media in Ireland at distinct moments of Irish modernization inform the production of meaning in processes through which old and new media diachronically and dialectically inform each other through regional contexts. Jay David Bolter and Richard Grusin define this form of remediation: "No medium today, and certainly no single media event, seems to do its cultural work in isolation from other media, any more than it works in isolation from other social and economic forces. What is new about new media comes from the particular ways in which they refashion older media and the ways in which older media refashion themselves to answer the challenges of new media."[29] Bolter and Grusin's understanding of remediation comes into sharp relief in my third chapter's analysis of Seán Ó Riada's 1960s radio program, *Our Musical Heritage*, and my fifth chapter's examination of Risteard Ó Domhnaill's 2010 documentary film, *The Pipe*. While Ó Riada innovates oral traditions on national radio to demonstrate alternative forms of modernization, Ó Domhnaill reworks picturesque visual depictions of rural Irish landscapes to assert multiple multispecies modernities thriving in a Gaeltacht, or Irish-speaking community, threatened by the building of an LNG pipeline.

The multiple modernities and instances of remediation in each of my chapters highlight modes of resistance and assertions of agency from human and more-than-human communities that permeate narrative forms and media in the twentieth and twenty-first centuries. Documentary photography, print, radio, and film inflect tensions between attempts to decolonize Irish cultural production and the media that were more established in the imperial centers of Britain and the United States. The use of documentary photography in Victorian-era imperial land reforms shaped the aesthetics of what modernity should look like, and these expectations resurface across media in depictions of postcolonial modernization projects. Similarly, print publishing, radio, television, and documentary film in Ireland invoke and subvert established forms and media histories developed earlier in Britain and the United States. My analyses reflect the relatively late development of infrastructure that Irish people and environments experienced over the twentieth century.

By elucidating multiple modernities and forms of remediation in Irish cultural production, *Irish Ecomedia* aligns with the overarching commitment of postcolonial ecocriticism to better understand and find just alternatives to the uneven distribution of the benefits and burdens of natural resource extraction and development across geopolitical hierarchies emerging out of ongoing colonial histories. Rather than theorizing new and supposedly more modern terms for analysis, this book, like the case studies in my chapters, reworks the established concepts of multiple modernities and remediation to reveal alternative and multimodal ways of reading postcolonial texts across multiple media in historically specific contexts. The multiple modernities in my analyses destabilize imperial-era structural inequalities in local and global relationships with material environments. The theories of remediation I develop revise and expand how scholars examine interactions among different media, environments, and multispecies communities over time. Analyzing multiple modernities and forms of remediation in Irish cultural production at distinct moments of modernization in the twentieth and twenty-first centuries provides a theoretical frame for better understanding and decolonizing the environmental impacts of empire globally and across the deep time of Earth's past, present, and future.

From Imperial-Era Land Reform to Twenty-First-Century Fossil-Fuel Extraction

Irish Ecomedia demonstrates how those most affected by development projects challenge dominant narratives of modernizing fisheries, agriculture, and energy infrastructure. To support readability, I chronologically trace modernization in Ireland from the late nineteenth through the early twenty-first century, but my case studies assert continually unfolding agential relationships among humans, more-than-humans, and their environments that diachronically challenge constructions of colonial, linear time. My case studies show multimodal representations of communities that present alternative relationships with material surroundings to those promoted by state-authorized modernization projects. These alternative environmental relationships remediate emerging media and give rise to multiple modernities that promise more just and enduring futures. Analyzing visual, aural, and print media through postcolonial and ecomedia methodologies, my research reveals how people and communities challenged, reworked, and remediated dominant narrative forms and emerging media to assert rival modern experiences across multiple modernities.

My first chapter examines photographs taken by the CDB between 1906 and 1914 of a variety of imperial-era projects for modernizing agriculture and fisheries, as well as for implementing land and housing reforms and relocation schemes. The 1891 Land Purchase Act, proposed in the British Parliament by Arthur Balfour, created the CDB, which existed as an independent development agency from 1891 to 1923.[30] The CDB applied agricultural and marine science in western Ireland to modernize agriculture, fisheries, and cottage industries, as well as to redistribute land.[31] Narrative elements in the CDB's photos reveal local resistance to imperial-era agricultural and fisheries reform under the CDB, defying how modernity should look even within the official photographic record. In contrast to modernization projects imposing a singular form of modernity upon people in the west of Ireland, my analysis exposes multiple modernities within the photographic frame that alter understandings of class, gender, nation, and environment in early twentieth-century rural Ireland. The multiple modernities in the CDB photographs challenge Victorian visual expectations for modern cultural practices and modernized environments. My analysis contributes to ecomedia studies by revealing how the limitations of photography in the early twentieth century interact with environmental conditions in Ireland but also with the global processes of extraction and exchange that made photography possible in rural Irish communities. This chapter also opens up understandings in postcolonial ecocriticism about how women's assertions of agency through the medium of documentary photography contested colonial power relations actively shaping the land and people's relationships to land.

My emphasis on visual representations of colonial progress in my first chapter persists in my second chapter's exploration of how picturesque landscapes in postcolonial Ireland become the object of satiric critique in Flann O'Brien's 1940 novel, *The Third Policeman*. Imperial-era depictions of a traditional Irish past informed racializing and gendered understandings of modernity and land reform projects as Free State Ireland moved away from the Anglo-Irish Trade War and the rest of Europe entered World War II. While focusing on a print text, this chapter reworks understandings of remediation for ecomedia studies. Remediation in this chapter indicates how formal narrative structures emerge across different media, environments, and communities undergoing development. As cultural and social relations changed through development projects, Irish communities remediated representational conventions across diverse media. In keeping with Siskin's definition of remediation, O'Brien integrates imperial-era aesthetic forms into the content of the novel to offer a postmodern view of how colonial narrative forms continue to shape expectations for how material realities in Irish-speaking regions should appear even after Ireland's partial independence. My analysis demonstrates how visual and print media interact in O'Brien's critique to disrupt an overdependence on visual representations in colonial discourse and expose failed opportunities to engage with existent modernities in Irish-language forms and culture.

My second chapter's decentering of idealized visual representations becomes the focus of my third chapter's analysis of orality in Seán Ó Riada's 1962 radio program, *Our Musical Heritage*, which aired at a moment when Irish radio was both modern and retro. Ó Riada describes oral traditions on national radio as television was increasing in popularity after the Broadcasting Authority Act of 1960. Ó Riada innovatively taps into both the technological advancement and practice in rural Ireland of listening to the radio to remediate oral cultures into a trusted modern medium.

Ó Riada's work demonstrates Bolter and Grusin's understanding of remediation through "the ways in which older media refashion themselves to answer the challenges of new media."[32] Radio was ubiquitous throughout rural Ireland in the 1950s and 1960s, but it was being superseded by the relatively late establishment of a national television network in the early 1960s during Ireland's intensified international economic expansion after 1959 under Taoiseach Seán Lemass. Ó Riada taps into this transitional moment, using interactions among orality, radio, television, and material environments to critically assess the rapid changes Irish modernization was bringing to rural Irish-speaking communities. Ó Riada critiques how Irish oralities are often depicted as part of a vanishing past in colonial and Irish revivalist representations, and his program shows how Irish oral traditions demonstrate alternative forms of modernization. As Ireland's media and natural resources were drawn into an economic and culturally European space, Ó Riada's natural and gendered metaphors assert a strategic distancing from Europe as they create an ephemeral environment for indigenous oral cultures, such as Irish traditional music, to innovate and expand on national radio.

Ongoing economic integration with Europe shifted Ireland toward technology-driven education and emigration during the recession after the oil crises of the 1970s, which combined with early discussions of climate change and a heightened perceived risk of nuclear energy. This complex moment is the premise of the dystopian future in Éilís Ní Dhuibhne's climate fiction novel, *The Bray House* (1990), in which nuclear technologies used to address the effects of global warming position Ireland as a sacrifice zone.[33] The novel critiques emerging forms of neocolonialism in an integrating Europe. These forms of neocolonialism reframe Ireland's relationship to territorial sovereignty and anticolonial resistance during the Northern Irish Troubles, emerging discourse on climate change, and the prevalence of nuclear energy in Anglo-US and Anglo-Irish relations in the 1980s. While Ní Dhuibhne critically invokes earlier literary forms like the unreliable and megalomaniacal narration of O'Brien's novel, she also reimagines ancient Irish writing etched into stone and natural springs in the Irish landscape to persist and protect in the face of nuclear apocalypse. This representation of ancient media and environmental resilience in *The Bray House* points to how colonial printing presses worked to eradicate the Irish language and traditional relationships with material environments. The remediation of ancient writing alongside enduring environmental systems in an apocalyptic future demonstrates multiple modernities embedded in material environments and geologic histories in Ireland. Such a representation rejects the implied advancement of colonial and neocolonial technologies, which fail to contribute to the world in the longue durée. Rather, the extraction, production, and consumption of modern media wreak havoc on multispecies material environments over the geologic deep-time scale of the planet. Through revising understandings of progress in representations of ancient media and alternative ways of knowing, *The Bray House* offers a glimpse of dimensions of Irish culture rooted in the material environment that continue to provide protective and enduring spaces in the wake of modernity's horrific collapse in the novel.

My final chapter develops an ecocinema studies analysis to reveal multiple multispecies modernities in the ongoing fossil-fuel extraction that marginalizes rural communities in the west of Ireland. Continuing to examine the legacy of colonial economies in geopolitical hierarchies, my final chapter shows how Risteard O'Domhnaill's 2010 documentary film, *The Pipe*, uses aesthetics that promote authentic local industries, such as those in the CDB photographs, to align the Irish government with a specter of multinational corporate power. A close analysis of the film reveals how Ó Domhnaill subversively invokes colonial-inflected romanticizations of Ireland's underdevelopment and gendered petromodernities. Like Ó Riada's use of radio and recording technologies, Ó Domhnaill reveals modernizing traditions in emerging digital technologies by remediating romanticized images of rural Ireland into a complex montage of multispecies modernities. While all the multiple modernities I discuss involve human and more-than-human relations, my framing of multispecies modernities in this final chapter shows the interrelated lives and afterlives of postcolonial communities, the environmental impacts of empire, and the material implications of old and new media through ongoing interactions that collapse divisions between human and more-than-human worlds. Filmed primarily with a handheld camera in Ó Domhnaill's own community, *The Pipe* follows local resistance against Shell's LNG development in Rossport, County Mayo, Ireland. *The Pipe*'s cinematography, sound design, and montage expose the ongoing environmental impacts of empire on postcolonial nations and state formation while revealing multispecies relationships and material agencies that challenge neocolonial regimes. Reworking understandings of progress and environmental justice within a postcolonial frame, the multispecies modernities in *The Pipe* revise how postcolonial ecocritical and ecocinema studies scholars read tradition and modernization depicted in postcolonial films as it honors the interconnected interspecies cultural relationships that sustain life.

Conclusion: Imagining More Socially and Environmentally Just Futures

Representations of development and modernization in twentieth- and twenty-first-century Ireland offer postcolonial ecocriticism and ecomedia studies new ways of recognizing resistance and apprehending the insidious and often unexpected effects of power on the planet, local environments, and multispecies communities in postcolonial contexts. While Ireland is a European island whose emigrants perpetuated settler colonialism across the British Empire and whose descendants currently benefit from hegemonic and racist constructions of whiteness, Ireland also comprises a postcolonial nation and a settler-colonial statelet whose histories challenge and nuance theories of race, gender, environment, and power in postcolonial ecocriticism, ecomedia studies, and Irish studies. My examination of how narrative forms and media interact with material environments and environmental development projects over time forces postcolonial ecocritical scholars like myself to reassess the tools through which we examine the ongoing environmental impacts of colonial regimes on people, places, and the planet in the current era of neocolonial economic globalization and globalizing environmental injustices. Examining narrative forms across media in depictions of modernization in Ireland over the past century shows how authoritative understandings of modernity during imperial-era development projects ripple out across social hierarchies and dehumanizing power relations.

Including Ireland in postcolonial ecocritical and ecomedia studies conversations expands the geographic and historical methodologies of these fields as it helps to address intensifying planetary crises and their uneven impact on marginalized communities across geopolitical hierarchies, transnational environmental injustices, ongoing histories of colonialism, and the environmental impacts of empire. By exposing the ways power strategically adapts to occlude modes of resistance, *Irish Ecomedia* bears witness to how multiple modernities and remediations in Irish cultural production imagine more environmentally and socially just futures.

Through distinct moments of modernization and Irish media histories, this book highlights how people drew on an array of cultural, material, and environmental resources to resist, remediate, and offer alternatives to the mechanisms of development that reproduce colonial relations to material environments in a neocolonial modernity. The historical arc of these multiple modernities emerges in resistance to the visual aesthetics of colonial modernity, a context to which I will now turn in my analysis of the CDB photographic archive.

1
1891-1922
PHOTOGRAPHY AND THE VISION FOR
MODERNIZED RELATIONSHIPS TO LAND

CAPPAGH VILLAGE did not meet the expectations of the Congested Districts Board (CDB) members for what modernity should look like in the early twentieth century (see fig. 1). That is, the village comprised a cluster of thatched cabins rather than the more modern slate-roof houses on parceled-out squares of land. Expectations of what was recognizably modern shaped how the increasingly prominent field of photography framed people and places. By the late nineteenth and early twentieth century, photography had come to play a complex role as, at times a conveyer of historical and scientific truth, an artistic medium, and a distrusted new technology. Photographs commissioned by the CDB between 1906 and 1914 documented its projects to modernize land and fisheries in the west of Ireland, including spaces that had yet to be modernized, like the village in the photo *View of Cappagh Village, Castlerea District, Co. Galway*.[1]

Taken from behind an uneven stone wall that forms a line across the bottom third of the image, the photograph of Cappagh divides the modernity implied by the camera on one side of the stone wall from the supposedly outdated patchwork of fields around the group of thatched houses on the other. This temporal division between the camera technology and the seemingly archaic forms of agriculture and ways of life in the photo's diegesis indicate, in the words of Mieke Bal, "a double focalization, hinging between internal and external and thus connecting the two worlds this work brings together."[2] Although Bal does not examine the CDB photographs, she presents a helpful framework for analyzing competing narratives in visual texts. The double focalization "hing[es] between" the material realities that the photo seeks to represent and the external world in which CDB members view and interpret the photograph to justify and promote modernization projects in the congested districts. A note on the back of the photograph emphasizes this external world by explaining that

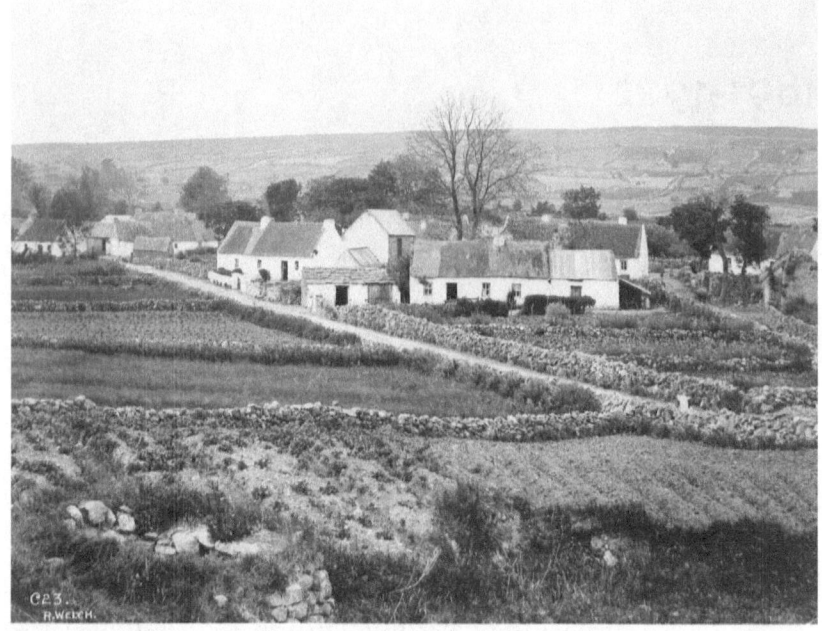

FIG. 1. Robert John Welch, *View of Cappagh Village, Castlerea District, Co. Galway,* ca. 1906–1914, CDB19. (Courtesy of the National Library of Ireland)

"the congested village of Cappagh [was] one of the worst the Congested Districts Board had to deal with in Mayo or Galway."[3] While this note underscores the materiality of the photograph, it also promotes the external focalization from the point of view of the CDB, the photographer, and the unknown author of the note.

The note's interpretation establishes an implicit hierarchy within the double focalization that favors the more omniscient narrative of the external focalizer and obscures complex discursive elements that internal perspectives might reveal. In doing so, the note tells the viewer how to read Cappagh not only in relation to other photographs in the CDB's collection but also in relation to other places in the west of Ireland. By reading this image in terms of a developmental teleology, ranging from "the worst" to an implied better and best, the note positions the photograph and the actual village within a comparative interpretative framework that separates the viewer from the viewed. Such comparative interpretations establish an external focalizer to monitor the progress that modernization projects make to draw supposedly obsolete ways of life into the CDB's vision of modernity. These implicit visual expectations for premodernity and modernity indicate how photographic realism shaped perceptions of existent material realities in the west of Ireland captured in the photographs.

The CDB's identification of the "worst" forms of poverty and underdevelopment in Cappagh was based on Victorian-era understandings of realism. The "larger culture of realism," Jennifer Green-Lewis explains, was structurally dependent upon divisions between the periphery and the imperial center: "Photography's contribution to instrumental realism was largely to preserve the horizon of bourgeois subjectivity by populating its nethermost regions with groups of persons whose very existence appeared to threaten the boundaries of culture beyond which they were perceived as living."[4] By framing the "boundaries of culture" through a technology that had the "moral purpose ... to relate the truth," the photo of Cappagh juxtaposes modernity with premodernity to justify the social and cultural implications of the CDB's modernization projects.[5] This implicit temporal division between the premodern and the modern reinforces comparative interpretive practices through which realist aesthetic conventions materially influence lived realities and actual environments.

Narrative Realities: Reading Rival Experiences of Modernization

The external focalization in the photograph of Cappagh Village articulates the larger project of improvement that the CDB and its collection of photographs sought to document, even as the internal focalizations expose a multiplicity of perspectives that reframe understandings of modernization and modernity. While the external focus in many of the CDB's photos associates the future with the horizon, the photo of Cappagh lacks this developmental movement toward an implied modernity. This image shows land communally divided through the clachan system in and around the group of houses in the village center, something the CDB associated with congestion. Indeed, the sparsely populated regions of the congested districts were deemed overcrowded, Ciara Breathnach points out, due to too many people living on land that was considered "unprofitable" and in austere, small houses that contributed to the spread of disease.[6] Breathnach explains that "the term 'congested' is misleading:

not all the areas in question were overpopulated. . . . In many respects, congestion was a euphemism for relative poverty stemming from an over-dependency on smallholdings (holdings in the congests were on average four acres)."[7] The two roads around Cappagh emphasize this congestion as they encircle and disappear on either side of the village rather than at a point on the horizon, and they are only partially visible, starting somewhere outside the frame on the right-hand side of the photo. The direction of the roads from right to left subtly guides the external focalizing gaze across the photo in the opposite direction of reading a Western text, thereby indicating the viewer is looking back from a point further along in the photographic text. This backward glance, combined with the absence of a clear direction to the horizon within the photo's frame, demonstrates the way of life in the village is literally and figuratively going nowhere but back across the material photograph and back in time, a view that many members of the CDB held of the clachan system in the early twentieth century.

Despite its positioning in the recesses of history behind the wall, the clachan way of life still clearly exists at the time the photograph of Cappagh was taken. A close inspection of the photo shows people walking along the road, and a young woman looks directly at the camera from a stone wall. This reversal of the camera's gaze reveals an internal focalizer who undermines the invisibility, or "disembodied point of view," of the photographer.[8] The internal focalization asserts that both the viewer and the viewed are in the same place at the same time. The implicit and possibly unintentional cooptation of the camera's gaze by the villagers ruptures the division of modernity and premodernity that the wall establishes. It also challenges the teleological construction of modernization encouraged by the external focalization and upon which its division of space and time relies. The double focalization "connecting the two worlds" between the external gaze of the implied viewer and the internal focus of those viewed becomes ambivalent. Attending to such instances of rupture in the photographs' narrative construction highlights complex negotiations of agency and relationships to land through the medium of photography.

The CDB photographs were taken by Robert John Welch, J. D. Cassidy, Valentine and Sons, and some unknown photographers between 1906 and 1914. Given the technologies of the time, these photographs were likely using dry-plate processes in which light imprints an image on glass plates coated with a gelatin emulsion of silver bromide.[9] The CDB commissioned Welch in 1914 to document many of their projects, and Welch's photographs comprise the majority of the images in the NLI collection "The Congested Districts Board Photograph Collection," which has been digitized and is available online.[10] While Welch is not the only photographer of the CDB's project, he offered an aesthetic, as Gail Baylis argues, in which people of the western counties are often "contained within the nature that surrounds them."[11] The aesthetic of the CDB's paternalism and Welch's implicit objectification of communities in the congested districts emerged alongside revivalist aesthetics that idealize an austere but authentic rural Ireland.

By analyzing narrative constructions of space and time in the CDB photographs, this chapter reveals rival experiences of modernity and modernization emerging in individual photographs as well as in sequences across the collection. Justin Carville has established the CDB's dominant narrative of modernity by showing how photography conventions reinforce the CDB's idealizations of modernization: "Progress was measured in terms of the visual idealisation and aestheticisation of the landscape. Nowhere in the CDB archive is this demonstrated more clearly than in the photographic representations of housing."[12] Yet the CDB's vision of modernity obscures discursive complexities in both the visual texts and the material world that is interpolated into the photograph for an external audience of, presumably, CDB members and government authorities sponsoring the modernization projects, though little evidence exists about the presentation or reception of the photos. Bringing a narrative approach to the CDB's agricultural and fisheries photos builds on Carville's work to show how, as Bal explains, "the analysis of visual images as narrative in and of themselves can do justice to an aspect of images and their effect that neither iconography nor other art historical practices can quite articulate."[13] The double focalizations in the CDB photographs individually and in relation to one another expose the presence of multiple perspectives on modernity and modernization, both at the time the photographs were taken and in their subsequent interpretation by viewers of the lives, traditions, and improvement schemes in the west of Ireland.

The multiple levels of focalization within and outside the photographic text recuperate multiple modernities and agencies of people in rural Ireland in the midst of shifting relationships to material surroundings. The multiple modernities emerging in "The Congested Districts

Board Photograph Collection" show how people experience modernization schemes differently and how the effects of such schemes splinter more singular understandings of modernity and modernization. Doreen Massey conceptualizes spatial organizations as always producing multiple temporalities and trajectories, "a simultaneity of stories-so-far," and "space as the dimension of a multiplicity of durations."[14] The "simultaneity of stories-so-far" in individual photographs and sequences in the collection highlight how those living in the congested districts, that is, those most directly affected by the CDB projects, disrupt dichotomies between premodern or authentic traditions as prior to and transcended by the CDB's conception of modernity. The double focalizations in the CDB photographs reveal, in Massey's words, "space as the dimension of a multiplicity of durations." The spatial and temporal elements in the photographs' focalizations expose processes of representation and assertions of agency that both legitimate the extraction of natural resources and illuminate modes of resistance, which, in turn, counter the erasure of multivalent regional histories. The multiple modernities in the CDB's archive of photographs expand our understanding of Victorian visual discourse in photographic representations of Irish material environments by challenging divisions of the modern and the premodern, the viewer and the viewed, and the center and periphery that legitimate constructions of progress.

Hierarchies of Progress: Developing Gendered and Classed Views of Modernity

The narrative of progress in the CDB's agricultural photographs rearrange people and places in the photos, the archive, and the west of Ireland into constructions of space and time that conform to Victorian understandings of gender roles, propriety, and sanitation. For example, the panorama *House on Cloonmore Grass Farm near Tuam, Co. Galway* depicts a man sitting on a pile of rocks on the far left (see fig. 2).[15] From the man, the external focalization follows the stone wall and horizon to an almost identical house behind the first house. Given the camera technologies of the time, the panorama comprises two photographs positioned side by side. The right-hand photo of the panorama shows four additional new houses, barns, and grass fields, giving a uniformity to the landscape that encourages the gaze to move from left to right across the panorama. This implicitly forward movement across the photographic text emphasizes the rationalization of space into parceled-out plots that multiply along the horizon across both photos in the panorama. Although it is unclear who this man is, or what relationship he has to the land around him, the external focalization represents him as overseeing a seemingly infinite series of grass farms. In situating the man in the field in front of the new house, the man's position directs the internal gaze to the new farms and the horizon, metaphorically associating both with the future. The double focalization in this panorama thus presents the modernized landscape under the purview of the man.

Women are notably absent from the panorama of the farms near Tuam and many of the other photographs of new farms.[16] In late nineteenth- and early twentieth-century rural Ireland, women's labor played a prominent role in household and regional cash economies as well as in domestic life.[17] Breathnach explains that "female inclination to engage in paid labor was considered a sensitive barometer of poverty" and negatively perceived in the Victorian period, but the CDB was one of the few Victorian-era land reform agencies to recognize the economic value of women's labor.[18]

Given the CDB's recognition of rural Irish women's labor, the absence of women from most of the new farm photographs raises questions about how the focalization in these images negotiates expectations of gender within the CDB's vision of modernity. Women's labor historically played an important role in establishing and growing colonial extraction economies. Seventeenth- and eighteenth-century colonial industries positioned both material environments and Irish women's labor as natural resources.[19] Donna Potts argues that "the feminization of Irish land and people had been used to justify its oppression," and contributed to women's "double colonization."[20] These longer histories of drawing feminized people and environments into extraction industries inform colonial gender hierarchies in the Victorian and Edwardian periods, in which, as Anne McClintock argues, "the problems of land and labor are rooted in the fundamental question of who was to control the women's labor."[21] The CDB sought to visually navigate the important role that women's labor had come to play in rural Ireland as it promoted a masculine-inflected vision of modernity emerging out of colonial gender hierarchies. Building on McClintock, Bliss Cua Lim discusses the "sexualization of national-historical time" in visual culture, noting that spatiotemporalities in teleologies of development implicitly "naturalize" gender hierarchies

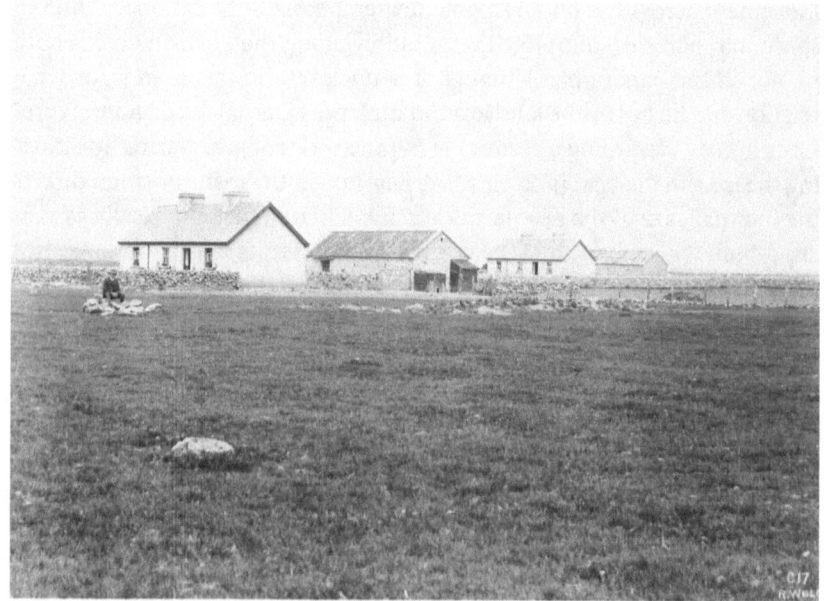

Fig. 2. Robert John Welch, *House on Cloonmore Grass Farm near Tuam, Co. Galway*, ca. 1906–1914, CDB15 and CDB16. (Courtesy of the National Library of Ireland)

through the erasure of women and feminized traditions from more masculine national modernization narratives.[22] The CDB's photographs indicate a conception of modernity that resolves gendered "problems of land and labor" across competing political perspectives by "naturaliz[ing]" Victorian gender relations in narratives of development.

Bringing McClintock and Lim's broader assessments of colonial gender hierarchies and visual culture into conversation with the gendered teleology of development in the CDB photographs elucidates how the CDB negotiated political tensions in Ireland in the early twentieth century amid constructive unionism, a rising separatist movement, and debates about Home Rule. Although the CDB operated as a politically independent entity, it was part of constructive unionism as it aimed to show the benefits of remaining part of the British Empire after Charles Stewart Parnell fell from favor, subsequently dying in 1891, and as the second Home Rule bill was defeated in 1893.[23] The CDB's constructive unionist vision emerges in its recognition of Cappagh as "one of the worst the Congested Districts Board had to deal with." In contrast to the CDB's vision of modernity,

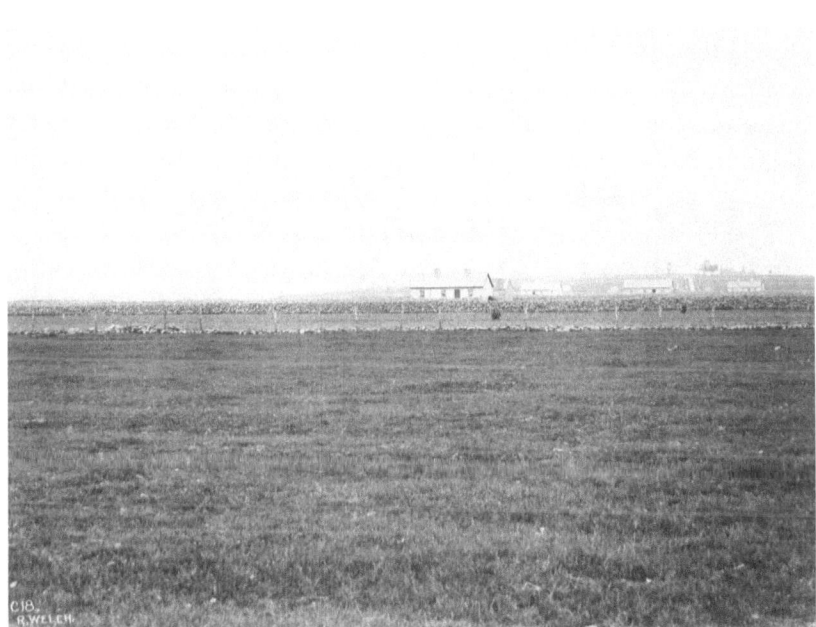

Cappagh was missing the slate-roof houses maintained by women's domestic labor while men worked the surrounding parceled-out squares of land. This vision assumes the authority to track improvements in rural Ireland through implicitly comparing this "worst" with other photographs in the archive like *House on Cloonmore Grass Farm near Tuam, Co. Galway*. The double focalization in the panorama of the farms near Tuam asserts that the CDB has accomplished its vision of a modern Ireland, a vision in which Victorian value systems render women's labor invisible and an implicit part of farming resources in the agricultural photographs. Despite the prevalence of women's labor in cash economies and the CDB's various training programs to improve women's earnings in wage-labor jobs, the CDB's agricultural photographs of modernized farms do not evince appreciation for the necessity of women's wage labor.[24] Rather, the pictures of new farms demonstrate that modernization projects should eradicate the need for women's wage labor and facilitate their full-time work in domestic and agricultural production upon which the modernized and undoubtedly male farmer relies.

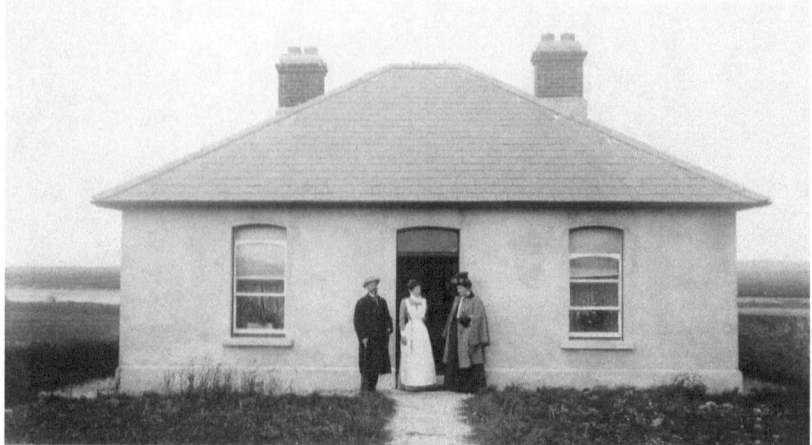

FIG. 3. Congested Districts Board, *Lord and Lady Aberdeen with Nurse, Outside House at Geesala, Ballina, Co. Mayo*, ca. 1906–1914, CDB56. (Courtesy of the National Library of Ireland)

In *House on Cloonmore Grass Farm near Tuam, Co. Galway*, the man's relaxed position sitting on the rocks asserts a confidence in the land's potential under this modernized management system, which metaphorizes women's labor with representations of new houses and farms. The door of the house is open, indicating ventilation. Properly ventilated homes reveal particular understandings of hygiene and sanitation in the late Victorian era that the CDB promoted in the west of Ireland through its 1897 Parish Committee Scheme and through working alongside the Lady Dudley District Nursing Scheme and the Women's National Health Association (WNHA) of Ireland.[25] In tracing the collaboration of the CDB and the Lady Dudley District Nursing Scheme, Breathnach describes expectations for nurses' behavior: "Nurses were nearly always female; they were perceived as maternal figures, and the remit of those engaged in the public health-care setting was broadly defined. On entering a household, a nurse was expected to conduct domestic duties, such as cooking and cleaning as well as caring for children."[26] Since women's wage labor was seen as an indication of poverty by Victorians, nurses working in the congested districts were expected to model domestic roles to establish gendered and socioeconomic class standards of sanitation and hygiene.

Certain photographs in the CDB collection reflect this transition into a modernity in which imperial agents collaborate with nurses to reinforce Victorian class and gender expectations for rural Irish women inside houses in modernizing regions. The photograph *Lord and Lady Aberdeen with Nurse, Outside House at Geesala, Ballina, Co. Mayo* (see fig. 3), indicates such intersections of class and gender in the CDB's vision of Victorian modernity.[27] This symmetrical photo centers a single-story modernized house with two chimneys and a slightly opened window on either side of the door, with the camera positioned on the path leading up to the door. Lord Aberdeen looks directly at the camera while Lady Aberdeen and the nurse appear to confer about something. Any rural Irish women who might come to dwell in this house are nowhere to be seen. The external focalization of the camera traces the path to the entrance of the house, where the nurse stands in the doorway. Her uniform contrasts with the darkened doorway and "was an immediate symbol of middle-class authority and respectability."[28] Lord Aberdeen's gaze into the camera reinforces the line to the house that the path creates, thereby guiding the external gaze to the internal focalization between Lady Aberdeen and the nurse. Their internal focus on each other frames the doorway of the house to show their attention to the inside. The nurse's position in the doorway presents her work to facilitate and monitor the threshold between the technological advancements that modernization projects were bringing to rural communities under the supervision of imperial agents like Lady Aberdeen while upholding the domestic expectations and social standards the nurse conveys to people within the house. The double focalization emphasizes the liminal role the nurse plays to establish a Victorian modernity through particular class and gender relations.

This photo thus documents the structural gender and class relations envisioned by the CDB for rural Ireland in a Victorian modernity while also suggesting the promise of class mobility. Breathnach explains that nurses had a pedagogical role as they worked to improve the health conditions of people in the congested districts: "In areas where nurses, unlike doctors, were accepted unequivocally, they had a twofold position, that of health-care provider and educator."[29] By teaching people in the west of Ireland how to improve their conditions, the nurses model the social and gender roles expected of a higher socioeconomic class. Breathnach asserts that "an obvious social and cultural gulf existed between the two classes—the educated nurses and the poor local people."[30] The elevated class position of the nurses above those whom they attended and taught suggests larger class formations that increasingly became part of Lady Aberdeen's programs in her absence. In 1886, Lady Aberdeen established, as Val McLeish explains, the "Irish Industries Association (IIA), which sought to help homeworkers develop skills in such crafts as lace-making, embroidery, knitting and spinning, and set up shops to sell their products in Dublin and London."[31] Two decades later Lady Aberdeen returned from Canada to Ireland and established the Women's National Health Association (WNHA), which reflected class divisions of the Victorian Order of Nurses that she had founded in Canada: "Most branches [of the WNHA] were run by the Anglo-Irish aristocracy and gentry. . . . Some Catholic women took part, although many preferred to join the United Irishwomen, a rural self-help group run by Sir Horace Plunkett."[32] Class relations in imperial-era efforts to ameliorate poverty and improve public health entrenched classed and gendered labor roles that are evident and subtly revised in this photograph of Lord and Lady Aberdeen with the nurse.

The gender and class relations in this image offer the possibility for class diversity and mobility for rural Irish people unconnected with the Anglo-Irish elite through the CDB's initiatives to, as Breathnach explains, "teach the people how to cultivate and maximize the output of their holdings."[33] Alongside the cottage industries Lady Aberdeen's initiatives supported, this picture emphasizes the potential to improve economic conditions through lifestyle changes in sanitation and health and medical practices that the nurse imparted inside the house.[34] Improving conditions through lifestyle changes was an aspect of modernization projects that both the CDB and Lady Aberdeen sought to promote in 1906 when the CDB photographs were initially commissioned. While the gender and class implications of the CDB's initiatives aligned with the overarching aims to ameliorate poverty through modernization under constructive unionism, they also informed how the CDB's photographs manipulate the double focalization to endorse the promise of class mobility within material realities sanctioned by the CDB's view of Victorian modernity in rural Ireland. The CDB photograph of Lady Aberdeen and the nurse emphasizes the potential to improve economic conditions through self-help strategies the nurse will share with those inside the house.

These implicit gender and class relations indicate how the CDB's vision for modernity both acknowledged and departed from Anglo-Irish revivalist aesthetics. The Protestant Anglo-Irish settler class benefited from Britain's penal laws, which systematically dispossessed Catholic people of their rights to accumulate wealth while prohibiting them from practicing their religion, and, in the case of indigenous Irish people, of speaking their native language. During their Ascendancy in the eighteenth century, the Anglo-Irish settlers owned most of the land and depended on indigenous Irish tenantry labor under oppressive conditions to continue to gain power and wealth until the Great Famine in the mid-nineteenth century. Anglo-Irish power and social positioning shifted after the Famine and the subsequent Land Wars.

As a result of this historical context, ideals of an authentic Irish tradition preceding colonial development in divergent relations to land, as Gregory Castle explains, historically separated indigenous Irish and settler Anglo-Irish people along socioeconomic and religious lines: "While Roman Catholic writers of the revival period seemed obsessed with the history of their land, to Protestant artists that history could only be, as Lady Gregory insisted, a painful accusation against their own people."[35] The process of romanticizing material and discursive relationships to place are implicit in settler-colonial pastoral narratives, as Graham Huggan and Helen Tiffin explain: "To assert one's right to live in a place is not the same thing as to dwell in it or inhabit it; for assertion is possession, not belonging, and dwelling implies an at-homeness with place that the genealogical claim to entitlement may reveal, but just as easily obscure."[36] Prominent Anglo-Irish revivalists such as Lady Gregory and W. B. Yeats demonstrate a conflation of possession with belonging. Lady Gregory's Big House at Coole and Yeats's home at Thoor Ballylee materially make a "genealogical claim" to an aesthetic of "at-homeness" that obscures the history of settler-colonialism from Cromwell's plantation system to the opulence of Anglo-Irish landlords in the eighteenth century. As Anthony Bradley points out, Yeats purchased property emblematic of his idealized notion of an authentic and ancient but vanishing Ireland from the CDB: "One is inclined to think of Coole, after reading Yeats, as a beautiful estate and countryside, but that beauty was based on the deprivation of many who lived in the region. The government agency from which Yeats had bought the tower at Ballylee, the Congested Districts Board, had been set up to deal with land reform and outdated agricultural practices in the western coastal areas of Ireland."[37] By buying Thoor Ballylee from the CDB, Yeats ironically participated in modernization projects that contributed to the eradication of the clachan system and the relocation of Irish-speaking populations, whose poverty in the west of Ireland has a long history in the Anglo-Irish Ascendancy. Yeats's purchase thus disrupted his own romanticized aesthetic of life in rural Ireland, which eulogized the quasi-feudal order of the Anglo-Irish Ascendancy in the eighteenth century.

The CDB photographs reflect this contradiction of modernization and preservation in Yeats's conception of rural life through romanticizing images of developed farms. Increasingly empty space and redivisions of fields connote a bucolic version of modernity. The photo *Two New Holdings in Cloonkeen, Castlebar, Co. Mayo* shows how the reorganization of the houses and land implied a reduction in the number of people living in an area.[38] The camera looks out from behind an overgrown wall at two new houses and accompanying barns on a distant hill. A handwritten note on the back of the photo notes: "Originally there were twenty-four tenancies in this village." Although the CDB policies aimed to encourage local prosperity to discourage emigration, its domestic migration schemes reshaped landscapes and people's relationships to the land, thereby raising questions about the connections between changing environments and ongoing migration from predominantly Irish-speaking regions.

The problem of emigration intersects historically with the visual discourse in some of the early photographs of the congested districts, which were taken to show the impoverished conditions of the west of Ireland at a time when emigration was seen as a viable solution by the British government for relieving poverty. As Frederick H. A. Aalen notes, assisted emigration was historically one way that government administrators saw of ameliorating acute poverty in the congested districts.[39] In the early 1890s, Major Ruttledge-Fair, the amateur photographer from County Mayo, took pictures for the Yorkshire Quaker philanthropist James Hack Tuke, who worked with Arthur Balfour in creating the CDB as part of the 1891 Land Act and who was also involved in emigration stimulus projects associated with the 1882 Arrears of Rent Act.[40] Tuke had visited the west of Ireland during the Great Famine of 1845–48, which decimated rural Irish communities as people either starved to death or fled the country on what were known as "coffin ships," or one-way journeys from which people knew they would never return. Witnessing this led Tuke to commit himself to alleviating poverty through economic reforms since he, as Breathnach puts it, "believ[ed] that Irish distress was due to economic and not to political causes."[41] Breathnach explains that congestion in rural Ireland in the late nineteenth century largely sought a

"Malthusian solution . . . to relieve the land of surplus population. Balfour favored this, and indeed both Tuke and Plunkett made strong petitions for emigration schemes, but nationalist opposition viewed these policies as legal deportation."[42] The photographs Ruttledge-Fair took for Tuke are housed in the Tuke Collection at the National Photographic Archive.[43] The Tuke Collection depicts the hardships, particularly in Connemara, of survival and of the heavy labor women often bore to contribute to this survival.[44] These photos document to a large extent why modernization and reform were needed as Tuke worked for various political actions to ameliorate impoverished conditions in rural Ireland up until his death in 1896.[45] Although the photographs comprising the Tuke Collection may have contributed to the foundation of the CDB, they do not document the CDB's modernization schemes.

The 1891 Land Purchase Act established the CDB to operate independently of Dublin Castle and to emphasize migration within Ireland rather than emigration.[46] The 1891 Land Purchase Act "sailed through the house," as Breathnach puts it, because the Irish Parliamentary Party was divided after the fall of Parnell, who established the Land League in 1897 to alleviate the distress of impoverished rural communities.[47] The CDB photographs support migration projects by promoting less congested spaces as more sustainable and modern. Although people resisted the CDB relocation schemes, they are invited by photos like *Two New Holdings in Cloonkeen, Castlebar, Co. Mayo* to step over the wall into an Irish modernity. From the unkempt grass and shrubbery on the camera's position in the photo, the manicured fields on the other side of the wall provide the external focalizer with a view of a more efficient and prosperous future. The crowded foliage in the foreground of the photo implies the congestion and austere poverty associated with the clachan villages away from which the CDB sought to transition people living in the west of Ireland.[48] Yet, just over the wall, the farms in the distance in this photo justify relocation and migration schemes.

The removal of people from villages and the eradication of the clachan system, which people used to communally divide land, was an explicit project of the CDB in their efforts to modernize industries and rationalize material environments in the west of Ireland. While the clachan system is often situated as symbolic of premodernity, David Lloyd notes that the regions of the congested districts had long been affected by various forms of modernization that led to more innovative divisions of arable land: "Over the previous century, the Irish poor, dispossessed by settler colonialism of the more fertile lands and driven onto the bogs and mountainsides, had developed what is now understood to be a sophisticated and ecologically inventive means of survival."[49] While the CDB positioned the clachan system as outdated, Jonathan Bell shows that a related system continues to work in Scotland today and suggests the clachan system in Ireland might have been incorporated into modernization schemes if the CDB had stigmatized it less: "CDB officials, like most Irish landlords whose attitudes we know of, were almost entirely dismissive of the rundale system of landholding."[50] Landlords and the CDB saw the clachan system as causing conflict and inhibiting efficient farming practices, but people in the west depended on it culturally and materially, as Bell explains: "People living in the Irish settlements valued the egalitarian aspects of the system, and were also very attached to the communal living associated with the *baile* [village]."[51] The clachan system arose out of the impacts of colonialism, but it reveals the way that subjugated populations in Ireland drew on their surroundings and each other to survive materially and flourish culturally. The baile at the center of the clachan system supported oral traditions like music and storytelling in the Irish language in addition to facilitating communal land use.

The CDB photographs support the erasure of the clachan system through framing implicit progress narratives that render material environments into natural resources. Formal elements in the photos assert how seemingly older ways of life can be transformed into prosperous grass farms by using existing resources in new ways. In *View of Flooded Areas in the Townlands of Clooneen and Knockatee East, Co. Galway*, a grassy floodplain or wetland covers the bottom two-thirds of the photo.[52] Cows graze in the distance, but, otherwise, there are no animals or people in this photo. The text on the back of the photo states: "Drainage improvements were to be carried out by a deep straight cut in July 1914."[53] The "improvements" made to the wetlands recall the enclosure movement, which displaced people in western Ireland, as Lloyd describes: "Improvement demanded the consolidation of landholdings into larger farms on English models, the concomitant enclosure of all but the most marginal wasteland, the turn to labor-extensive grain-farming and grazing, and the eviction of the smallholding tenants."[54] Although the eradication of the clachan system was an explicit project of the CDB in their efforts to modernize industries and landscapes in the west of Ireland, these efforts molded material environments to support existing extraction economies, thereby ensuring that, in the words of Frantz Fanon, "the young independent nation is obliged to keep the economic channels established by the colonial regime."⁵⁵ Modernization projects shaped Irish land to ensure money continued to flow to the imperial center regardless of the outcome of debates around devolvement or independence.

The latent potential of environments being rendered into extractable natural resources also emerges in the photograph *Extensive Marl Beds at Moorehall, North East Corner of Lough Cara, Co. Mayo*, which shows a bed of calcium carbonate used for neutralizing the soil pH in agricultural fields.⁵⁶ The photo echoes geological illustrations, such as those by George Victor du Noyer, who worked for on the Ordinance Surveys in the mid-nineteenth century.⁵⁷ Like the Ordinance Surveys and geological surveys of Ireland for the expansion of the railroads, this photo documents the land's potential to be modernized and rendered productive for an industrialized British economy. Visual depictions of material environments combine with the professionalization of geology to encourage viewing landscapes for their potential as extractable materials to support industry and economic growth.⁵⁸ Such entanglements coincide with the material history of photography and the extraction of elements like silver required to create photographs.⁵⁹ These histories collectively cultivate what Siobhan Angus defines as the "extractive gaze," which is a "way of seeing the world [that] recasts environmental degradation as progress under the guise of technological innovation, economic development, and increasing quality of life," while it also "appeals to ideas of nature and the natural to legitimize the exploitation of humans and the natural world."⁶⁰ The framing, contextualization, and materiality of the photo rely on an extractive gaze in which the marl beds materially and semantically indicate the modernizing potential of rural Ireland. The photo frames the congested districts in a modernization narrative in which natural but supposedly unproductive land could be enhanced by relocating and rearranging the land and the relationships people and animals have with their environments. The extractive gaze evinced in this photo facilitates colonial-era economies and the rendering of material environments into natural resources. This visual culture of seemingly transparent photographic views of seemingly unused land and resources obscures alternative ways of viewing the landscape. The use of the relatively new medium of documentary photography in the CDB archive and photos like that of

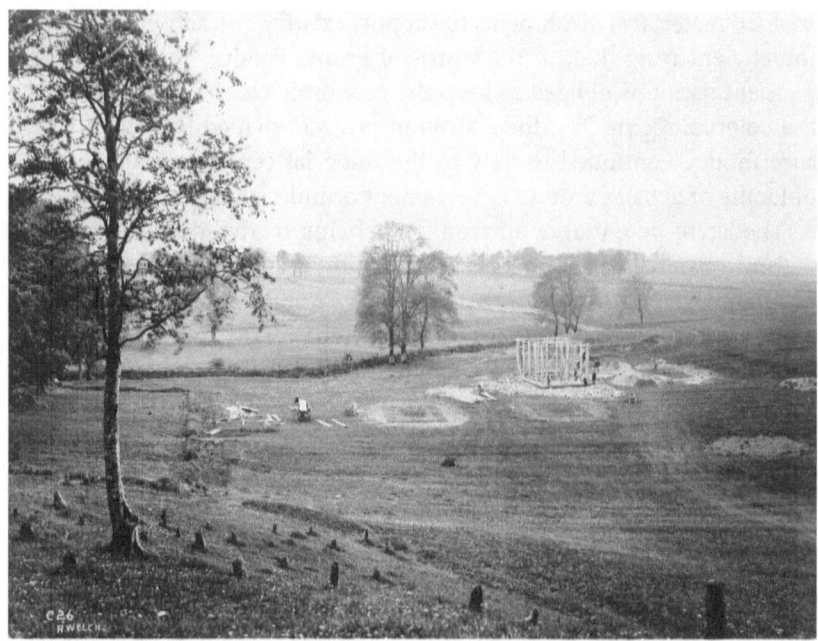

Fig. 4. Congested Districts Board, *Frame for a New Concrete House on a Grass Farm in the Castlerea District, Co. Galway*, ca. 1906–1914, CDB21. (Courtesy of the National Library of Ireland)

the marl beds indicate how as-yet-untapped resources in the west were readily available if the space was rationalized temporally into the bucolic future of an implied masculine modernity.

This implied modernity requires male farmers to oversee the management of women's labor and feminized material environments that have been rendered into natural resources. CDB photographs of houses being built captures the processes through which the CDB sought to realize modernized landscapes. The photo *Frame for a New Concrete House on a Grass Farm in the Castlerea District, Co. Galway* is a long shot of a house being built by the CDB (see fig. 4).[61] The position of the camera in this photo is just to the right and behind a tree on a small hill, looking down at squares on the ground and part of the wooden framing of a new house. The external focalization encourages viewing this photo from left to right, following several tree stumps and the old foundation of a building, which has long since ceased to exist given its erosion, to the men who work on the frame of the house. Beyond the house frame, a stone wall leads the eye to enclosed grass fields where animals graze. The "spatio-temporal event," to quote Massey, articulated in this photograph reveals the benefits of extracting and refining natural resources like trees into "ready-made building materials," like lumber, which Breathnach noted, were in "short supply" in the west.[62] The misty and implicitly productive grass fields in the distance offer a romanticized view of rendering living beings into exploitable resources, which, in turn, supports supposedly modernized relationships to land through gendered labor roles on grass farms.

Developing material environments into natural resources of economic value was a decidedly gendered project. In contrast to the masculine modernity shown in *House on Cloonmore Grass Farm near Tuam, Co. Galway*, the *View of Flooded Areas in the Townlands of Clooneen and Knockatee East, Co. Galway* implicitly feminizes the land by calling for its enclosure into a domesticated grass farm.[63] In addition to legitimizing the erasure of the clachan system, as I discuss above, the photographic frame of this image positions the camera dangerously close to the flooded area that spills across the photo and pushes the cows and more profitable forms of land use far into the distance. The flat horizon does not provide the external focalizer with a clear direction for progress. Rather, the displacement of people and cows through the natural water deposits promotes a notion of progress that promises class mobility through developing the wetland into a profitable grass farm and embracing the gendered forms of labor evinced in many of the agricultural photos across the collection. Through the photo's enclosure of the apparently feminized, superfluous, and unruly wetland, it promotes the region's imminent enclosure into a natural resource that will benefit a beef economy and maintain the empty promises of class mobility in a masculinized modernity.

Photographs of regions that have yet to be modernized often invert the gender and class roles expected of modernity in the early twentieth century. This inversion asserts the need for the modernization projects and domestic relocation schemes that the CDB facilitated. In response to rising nationalist concerns that assisted emigration was "legal deportation," Breathnach explains that relocating people from congested villages within Ireland became an explicit project of the CDB's agricultural modernization.[64] For example, *View of Congested Village of Graigue, Co. Galway, from Where Migrants Were Taken to Holdings in Graigueachuillaire* shows a circular road that presents the villagers' way of life as a literal

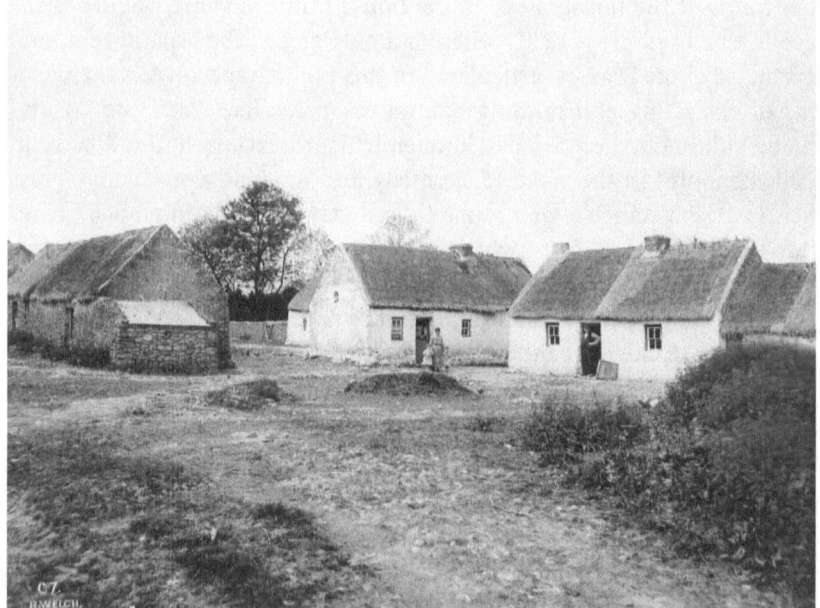

FIG. 5. Robert John Welch, *View of Congested Village of Graigue, Co. Galway, from Where Migrants Were Taken to Holdings in Graigueachuillaire*, ca. 1906–1914, CDB7. (Courtesy of the National Library of Ireland)

and figurative dead end (see fig. 5).[65] The six people in the photograph stand in or near two thatched cottages that depict the kind of poverty that the CDB aimed to ameliorate and that Carville critiques as a colonial stereotype.[66] The CDB considered houses with thatched roofs uneconomical and unsanitary, so part of their project was to rebuild houses with slate roofs.[67] The baile, or village, of the clachan grouped houses together, and this connoted overpopulation and crowded conditions for the CDB, thereby providing an implicit justification for the CDB's projects to eradicate clachan systems in the west of Ireland. All the people in the photograph offer restrained and serious expressions as they pose for the camera, a countenance that was expected of portrait photography but in this photo may just have been the result of the extended exposures necessary for camera technology in the early twentieth century.[68] The camera is positioned on a rough road that leads into the village and circles around a worn dirt mound at what appears to be the literal and figurative end of the road. No productive farming is visible, and the top half of the photo is just a blank, gray sky. The sky is inevitably blank due to the camera technology at the time, which did not comprise the light sensitivity or color spectrum to capture the sky in landscape shots until the 1920s and 1930s, when exposure meters, flashes, and film sensitivity to a broader range of light improved.[69] Like the photo of Cappagh, this image's composition of blank sky, dead-end road, and people crowded into and out of thatch houses lacks any developmental movement toward an implied modernity. The woman, who has a child holding each hand, seems forced out of the house and into the dead end, circling road while the men are in the houses, one of whom is holding a child, implying a need for men to care for the children. By associating the men's labor with childcare in the home while the woman leaves the domestic space of the house, this photo inverts representations of domestic gender roles expected of an agricultural modernity envisioned by the CDB.[70] This inversion of expected gender roles offers evidence that population congestion undermines normative Victorian gender and class relations.

The photo of the Graigue villagers demonstrates the need to redistribute people onto farms in which men will come out of the houses to maintain the land and women will disappear into well-ventilated and modernized homes like in the panorama of the new farms near Tuam (see fig. 2).[71] A handwritten note on the reverse side of the photograph of Graigue indicates that the six people in the picture will be relocated to new houses and farms in Graigueachuillaire: "Migrants are being taken to holdings shown in C4-C5." This note foregrounds the power of the implied CDB viewer to move people rather than acknowledge their agency to decide for themselves whether they move to new grass farms that other photographs depict or whether they innovate their traditional holdings and relationships to land. The external focalization of the material photograph and the note both encourage the CDB's subordination of the people in the photograph to objects of the CDB's gaze. This external gaze implicitly justifies the relocation of the people in Graigue out of their material realities and onto modernized grass farms. The reverse gaze of the six villagers on the camera establishes an internal focalization on the modernity signified by the respective positions of the viewer and the photographer outside the photograph and its frame. The external focalization thus materially and discursively relocates the villagers' internal gaze to the modernity envisioned by the CDB in two photos of new farms (see figs. 6 and 7). By deferring the internal focus of the villagers in Graigue to the new

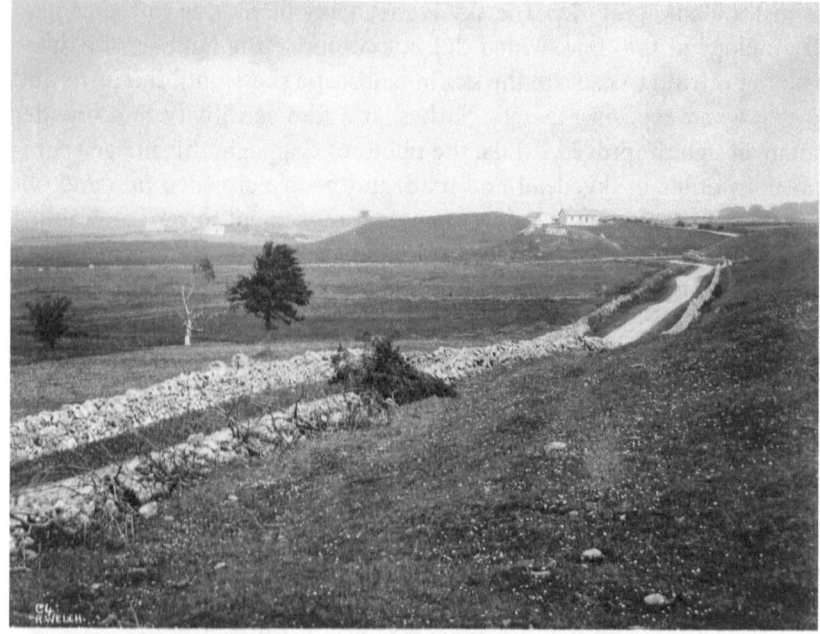

FIG. 6. Robert John Welch, *A Grass Farm in Graigueachuillaire, Seven Miles North of Tuam, Co. Galway*, ca. 1906–1914, CDB3. (Courtesy of the National Library of Ireland)

farms, the external focalization demonstrates a narrative of modernization not only within individual photographs and through the medium of photography but also through sequences across the collection.

Splintered Modernities: Two Distinct Viewers Look upon a Modernized Landscape

The photographs of the new farms where the people of Graigue will go are both called *A Grass Farm in Graigueachuillaire, Seven Miles North of Tuam, Co. Galway*, and they demonstrate what modernization should start to look like in the west of Ireland. Reading the photos together presents a sequence through which the landscape becomes increasingly efficient and rationalized. The first photo shows a partially visible road winding up to new houses on an uneven horizon (see fig. 6).[72] Although this photo indicates improvements are being made, it seems like a work in progress when compared to the second photo. While there are not yet

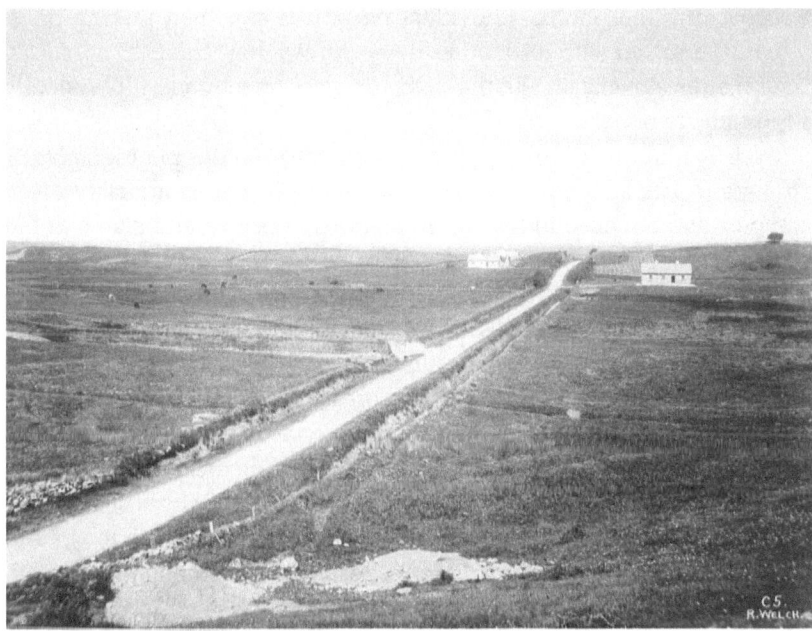

FIG. 7. Robert John Welch, *A Grass Farm in Graigueachuillaire, Seven Miles North of Tuam, Co. Galway*, ca. 1906–1914, CDB5. (Courtesy of the National Library of Ireland)

driveways and crops adjacent to the new houses in the first photo, the straight lines of crop rows and driveways in the second photograph run parallel to the road, foregrounding the increasingly straight lines emerging across these two photographs.

The second photograph's formal composition gives the landscape a controlled and uniform structure that matches the grid-like parcels into which the CDB enclosed land (see fig. 7).[73] The road and the horizon divide the photo into a grid that offers a rationalized space in which people can produce more with less effort. The external focalization follows the road to a point among the new houses on the horizon, thereby guiding the viewer to traverse the vast expanse of grass farms. The creation of grass farms would regenerate the soil and supply fodder to support the beef and dairy industries, which were important agricultural products in Ireland at this time.[74] The composition of each photo, as well as the sequence of the two photographs together, asserts a narrative of progress that teleologically moves toward more efficient and rationalized spaces.

Approaching the photos' individual narratives and then putting them into conversation with each other demonstrates how the external focalization often associated with the CDB's conception of modernity conceals a multiplicity of perspectives.

Such a multiplicity of perspectives emerges in the photography of writer and Anglo-Irish revivalist J. M. Synge. Synge is arguably more complex and nuanced in his representations of people and places in the west of Ireland than many of his Anglo-Irish contemporaries. He offers insight into how revivalist photography engaged with Victorian visual discourse like that of the CDB to deliberate and counter the effects of modernization on local communities and ways of life. Indeed, Synge was highly critical of the CDB's efforts to break up the clachan system and impose different forms of agriculture and land practices on rural communities rather than economically support existing local industries. P. J. Mathews summarizes Synge's general critique of the CDB in the articles that *The Manchester Guardian* commissioned Synge to write in 1905: "The point is clear: people are more likely to thrive by developing pre-existing native industries than throwing them over for new economic practices of which they have little or no experience or expertise."[75] This critique emerges in Synge's photographs, some of which were taken as inspiration by Jack B. Yeats to illustrate Synge's autoethnography, *The Aran Islands*.[76]

Divisions of space and time in photographic representations of an idealized but apparently vanishing authentic Ireland appear in Synge's photography. Both Giulia Bruna and Carville discuss Synge's photographs of the Aran Islands as what Christopher Pinney calls "salvage photography," which Bruna defines as "a specific use of photography in ethnographic study aimed at visually preserving ethnographic knowledge that is on the verge of extinction."[77] Carville points out that Synge brought modern technologies to the Aran Islands that helped him navigate Edwardian modernity: "Taking a camera and a clock onto Aran, he [Synge] brought with him two technological forms of modernity that emphasized in the most extreme way the different temporalities between inland and Island life. Photography, the standard mechanization of time, and cinema, had all initiated the most radical ruptures to temporal experience in the Edwardian era."[78] Carville sees Synge's use of photographic technology as a means to juxtapose his own modernity with what he perceived as primitive on the Aran Islands: "Synge, of course, emphasized these technologies and his introduction of them into the Aran Islands as a textual strategy to reinforce his own modernity by primitivizing the pastoral existence of the Islands' inhabitants."[79] While Synge's camera facilitated changing habits of looking amid the modernity of rising tourism on the Aran Islands, it also aided Synge in his desire to document the people and ways of life on the islands as part of an authentically Irish and premodern way of life.

Unlike the history of Anglo-Irish photography that Carville describes in terms of the "colonial picturesque," Synge openly discusses the negotiations involved in photographic representation.[80] In his 1907 autoethnography, *The Aran Islands*, Synge recounts his visits to Inishmaan, the middle island in the Aran Islands, during the last few years of the nineteenth century, and he shows the role that photography was starting to play in shaping realist and romantic representations of rural Ireland. Synge's descriptions of photographs in *The Aran Islands* suggest he was aware of the role his photographs would play in constructing the west of Ireland as primitive and in providing lasting representations of a place and way of life that he wanted to show as authentically Irish. In depicting a disagreement he had with a young boy about what clothes the boy should wear for a photograph, Synge implicitly admits that his representation of Aran Islanders and their own self-representation were not the same: "We nearly quarreled because he [the young boy] wanted me to take his photograph in his Sunday clothes from Galway, instead of his native homespuns that become him far better, though he does not like them as they seem to connect him with the primitive life of the island. With his keen temperament, he may go far if he can ever step out into the world."[81] The photograph in question shows a man, Martin McDonagh, leaning against the stone wall upon which the boy sits in his "homespu[n]" clothes that fit Synge's conception of how people from the Aran Islands should look.[82] Synge acknowledges the boy's reticence to wear attire for a photo that "connect[s] him with the primitive way of life of the island," a sentiment indicating the boy's recognition of hierarchies of tradition and modernity that justified so many imperial-era modernization projects in the west of Ireland. The boy's desire to wear clothes that were seen as more modern demonstrates that he is already aware of and in "the world." Although Synge acknowledges the boy's feelings, he does not admit that these feelings show the boy's culture and traditions are dynamically changing with shifting sociocultural contexts. Indeed, the boy's request to wear "his Sunday clothes from Galway" for the photograph reveal the boy is cognizant of how external viewers see him, his home, and his clothes. The boy seeks to negotiate with Synge what meanings the photograph will create for an external focalizer, thereby indicating multiple modernities splintering across the materiality of the photo and Synge's autoethnographic text. Synge's negotiations with the young boy in his photo deliberate degrees of modernization on the Aran Irelands, but Synge does not engage with the multiple modernities already existing on Inishmaan. Synge's photographs and writing implicitly seek to preserve binary divisions between traditional ways of life on the Aran Islands and the modernity of "the world" into which he thinks the boy may "step." Synge implicitly undercuts the boy's ability to "go far" within the traditional ways of life on the Aran Islands by overlooking how traditions can innovate and "go far" through the alternative forms of modernity and development they embody and demonstrate.

Synge's photograph and its description imply that he was mindful of the difference between himself as viewer and the Aran Islanders as viewed in photographic constructions of rural Ireland. Synge subtly embraces his role to construct broader understandings of tradition and modernity for an external and probably urban viewer associated with an advancing colonial modernity. Through Synge's recognition of his role in creating representations of a primitive traditional Ireland, Synge's photography, to use Bruna's words, "participate[s] in Revival activism in a more oblique way."[83] Bruna contends that Synge's largely unpublished photographs foreground the communities he photographed "to reflect... Irish national life."[84] Synge's photographs depict communities in ways that are "arguably objectified and abstracted into a revivalist idea of peasant Irishness," but these objectifying tendencies are tempered by "his photographic negotiations with locals on the islands."[85] Synge's more nuanced photographic aesthetic and candid descriptions of conversations in his writing offer a multimodal instance of what Bruna calls his "dialogic practice."[86] This multimodal "dialogic practice" helps frame the critique Synge explicitly voiced about the CDB's projects. In his *Manchester Guardian* articles, Synge critiqued the CDB for neglecting the potential of local industries and for their inability to stop "one of the chief problems that one has to deal with in Ireland"—namely, the erasure of indigenous Irish traditions and the Irish language through emigration.[87] Synge's critique expresses a desire to preserve traditional practices and communities. Although Synge ultimately reinforced tradition and modern binaries in his photographs and writing, the "dialogic practice" between his writing

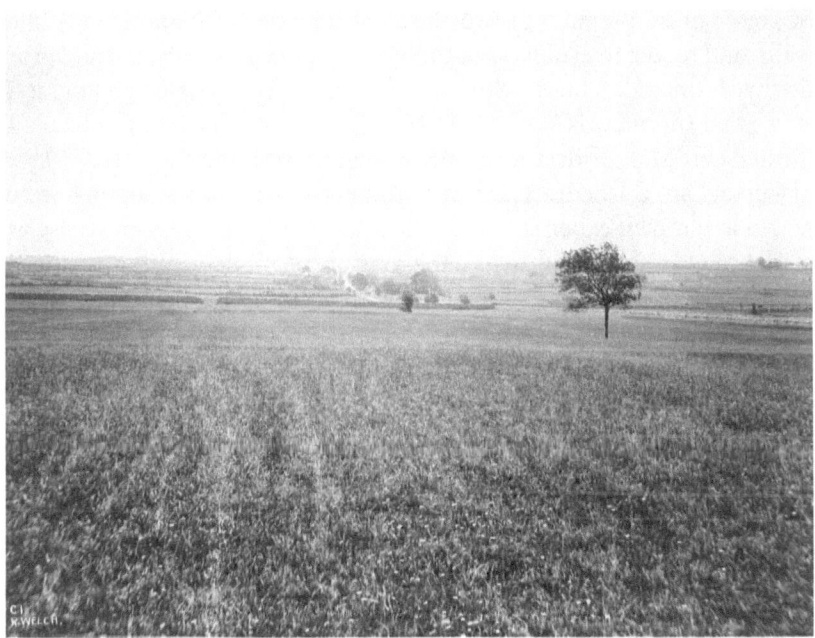

FIG. 8. Robert John Welch, *View from the New Dwelling House of Mrs Bridget Kelly, Lisvalley Vesey, near Tuam, Co. Galway*, ca. 1906–1914, CDB2. (Courtesy of the National Library of Ireland)

and photographs indicates the existence of multiple alternative modernities innovating alongside sanctioned visions of modernity and forms of development.

In contrast to Synge's more nuanced photographic negotiations of a modernizing rural Ireland, many of the CDB's photographs reinforce divisions between a seemingly vanishing traditional past and colonial modernity. Carville has documented ideological emphases that consistently emerge in the CDB's photographic archive through an approach that centers the aesthetic and historical elements of the images. A narrative approach, however, reveals how certain pictures in the CDB photographic archive rupture the developmental teleology of gender and class expectations implied in the CDB's understanding of modernity.

The photo *View from the New Dwelling House of Mrs Bridget Kelly, Lisvalley Vesey, near Tuam, Co. Galway* initially suggests, as Carville puts it, a "picturesque view of the Irish countryside" (see fig. 8).[88] A large expanse of grass covers the bottom two-thirds of the photo. The horizon, stone walls, and road parcel out a seemingly endless stretch of efficient and productive farmland. A handwritten note on the back of a related photograph states that this view is available to Mrs. Kelly through windows she paid for herself: "Mrs. Bridget Kelly was a migrant from the congested village of Curraghan, Co. Leitrim. The bay windows seen in the photograph were added at her own expense."[89] Carville interprets Mrs. Kelly's purchase as evidence that she found the CDB's version of modernization aesthetically pleasing: "The fact that Mrs. Kelly has contributed financially to this visual amenity merely serving to reinforce the idealised visualization of rural space as a signifier of modernization."[90] Carville's analysis asserts that Mrs. Kelly's view exposes "a signifier of modernisation" in a larger teleology of development and class mobility. Attending to the double focalization in the photograph builds on Carville's analysis, however, because it demonstrates additional discursive complexities within the photographic frame that interrupt the CDB's conception of modernity.

A slippage within the double focalization in the photo through Mrs. Kelly's window exposes tensions between an ostensibly premodern condition that the CDB's modernization projects sought to replace and an extant rural Irish modernity that precedes the CDB's interventions and effectively incorporates the opportunities it provides. Unlike the CDB photographs in which the external focalization overwrites or appropriates alternative views to reinforce a particular conception of modernity, the double focalization from Mrs. Kelly's window reveals two distinct focalizers. The external gaze guides the implied CDB viewer to look out upon a modernized landscape that, in Carville's words, "reinforce[s] the idealised visualization of rural space." This external view is in keeping with the CDB's overarching project and progress narrative throughout the archive, including in its avoidance and erasure of internal perspectives. Yet the internal focalization frames the perspective of one who is typically viewed, that is, the perspective of "a migrant from the congested village of Curraghan, Co. Leitrim," as the anonymous note states.

This internal view claims an alternative relationship to modernity that is only possible because Mrs. Kelly already skillfully navigates modernization initiatives in her region. Breathnach explains that migration schemes required either capital or land to exchange as the CDB moved people "from small to larger holdings."[91] These requirements suggest that Mrs. Kelly used her financial wherewithal to purchase not only her new house and farm but also the bay windows "at her own expense" to ensure a view framing her own perspective. The internal focalization of this image thus asserts an agency that the external focalization in most of the agricultural photographs elides. This photo reveals a double focalization that separates, rather than "hing[es]," in Bal's words, "the two worlds this work brings together."⁹² The rupture in the double focalization interrupts the CDB's teleological narrative, which relies upon a supposedly premodern condition that land reform projects seek to render into a future modernity.

Mrs. Kelly's view also thwarts the CDB's expectations for modernity established in other agricultural photographs, in which an external focalization associates a future modernity with the horizon. In contrast, the view from Mrs. Kelly's windows frames a subtle zig-zag movement that guides the eye both forward and backward across the photographic text. The stone wall in the distance initially seems to lead the viewer from left to right, reading the landscape like a narrative of development that moves forward in linear time. However, upon reaching the road, the wall intersects with it, and there is no clear direction for the gaze to follow. If the gaze moves away from the window upon reaching the road, it must move back across and deeper into the photo's diegesis along a curving path, thereby disrupting a clear direction for the rationalization of space to follow. If the gaze follows the road toward the viewer's position, it comes to Mrs. Kelly's own point of view, a view around which she chose to frame her window at personal cost. This act in which Mrs. Kelly demonstrates her ability to work within the constraints of modernization projects interrupts the CDB's paternalistic vision of establishing a Victorian modernity in an ostensibly premodern rural Ireland as it also allows Mrs. Kelly to oversee the modernization projects in her immediate surroundings.

Demonstrating that the CDB's projects were improving the lives of people in the congested districts would have been particularly pressing at the time the CDB photographs were initially commissioned in 1906, when it came under review by the Royal Commission on Congestion for Ireland (RCCI). The review was at the request of CDB members who felt curtailed in their ability to ameliorate poverty by legal limitations on purchasing land.⁹³ After three years, the RCCI increased the CDB's budget and authority to manage the acquisition and redistribution of lands in the congested districts, concluding in the RCCI's Final Report that, as Breathnach cites, "great is the difficulty that will beset any body in the work of relieving congestion (involving as it does the shattering the hopes of those who have so long cast their eyes upon the promised land)."[94] The language of the report leads Breathnach to conclude that "the paternalistic image of the board that Horace Plunkett abhorred so much was eventually its saving grace."[95] The imperial burden of the CDB to "shatte[r] the hopes of those who have so long cast their eyes upon the promised land" was apparently necessary to establish more modern and therefore supposedly better relationships between people and their immediate environments in rural Ireland. The CDB's teleology of development purports to draw seemingly premodern places and ways of life into its vision of modernity. By 1914, when the photographs of Mrs. Kelly's view and house were taken by Robert J. Welch, the CDB could document its success of having accomplished this implicitly paternal role of modernizing people and places in rural Ireland.

Yet the view from Mrs. Kelly's windows interrupts the CDB's success story by foregrounding the unsteady double focalization in which

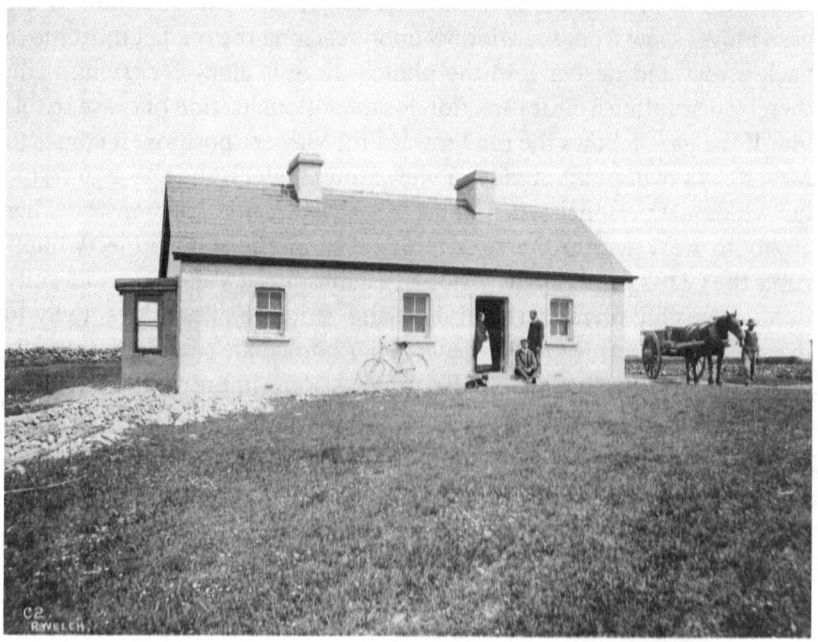

FIG. 9. Robert John Welch, *House of Mrs Bridget Kelly, Lisvalley Vesey, near Tuam, Co. Galway*, ca. 1906–1914, CDB1. (Courtesy of the National Library of Ireland)

the external and internal focalizations teeter uncomfortably between two distinct viewers: the dominant focus of the CDB's external viewer on a modernized landscape, and Mrs. Kelly's internal view of the rural Irish modernity in which she already lives. The photograph captures a moment of this rural modernity through which Mrs. Kelly was able to purchase the windows that frame her view. This purchase shows that Mrs. Kelly knew how to negotiate land reform initiatives in her region to actively participate in the construction of the rural Irish modernity that she can monitor from her windows. The existence of this rural Irish modernity counters the CDB's teleology of development by demonstrating, in Massey's words, "space as the dimension of a multiplicity of durations."[96] The view through Mrs. Kelly's windows evinces the existence of an alternative modernity, one that existed in the view from her windows and is also captured in the photograph. The double focalization in the photograph thus exposes the "two worlds" that the view frames, thereby revealing multiple modernities unfolding across the same piece of land.[97]

Like the view through the windows, the photo of Mrs. Kelly's house establishes her as the overseer of her farm and of the men who work there (see fig. 9).[98] This semi-low-angle shot is taken from slightly left of the new house, a position that foregrounds the bay windows, and shows Mrs. Kelly in the doorway with three men, a dog, and a bicycle outside. A low stone wall draws the eye from left to right, thereby moving forward in the narrative text of the image until the wall intersects with the horizon, perpendicular to which Mrs. Kelly stands. This intersection situates Mrs. Kelly's position in the doorway of her new house as the focal point of the external focalization. Mrs. Kelly leans against the doorframe, and the horizon coincides with her internal focus. The step upon which she stands elevates her above the men. While a man stands facing her, another sits on the step next to the dog.

Following Mrs. Kelly's internal view to the man leading a horse and cart down the driveway draws the external gaze across the photo from left to right, thereby establishing a double focalization in which Mrs. Kelly consents to forms of modernization that the CDB promotes. Yet her relaxed position against the doorframe asserts that she inhabits a liminal space in which she claims her position in the house but will not disappear inside it. The man's position next to the cart suggests he will remain within Mrs. Kelly's gaze even if his movement down the road leads him out of the photographic frame and beyond the scope of the external narrative framed by the photographer for the CDB. The internal focalization shows Mrs. Kelly to have a more complete and enduring view of the modernization of the west of Ireland than the sanctioned efforts of the CDB.

The photo of Mrs. Kelly's house also reveals a slippage in the double focalization that interrupts the external gaze from overwriting Mrs. Kelly's internal point of view for an implied CDB viewer. While the double focalization shows Mrs. Kelly willing to supervise her modernized farm, it also reveals her to refuse what Lim called the "sexualization of national-historical time" at a moment in which particular forms of modernization were undermining the role of women in regional cash economies.[99] This refusal to be subsumed into the dominant and colonial conception of modernity breaks down teleological narratives of modernization into what Massey has called "a simultaneity of stories-so-far," and it shows Mrs. Kelly to construct her own version of modernity within the constraints of modernization projects in her surroundings.[100] Regardless of whether she stands at her bay windows or in the doorframe of her house, Mrs. Kelly can inhabit multiple modernities that undermine implicit teleological divisions between the premodern and the modern, upon which the CDB's narratives of modernization relied. The multiple modernities evinced in the photographs of Mrs. Kelly's house and her view subvert gendered and classed understandings of the CDB's subscription to a Victorian vision of modernity and reveal Mrs. Kelly's relationship to modernity to be under the purview of her own gaze.

Unexpected Effects: Power and Progress in the Gendered Labor of Commercial Fisheries

In contrast to the gendered and classed constructions of modernity across rationalized agricultural spaces, the CDB's fisheries photographs depict communities' active adoption of commercial fisheries as a natural progression toward modernity, one that depends upon women's wage labor at fisheries stations while men partake in deep-sea fishing. This seemingly natural transition to commercial fishing was supported by the CDB's use of scientific evidence from marine biology to recommend particular kinds of development in the west of Ireland, including the types of nets and fishing boats that would be most productive at extracting fish.[101] Scientific understandings of the fisheries promised economic prosperity, and, as Niamh Connolly notes, "the people of Donegal in particular wholeheartedly embraced the ethos of the CDB and the changes it suggested and implemented, with the result that viable fishing communities grew and prospered."[102] Connolly asserts that "substantial social improvement" came from projects in which "piers were built and loans provided for boats, nets, and the necessary equipment."[103] However, Seán Beattie notes that Donegal fishermen had "a desire to cling to the traditional currach and open boat" and resisted full-time commercial fishing: "Estimates suggest that only 6 per cent of fishermen were engaged in fishing throughout the year, providing a supply mainly for the home market."[104] CDB member William L. Micks notes the "bitter disappointment" of Donegal fishermen as "over 200" British steam drifters might fish off the coast of Donegal at a time.[105] This instance of primitive accumulation meant the fisheries in Donegal were in decline by the start of World War I.[106] Steam drifters, which allowed for year-round fishing and the possibility of competing with already industrialized fisheries, required an investment that only full-time fishing could repay.[107]

Given this historical context, it is unsurprising that the CDB fisheries photographs make an implicit call for year-round fishing and the adoption of new fisheries technologies. The CDB encouraged full-time farming and fishing even as they also offered a variety of training programs to enhance the wages men and women could earn through seasonal migrant labor, which was an important source of income for people in the west at this time.[108] Yet the conditions of migratory labor were often premised on low wages, as Breathnach explains: "Western smallholders were guaranteed work on large British and Scottish farms because they worked for a lower wage than native farm workers. . . . Surplus children (those other than the inheriting son) migrated seasonally to contribute to the household budget."[109] Such forms of income would need to be replaced by a more vibrant, full-time fishing industry. The active participation of communities to create a full-time commercialized fishing industry was an integral part of the CDB's modernization projects in different coastal regions of Donegal.

Photographs of fisheries consequently demonstrate that the road to prosperity in Donegal runs in the direction of full-time deep-sea fishing in the waters beyond. One of several photos called *Downings Pier, Co. Donegal* offers an overview of the Downings fish curing station and pier.[110] Hundreds of barrels are stacked up as high as the warehouses, and boats are in the bay and tied up beam to beam on the dock. These stocks of supplies, facilities, and boats confirm the potential of this place to grow as a prosperous fishing community. The water, which performs a similar role to the roads and driveways in the grass-farm photos, encourages the external focalization to follow a particular direction. When read from right to left, the lines of the photo lead nowhere, as the hill abruptly ends before it reaches its peak at the edge of the frame. Instead, the external focalization guides the gaze in the other direction, toward the economically promising full-time deep-sea fishing. In both directions, the viewer must observe the modernized fisheries station that frames the water, thereby positioning modernized fisheries as inevitable. This inevitability of commercial fisheries overwrites possible internal perspectives comprised within the actual space the photograph captures. Regardless of which direction the external focalization takes, modernization projects bringing new technologies to the area will play a role.

The photographs' implicit encouragement to commercialize the fisheries into a full-time operation situates the choice with the people of Donegal while showing that the fisheries are sitting atop untapped marine resources. This move to position modernization projects as a choice indicates the political climate in which the CDB sought to negotiate a place among other movements to ameliorate poverty in rural Ireland. As separatist, constructive unionist, and Home Rule movements in Ireland began to crystallize into distinct political positions in the wake of the late nineteenth-century Land Wars, organizations emerged alongside the CDB to counter many colonial forms of modernization while postulating alternative and specifically Irish modernization projects.[111] The CDB's fisheries photos regularly assert the potential of the community to achieve prosperity within a constructive unionist vision, a view that sought to highlight the benefits of remaining part of the British Empire under terms established by the 1801 Act of Union.

Examining how narrative elements focalize space and time in several photos called *Fishing Vessels at Sea* confirms the CDB's vision that more could be happening in Downings.[112] There are few people in these images, and some show no people at all. Despite the pictorial influences these photographs exhibit, the relatively glassy water indicates a lack of wind that would stagnate even the boats with raised sails from moving in any particular direction. These environmental conditions combined with the inevitably overexposed sky above the distant hills draw the eye to an untapped potential both on and below the waterline. The distant

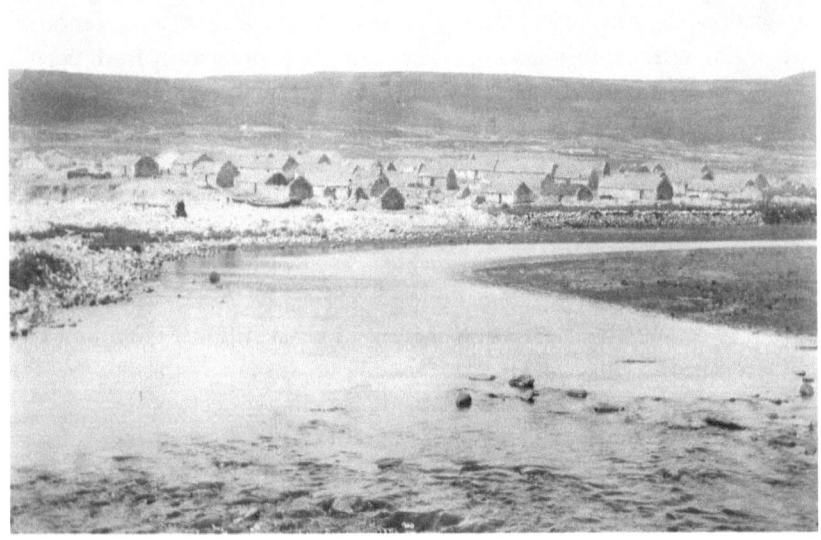

FIG. 10. Congested Districts Board, *Group of Cottages Beside the Sea*, ca. 1906–1914, CDB102. (Courtesy of the National Library of Ireland)

hills offer an uneven horizon that dissects the photograph into sea and sky, thereby emphasizing the glossy water of a low-wind day. The composition of the photo establishes an external focalization that forces the viewer to scan the watery space in abeyance of temporality. The atemporal space in *Fishing Vessels at Sea* reveals an unresolved tension between modernity and existing ways of life that the people in Donegal themselves must resolve.

A solution to this tension between seemingly natural processes and cultural relations is offered in the photo *Group of Cottages Beside the Sea*, in which the camera looks from a position in a stream that literally flows away from the ways of life in the village and out to sea (see fig. 10).[113] The position of the camera frames the turn away from the village toward modernized commercial fisheries as natural. While the stream comprises the bottom third of the photo, the middle third shows several thatched stone cottages, some of which appear to be falling down. This indication of collapse is in keeping with Carville's argument that the CDB archive foregrounds poverty rather than traditional ways of life to legitimate its modernization projects.¹¹⁴ Indeed, the composition of the photo shows that there is nothing beyond the village should the viewer's gaze move against the stream's natural flow. This absence of a clear vision of modernity in the external focalization evokes a desire to pivot away from the old houses and turn toward the modernity implied by the camera.

The tension between an existing culture and the seemingly natural flow out to sea is structurally dependent upon a narrative of modernization in which there are supposedly only two directions. This bifurcation of time and space is ruptured, however, upon close inspection of *Group of Cottages Beside the Sea*, which reveals some blurry figures that other photographs in the collection indicate to be a cow and two women standing or walking near the village.¹¹⁵ Even while life is still clearly going on in the village at the time the photo was taken, the external focalization from the stream frames the village in a process of decay as the photo blurs the potential agents of internal focalization. This erasure of possible alternative perspectives enhances the implicit call to turn away from the houses in the village and the supposedly collapsing ways of life they contain.

The call to turn toward an implied modernity finds a response in many of the fisheries photographs that emphasize women's wage labor as an integral part of modernizing fisheries. Although many people in western Ireland engaged in both farming and fishing, connections between gendered domestic labor on the farm and gender hierarchies in the wage labor of the fisheries are not made explicit in either the CDB's fisheries or agricultural photographs. Unlike the gendered constructions of modernization in the agricultural photographs, in which women and their labor disappear within the modernized houses, women in the fisheries pictures are not metaphorized as houses because women's labor in the fisheries took place outside the home. The turn to flow downstream and out to sea thus implicitly promotes gendered labor roles associated with a full-time fishing industry.

Despite the limited work actually available in fish production facilities, gendered labor became the focus of many of the CDB's fisheries photographs.¹¹⁶ Five photographs all called *Curing Fish, Downings Pier, Co. Donegal* frame the processes through which gendered labor modernizes the fisheries in real time.¹¹⁷ These five candid photos show a fish preparation table from various angles, establishing a broad overview of the scene that

1891-1922   61

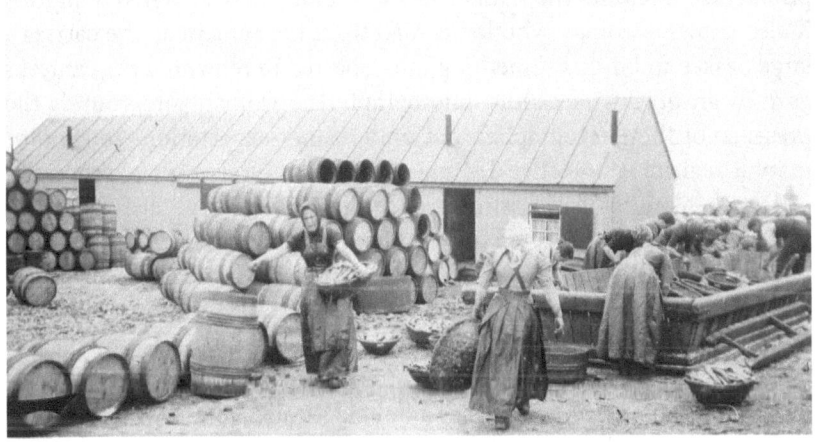

FIG. 11. Congested Districts Board, *Curing Fish, Downings Pier, Co. Donegal*, ca. 1906-1914, CDB71. (Courtesy of the National Library of Ireland)

is in keeping with Carville's analysis of CDB panoramas, leading him to conclude: "The CDB photographic archive is then yet another instrument of the society of surveillance identified by Foucault, invested with power relations that produce a correlative 'field of knowledge' of its subject."[118] Carville examines how the panorama photos document forms of modernization that endorse the CDB's vision of modernity and the power formations it entails. Although the pictures of the fish-curing station at Downings Pier are not panoramic shots, their dimensions and various angles institute an omniscient realism through the external focalization to produce knowledge that justifies gendered labor hierarchies in the commercializing fisheries.

The general tendency in the photographs is to situate rural Irish women's labor at the fisheries in supportive but subordinate roles. Yet certain photographs complicate how women's labor in the fisheries is valued or positioned in socioeconomically stratified gender hierarchies. In all five of the photographs, the women are bent over the table while a male supervisor oversees the process, and four of the images position the women literally lower than the man on the two-dimensional surface of the material photograph.[119] One photo positions the man as the same size and on the same level as the women, though he still stands on the fish-curing table while the women stand on the ground (see fig. 11).[120] Although this photograph presents the man's labor as literally and figuratively higher, it also shows a woman who looks directly at the camera as she carries a large basket and drops something into a barrel. In returning the camera's gaze in an otherwise candid photograph, the woman foregrounds the presence of the photographer and undermines expectations for photographic realism as objective documentation of natural or social processes.

Details like this woman's reversal of the camera's gaze disrupt narrative conventions established for women and rural spaces in other CDB photographs. The woman's gaze asserts an internal focalization that both affirms the external focalization on the gendered modernization projects at the fisheries station and asserts her agency in teleologies of development that pushed particular subjects to the periphery of progress narratives. This photograph establishes a double focalization in which there is mutual acknowledgement of the viewer and the viewed. Although this double focalization indicates forms of power that Carville observed in the panoramas as surveillance, it also demonstrates the unexpected effects that power relations produce. Foucault analyzes how power evokes assertions of dissent and evasion that, in turn, reinforce existing power structures in ongoing relational processes.[121] These processes inform the interlocked relationship between the photograph's double focalization and the modernization processes it represents. The photo indicates an

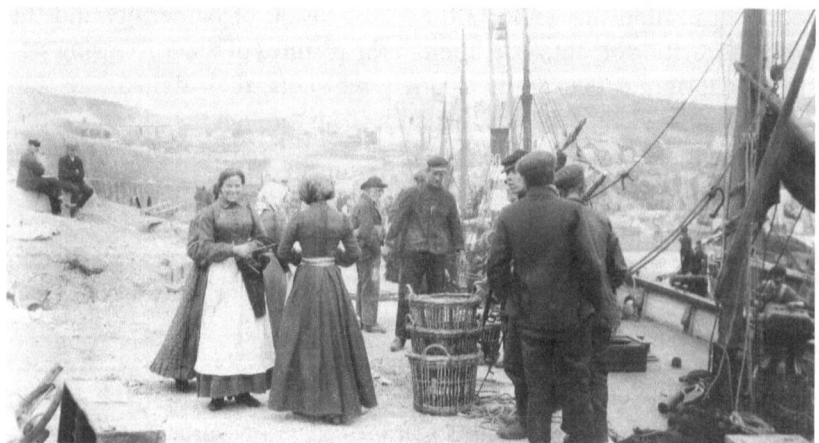

FIG. 12. Congested Districts Board, *Downings Pier, Co. Donegal*, ca. 1906–1914, CDB47. (Courtesy of the National Library of Ireland)

implicit attempt to document consent to modernization projects in the fisheries from those actively participating in them. Yet the tensions and contradictions within such a project create space in which multiple forms of agency arise to complicate the CDB's singular conception of modernization and modernity.

Many people whom the CDB photographed may not have had access to cameras or the material photographs, but they could draw on the mechanics of the photographic process to intentionally or unintentionally interrupt supposedly natural transitions into the CDB's vision of modernity. Such a disruption is exemplified in two related photographs, *Group Gathered on Downings Pier, Co. Donegal* and *Downings Pier, Co. Donegal*.[122] These images frame the processes of modernization in Downings by showing the burgeoning industry to occlude the material surroundings. In both photos, a group of women stands near the center of the frame, with one woman smiling directly at the camera. In *Downings Pier, Co. Donegal*, the dock has several fishing boats lined up, and some men are working on the boats or the dock (see fig. 12). These activities indicate the community's collective participation in the processes through which the commercial fisheries overwrite the surrounding material environment. Some people in the photograph do not labor explicitly, but all are engaged in some form of activity that contributes to the fisheries. Even two men sitting above the rest, arms folded, seem to oversee the work on the boats and dock, thereby implying their participation in the processes of modernization.

These processes demonstrate how the interpretive practices for reading the CDB's photographs often privilege an external focalization that obscures complex relationships to modernity presented by internal perspectives. Indeed, the bustle on the dock organically takes over the entire frame of the photo and the surrounding space it documents, thereby establishing an external focalization that monitors the expansion of industry as it overwrites preexisting relationships with the material world. Most of the women avoid the camera's gaze, but the smiling woman's face is completely visible. Her white apron draws the viewer's attention to her and to the knitting she holds idly in her hands, indicating the work she has stopped doing to smile at the camera.

The leisure the smiling woman flaunts by taking the time to smile for the photograph asserts her ability to counter gendered constructions of labor and their role in modernization narratives. As Sarah Jane Edge notes, people generally avoided smiling in portrait photographs in the Victorian era because it might be seen to invite the mockery of viewers, whereas serious expressions elicited respect.[123] Neither of these photos is a portrait, but questions remain as to what motivated the woman to smile so visibly at the camera for the duration it took to create these photographs. The woman's smile interrupts the more disciplined and sober expression she is ostensibly expected to perform based on the faces of the other people, particularly the women, in the images in which she appears. The woman's smile establishes an internal focalization that coopts the photographer's attempt at a quotidian scene that several other candid photographs evince.[124] In doing so, her smile counters any possibility for the external focalizer to overwrite her experience or to document an anonymous glimpse of the everyday lives of a community in transition. The woman makes both photos in which she appears moments of pause. Her smile consequently arrests the processes of modernization for the time it took to take these two photographs.

Although the lives and traditions of Irish-speaking populations were changing with the CDB projects, they were not, in the words of Luke Gibbons, "a whole way of life before it passes into oblivion."[125] The woman's smile disrupts expectations of an invisible and omniscient photographer whose documentation of modernization projects would frame technological changes to the existing fisheries as the supposedly natural next step toward a homogenizing modernity. In reappropriating the moment captured in the photo, the smiling woman claims a moment to say, as Roland Barthes writes, "only and for certain what has been."[126] That is, her smile asserts the presence of multiple modernities that counter singular conceptions of modernization and assert the potential for multiple perceptions and experiences. The woman's smile demonstrates that multivalent histories existed and continued to emerge in the CDB's agriculture and fisheries projects. As a result, her visage establishes an index for the myriad multiple modernities implicitly documented in the CDB photographic archive.

Conclusion: Power and Agency Across Multiple Modernities

Photographers for the CDB documented how its modernization projects drew on advancing fields of science and technology to change landscapes and material environments, as well as people's relationships to each other and their surroundings, under the aegis of progress. Analyzing narrative constructions of focalization inside and outside the space and time in which the photographs were taken and viewed reveals how different groups of people perceived and experienced modernization projects differently, thereby indicating rival modern experiences lived by those outside of the state authorized modernization efforts. The multiple modernities in photos from the CDB archive complicate constructions of realism and modernity in visual texts to demonstrate modes of resistance upon which those photographed drew to assert agency in their relationships to land and the material environment.

These assertions of agency in the CDB photographs resist inclusion into idealized economic and technological forms of modernization associated with commercial resource extraction and gendered constructions of modernity. They expose implicit gender and class relations and hierarchies that subtend the project of modernization which the CDB and related land reform projects sought to normalize. Consequently, the multiple modernities in the CDB photographs rework understandings of Victorian and Edwardian visual discourse, conceptions of modernization and modernity, and the resources upon which people in the west of Ireland drew to negotiate power and agency amid their changing relationships to the material environment in the early twentieth century.

2

1922–1950

A CRITIQUE OF PICTURESQUE POVERTY AS PROGRESS IN
FLANN O'BRIEN'S *THE THIRD POLICEMAN*

IMPERIAL-ERA VISUAL representations of rural regions paradoxically inform conceptions of what a decolonized Ireland should look like after the partition of the industrialized north from the colonially underdeveloped south in 1922.[1] The violently contested Anglo-Irish Treaty of Independence established the Irish Free State, which sought to modernize Irish landscapes in similar ways to the Congested Districts Board (CDB), with the Irish Land Commission adopting many of the same economic and land reform policies, such as relocating people domestically and reorganizing their relationships to land through, as David Lloyd put it, "larger farms [based] on English models."[2] The Free State's first government, led by the pro-Treaty Cumann na nGaedheal party, supported larger farms and sponsored domestic industrialization projects in the nation's first decade, thereby asserting the Free State's sovereignty and modernity. After rising to power in 1932, the anti-Treaty Fianna Fáil government under Taoiseach Éamon de Valera strove to preserve supposedly more authentic Irish landscapes and ways of life. Yet both governments inflected norms internalized during the era of British colonization and modernization projects. As Britain's oldest colony, colonial strategies to develop Ireland's environments arose alongside campaigns and legislation to eradicate the Irish language, oral traditions, and traditional relationships to the land. This resulted in the fact that many aesthetic and narrative forms available to Irish people by the early twentieth century reflected English norms and values, something Maria Tymoczko shows through postcolonial translations of Old Irish.[3] The Free State and later the Republic of Ireland's attempts to reawaken sleeping languages and traditions consequently often relied on picturesque precolonial cultural ideals that obscured rural poverty and embraced primitivist representations of Irish cultural traditions in Irish-speaking regions. The implicit focus on precolonial and colonial relationships to the environment overlooked more-than-human agencies and communities' material relationships to the land, both of which offered existent and alternative modernities to that endorsed by the state.

The irony of trying to decolonize through colonial understandings of modernity and picturesque aesthetic forms is the subject of critique in *The Third Policeman* by Flann O'Brien, the pen name for Brian O'Nolan's English-language texts.[4] Although *The Third Policeman* was published posthumously in 1966, it was written in the late 1930s as the Fianna Fáil government's Irish Land Commission adopted divisions between tradition and modernity in land reform and relocation schemes, which constituted a prevailing logic for land reform projects since the 1890s. Like the imperial governments before it, the Free State's understanding of a sovereign and modern Ireland supported ranchers under the Cumann na nGaedheal government, but under the Fianna Fáil government of the 1930s and 1940s, it implicitly idealized poverty as authenticity, consequently contributing to the erasure of Irish-speaking communities. *The Third Policeman* satirically critiques the persistence of imperial-era logics and aesthetic forms in the Free State's embrace of a seemingly authentic, premodern rural Ireland in the 1930s.

Written in just five months, from late 1939 to early 1940, O'Brien's novel scrutinizes the aesthetic forms of the picturesque and modernization narratives, as well as the relationship between these seemingly opposed depictions of place. *The Third Policeman* exposes processes that Clifford Siskin defines as remediation, which occur "in moments of change [when] the older *form* of reality becomes the *content* of the new one."[5] Through remediation, *The Third Policeman* shows how imperial-era aesthetic forms distort depictions of rural Irish modernities to maintain colonial socioeconomic hierarchies in a postcolonial Ireland. O'Brien's novel satirizes the continuation of colonial logics of development in Free-State modernization projects and efforts to decolonize Irish ways of life economically, culturally, and materially. The distortions that O'Brien's critique brings to light reveal how aesthetic forms materially establish a neocolonial modernity in postcolonial Ireland. Such a neocolonial modernity remediates colonial strategies of assimilation and eradication to further undermine the Irish language and oral traditions, traditions that O'Brien shows to offer alternative aesthetic forms and understandings of modernity and modernization. Having spent much of his youth in Irish-speaking communities, or Gaeltachtaí, and later working as a civil servant for the Free State, O'Brien had a clear view of multiple and often conflicting modernities as well as the aesthetic forms Irish literature invoked to contest ongoing poverty and injustices in the new postcolonial nation.

While ecocritical analyses of O'Brien's work are expanding, scholarship on *The Third Policeman* largely examines the novel as a satire of narrative forms that construct perceptions of reality.[6] M. Keith Booker and Keith Hopper have each pointed out that *The Third Policeman* is a Menippean satire, in which, to quote Mikhail Bakhtin, "the subject moves with extreme and fantastic freedom; from heaven to earth, from earth to the nether world, from the present into the past, from the past into the future" in a quest to comically "expose ideas and ideologues."[7] The "ideas and ideologues" that Hopper identifies in *The Third Policeman* show how O'Brien "sets out to undermine accepted conventional modes of discourse by concentrating on their inherent linguistic instability. Metafictions focus on representational form, and eschew 'meaning' in favour of poetics, i.e. the ways in which meanings are constructed and transmitted to the reader."[8] Hopper theorizes this self-reflexive critique of "conventional modes of discourse" as "metafiction," which, in turn, lead to "frame-breaking techniques in fiction [that] help us map the inescapable 'writtenness' of all constructed reality through self-awareness of literary practices."[9] Hopper shows O'Brien's novel to defamiliarize the literary frameworks through which it becomes impossible to imagine anything exterior to the text. Such literary frameworks reify "the cult of authorship and the tyranny of Cartesian thought," or the implicit separations between the supposedly real world of the author and the author's textual representations.[10] Tensions between material infrastructures and aesthetic forms and representations are the focus of Michael Rubenstein's analysis of *The Third Policeman*, in which he argues that the novel is a parody of James Joyce's depictions of public waterworks in *Ulysses*.[11] Drawing on biographical details of O'Nolan, who was a civil servant for the Irish Free State and worked "in the water-and-sewage department of the Office of Public Works," Rubenstein shows how O'Brien connects literary forms and public utilities, from roads and pipes to electrical grids, to demonstrate "that Irish modernism was largely a literary engagement with the problem of how to forge an Irish modernity after colonialism."[12] The connections between aesthetics and built environments in O'Brien's work raise questions about how narrative forms, media, and postcolonial modernization projects interact to reinforce or rework entrenched colonial-era aesthetic forms imposed onto the material environments of the postcolonial Irish nation.

Bringing Siskin's definition of remediation to an analysis of O'Brien's novel builds on Hopper and Rubenstein by demonstrating how *The Third Policeman* embraces a postmodern disintegration of the formal separations between the material world and interpretive practices that shape the world. This disintegration registers an Irish environmental consciousness in the material agencies of the land and people's relationships to their material environments. O'Brien implicitly points to this environmental consciousness in his remediation of picturesque and modernizing landscapes ripe for economic development in the content of *The Third Policeman*. Through processes of remediation, O'Brien offers a postmodern novel that documents the agency of material environments while satirically critiquing underlying narrative forms that structure perceptions of the real through colonial subject-object hierarchies. Such hierarchies erase alternative possibilities and more enduring human and more-than-human relationships to land and place. *The Third Policeman* contests what Siskin describes as "the premise of that century's Enlightenment ... that the world *can* be known—known *because* the representations we call knowledge seem to resemble it so closely.... The real was up for grabs in the eighteenth century *because* the rise of a technology [in printing] that seemed capable of simulating it."[13] In contesting representations of the real in the early twentieth century, *The Third Policeman* defamiliarizes colonial-era representational strategies that simulate the real, but it does so by exposing how established aesthetic conventions continue to shape expectations for what postcolonial material realities in 1930s rural Ireland should look like. The implicit comparisons that *The Third Policeman* draws between imperial-era aesthetic forms and Free-State ideals of Irish rural life expose colonial hierarchical relationships between viewer and viewed, narrator and narrated, and human and more-than-human (and often dehumanized) communities that mark marginalized peoples and places as premodern. O'Brien critiques how such colonial logics continue to structure postcolonial modernization projects through the hierarchical positioning of a modernizer as an authoritative subject who subordinates and objectifies rural communities and their surroundings, as well as their ways of making meaning and producing knowledge within those surroundings. While acknowledging the material agencies and multiple modernities in human and more-than-human communities across rural Irish landscapes, my analysis of *The Third Policeman* shows how the novel critiques persisting colonial divisions of an idealized precolonial past and postcolonial sovereign future to ultimately foreclose alternative ways of narrating or constructing rural Irish modernities after independence.

Reproducing "the Colonial Mindset": Narrative Forms That Perpetuate Poverty as Progress

The Third Policeman registers a tension between actual environments and their aesthetic representations, a tension that was an explicit interest of O'Nolan (O'Brien) in the master's thesis he completed in 1935 on Irish language nature poetry, "Tráchtas ar Nádúir-fhilíocht na Gaedhilge."[14] Raised in an Irish-speaking household, O'Nolan regularly visited Gaeltachtaí in Donegal, building experiences that informed his research at University College Dublin.[15] Carol Taaffe describes how O'Nolan's thesis "divides Irish nature poetry into two types—that which solely concerns the natural world, rather than the poet himself, and a later (inferior) poetry in which nature imagery is used to mirror the state of the poet's mind."[16] O'Nolan critiqued poetry that used representations of nature to describe the author instead of depicting the material environment itself.

The Irish-language poetic forms that O'Nolan emphasized in his master's thesis reveal a specifically Irish-language environmental consciousness. Louis de Paor's analysis of O'Nolan's thesis asserts that Irish-language poetic forms constructed an alternative relationship between the poet and the material environment that is distinct from forms in English-language poetry: "[O'Nolan] distinguishes the Celtic Irish attitude from the English perceptions of the natural world, suggesting that where there is a similarity between the two it is due to the pretense of Irish influence in the English material."[17] The Irish-language environmental consciousness O'Nolan analyzed in his master's thesis differed from English-language poetry. These differing forms represent or recognize the agency of the material world in divergent ways, as Taaffe explains: "O'Nolan approvingly quotes Ruskin on Walter Scott: 'He conquers all tendencies to the 'pathetic fallacy' and instead of making Nature anywise subservient to himself, he makes himself subservient to Nature . . . and appears therefore at first shallower than other poets, being in reality wider and healthier.'"[18] Although O'Nolan's thesis, in Taaffe's words, "argued that Irish nature poetry had already reached its peak in the twelfth century," it saw many English-language depictions of the natural world projected onto actual material environments.[19] As Adrian Naughton describes: "Nature has now become a means of expression, a device, rather than a reason for writing poetry in itself."[20] Through examining how literary forms construct relationships among people, literature, and their surroundings, O'Nolan distinguished distinct and divergent interactions with material environments that different poetic forms either promote or preclude.[21] O'Nolan's thesis contended that English-language poetic forms perpetuate conceptions of nature in the text that reflect the poet's own interior mind without actually engaging with the material realities to which the poem purportedly refers.[22] By contrast, Irish-language poetry offered O'Nolan ways to recognize how the poet is part of the material world about which the poet writes. The need to embed oneself in the material conditions and environments about which one writes became particularly important to O'Nolan in depictions of Gaeltachtaí, as Irish-speaking communities were regularly divided, relocated, and undermined through modernization projects, as I discuss in chapter 1.

Representations of Gaeltachtaí in which an authority objectifies and consequently misrepresents the lived experience of peoples and material environments in rural Ireland remained a concern for O'Nolan during his career as a civil servant. In an unpublished manuscript written nearly a decade after *The Third Policeman* called "What Is the Position of the Gaeltacht?," O'Nolan critiques Free-State land reforms.[23] His critique indicates that independent Ireland continued to rely on imperial-era representations that ignored the lived experience and material realties of Gaeltacht communities and their material environments. Land reforms, first under the CDB and later through the Irish Land Commission, reveal a continuity across imperial and independence-era expectations for what a premodern or modernized rural Ireland should look like. Both institutions failed to apprehend and address the material needs and lived experiences of Irish-speaking communities. O'Nolan writes that the CDB "made no attempt to alleviate the conditions of the inhabitants" of "Irish-speaking districts... duly found and recorded on a large-scale map which, though much out of date, is still in use officially."[24] O'Nolan goes on to write that land reform policies in an independent Ireland perpetuated imperial-era policies by associating poverty with a kind of premodern, precolonial authenticity.

While land reforms after independence sought to decolonize Irish ways of life economically and culturally, such reforms thwarted innovation. New industries, O'Nolan indicates, might have helped Gaeltacht communities to flourish and stay together rather than be undermined through domestic migration and emigration: "Instead of considering the problem *de novo* and seeing whether the Gaeltacht congests could be given an entirely new way of living, the commission concentrated its attention on trying to patch up a pseudo-agricultural economy compounded of attempts at mixing farming on nearly useless soil, fishing, the sale of turf to islands and migratory absences to labour abroad on other people's farms."[25] The poverty that traditional industries seemed to produce contributed to seasonal and domestic migration, as well as emigration, which O'Nolan's manuscript shows through statistical evidence.[26] His critique highlights persistent concerns about emigration that J. M. Synge's photographs and writing also expressed (see chapter 1). Yet, in contrast to Synge's desire to preserve preconceived notions of seemingly ancient but vanishing ways of life on the Aran Islands amid ongoing emigration, O'Nolan calls for more modernization in Gaeltachtaí. He advocates for forms of modernization that innovate rather than replace traditions with colonial relationships to material environments. In this way, O'Nolan demonstrates less interest in pretending rural ways of life are somehow authentically Irish or premodern. Rather, he expresses more interest in embracing the continual changes and multiple modernities already existing in Irish-language communities.

Writing this manuscript in the late 1940s, O'Nolan asserts that land reform after independence implicitly maintained poverty because "the status of the Irish language [acts] as the badge of poverty as well as of nationhood."[27] Representations of Gaeltacht communities as inherently impoverished came to be associated with understandings of seemingly timeless traditions and authentic ways of life in the early Free-State land reforms to which a national and postcolonial Irish identity should supposedly strive. O'Nolan critiques persisting ideologies that prevented the Irish Land Commission from looking for alternatives that would bring prosperity to rural communities. Rather, colonial ideologies perpetuated the narrow visions of modernization of imperial-era land reform projects in the Free State. These enduring imperial aesthetics juxtaposed a supposedly picturesque underdevelopment with modern developed spaces. The implicit opposition from conceptions of undeveloped and developed regions foreclosed the possibility that Irish-speaking communities might comprise elements of both tradition and modernity. This foreclosure obscured multiple modernities existent in rural Ireland that offered alternative trajectories for modernization through which Irish culture and Gaeltacht communities would survive and flourish.

O'Nolan's master's thesis and manuscript on Gaeltacht policies reflect his decades-long interest in the relationship between representation and material reality during ongoing attempts to decolonize through modernization projects in Free-State Ireland. The Land Commission took over projects from the CDB, and the 1923 Land Act ensured that the Land Commission adopted many of the CDB's understandings of land reform and agricultural and fisheries modernization.[28] Efforts to decolonize through land reforms reflect how the legacy of imperial-era modernization projects was both material and aesthetic. Understandings of what modernity should look like, as I show in my analysis of the CDB photographs in chapter 1, relied on narrative elements that implicitly categorized regions and ways of life as undeveloped and developed.

Besides the formal, developmental narrative elements of visual culture discussed in the previous chapter, *The Third Policeman* takes issue with picturesque aesthetics that positioned Irish-speaking communities in a vanishing past to implicitly promote imperial-era modernization projects, such as those of Lady Aberdeen. Val McLeish describes how many of the imperial-era schemes to economically improve cottage industries or enhance hygiene and sanitation in homes through nursing programs were part of initiatives established by Lady Aberdeen across the British Empire: "The Aberdeens represented the crown in Ireland and Canada, and Lady Aberdeen set up organisations to improve health and rural welfare in both places."[29] The Aberdeens were in Ireland for half a year in 1886, Canada from 1893 to 1898, and then again in Ireland from 1906 to 1915.[30] Lady Aberdeen's projects exposed transimperial ideologies implicit in visual representations and their aesthetic forms. Bringing a transimperial approach to Lady Aberdeen's work in Ireland and to understandings of the picturesque in the early twentieth century exposes, in David Lambert and Alan Lester's words, the way "a networked notion of empire" reveals the "differential mappings of race, class, gender and religion across the empire."[31] Picturesque aesthetics defined ongoing formations of "racial otherness," as McLeish explains: "What she [Lady Aberdeen] was happy to see as 'picturesque' in Ireland, or amongst non-white Canadians, she clearly thought would have been a disgrace—for which she felt personally responsible—amongst white people in Scotland and Canada."[32] These emerging racial hierarchies impose divisions of native versus settler populations as well as ideas of premodernity and modernity and undeveloped and developed environments onto peoples across devolving British colonies.[33] As a result, Lady Aberdeen's racialized use of the picturesque indicates how colonial relationships to material surroundings entrench social and economic hierarchies and render environments into natural resources.

Implicit in the racializing aesthetics that Lady Aberdeen maps onto particular regions is a justification for emigration. As David M. Smith shows, Sir Horace Plunkett, who was an MP, landlord, CDB member, and avid promoter of the cooperative movement, "went on an extensive fact-finding mission to Canada to evaluate the potential for emigration to that country."[34] In keeping with the various programs for social mobility that Lady Aberdeen sponsored, which I discuss in chapter 1, colonial projects encouraging migration from Ireland to other colonies and settler-colonies were founded on evolving colonial racial hierarchies. McLeish argues that Lady Aberdeen "did not consider Ireland to be an equal partner in the United Kingdom, but a nation of dependent, and probably inferior people. It was in marked contrast to her representations of the new Canadian nation, and the way she described the white settlers of Canada."[35] Lady Aberdeen's perception of primitive but picturesque Irish-speaking communities demonstrates colonial connections between British understandings of land management and racial formations across the empire that economically subsidized emigration schemes helped to cultivate and reinforce.

Despite Lady Aberdeen's depiction of Irish relationships with land as somehow precolonial and racialized, land reform projects in Ireland after the Land Wars in the mid-nineteenth century redistributed wealth to ensure British economic interests.[36] The redistribution of land, property ownership, and people after the Land Wars ensured that extractive colonial economic channels would remain in place regardless of who governed Ireland amid debates about Home Rule and an intensifying independence movement. John Regan asserts that "any chance of real social revolution had been substantially undermined by land reform and the creation of an increasingly conservative peasant proprietorship in Ireland sponsored by various British Governments in the four decades before independence."[37] Imperial-era land reforms thus established relationships with material environments that constrained Ireland's agency to decolonize culturally or economically because of land relations and material environments shaped during the nineteenth and early twentieth centuries.

Picturesque aesthetics appeared under the aegis of decolonization by purportedly preserving an idealized understanding of a precolonial Irish authenticity. As I discuss in chapter 1, revivalist expectations for a supposedly traditional and authentic past implicitly perpetuated imperial-era romanticizations of Gaeltachtaí as a disappearing way of life, a narrative trope seen in the way colonials and settler-colonials across empire visualized Indigenous populations.[38] Even as revivalists lamented this disappearance, the preservation of a picturesque ideal of an ostensibly vanishing Irish culture and language willfully overlooked how policies preserved the poverty that perpetuated the erasure of Irish-speaking communities through emigration. After coming to power in 1932, Fianna Fáil refused to pass on the land annuities they collected to the British exchequer, thereby taking a moral stance not to pay Britain back for land it had colonized for centuries. Despite a repressed economy during the ensuing Anglo-Irish Trade War of the 1930s, the 1933 Land Act aimed to intensify land redistribution and support small farms and rural lifestyles associated with an idea of authentic Irishness.[39] As Donal Ó Drisceoil explains, "The thrust of government agricultural policy was the reorientation of production away from the cattle and exports and towards tillage and the home market."[40] Although such a shift might seem to counter imperial-era projects, it maintained the socioeconomic hierarchies of the colonial era in an independent Ireland by structurally marginalizing Irish-speaking communities.

O'Brien's *The Third Policeman* calls attention to how this shift from imperial extraction economies to postcolonial protectionist policies continues to favor picturesque notions of precolonial authenticity that sustain the erasure of competing modernities. The ways that the picturesque implicitly racialized and othered populations across the British Empire maintain the ongoing marginalization of existent rural Irish modernities in Gaeltacht communities. *The Third Policeman* remediates imperial-era picturesque views of rural Ireland into the text to satirically expose how such colonial relationships to land ironically became the aesthetically pleasing versions of an Irish authenticity in the Free State. O'Brien's critique of how the Free State and Irish-language revivalists idealized poverty in Gaeltacht communities is one he continued to pursue just a year after writing *The Third Policeman* in *An Béal Bocht* (1941). Published under O'Nolan's pseudonym for writing in Irish (Myles na gCopaleen), *An Béal Bocht* (translated as "The Poor Mouth") satirizes how revivalists took up Irish-language autobiographies like Tomás Ó Criomhthain's *An tOileánach* (1929). Na gCopaleen critiques how Irish-language autobiographies were coopted by revivalists to idealize forms of poverty as authenticity. Yet many of these texts had already been edited to impose notions of propriety and chastity, which revivalists associated with a pious rural Ireland.[41] Na gCopaleen did not want *An Béal Bocht* translated into English, thereby indicating that his audience, including revivalists, was Irish speaking. Through the Irish language, na gCopaleen exposes how, in Sarah E. McKibben's words, "the colonial mindset and its strangely similar nationalist obverse, which recycled and perpetuated it," come to "replicat[e] the inequalities of colonial relations."[42] While *An Béal Bocht* satirizes "the colonial mindset and its strangely similar national obverse" in revivalists' reception of Irish-language autobiographies, *The Third Policeman* offers in English a complex critique of the aesthetic forms of picturesque and modernizing landscapes that led to this mindset.

O'Nolan's sustained engagement with distinctions between aesthetic forms in English and Irish acknowledges processes through which colonialism and cultural genocide in Ireland materially altered environments and people's relationships to their surroundings. Tymoczko explains how "the Irish were such a people whose ideas of land tenure were radically different from those of the English, and the success of the legal conquest of the Irish and their dispossession from their own lands during the Tudor period and thereafter anticipates policies adopted by the English in the New World and elsewhere."[43] The Irish-language environmental consciousness that O'Nolan reveals in his master's thesis and then remediates into *The Third Policeman* apprehends the differences in Irish and English relationships to land and property ownership that emerged materially and aesthetically during the era of colonialism and in postcolonial land reform projects. Postcolonial modernization projects reshaped material environments and more-than-human agencies embedded in the land. Material agencies in *The Third Policeman* rework anthropocentric logics that divide people from the more-than-human world, divisions wrought by centuries of colonial logics and modernization projects imposed on and internalized by postcolonial peoples and places. *The Third Policeman* incorporates Irish- and English-language forms to satirize how relationships between colonialism and the environment rearticulate themselves in picturesque idealizations in the modern era as British colonies devolved or gained national independence. O'Brien remediates the Irish-language environmental consciousness he elucidates in his master's thesis and the picturesque into *The Third Policeman* to recognize ongoing interactions between people and place and to indicate obscured or oppressed aesthetic forms with the potential to cultivate different and potentially more enduring modernities in rural Ireland.

Underlying Infrastructure: Producing a Picturesque Scene of Progress from the Road

The Third Policeman uses the road to demonstrate how imperial-era picturesque aesthetics shape expectations for what the landscapes of rural Ireland should look like through land reform projects in the Free State. The road infrastructure presents the narrator with a "pleasing picture" of the surrounding landscape as it also maintains binary divisions between the viewer and the viewed.[44] As I argue in chapter 1, the CDB built many roads, and the direction these roads take in the CDB's documentary photographs indicate spatial and temporal trajectories of modernization that guide the viewer's gaze. Roads that lead from left to right toward a vanishing point on the horizon indicate a literal road to modernity. A developed modernity is the supposedly correct direction, according to O'Brien's narrator, as "a good road will have character and a certain air of destiny, an indefinable intimation that it is going somewhere, be it east or west, and not coming back from there."[45] The "air of destiny" that the direction of the road suggests demonstrates the inevitable direction modernity will take, a direction in which the past is definitively left behind.

Going in the opposite direction of how a road is intended to progress, however, will lead the traveler to "marvel at the unfailing bleakness" of the implied premodern past.[46] The road ironically preserves the premodern past for the viewer, whose position on the road spatially removes them from the supposedly authentic scene they oversee. A good road takes one out of the "tangled town" of the clachan, or village, but a bad road reveals "the unfailing bleakness" of a premodern past that was paradoxically valued culturally and modernized materially in Ireland in the 1930s.

Rationalizing space through building roads facilitated the modernization of housing and agriculture which undergirded part of the CDB and later the Irish Land Commission's rationale for breaking up practices of communally sharing lands in the clachan system.[47] Prejudices led the CDB and later the Irish Land Commission to deliberately break up the clachan system, which they associated with decidedly unmodern ways of life. The eradication of the clachan disrupted oral traditions, the Irish language, and social relations, particularly in Irish-speaking communities.[48]

The prejudiced habits of looking evinced by the CDB and Irish Land Commission emerge in *The Third Policeman* through how the road provides the narrator with picturesque views in addition to how the text naturalizes roads as the foundation of civilization, even of an idealized and ancient Celtic civilization. The narrator paraphrases theories of the novel's overtly absurd pseudoscientist, de Selby. De Selby holds a theory that roads are an ancient and natural part of the landscape, as the narrator describes: "Roads he regards as the most ancient of human monuments, surpassing by many tens of centuries the oldest thing of stone that man has reared to mark his passing."[49] The idea that "man has reared" roads throughout time emphasizes their apparently natural reproduction and the need to care for this built infrastructure. The narrator goes on to explain that even "the Celts had in ancient times" used the roads, thereby showing roads were already well established in the Celtic people's own early culture.[50]

Conceptions of an ancient Celtic people formed a foundation for understandings of postcolonial Irish identity because it indicated a high civilization that preceded colonial occupation. In suggesting that roads are even older than the "the Celts . . . in ancient times," O'Brien's text uses the narrator to parody how the imperial-era aesthetics of the picturesque and modernity are uncritically incorporated into postcolonial understandings of premodern and precolonial Irish cultures. The narrator confers the national pride associated with being descended from a civilization in antiquity to the road infrastructure itself, a product of British land reforms on the Irish landscape rather than part of supposedly ancient Celtic traditions. The text thus parodically conflates imperial-era infrastructure with possibilities for decolonization through an implied antiquity and authenticity of the road.

This conflation exposes a fake dynamism associated with the history of land reform and modernization projects in Ireland. The roads built during land reform projects indicate forms of progress that do not change but rather entrench the status quo across time and space. The spatiotemporal stasis of modernization comes into sharp relief in the narrator's description of the region from the road: "I looked blankly and carefully everywhere, seeing for a time no difference between any different things, inspecting methodically every corner of the same unchanging sameness."[51] This sameness satirizes the change implied by developmental narratives and understandings of progress associated with modernization projects like the building of roads. The text challenges the implied change modernization supposedly brings when the narrator realizes that progress and preservation produce meaning similarly everywhere and ironically at different historical moments, so that "ten minutes or ten years" made no difference.[52] The text's depiction of the constancy of modernization satirically inverts the timelessness that revivalists attributed to Irish traditions and the developmental temporalities associated with ideas of progress. In contrast to seemingly ahistorical forms of cultural authenticity, *The Third Policeman* indicates that modernization projects actually produce the same forms over and over again through built infrastructures and their representations of implied progress. This is in keeping with Rubenstein's argument that built infrastructures like roads "arrang[e] agency" as well as Jonathan Foster's analysis of the road in *The Third Policeman* as "that which endows nature with meaning" and reflects the narrator's state of mind rather than the material world.[53]

While the narrator's view mirrors his mind, the text also shows the road to have its own material agency in both depicting and shaping surrounding environments that exceed the narrator's control or imagination. The road facilitates progress narratives that ultimately produce "the same unchanging sameness" so that the narrator "felt that every day would be the same always."[54] This idea of progress as stasis contrasts with the implied dynamism progress supposedly creates. The changes that progress implies and that modernization projects ostensibly bring to rural Ireland shape the reader's expectations as well as the lives and realities of peoples and places. Yet the conception of progress as stasis in "the same unchanging sameness" recalls roads built during the Great Famine of 1845–48, in which people who were starving were forced to work in order to obtain aid, often by building roads that went nowhere.[55] The cultural memory and meanings attached to roads in rural Ireland combine with the road's agency in *The Third Policeman* to direct the narrator's gaze, thereby influencing the shape of the story and, by extension, determining the possibilities of what progress can mean in particular material and built environments. Through foregrounding the agency of the road, the text undercuts the myth of progress as advancement. Rather, O'Brien shows modernization to recycle static aesthetic forms and colonial histories to construct the same old newness every time.

This paradoxically ahistorical progress narrative emphasizes the implicit division between the viewer and the viewed as the narrator looks out at the undeveloped and developed spaces in lands surrounding the road. The sameness of the material environments viewed from the road (which itself was built as the product of modernization projects) demonstrates how the land and cultural relationships to the land have already been homogenized by limited visions of what modernity is and how accompanying modernization projects should structurally integrate material environments into that vision of modernity. The narrator's description indicates how the road establishes a view that implicitly forecloses the possibility of an alternative modernity. The road facilitates views of picturesque and modernized landscapes, both of which implicitly justify modernization and preservationist projects in the name of progress and decolonization, respectively. By showing the activities comprised in postcolonial progress narratives to only structurally reproduce similar realities to those undergirding colonial-era land reform projects and policies, *The Third Policeman* exposes how hegemonic expectations for rural spaces continue to interpolate dynamic material environments into static picturesque landscapes, thereby shaping postcolonial Ireland.

Through depicting the road as an agent able to shape the narrator's understanding of his surroundings, O'Brien remediates the underlying forms and the built infrastructure of seemingly successful progress narratives into the content of the novel. The narrator becomes the viewer of picturesque scenes that position him within hierarchical relationships to his surroundings through the landscapes shaped by, and that subsequently promote, specific understandings of modernization. The view from the road reflects the temporalities of progress in which tradition transitions into modernity. The seemingly inevitable trajectory of linear colonial time undergirds how revivalists sought to fix Irish traditions in the past and preserve them under the aegis of authenticity associated with specifically Irish ways of life, which O'Nolan pointed out were often impoverished.[56] Such acts of preservation ironically ensured the ongoing erasure of dynamic Irish traditions. Like the English-language poetic forms that O'Nolan (O'Brien) critiqued in his master's thesis, the narrator's observations from the road reveal how "imagery is used to mirror the state of the poet's mind."[57] The narrator's view mirrors his own state of mind, but only through the way in which the road guides his gaze. The road produces and reproduces the hierarchies of a viewer-subject who subordinates the viewed object in a picturesque image. This image obscures the communal forms of living and existent modernities in Irish-speaking communities as it also calls for modernization projects that seek to develop or preserve rural poverty.

These processes of remediating the picturesque and modernization projects like the road into *The Third Policeman* raise questions about the extent to which national independence or protectionist policies can alter colonial, socioeconomic hierarchies written into the material environment and communities' relationships to the land. The ongoing material impacts that land reform laws and legislation have on Irish landscapes correspond to what Daniel Shtob and Jordan Fox Besek theorize as "environmental precedent," which refers to how "a wide variety of legal decisions and practices have environmental consequences that may not be fully under social control, and that these consequences often structure future socio-legal and socio-environmental relationships."[58] In highlighting the environmental precedent of colonial land reforms and modernization projects, *The Third Policeman* demonstrates how the environmental impacts of empire emerge out of ongoing interactions between hegemonic aesthetic expectations for tradition and modernity and material agencies in natural and built infrastructures. O'Brien's novel draws an implicit comparison between the formal aesthetic elements undergirding imperial-era infrastructure projects in a colonial context and Free-State policies materially shaping rural regions in postcolonial Ireland. Although O'Brien's narrator attests to the "fine views of the bogland," the narrator's view indicates picturesque aesthetics that idealize poverty and position rural Irish-speaking communities within views of a seemingly premodern and inevitably vanishing way of life: "Everything seemed almost too pleasant, too perfect, too finely made."[59] The road infrastructure and the picturesque views the road offers in *The Third Policeman* expose how modernization projects and their aesthetics combine to maintain social and economic hierarchies that continue to subordinate, marginalize, and eradicate human and more-than-human relationships with material environments in rural Irish modernities already present in Gaeltachtaí throughout multiple generations of imperial-era modernization projects.

O'Brien's remediation of the picturesque form into the content of his novel demonstrates how imperial-era aesthetic forms disfigure existent rural Irish modernities in the Gaeltachtaí. The picturesque views from the road shape what the narrator describes as "reality," in which he sees "far away near the sky tiny people were stooped at their turf-work, cutting out precisely-shaped sods with their patent spades and building them into a tall memorial twice the height of a horse and cart."[60] This image recalls the connections between imperial-era modernization projects to build roads and technological developments to extract resources from the earth, as Donna Potts explains: "During the late eighteenth and early nineteenth centuries, the reclamation of bogs was facilitated by a program of road building throughout Ireland, which increased the potential value both of existing agricultural land and of adjacent areas of as yet undrained bog."[61] Potts goes on to describe the subsequent industrialization of bog extraction: "The first turf sod machine was invented in 1844, followed by Charles Hodgson's 1860 perfection of a way of milling peat and turning it into 'briquettes.'"[62] These histories of imperial road building and fossil fuel extraction resonate in the narrator's description of the picturesque view that the road offers of local people cutting turf in a seemingly traditional and timeless way.

The position of the people "near the sky" indicates how multivalent traditional practices like turf cutting are manipulated into a two-dimensional picture through representational forms that erase complex cultural and environmental histories and material agencies, including those of the road. Although turf cutting continues to have strong cultural significance in rural communities, it also involves a colonial history of industrial extraction for energy production, as Derek Gladwin explains: "Hand extraction of peat reached its apex in the nineteenth century, after which mechanised peat removal appeared. Despite the level of industrialised production over the last 200 years, around 3,000 people still cut turf by hand."[63] Twentieth-century depictions of bogs and turf cutting, such as in the paintings of Paul Henry and Maurice MacGonigal, thus refract both traditional and modernizing projects across a colonial and postcolonial landscape.[64] The flattened image of people cutting turf in O'Brien's novel exposes the narrator's distorted view of these competing histories of rural life in the Gaeltachtaí by the 1930s. Indeed, the hardships of the economic war with Britain and the start of World War II in the 1930s did put pressure on boglands since coal from England was more difficult to get, and many migrated to cut turf during World War II.[65] Picturesque descriptions of turf cutting in *The Third Policeman* connect these extraction economies with representations of material environments. Through these connections of extraction and representation, *The Third Policeman* demonstrates how formal elements in visual and print media shape understandings of culture and place to contribute to the ongoing environmental impacts of empire. Within the context of turf cutting in the 1930s, the "canopy of lazy smoke ... erected over the chimney" indicates the burning of turf as well as its extraction. The idealized image of turf cutting and burning misrepresents how Ireland's newly sovereign land is literally dispersing into the air.[66]

O'Brien points to the promises of Irish independence evaporating through the carefully constructed artifice of an idealized rural life that distracts from the material realities such misrepresentations obscure. O'Brien's megalomaniac narrator obtusely overlooks the ongoing histories of colonialism and extraction right in front of him and upon which he stands on the road. Through this narration, *The Third Policeman* satirically critiques the Free State's implicit promotion of particular picturesque aesthetics through land reform policies that ignore the material realities impacting the everyday lives of people in Irish-speaking communities and their environments in the 1930s. Rather than grapple with these realities, O'Brien's narrator describes a deliberately constructed but superficial scene. The superficiality of the narrator's perspective mocks Free-State attempts to decolonize through enshrining poverty as an authentically Irish way of life in the Gaeltacht. O'Brien thus critiques the erasure of depth and dynamism that he knew from his Irish-speaking upbringing and research to exist in Gaeltachaí and the material environments of rural Ireland. Consequently, *The Third Policeman* implicitly calls on its readers to heed the economic constraints in which actual people live and labor and the environmental histories of empires that inform the future of postcolonial economies and ways of life.

The artificially constructed scene the narrator describes of the turf cutting and burning is reminiscent of the Postimpressionistic paintings of Paul Henry, whose depictions of Connemara emphasize the pictorial elements of the image over any attempt to realistically represent rural Ireland. Henry's painting *Connemara Cottages* (1936–37), created just a few years prior to O'Brien's *The Third Policeman*, offers a view from the road of thatched cottages and piles of turf stacked in some cases as high as the cottages themselves (see fig. 13).[67] Like the road in O'Brien's novel, the road in Henry's painting shows the viewer an image of rural Ireland that flattens the material realities of the people who live there into a picturesque scene. Billowing above the village are enormous clouds that cast a shadow over the position on the road from which the viewer's perspective starts. The road guides the viewer's gaze to sunnier hills and cottages just beyond where the viewer seems to stand, indicating that Henry's viewer, like O'Brien's narrator, is on a "good road" that "run[s] swiftly across the flat land and paus[es] slightly to climb slowly up a hill" into the sunny modernity beyond—that is, to a vanishing point that "goes somewhere" and does "not com[e] back from there."[68] Recalling the piles of turf in Henry's painting, the road in *The Third Policeman* also guides the narrator's gaze in a particular direction to see how the piles of turf become "a tall memorial twice the height of a horse and cart" and

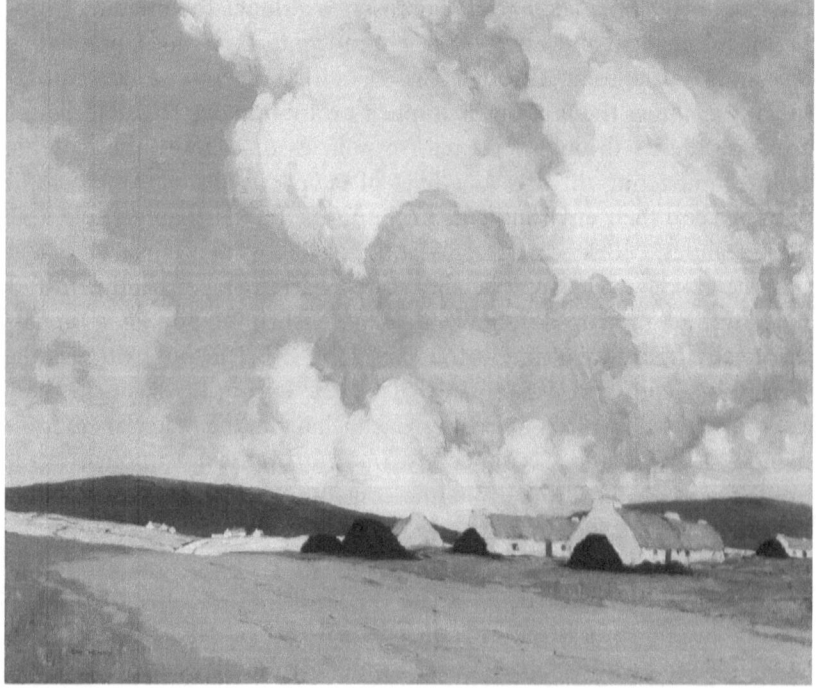

FIG. 13. Paul Henry (1876–1958), *Connemara Cottages*, ca. 1936–1937. (Courtesy of the National Gallery of Ireland, © Paul Henry, *Connemara Cottages*, c/o Pictoright Amsterdam 2025)

"arranged neatly on each side of the road."[69] The scene in *The Third Policeman* and in Henry's *Connemara Cottages* both offer picturesque images of traditional turf cutting that conceal the colonial and environmental histories of the extraction of the bog.

The remediation of such picturesque images in O'Brien's novel satirically exposes how aesthetic forms and depictions of authenticity and progress distort rural Irish modernities. The road guides the narrator's gaze in a particular direction to see how turf is "cu[t] out [in] precisely-shaped sods with their patent spades and building them into a tall memorial twice the height of a horse and cart."[70] The text implicitly exposes the irony of creating a "memorial" by destroying what it memorializes. Through this irony, *The Third Policeman* registers how aesthetic forms exaggerate rural Ireland's culture, language, and traditions into misleading shapes that undermine material realities for people and environments in the Gaeltachtaí. Picturesque aesthetics idealized, indeed even celebrated, rural poverty to establish divisions of premodernity and modernity that replicate the binary logics and material contexts of colonial-era underdevelopment and later justifications for coerced forms of modernization into a globalizing, neocolonial economy. These binary logics reinforce hierarchies between human and more-than-human worlds, as the bog only takes on cultural meaning when it is rendered into a natural resource—that is, when it becomes turf for burning to warm homes or to cook. Consequently, the cultural and economic value of unique and multispecies boglands satirically emerges in O'Brien's novel only as a larger-than-life "memorial" after it is extracted from the earth and prepared as a fuel resource for industry or in human homes.

O'Brien thus satirizes how these colonial mindsets and hierarchies persist in the Irish Free State and its land reform projects. The Free State attempted to preserve a picturesque conception of Irish authenticity that O'Brien's novel satirically challenges through the narrator's distorted views. As Hopper explains, the preservationist attitude toward the Irish language came, according to O'Nolan (O'Brien), at the expense of the Gaeltacht communities through relocation and land redistribution efforts: "For Myles [O'Brien/O'Nolan] the net result of the revival's nationalist agenda was that it had privileged an imagined peasant lifestyle, and through its promotion of this dubious fairytale it had inadvertently enshrined the parochial shibboleths of a conservative order."[71] Efforts to preserve an imagined rural Ireland reveals the persistence of imperial-era aesthetic forms in the Free State's attempts to culturally and economically decolonize. The flattened picturesque view that the road creates for the narrator of the material bog rendered "into a tall memorial twice the height of a horse and cart" misrepresents rural Irish modernities.[72] Instead of showing the dynamic modernities and innovating cultural traditions of actual Gaeltachtaí and their material environments in postcolonial Ireland, O'Brien's depictions expose how picturesque views distort Gaeltachtaí into "an imagined peasant lifestyle" and render boglands into an extractable resource.[73] O'Brien's remediation of the picturesque and progress narratives into *The Third Policeman* critiques how the Free State's policies rely on imperial-era aesthetic forms that contort lived realities and material environments into colonial tropes of vanishing civilizations with imagined authenticity.

Besides the irony of memorializing a multispecies bog environment by extracting it into "precisely-shaped sods," O'Brien shows picturesque scenes of modernized farms to also erase women from the record. This erasure of women's labor within houses persists in the work of the Land Commission after the 1933 Land Act, which relocated people from Irish-speaking regions in the west to County Meath. As Suzanne Pegley notes, when people from rural communities in the west were moved to the Gaeltacht colonies in County Meath, the Land Commission did not keep track of the number of women: "The Land Commission officials erred in the number of children, perhaps understandably, but it was questionable not to include wives, even for the time."[74] Wives were implicitly considered a necessary part of a man's farm; women were not seen as independent agents in the work the Land Commission carried out under the 1933 Land Act, a fact that echoes the rendering of women as natural resources in colonial Ireland.[75] In *The Third Policeman*, the "canopy of lazy smoke [that] had been erected over the chimney" asserts a modernized house implicitly participating in forms of progress that rely on women's labor and natural resources extracted from the bog, which are both concealed within the house. "The happiness of a coterie of fowls" who are "unrelenting [in the] manufacture of their eggs" depicts feminized labor as literally dehumanized.

By describing the hens' labor of production and reproduction and not representing the domestic labor inside the house, O'Brien points to how picturesque images of premodern and modern rural lifestyles obscure the subordinated gender roles of women. The text's recognition of this subordination and erasure of women in nation building is in keeping with Maebh Long's assertion that O'Brien often satirically repeats stereotypes to expose gender hierarchies and does not censor the physical hardships women in Ireland bore, but he also does not imagine alternatives.[76] Certainly, the narrator's personal reflections indicate this tendency, such as when he shares that he "never saw [his] mother outside the kitchen in all [his] life," and "her face was always red and sore-looking from bending at the fire."[77] The text implicitly recalls this memory of the narrator's mother as he views the idealized landscape in which chimney smoke "indicate[s] that people were within engaged on tasks."[78] Rendering the material and embodied experiences of women and land into metaphors of houses and rationalized space satirically critiques an imperial-inflected vision of rural modernity in postcolonial Ireland.

This reference to "the happiness of a coterie of fowls" also implicitly points to successful forms of modernization in the seemingly timeless picturesque vista the narrator views from the road. Women in rural Ireland historically controlled the buying and selling of eggs and poultry, though the Irish Agricultural Organization Society and the Department of Agricultural and Technical Instruction unsuccessfully encouraged men to take over these cash economies.[79] As Smith and Ciara Breathnach separately explain, the CDB stood out among these improvement initiatives in its acknowledgment of women's roles in the production and management of household funds in rural economies by seeking to enhance these rural economies.[80] Indeed, the prominent role of women in the rural Irish egg and poultry economies consequently feminized the industry, leading to, as Maureen O'Connor describes, "an obscure literary genre in late nineteenth- and early twentieth-century Ireland, the 'chicken novel', a series of texts with 'poultry themes.'"[81] O'Connor notes that the "chicken novel" offers a response to "male anxiety" at the way this women-led industry "traditionally represented some small measure of independence for women living and working on Irish farms."[82] Reading *The Third Policeman* in light of these historical and literary contexts deepens O'Brien's satiric critique of the picturesque by pointedly excluding actual women in favor of the "happy coterie of fowls." The novel demonstrates a continuity of the picturesque aesthetics of modernized farms from imperial-era land-reform initiatives to Free-State modernization projects, many of which sought to preserve a picturesque rural idyll that undermined women's autonomy in household economies.

Like the agricultural photographs in the CDB photographic archive, people generally (and women in particular) are not included in visual representations of postcolonial Irish modernity. The people in the houses in the narrator's description are presumably women, and they become metaphorized as homes, apparently "engaged on tasks" that would contribute to a romanticized rural space the narrator describes as "the reality of all the simple things my eyes were looking at."[83] Bronwen Walter explains how understandings of home and family in Free-State Ireland in the 1920s and 1930s perpetuated the erasure of women from representation: "The cottage in the landscape became a symbol of women, who were absent from the frame yet understood to be present within the walls, essential both to the operation of the enterprise and to the continuation of the nation, fixed yet dispossessed."[84] The view from the road invokes a picturesque image of rural Ireland that dehumanizes and erases women's labor as it conceals gendered forms of exploitation within the houses through the metaphorization of women as a rural cottage. Such depictions of women as houses also occurred in the CDB agricultural photographs to connote forms of progress, as I argue in chapter 1, thereby indicating longer histories of aesthetic representations that shape gendered understandings of modernity and tradition. O'Brien reveals a parallel between metaphorizing women as houses or hens and depicting the bog as "precisely shaped sods" that "memorialize" an imagined past foreclosed from existing in a neocolonial modernity after independence. The dehumanization of gendered labor indicates, to use Sarah Townsend's words, "how processes of modernization deteriorate humans' relationships to their fellow animals in order to secure further their consent."[85] The imperial mindsets that divide humans from the more-than-human world and shape environments into particular conceptions of modernity continued after independence to maintain and even exacerbate colonial gendered hierarchies in postcolonial modernization projects.

Through satirically remediating imperial-era forms into the novel, *The Third Policeman* points to how modernization narratives and the implicitly picturesque aesthetics associated with premodern and modern landscapes actively shape postcolonial Irish histories and identities in ways that perpetuate the erasure of multiple modernities existing in Irish-language communities and literary forms. The focus on rendering forms like the picturesque into the content of the narrator's descriptions in *The Third Policeman* echoes the focus on poetic forms in O'Nolan's (O'Brien) master's thesis. Where O'Nolan interpreted English-language poetry as constructing the material world into preconceived forms for how the poet-subject identified themself in idealizations of nature, the

Irish-language poet "makes himself subservient to Nature" in ways that respect agencies in the material and more-than-human environment.[86] O'Brien's narrator envisions rural Ireland through the lens of an English-language poet, but the absurdity and irony in the narrator's descriptions implicitly invite the reader to adopt a worldview that heeds the obtusely overlooked presence of multiple modernities experienced and lived by Irish-speaking communities and in their relationships with material environments.

The remediation of imperial-era forms in *The Third Policeman* satirizes the Free State's policies to preserve and modernize rural Ireland in the image idealized by its colonial oppressor. These imperial images and forms justify paternalistic programs and the erasure of supposedly premodern ways of knowing and living. The text exposes picturesque aesthetics and modernization narratives to sustain colonial hierarchies and racial formations across the British Empire through representational forms that distort depictions of supposedly static traditional ways of life in Irish-speaking communities. Such forms sought to eradicate the Irish language and the cultural practices embedded in the Irish language and people's relationships to land under colonial rule. While gesturing to dynamic multiple modernities present in material landscapes rather than their picturesque representations, O'Brien's remediation of the picturesque aesthetics and modernization narratives into the content of his novel critiques formal elements that inform perceptions of the land and policies shaping material environments. By exposing these formal elements, O'Brien shows how they collectively continue to erase Irish-speaking communities and gendered labor in the Free State.

Misguided Plans: An Overdependence on Colonial Ways of Knowing

Through the character of de Selby, *The Third Policeman* satirically challenges how picturesque landscapes and modernization narratives distort human and more-than-human environments, cultures, and agencies. It does this through attributing authority to misguided plans that structurally maintain colonial hierarchies between the viewer and the viewed, the modernizer and the modernized, the human subject and an objectified material world. One way the text critiques misguided plans is by showing de Selby's supposedly innovative designs for modern housing to rely on mistaking his "absent-minded practice known generally as 'doodling'" for "the plans of a type of dwelling he always had in mind" and for which he "immediately wrote many pages explaining the sketches."[87] Ironically, de Selby's innovative ideas replicate the conditions of a supposedly premodern past that they purportedly supersede through new science on hygiene. The narrator describes the "therapeutic values—chiefly pulmonary" that de Selby's "habitats" would apparently provide, because these "habitats" lacked either roofs or walls.[88] As I discuss in chapter 1, many of the hygiene guidelines for what the CDB called "dwellings" (as opposed to de Selby's more dehumanizing term, "habitats") did indeed call for more ventilation, but the addition of windows is less extreme than de Selby's partial houses.[89] De Selby's designs for "habitats" were also "surrounded by a diminutive moat or pit bearing some resemblance to military latrines."[90] De Selby's idea contrasts with efforts by the CDB to eradicate cesspools of pig or cow urine, which were outside some houses in the congested districts, and which Breathnach points out actually eliminated certain harmful bacteria, despite the disapproval CDB members had for that arrangement.[91]

A note by the narrator indicates that de Selby's houses would be "the last place where one would think of keeping even cattle," which suggests that no one, human or animal, would want to live in such houses.[92] Moreover, it satirizes the prominent role of cattle in socioeconomic hierarchies in which the state values ranchers, like Mathers in the novel, more than people in the picturesque representations of Irish-speaking communities that the road envisions. The irony that de Selby's modernized housing would actually make conditions worse according to colonial-era evaluations of supposedly premodern housing conditions subverts the implicit linear time that modernization narratives impose on actual spaces and lived experience. The text invokes de Selby's confusion of undeveloped and developed and premodern and modern forms of housing to expose how particular ideas or symbols signify progress in a seemingly arbitrary arrangement that strategically maintains social hierarchies rather than promotes any actual material changes. Indeed, those living in de Selby's houses would likely be worse off than they were before his so-called improvements were made. This assessment of housing improvements is in keeping with Colleen Taylor's biosemiotics analysis of the benefits of the traditional mud cabin, which "contains an internal ecosystem where soil, oxygen, fire, human, and pig interact, provoking change and contributing toward continued survival and revival."[93] While Victorian ideologies of hygiene and colonial forms of modernity and modernization continued to deride mud cabins in the early twentieth century, traditional mud houses were in many cases more durable and healthier than their modernized replacements.[94] By exposing the absurdity of de Selby's alleged improvements to eradicate walls and confusing his "doodl[es]" with modernization schemes, O'Brien satirizes the array of colonially inflected aesthetic forms and representations of Irish-speaking communities upon which the Free State relied to envision postcolonial or even decolonial progress. The Third Policeman critiques how the environmental impacts of empire have an agency, like that of the road, to constrain the imaginative possibilities for representing and empowering rural Irish communities. Rather, the aesthetics of the colonial picturesque and conceptions of modernity recur in Free-State efforts to effect presumed improvements and preservationist policies made for Gaeltachtaí in 1930s Ireland.

In highlighting de Selby's confusion about what constitutes improvement in misunderstandings of his drawings, The Third Policeman also critiques the sociocultural value and authority given to misguided notions of progress. The text shows through the character of de Selby that imperial-era aesthetic forms do not just inform picturesque views of primitivized peoples and landscapes; they also inform the scientific expertise that sustains subject-object hierarchies in who writes and who is written. Rather than heed material realities in which space and time mutually constitute each other, de Selby abstracts time and space into discrete and separate points. This act of separation empties meaning out of spatiotemporalities of development and shows ideas of progress to superimpose superficial representational structures onto a dynamic and interactive material world. The severing of space from time emerges through de Selby's theory of "human experience . . . 'as a succession of static experiences each infinitely brief.'"[95] To prove his point, de Selby attempts to travel from Bath to Folkstone by "shut[ting] himself up in a room in his lodgings with a supply of picture postcards of the areas which would be traversed on such a journey, together with an elaborate arrangement of clocks and barometric instruments and a device for regulating the gaslight in conformity with the changing light of the outside day."[96] De Selby's elaborate contrivance ultimately leads nowhere, of course. Instead, it displays de Selby's confusion of representation with reality. It conflates progress narratives with actual progress and changes that might improve the lives of people in rural Irish modernities. For de Selby, "picture postcards" and the places they represent are interchangeable. The conflation of signifier and signified into a single entity allows de Selby to separate time and space into "a succession of static experiences each infinitely brief" that builds "human experience" as a cherry-picked selection of details for constructing a progress narrative.

The text emphasizes the confusion of reality with representation when the narrator notes that de Selby's theory of human experience is derived from his misunderstanding of how cinema works. Having broken film into individual frames, the narrator asserts that de Selby has considered the "strong repetitive element" in cinema to be "tedious," but de Selby concludes that the serial repetition of frames is synonymous with reality, leading him to assert that progress and motion are "illusion[s]."[97] Through these representations of de Selby, *The Third Policeman* critiques the seemingly transparent access to material reality that documentary photography and film supposedly offer. De Selby ignorantly interpolates the structural elements of imperial space and time into theories he derives from a relatively new medium indicative of modernity. This situation of breaking film into its constituent elements of repetitious frames foregrounds what Jay David Bolter and Richard Grusin theorize as the paradoxical dual logic of remediation.[98] The immediacy of film to offer a window into the world is at odds with the hypermediacy of film's materiality. De Selby's focus on the hypermediacy of cinema enables him to deconstruct the film into a series of stills. *The Third Policeman* thus playfully remediates older media for documentary photography into the relatively new medium of cinema, thereby exposing how older forms rearticulate themselves through newer media and material environments in the postcolonial state.

Through these representations of de Selby, O'Brien gestures to how evolving media in the Free State inflect the imperial-era aesthetic forms of modernity and modernization and contribute to colonial and neocolonial forms of extraction. Cinema was becoming increasingly popular in 1930s Ireland, and it connotes a relatively new and thus modern medium.[99] De Selby's misunderstanding of how cinema works or how to consume it highlights the implied newness of this modern medium as it also exposes the way in which de Selby's supposed authority on improvements in the modernizing world of science maintain deteriorating conditions in material environments. The text thus points to how older narrative forms are continually remediated into new media to perpetuate "the same unchanging sameness."[100] The parodic remediation of the older forms into newer media in de Selby's flawed conclusions critiques how so-called experts reproduce the status quo by recycling the lenses through which they view the world and retain a continuity across colonial and postcolonial contexts.

The dead narrator's unwavering faith in de Selby's ideas perseveres, even as those ideas contradict his ironically lived experience in his hellish afterlife. This blind faith in de Selby satirically critiques the Free State's uncritical acceptance of imperial logics of time and space in land and economic reforms of rural Ireland that produce misrepresentations of Gaeltacht realities. Imperial logics reproduce colonial-era social and material relations through an engrained deference to authoritative, colonial expertise. De Selby's authority goes unquestioned even as the narrator finds "his theory ... at variance with everything I have learnt myself on a country walk."[101] The narrator's "country walk[s]" even before death indicate he has learned something from observing his material surroundings. Yet he privileges de Selby's authoritative knowledge over the knowledge to which he bears witness in the land.

Like the English-language poetry that O'Nolan (O'Brien) critiqued in his master's thesis, the narrator's relationship to land facilitates a hierarchy between an authoritative subject who objectifies the land as well as the animals and people who live there. This hierarchical relationship between the narrator and his surroundings renders the material environment and the rural communities in the locality as inert matter and static traditional cultures. By subordinating the agency of land and rural communities to the authoritative view the road produces, the narrator inhabits a hierarchy of viewer and viewed. The view from the road shapes the environment and traditional ways of life into preconceived images that establish the eye of the beholder and its position on the road to modernity. The narrator, de Selby, the policemen, the Land Commission, and revivalists in the Free State incorporate colonial environmental histories and infrastructures that inform their interpretations of what authentic rural Ireland is. Rather than recognize the land and Gaeltacht communities as having agency or the ability to modernize in alternative ways to those sanctioned by inherited imperial ideology, the narrator's interactions with his surroundings reinforce colonial logics, even when these are "at variance with everything" he encountered "on a country walk." *The Third Policeman* critiques how these colonial logics insidiously and ridiculously undergird de Selby's flawed theories and the ways in which those with authority can deputize arbitrary forms of knowledge to maintain colonial hierarchies in the novel or in the Free State's 1930s land reforms.

Such colonial logics emerge in how the policemen maintain socioeconomic hierarchies through manipulating material realities rather than attempting to work within the constraints of physical systems. Instead of making themselves "subservient to Nature" as O'Nolan found Irish-language poetic forms to encourage, the policemen surveil bodily and social boundaries to maintain a picturesque but impoverished and consequently vanishing rural idyll.[102] People and their bicycles are physically permeable bodies that exchange atoms and become increasingly like one another, a phenomenon that the character Sergeant Pluck describes as the Atomic Theory.[103] The Atomic Theory is in keeping with modern physics, which shows that boundaries and bodies are not contained. Rather, bodies are in ongoing interaction with one another and their material environments. These ongoing interactions correspond with what Stacy Alaimo terms "trans-corporeality," which "reveals the interchanges and interconnections between various bodily natures."[104] They also conform to Karen Barad's theories of intra-activity and agential realism in which "there are no intrinsic boundaries."[105] The shifting of atoms among the characters and environments in *The Third Policeman* resists Pluck's efforts to police artificial boundaries and material realities.

The Third Policeman shows how officials and experts, such as the policemen and de Selby, willfully ignore lived experiences and material realities to impose and control artificial boundaries. These boundaries, in turn, strategically maintain the authority of the police and colonial-era socioeconomic hierarchies. The police preserve poverty in the region by ensuring that people and bicycles do not exchange atoms. Policeman Pluck patrols the boundaries between bodies and bicycles, even as spending too much time "walking [on a road] fills you up with clay far sooner (or buries bits of you along the road) and brings your death half-way to meet you."[106] Despite the ongoing entanglement of material agencies and constant exchange of atoms, Pluck successfully prevents people who cannot afford more than one bicycle per family from obtaining the means to acquire more bicycles. Pluck explains that the O'Feersa brothers have a lower percentage of bicycle in them "due to the lucky fact that there are three similar brothers in the house and that they are too poor to have a separate bicycle apiece."[107] Pluck goes on to remark: "Some people never know how fortunate they are when they are poorer than each other. Six years ago one of the three O'Feersas won a prize of ten pounds in *John Bull*. When I got the wind of this tiding, I knew I would have to take steps unless there was to be two new bicycles in the family, because you will understand that I can steal only a limited number of bicycles in the one week. I did not want to have three O'Feersas on my hands."[108] The text indicates that Pluck cannot tell the O'Feersa brothers apart from each other or from their bicycle, as he conflates the potential of three bicycles with "hav[ing] three O'Feersas on [his] hands." Despite this ambiguity among the brothers and between the brothers and their bicycle, Pluck actively polices their poverty to prevent them from obtaining more bicycles or becoming more like their bicycle. The irony of Pluck policing artificial and seemingly arbitrary boundaries that he cannot visually observe critiques the absurdity of imposing authoritative forms of knowledge, picturesque aesthetic conventions, and imperial-era progress narratives on Gaeltachtaí. The text critiques how colonial power relations persist through the production of scientific knowledge and aesthetic conventions used to preserve rural Ireland in picturesque, romanticized poverty. Established aesthetic forms facilitate the perception and representation of arbitrary boundaries between bodies and material environments. Pluck is only concerned with policing the bodily integrity of these forms, thus producing and reproducing the predefined shapes that metaphorize and dehumanize rural women, the bog, and Gaeltacht communities.

In policing preconceived forms of what bodies should be and how places should look, Pluck ironically fails to see the material conditions that would allow the O'Feersa brothers to remain in the parish. Indeed, he does not anticipate how the community will be absorbed into other countries through emigration to England, Canada, or the United States, where they could, in Lady Aberdeen's view, potentially "overcome their difficulties and this would produce the strong characters that Canada needed."[109] The fact that the brothers obtained British pounds, or *"John Bull,"* indicates they were in England, probably for work, as migrating to England seasonally or permanently remained a necessary avenue for impoverished communities in rural Ireland even after Ireland's partial independence. This policing of poverty in the rural community aligns with O'Nolan's larger critique that "an almost intractable anomaly arises in devising a plan to preserve Irish by economically rehabilitating people whose retention of Irish is to be ascribed to poverty."[110] The text exposes authorities like Pluck to manipulate understandings of material relations to preserve the O'Feersas' poverty and render them and their ways of life into a disappearing premodernity based on colonial divisions of undeveloped and developed peoples and places.

Like the memorial of the bog or the metaphorization of women as houses, the preservation of the picturesque image of the O'Feersas' poverty misrepresents life in the parish as it erases the O'Feersas themselves. Indeed, the O'Feersa brothers ultimately and ironically only exist in the text through Pluck's description of them. The aesthetic forms maintain the bodily integrity and impoverished rural lifestyles that the police surveil as they occlude alternative forms of self-determination and autonomy through which people and communities might represent themselves. The aesthetics of modernization structurally marginalize and silence rural communities and their relationships to material environments and built infrastructure. The police contain the O'Feersas within the image of picturesque poverty that they perceive as more valuable than the O'Feersas' ability to stay in the region. Pluck's work and his description of the O'Feersa brothers overwrite their lived experiences in favor of a picturesque ideal that ascribes them to poverty. Rather than heed the dynamic cultural and material relationships between people and material environments that construct rural Irish modernities, the policemen recycle old forms and aesthetic conventions to sustain clearly defined boundaries. Through this depiction of the policemen, *The Third Policeman* critiques how Free-State authorities distort material realities by reproducing imperial-era aesthetic forms and colonial power relations under the guise of scientific, economic, and social progress.

The Limits of Decolonization: Enacting Divisions in Two-Dimensional Spacetime

By exposing how the police manipulate material realities to normalize social hierarchies, the text critiques the Free State's embrace of imperial-era aesthetic forms in its modernization projects. While the Free State sought to economically and culturally decolonize, its conception of progress relied on imperial-era aesthetic and narrative forms that subordinate the material world into a relatively narrow view of Western modernity. *The Third Policeman* exposes how aesthetic expectations of modernity promote hierarchies between modernizing subjects and modernized objects that force an independent Ireland into grotesque versions of what the postcolonial nation potentially could be. In a scene in the novel that is repeated twice verbatim, the narrator describes a police station, claiming that he "had never seen with my eyes ever in my life before anything so unnatural and appalling and my gaze faltered uncomprehendingly as if at least one of the customary dimensions was missing," and that he "had never seen a police station like it."[111] Like picturesque scenes the narrator sketches at other moments, this repeated scene exposes the two-dimensionality thereby indicating how "at least one of the customary dimensions was missing," thereby indicating how imperial-era forms distort representations of rural Ireland. The repetition of this passage in the middle and end of the text exposes how the narrator has seen the very "unnatural and appalling" scene innumerable times, but he has been conditioned by habits of looking and expectations of specific aesthetic forms to see the station each time anew, with a similar level of disgust. Indeed, Long notes that the narrator tells the story in the past tense, indicating that the narrative might not even be the first occurrence of the story.[112] This repetition emphasizes and echoes the distorted formal and representational elements through which the novel asserts a postmodern disintegration between the material world and its aesthetic representations. The narrator experiences these repetitious and grotesque views as uncanny, thereby exposing how imperial-era forms haunt the Free State's attempts to decolonize through land reforms that ostensibly preserve idealized precolonial and supposedly traditional ways of life.

By distilling the aesthetic and narrative forms that promenade as economic or social progress in attempts to culturally decolonize Irish traditions, O'Brien remediates imperial-era forms into the content of *The Third Policeman*. His novel thus challenges the underlying structures of development that were entrenching social hierarchies in 1930s Ireland and further rendering material environments into extractable and exploitable natural resources. O'Nolan (O'Brien) saw these underlying structures of development to perpetuate the ongoing erasure of Gaeltachtaí through Free-State land reforms. The processes of remediation in which O'Brien critically reframes the picturesque and modernization narratives in land reform, scientific authority, and police surveillance in the novel expose what Priya Satia theorizes as the "institutional stickiness" of "the disciplines and modes of thought that enabled colonialism."[113] *The Third Policeman* shows the limits of decolonization within the constraints of imperial-era mindsets that perpetuate hierarchies of an authoritative subject over objectified people, places, and the relationships between them. The sanctioned colonial view of modernity implicitly enacts spatiotemporal divisions of the present into a premodern past and an implied future modernity that are at odds with the physics of the agential realisms that Barad theorizes and Alaimo's transcorporeality conceptualizes. O'Brien satirizes colonial spatiotemporal divisions implicit in the policemen's attempts to wield the Atomic Theory as a means of control and the narrator's religious adherence to de Selby's pseudoscience. Despite the physical realities in material environments that contest and counter such spatiotemporal divisions, modernization narratives rely on the transition from a premodern past into a postcolonial future. This transition is understood as progress toward a supposedly more socially, economically, and technologically advanced way of being. These conceptions of progress overwrite lived realities and multiple modernities in the Gaeltachtaí to maintain a colonial modernity that embraces subject-object hierarchies, a structuring relationship more in line with the English-language forms O'Nolan (O'Brien) critiqued in his master's thesis.

O'Brien (O'Nolan) implicitly invokes the more relational creation of communities and their environments in *The Third Policeman* that he noted in Irish-language poetic forms in his master's thesis. He does this by exploring the liminal spaces in *The Third Policeman* where meaning gets made from the seemingly infinite possibilities symbolized by the mythical but powerful natural resource of omnium. Although "one of the customary dimensions was missing" in the town's built infrastructure, this seemingly "missing" dimension is inhabited by Policeman Fox, who works and lives literally in the liminal wall space between the "natural order" outside and the cultural interior of the rancher Matherss's Anglo-Irish Big House, a structure that recalls the dispossession of Catholic and Irish people and the rationalization of environments under the Anglo-Irish Ascendancy landlords during the eighteenth century.[114]

Within this liminal space between material environments and infrastructures of settler colonialism, Fox possesses four ounces of the mysterious omnium with which he "calmly mak[es] ribbons of the natural order, inventing intricate and unheard of machinery to delude the other policemen, interfering drastically with time to make them think they had been leading their magical lives for years, bewildering, horrifying and enchanting the whole countryside."[115] The liminal space Fox inhabits in the wall and the omnium he possesses indicate the potential for new forms of modernization, representation, and decolonization between twentieth-century Irish cultural relations and dynamic material environments. This space in the wall demonstrates an opening for subverting implied hierarchies between the poetic subject and objectifying representations of material environments. *The Third Policeman* thus indicates unrealized possibilities for the Free State to embrace the more Irish-language environmental consciousness that O'Nolan admired in his master's thesis. Such an Irish cultural consciousness in the text demonstrates the possibility of coconstructing communities and cultural traditions within material constraints rather than endeavoring to dominate the omnium and the material agencies it represents.

Although *The Third Policeman* implicitly points out the promise of alternative modernities, the novel ultimately shows Fox to perpetuate the hierarchical forms that maintain the authorities and authorial structures controlling the material world. Fox only uses the elusive omnium and the potential of his in-between office "to delude the other policemen" and manipulate their perception of time and space, "interfering drastically with time to make them think they had been leading their magical lives for years." Through Fox's manipulation of the other policemen and their struggle to enforce artificial social boundaries on dynamic material environments and cultural relations, Fox embraces his power to create and recreate divisions between the maker and the made, the viewer and viewed, and the past and the future. Such divisions entrench structural elements of picturesque aesthetics and modernization narratives in which seemingly past, premodern spaces are preserved in a colonial modernity in ways that constrain the material, economic, and cultural potential of the postcolonial nation.

The structuring relationships in which a subject-authority dominates an objectified other, be it omnium or the social and environmental relations of postcolonial Ireland, emerge in Fox's despotic manipulation of space and time in the cabinet in eternity. The cabinet can produce any object the narrator and policemen might desire. Before "the articles" take known shapes, they have "no known dimensions" nor "an essential property of all known objects," thereby indicating endless potential that is never realized.[116] Indeed, the narrator clarifies that "their appearance . . . was not understood by the eye," and he can only know and describe what he already knows and has the vocabulary to articulate. His inability to recognize the objects leads to a lack of language. This inability to identify the omnium's material shape leads the narrator to conclude that it "was in any event indescribable. That is enough to say."[117] The text shows the matter in the cabinet to have the agency to silence the narrator, which, in turn, interrupts even Fox's attempts to control the material world.

O'Brien draws an implicit comparison between how Fox appropriates the omnium and how land reform policies of the 1930s appropriated Irish-language lifeways and culture to create delusions and distortions of Irish authenticity and modernization in the Free State. The infinite possibilities of the omnium and the meaning it might make indicate material agencies and possible futures that could emerge out of the Gaeltachtaí and the aesthetic forms the Irish language offers, including those O'Nolan (O'Brien) studied just a few years prior in his master's project. Rather than engage with forms in which the poet collaborates within material constraints and changing cultural relations, the narrator, de Selby, and the policemen try to manipulate material agencies into preconceived images that reflect only their own entrenched and implicitly colonial understandings of the world. They all lack the conceptual tools to apprehend or know anything outside the preexisting, exploitative colonial relationships that structure their realities, which they then internalize, inhabit, and reproduce. As a result, their observations, interpretations, and actions further embed colonial relations inherent in the picturesque and modernization narratives. Through critically remediating such aesthetic and narrative forms into *The Third Policeman*, O'Brien scrutinizes the structuring relationships through which the Free State's efforts to preserve the Gaeltachtaí ensures their misrepresentation and consequently the ongoing eradication of multiple human and more-than-human agencies and modernities existent in rural Ireland and the Irish-speaking world.

Conclusion: Remediating Postmodern Relations into Environmental Development

The Third Policeman responds to Ireland's marginalized cultural and economic position in emerging geopolitical hierarchies by exposing the underlying relationships that formally structure material realities and their representations in historically specific ways. These structuring relationships emerge through developmental narrative forms and picturesque aesthetics that informed land reform projects after the Land Wars. The material implications of imperial-era aesthetic forms in print and visual media involved influencing how rural Ireland was modernizing in the 1930s. *The Third Policeman* draws on processes of remediation to satirically expose how formal structures repeat imperial-era understandings of development, tradition, and authenticity in a postcolonial Irish modernity that reflects the aesthetic conventions of colonial-era modernization. By exposing the Free State's overdependence on imperial-era forms that entrench hegemonic understandings of modernity and modernization, as well as colonial-era social and racial hierarchies, O'Brien's novel focuses the reader's attention on structural elements through which alternative forms of representation could potentially emerge for cultural and environmental revitalization and decolonization in the late 1930s.

In doing so, O'Brien's text seeks to establish specifically Irish cultural forms and media for producing material and discursive texts in the Free State that resist how the forms of old and new imperial centers were being remediated into the content of independent Ireland by the start of World War II. As Clair Wills shows, negotiating a postcolonial Irish identity "in the absence of indigenous Irish versions of progress [where] becoming modern ... seemed hopelessly entangled with importation from abroad" revealed preestablished forms into which Irish cultural production, as well as the new Irish nation-state itself, had to fit.[118] Those who attempted to modernize Irish cultural production found themselves ignored in the larger literary and film markets of Britain and the United States. As Wills asserts, "The attempt to create a new, modern, and national film, theatre, and literary culture, to put the centre of cultural gravity in Ireland rather than England, meant turning away from an international audience. The sense of being 'cut off' in Ireland spoke of a fear that no one outside Ireland was listening, or no one who mattered."[119] The idea "that no one outside Ireland was listening, or no one who mattered" indicates the rising cultural hegemony of the United States and Britain in which Irish cultural formations played only a peripheral role if they played one at all. The insularity of protectionist economic policies and neutrality during World War II did not decolonize the imperial-era land reforms that the Free State ostensibly sought in its assertions of territorial and resource sovereignty. Rather, tensions between insularity and the ongoing cultural and economic influences of Britain and the United States continued to inform modernization efforts in the emerging Irish nation. These cultural influences from abroad intensified as Ireland turned away from protectionism and strove to privatize natural resources in an effort to economically integrate with the rest of Europe, a context to which I will now turn in my examination of radio and the media of Irish traditional music.

3
1950–1970
ORAL TRADITIONS ON RADIO AS ALTERNATIVE FORMS OF DEVELOPMENT IN SEÁN Ó RIADA'S *OUR MUSICAL HERITAGE*

IRISH TRADITIONAL music is one of the most visible and audible articulations of Irish oral tradition in the late twentieth and early twenty-first century. While it has persisted despite long histories of colonial land reforms and cultural oppression and postcolonial modernization projects, Irish traditional music has also innovated and developed alongside and in ongoing interaction with colonial and postcolonial modernities. It simultaneously signifies an older way of life and the commodification of Irish culture, especially since the mid-century shifts under Taoiseach Seán Lemass to globalize Ireland's economy through the privatization of natural resources and foreign direct investment (FDI). The presence of Irish traditional music in Irish pubs (another visible marker of the commodification of Irishness in the transnational cultural imaginary) positions the ephemerality and dynamism of Irish traditional music within seemingly fixed material and built environments. The paradoxical idea of Irish music as both a preserve of authentic traditions and a product of Ireland's embrace of the global economy recalls other efforts by the postcolonial nation to decolonize and modernize through the privatization of natural resources. Bord Fáilte Éireann, which became Fáilte Ireland in 2003, has promoted tourist campaigns since the Irish music revival of the 1960s and 1970s to establish a seemingly authentic Irish heritage to which an implicitly white Irish diaspora in settler-colonial nations like the United States, Canada, Australia, and New Zealand can return when visiting Ireland. While Irish traditional music (or at least stereotypes of it) has fed into this idea of a seemingly unchanging and unchanged authentic past, it also has modernized and evolved through its interactions with extraction economies, changing environments, and shifting media landscapes. Using ecomedia, ecomusicology, and postcolonial ecocritical lenses to examine the remediation of Irish music into modernization projects in mid-century Ireland demonstrates connections between colonialism and environmental development projects as it also reveals Irish traditional music as an alternative form of development. While the environmental impacts of empire persist and intensify in development projects in the aftermath of World War II, a time when emigration increased as a result of a severely depressed economy, different forms of music proliferated across expanding broadcast media. This gave rise to debates about which kinds of music best reflected modernity and the modern Irish nation.

The influence that musician, composer, and producer Seán Ó Riada has had on how Irish music should sound in Irish modernity is hard to overstate. Alongside the formation of the environmental movement and a rise in the popularity of folk music across the West in the 1960s and 1970s, the Irish traditional music revival became an international phenomenon in the 1970s after renowned groups like the Chieftains began touring abroad. The Chieftains built on Ó Riada's work, drawing members and arrangements directly from Ó Riada's earlier group, Ceoltóirí Chualann, which only performed in Ireland. While Ó Riada has had a tremendous impact on the sound of Irish traditional music, he also composed pieces in the Western classical tradition, pieces that sparked the interest of prominent Irish writers such as Brian Friel, Thomas Kinsella, John Montague, and Seamus Heaney.[1] Damien Keane contends that "music remains a potent symbol in Irish poetry," particularly for Ó Riada's "immediate male poetic contemporaries."[2] Keane points out that "Montague, Thomas Kinsella, Seán Lucy, and Pearse Hutchinson have all written elegies for him [Ó Riada], as has the younger Seamus Heaney."[3] Implicitly countering the feminized ways of life that modernization projects historically sought to replace, male writers in Ireland recognized the formation of a masculine-inflected modernity that fostered innovation and dynamism in postcolonial Ireland. This implicit recognition reflects mid-century debates about what kinds of economic and cultural development Ireland should preserve or modernize after the protectionist economic policies of its early decades. Ó Riada's work on national radio reveals tensions between feminized traditions and a masculinized modernity in shifting conceptions of Irishness and postcoloniality as economic policies moved away from protectionism and toward attracting FDI into the country after 1958.

Despite Ó Riada's prominence as an Irish musician on Irish national radio, television, and stage, Ó Riada initially held no special interest in

Irish traditional music. Indeed, he performed and composed several different types of music throughout his life, including classical, jazz, and showband music in Ireland and Europe.[4] Some of Ó Riada's more famous compositions, such as *Hercules Dux Ferrariae*, are based on the modernist, twelve-tone system from Arnold Schoenberg.[5] After working on films for Gael Linn, including *Mise Éire* (1959) and *Saoirse?* (1961), Ó Riada increasingly came to value the Irish language and traditional music in the late 1950s. He spent time in Dún Chaoin (Dunquin) with Thomas Kinsella and increasingly felt Irish traditions had an unruptured continuity there.[6] In his performances, such as his fourteen-episode 1962 national radio series *Our Musical Heritage*, Ó Riada recognized certain Gaeltacht areas as comprising indigenous populations that cohered culturally and had the potential to form political coalitions to represent the importance of dynamic and ever-changing cultural traditions nationally, even as these traditions were being commodified as seemingly fixed relics of the past through which tourists of Irish descent could connect with their real and imagined Irish heritage.

Although Ó Riada is a prominent figure in the history of Irish music and broadcast media who influenced some of Ireland's most celebrated writers, Ó Riada's work has not been analyzed in scholarship as rigorously as literary figures like Friel, Kinsella, and Heaney. Moreover, little scholarly work exists on Ó Riada's 1962 national radio program, *Our Musical Heritage*, and no extended analysis has been made of the program, even in more sustained studies of Ó Riada's work. Scholars have generally used *Our Musical Heritage* as an example of insular or bounded conceptions of cultural tradition. Joe Cleary juxtaposes *Our Musical Heritage* with resistance to cultural conservativism in the Pogues.[7] Richard Pine situates the ideas in *Our Musical Heritage* as Ó Riada's "idiosyncratic beliefs about Irishness," and Harry White summarizes the radio program as stemming from "the worst traditions of defensive, jingoistic insularity."[8] Although these assessments recognize a dogmatic tone Ó Riada used in the program, further examination of the complex and often intentionally contradictory assertions of identity, history, and traditions in *Our Musical Heritage* exposes an active renegotiation and remediation of understandings of nation, progress, cultural identities, and environment on national radio as the Republic of Ireland opened up to world markets and as Northern Ireland entered the Troubles.[9]

Instead of an insular, bounded, and fixed cultural tradition, I argue that a closer reading of Ó Riada's *Our Musical Heritage* within the sociohistorical context of 1950s and 1960s Ireland reveals alternative paths for cultural and environmental modernization to take through dynamic oral traditions, like Irish traditional music, that continue to innovate alongside neocolonial economic integration. Ó Riada's *Our Musical Heritage* strategically draws on the aural medium of radio to reimagine oral traditions in Irish culture as dynamic, ephemeral, and modernizing practices at a moment when geographies of decolonization, media landscapes, material environments, and national resources were beginning to be redefined in relationship to a global economy. Later iterations of *Our Musical Heritage* at the twenty- and fifty-year anniversaries of its first airing demonstrate changing understandings of identities and traditions, from indigenous Irish cultural practices to more cosmopolitan communities in European and international economies. These shifts in conceptions of identity during the Troubles, amid the rising environmentalist movement in Ireland, and in the aftermath of the Celtic Tiger continue to draw on the aural ephemerality of radio and evolving recording technologies to foster dynamic and ongoing innovations in Irish traditional music, even as memories of Ó Riada himself become increasingly fixed. Yet, as my analysis demonstrates, in 1962 Ó Riada's *Our Musical Heritage* showed how Irish traditional music continually and intrinsically modernizes and innovates, thereby offering an alternative model for Irish modernization after World War II.

A closer examination of Ó Riada's *Our Musical Heritage* shows how Ó Riada remediates Irish traditional music into the medium of national radio to counter material changes to culture and environment. Through these remediations, Ó Riada's program revises current and historical definitions of tradition as implicitly fixed or static. After contextualizing hierarchies of classical and traditional music, performance, and art alongside modernization projects in mid-century Ireland, my analysis shows how Ó Riada disrupts Western forms of development that obscure multiple modernities and potentially more environmentally enduring ways of life and relationships to material environments existing in Irish-speaking communities. The final parts of this chapter explore how the critique that *Our Musical Heritage* initially made about the adverse impacts of economic development projects in mid-century Ireland on indigenous traditions and knowledge systems is reworked by later iterations of the program's content in different historical contexts and through different media. Throughout my chapter, I establish the role gender hierarchies implicitly play in conceptions of tradition and modernity across the environmental impacts of empire. My reading reframes Ó Riada's complex career and role in redefining Irish cultural traditions and identity during early modernization projects under Taoiseach Lemass. By attending to these revised definitions of tradition and modernity, my analysis shows how modernizing traditions influenced Irish identity formations and multispecies relationships to land and environment across the second half of the twentieth century.

Media in Lemassian Modernity: Negotiating Place and Identity on Stage, Radio, Television, and Film

A series of letters from Brien Friel to Ó Riada at the end of 1967 through 1968 demonstrate ongoing collaborations across media and art forms for negotiating narratives of place and identity in Ireland in the 1960s. In Friel's first letter from November 8, 1967, Friel explains meeting Ó Riada years before when Friel's play *The Enemy Within* was produced by the Abbey Theatre in 1962. Friel describes his admiration for Ó Riada's work, noting how he felt "an intuition that our attitudes to the country that made us are very close."[10] This similarity in "attitudes to the country that made [them]" is a primary reason why Friel wanted to "produce something in cooperation" with Ó Riada, asking if he would like to make "a folk opera? A profane oratorio? A musical? Have you ever thought of something like this? Have you ever thought of an Irish drama-with-music?"[11] Ó Riada conducted orchestral pieces from Mozart and Grieg, as well as a piece he composed himself, during the intervals of Friel's *The Enemy Within*, performed at the Queen's Theatre in 1962, indicating that Ó Riada had probably thought about combining drama with music before. Indeed, Ó Riada's earlier work on films like *Mise Éire* (1959), *Saoirse?* (1960), and the feature film adaptation of J. M. Synge's play *The Playboy of the Western World* (1962), all show Ó Riada's ongoing engagement with different forms of history, literature, and music across media. Yet Friel's comment shows that Friel favored stage productions over the range of media in which Ó Riada was willing to work, including collaborating on an Irish opera with Friel.

The period in which Friel and Ó Riada corresponded about their possible collaborative production, *Grania*, was a time of intense change in Ireland as early Lemassian modernization and intensified natural resource extraction got underway on the cusp of the Troubles. After the historic meeting between the Northern Irish prime minister Terence

O'Neill and Taoiseach of the Republic of Ireland Seán Lemass in January 1965, the 1965 Anglo-Irish Free Trade Agreement precipitated Ireland's entry into the European Economic Community (EEC) in 1973.[12] These political events indicate tensions between understandings of a traditional cultural identity and emerging economic relations in the modernizing postcolonial nation. While Friel and Ó Riada discussed possibilities, including a musical version of Brian Merriman's eighteenth-century poem *The Midnight Court* (*Cúirt an Mheán Oíche*), which Friel noted they both found "too cerebral" for drama, the letters and early drafts that Friel includes in later correspondence show that Friel and Ó Riada began but never finished a production called *Grania* about Grace O'Malley.[13] Friel's articulation of how their "attitudes to the country that made [them] are very close" positions the often misunderstood figure of Ó Riada alongside Friel and other writers and artists of the mid-century who grappled with shifting conceptions of postcolonial Irish identities during the Northern Irish civil rights movement, the start of the Troubles, and as the Republic of Ireland increasingly turned toward international markets and the privatization of material and multispecies environments into natural resources.

Particular art forms and media as well as understandings of environments as national resources signified Ireland as a modern and modernized state that could globalize through European economic integration and FDI. In 1960s Ireland, energy extraction through hydroelectric dams and the burning of fossil fuels, including turf, coal, and oil, facilitated the expansion of the electrical grid and the relatively late development of national television in the early 1960s. Television increasingly connoted economic development and modernity, thereby superseding radio, even as national radio had once been indicative of Irish national sovereignty. Policies under Lemass aimed to promote Ireland as a forward-thinking, developed, and independent nation with a wealth of resources. Lemass, in John Horgan's words, "wanted the new television service to present, and perhaps even in part engender, an image of Ireland as a progressive, scientifically inclined, modern industrial nation."[14] Already in 1953 when Lemass worked in the Ministry of Industry and Commerce, he famously asked about the national radio station: "How's the hurdy-gurdy?"[15] This notion of national radio as the mouthpiece of parochial folk music from rural regions indicates the perception of Irish traditional music and rural Ireland as premodern and undeveloped. Such perceptions connect music and rural environments with the conservative understanding of cultural preservation that protectionist economic policies in the 1930s and 1940s encouraged. These policies failed to bring prosperity or cultural decolonization to Ireland after independence, however. New government policies after 1958 reframed Irish oralities and the Irish language in rural regions as behind the times but also as preserves of a seemingly authentic and conservative Irishness fixed in the past.[16] These tensions between an authentic, traditional past and an Irish modernity rooted in expanding extraction economies inform mid-century media landscapes and cultural understandings of radio and television.

While radio and television may have had different connotations in modernization efforts in the 1960s, both were seen as less artistically significant than stage productions of plays, operas, and musical performances. Indeed, Friel critiqued Ó Riada's focus on national broadcast media as a disservice to his talents, particularly when Ó Riada seems to have lost interest in the *Grania* project by the end of 1968: "If you are filling your life with TV and radio work, . . . may I suggest that this is a total waste of your real talents and energy. *You should be composing*, not spending yourself on journeyman work. You are an artist—not a TV link man on genteel programmes."[17] Although Friel takes issue with Ó Riada's focus on national broadcast media and their audiences, his criticism of and concern for Ó Riada's career highlights larger frameworks that were available for discussing art, music, and tradition in mid-century Ireland. Like the picturesque aesthetic and modernization narratives Flann O'Brien critiqued in *The Third Policeman*, as I discuss in chapter 2, theoretical frameworks for understanding art, music, and culture inflected imperial-era mindsets and structures for constructing subject-object relations informing what modernity looks or sounds like.

Ó Riada's oeuvre both invokes and challenges these frameworks to provide a multivalent approach that destabilizes imperial logics and hierarchies persisting in popular understandings of cultural traditions and high art. Friel's comment overlooks Ó Riada's explicit choice to promote new forms of Irish traditional music on popular media like national radio, thereby altering perceptions of both traditional music as premodern and national radio as an unsophisticated and outdated medium. Indeed, many of Ó Riada's programs on national radio challenge ideas of tradition as a fixed practice associated with particular gender and class connotations that, in turn, inflect upon communities' relationships with their material environments. Using the medium of radio and its cultural and material connotations, Ó Riada's 1962 version of *Our Musical Heritage* renegotiates fixed understandings of tradition as stuck in the past and remediates traditional forms as fluid, dynamic, and serious art forms on national radio to rework understandings of orality, culture, and nature. Through these remediations, Ó Riada demonstrates how the aurality and ephemerality of Irish traditional music has the potential to modernize across media like radio as it imagines alternative forms of national development and modernity. The alternative forms of development Ó Riada shows Irish traditional music to embody offer more socially and environmentally enduring alternatives to the linear and neocolonial conceptions of progress increasingly promoted by a US-led globalized petroeconomy.

"A Stand Against the Onslaught of Western Culture": Resisting Neocolonial Environmental Development

Tracing Ó Riada's work through his 1962 national radio program *Our Musical Heritage* and the history of national radio in Ireland reveals the role music played in constructing understandings of Irishness in Irish culture and relationships to material and multispecies environments. When *Our Musical Heritage* aired for the first time, Ireland was turning away from protectionist measures and efforts to culturally and economically decolonize as it moved toward economic expansion through multinational capital and European integration. In the early 1960s, to use Brian Girvin and Gary Murphy's words, "state resources [were being used] to attract foreign investment and to base policy on an export strategy."[18] The effects of T. K. Whitaker's 1958 report on economic development shifted Ireland away from attempts to decolonize through territorially bounded understandings of cultural revival and land redistribution based on Éamon de Valera's conceptions of Irish identity during earlier Fianna Fáil governments. Although the protectionist policies of the first decades of Irish independence failed to stop emigration out of rural and largely Irish-speaking communities, European economic integration positioned those communities as regions ripe for development under a neocolonial conception of modernity. Throughout these changes, national radio played an important role in modernization projects, cultural conceptions of Irishness, and people's changing relationships with their material environments and multispecies surroundings.

After independence in 1922, the Irish Free State used modernization projects to assert national sovereignty and industrialize domestically in efforts to decolonize culturally and materially. Despite a small state budget, the Free State launched the Shannon Scheme in 1925 in collaboration with a German company, Siemens Schuckert, to build what became, at least briefly, the largest dam in Europe.[19] The Free State's choice to build the hydroelectric power station in Ardnacrusha with a German company less than a decade after the end of World War I pointedly asserted Ireland's sovereignty from Britain through its choice to work with Britain's wartime enemy. This decision also meant that Ireland originally adopted different systems, such as a 110kV transmission system instead of the 132kV system historically used in Britain.[20] The Shannon Scheme led to the establishment of the Electricity Supply Board (ESB) in 1927 and the ESB's subsequent Rural Electrification Project, starting in 1946, which gradually brought electricity and plumbing to rural Ireland.[21] As the Republic of Ireland expanded its electrical grid, the state intensified its industrial extraction of peat from bog ecosystems and increasingly imported oil in the 1960s.[22] Concurrently, the Irish Land Commission, which took over from the Congested Districts Board (CDB) in 1923, worked to redistribute land and move people onto more viable farmland until shortly after Ireland joined the European Economic Community in 1973.[23]

These modernization projects to develop Ireland's environments and promote energy extraction had a cultural counterpart in the establishment of the national radio station 2RN in 1926, which would become Raidió Éireann.[24] After 1932, national radio under Taoiseach Éamon de Valera's Fianna Fáil government aimed to make 2RN "one of the chief agents in the legitimation of the modern Irish state."[25] De Valera's government strove to intensify the work of the Land Commission to foster small family farms seen as indicative of a bucolic ideal of traditional Irish ways of life and to revive the Irish language and culture. 2RN was intended to represent this emerging postcolonial Irish identity in the early decades of the Free State through Irish cultural programming. Although establishing the national radio service asserted sovereignty after independence, the Irish state's autonomy was constrained by international regulations for radio wavelengths that were being drawn up by the European Broadcasting Union and the League of Nations between 1922 and 1924.[26] Ireland's national radio broadcasting capability was consequently and ironically under the purview of Britain when 2RN was launched in 1926: "Since all Irish radio allocations remained within the remit of the British Post Office, the designation of '2RN' was decided in London."[27] Although 2RN signifies, as Horgan points out, "to Erin," a nationalist name for Ireland, parameters for national radio in Ireland were included in the 1921 Anglo-Irish Treaty of Independence, which created the Irish Free State and initiated Ireland's partial independence: "British negotiators, conscious as ever of Ireland's place in the scheme of imperial defense, had included a clause (not published at the time) restricting the right of the new government to establish radio stations with a capacity for broadcasting outside the national territory."[28] These restrictions became a point of contention when de Valera wanted radio broadcasts to reach the Irish diaspora in the United States in the late 1930s and later in the early 1990s, when commercial radio began to be regulated in Ireland.[29] Though the legacy of colonialism persisted in broadcasting constraints in Ireland from Britain, the first 2RN broadcast was a speech in Irish by Gaelic League cofounder Douglas Hyde on January 1, 1926. The announcement was primarily, as Horgan explains, "in Irish (after an introduction in English 'for any strangers who might be listening in')."[30] The launch of 2RN thus used the medium of radio to resist imperial pressures and carve out an anticolonial space where a specifically Irish language and culture could flourish.

This assertion of a uniquely Irish identity on national radio through Hyde's speech inverted colonial hierarchies to privilege the Irish language over English, a move that echoed anticolonial ideas about the Irish language in the 1920s—for example, in the writing of Daniel Corkery. Valuing the Irish language, to use Heather Laird's words on Corkery, "challenges the dominant narrative of Ireland's cultural past by constructing an alternative narrative of a cultural past that it omits . . . [and later calls] into question the nature and value of the cultural past that [the dominant narrative] documents."[31] Corkery's ideas on the Irish language in the 1920s contextualize Hyde's 1926 speech on 2RN and the initial role national radio was to play in cultural and language revival after independence. Hyde's introduction asserts the Irish language as indicative of national belonging that, like radio waves, has the potential to expand beyond and across the territorial borders of the Free State. Radio's ability to permeate national borders implicitly challenges imperial logics of containment and control over specific territories while it also points to radio's intrinsic relationship with material environments. Radio transmissions rely on electromagnetic fields surrounding the planet, and listeners would have encountered the aeolian sounds of the ionosphere that radio transductors made audible well into the twentieth century, something that influenced mid-century composers, like John Cage.[32] These implicit connections between material environments and cultural expression in the medium of radio inflect Hyde's assertion of a uniquely Irish identity embedded in the Irish language and broadcast over the entire island on Irish national radio. By establishing the ephemeral space of radio as a place to implicitly challenge cultural imperialism and develop Irish culture, national radio became an important medium through which to debate what cultural preservation even meant as the Free State moved away from protectionist economic policies.

Music was central to these debates. Different forms of music found a place on national radio, from traditional and *céilí* bands to Western classical, jazz, and showband music.[33] The place of Irish music in Ireland and how broadcast networks should promote particular forms of music was unclear in the 1950s and 1960s. A January 1951 article in *The Bell* by renowned Irish art-music composer Brian Boydell reveals how music promotion in national broadcasting relied on seemingly opposed notions of an ever-evolving art music and the fixed cultural practices of traditional or folk music. Boydell notes that "by far the greatest power in the field of professional music is the broadcasting service, which holds a large share of the responsibility for the future of Irish music."[34] Boydell laments a stagnating Irish art music (as opposed to Irish traditional music) due to "the national characteristic of thinking in terms of the past."[35] This failure to cultivate forms of Irish art music on broadcast media hindered music training at school and conservatoria levels in Ireland, according to Boydell, thereby undermining "a public who will listen to the performances" and forcing musicians and composers to look abroad to further their careers.[36] A respectable and respected national radio orchestra would go a long way in reinstating interest in Irish art music, Boydell asserts, something that is only financially possible through "hav[ing] broadcasting vested in an independent corporation."[37] Boydell's article demonstrates a persistent division between art and folk music in Ireland in the 1950s and 1960s. Irish art music was perceived as a more cultivated form of music that could continue to develop and engage internationally through European classical music while Irish traditional music was not considered a serious art form and was seen as mostly a local practice.

This division between art music and traditional music implicitly informs debates about the role music should play in Irish cultural modernization as the Irish economy shifted toward international markets after decades of protectionist economic policies. These debates occurred

on and about national radio on a variety of programs, many of which
Ó Riada contributed in the 1950s and 1960s about different kinds of music,
including traditional, jazz, and European classical music. Just a year after
Boydell's article appeared in *The Bell*, Ó Riada graduated from University
College Cork (UCC) and became assistant director of music at Raidió
Éireann in 1953, a position he held until 1955.[38] Despite his relatively short
time with a salaried position, Ó Riada wrote and produced radio programs on various kinds of music throughout the 1950s and 1960s, in addition to composing and arranging music for film and television programs.
While continuing to compose, perform, and teach various kinds of music
at UCC from 1963 until his early death in 1971, Ó Riada's innovations
in and frameworks for theorizing Irish traditional music reflect tensions
between conceptions of Irish modernity and tradition amid European
cultural and economic integration.

Through his experiences with Gael Linn and in the Gaeltacht on the
Dingle Peninsula, Ó Riada came to understand Gaeltacht communities
as having indigenous cultural traditions that should, to use the words
of Ó Riada's former student and well-known musician and musicolo-
gist, Mícheál Ó Súilleabháin, "'mak[e] a stand' against the onslaught of
Western culture."[39] Ó Súilleabháin explains that while Ó Riada's contemporaries, including Cage and Karlheinz Stockhausen, sought to integrate
non-Western musical traditions into Western music, Ó Riada aimed to
"avoi[d] ... [the] Western classical tradition in favour of the development
of a 'native Irish classical music' out of the soil of oral-tradition music in
Ireland."[40] Ó Riada saw Gaeltacht communities as having dynamic cultural traditions that could not be understood through frameworks for
studying European classical art and music.

Aligning Ó Riada alongside Cage and Stockhausen and as a successor
to Schoenberg indicates Ó Riada's engagement with developments in a
broad range of European music. In contrast to his contemporaries, however, Ó Riada attempted to decenter Western music rather than have it
absorb alternative and non-Western forms he recognized in Irish traditional music. Ó Riada aimed to move "Gaelic culture out into a new field
of vision that would reposition Ireland in the context of a world of music
rather than within European tradition."[41] Instead of being overwhelmed
by European forms and frameworks for understanding music, Ó Riada
asserts Irish traditional music as having its own complex and developed system to rival that of the sophistication and implied civilization of

European classical music. According to Ó Riada, the system of Irish traditional music could influence forms of music that were valued in 1960s Ireland as more modern and artistic, such as jazz, classical, or showband music. Ó Riada's parallel but different approach to Cage and Stockhausen indicates an attempt to counter fixed understandings of tradition that framed Irish art and traditional music in binaries of Western development and supposedly premodern practices.

Ó Riada's reframing of cultural traditions in this way in the 1950s and 1960s resisted forms of nationalism that idealized cultural traditions within a vanishing past, which echoed colonial tropes used in settler-colonial states around the world to justify the erasure of Indigenous ingenuity and ongoing lifeways. Pushing back on this trope also distanced Ireland from being part of an emerging conception of a cohesive Europe, in which local cultural traditions might evolve into the supposedly more complex European classical tradition. Tropes of a vanishing past emerge across genres and media. Harry White shows, for example, how the literary revival fixed Irish traditional music as a symbol of anticolonial struggle that persists today.[42] Ó Riada identified such fixed conceptions of Irish traditional music as symbolic of precolonial authenticity to subscribe to colonial binaries. Logics of imperialism situated Irish oral traditions, as well as the connections to place and environment that those traditions articulated, as a precolonial authenticity to which communities might return—for example, through land-reform projects under de Valera or by embracing specific performative renditions of the Irish language or of traditional music. Yet the idea of "return" assumes such traditions do not continue to innovate and give rise to multiple modernities with the potential to compete with and offer alternatives to colonial and neocolonial conceptions of Western modernity. This positioning of Irish oral traditions as precolonial relies on binary thinking and linear conceptions of time and modernization in which the past remains a snapshot in the present to which cultural revivalists can work toward in the future. Ó Riada recognized this structure as the same imperialist logics that undergirded Western forms of development impacting Irish environments in the 1960s. Ó Riada connects these forms of development to the structure of classical music associated with a larger European tradition. European classical music was at odds with the dynamic and innovative art forms Ó Riada apprehended in Irish traditional music in Gaeltacht communities, and he moved with his family to the Gaeltacht in West Cork the same year he produced *Our Musical Heritage*.

Ó Riada's work indicates that Irish traditional music was only deemed a symbol of the past because the frameworks for understanding European music in the classical tradition were inadequate for recognizing the complexity and ongoing innovations in Irish traditional music and other Irish oral traditions. Ó Riada sought to theorize modern forms of development based on Irish traditional music rather than European classical music. Ó Riada's theorization offers an alternative to imperial logics of either reviving supposedly premodern traditions or embracing Western modernization. The Republic of Ireland's assertions of sovereignty within cultural nationalism or by embracing a European identity situated cultural traditions in the past. Indeed, both revivalists and Lemass's modernization projects relied on conceptions of a supposedly premodern past that modernizing Ireland either threatened or promised to transcend through economic development projects and European integration in the 1960s. Viewing Irish traditional music as a symbol of the past allowed for a shift toward an implied Western modernity under Lemassian modernization schemes in the 1960s that Ó Riada saw as actively working against existing and innovating but threatened rural modernities in Gaeltacht communities.

In Ó Riada's view, Irish people needed to see and hear Irish traditional music as completely separate from classical music in the European tradition to understand its potential as an alternative form of modernization. Irish traditional music, according to Ó Riada, required its own theoretical lenses rather than negatively defining what Irish traditional music was not by using theories and heuristics built to understand classical music. Ó Riada demonstrates the futility of applying theory for one kind of music onto another in the first episode of *Our Musical Heritage* by defining Irish traditional music through what it is not, a point I discuss later in this chapter. Indeed, to set Irish traditional music apart from European classical traditions, Ó Riada claims that "[Irish music] is, indeed, much closer to some forms of Oriental music than to European music."[43] This assertion points to the repetitions and modalities in Irish traditional music as well as the oral traditions that may indeed make Irish traditional music more akin to certain forms of music outside Europe's classical traditions. Yet Ó Riada's reference to "Oriental music" strategically reclaims literary and cultural histories that have positioned Ireland and Irishness on the periphery of the habitable world.[44] Aileen Dillane and Matthew Noone theorize how Ó Riada's use of Orientalism to distance Irish culture from colonial cultural forms contributes to the role "music has had, and continues to have, . . . in the shaping of Irish cultural identity through subversive recontextualizations of dominant Orientalist tropes."[45] Ó Riada's "subversive recontextualizations" of Anglo-French forms of Orientalism to distance Ireland from the rest of Europe and to compare Irish traditional music to cultures outside of Europe also emerge in his alignment of Gaeltacht traditions with indigenous cultural practices around the world. Ó Súilleabháin describes how at a concert at UCC, Ó Riada "explained that this group [Cór Chúil Aodha] had come from the West Cork Gaeltacht just as American Indians might appear from their reservation to perform for 'outsiders'. The 'Pale', he explained, had now progressed to cover almost all Ireland with the exception of such small Gaeltacht areas as Cúil Aodha and others."[46] Ó Súilleabháin remarks that the group was "exclusively male," and that "Ó Riada was positioning himself with indigenous population groups globally."[47] Ó Riada's group maintains particular narratives of a masculine-inflected modernity as it also strategically inverts colonial gender hierarchies that would feminize indigenous practices to legitimate a turn toward economic and environmental developments.

Ó Riada asserts that "the 'Pale,'" or the area in and around Dublin where imperial control and culture are assumed to be hegemonic, threatens to overwhelm and erase what he identified as modern indigenous Irish traditions. Ó Riada felt the independent, postcolonial Irish state was recolonizing Gaeltacht communities through government initiatives and formations of national identity. This recolonization was possible because of the implied imperial-era contrast between a seemingly civilized eastern region of the country and the supposedly undeveloped west. While Gaeltacht communities did not become part of global Indigenous-rights movements, these movements, as well as the civil rights movements occurring in the United States and Northern Ireland in the 1950s and 1960s, most certainly would have informed Ó Riada's comparison.[48] In his appeal to a national audience, Ó Riada thus draws on both national and international identity formations to assert cultural resistance to neocolonial forms of economic development and modernization. In doing so, Ó Riada reveals Irish traditional music as a decolonial practice that imagines alternative forms of development for the postcolonial state to follow and use as a model to modernize and decolonize Irish cultures and environments.

Destabilizing Decolonization: Inverting Hierarchical Imperial Logics in Postcolonial Ireland

Ó Riada's radio programs of the 1950s and 1960s invoke and challenge the implicit gendering and trajectories of progress in understandings of a postcolonial national modernity in mid-century Ireland. Ó Riada's reluctance to work for international "fame and fortune," as Michael Emmerson put it in a 1968 letter to Ó Riada, stemmed perhaps from Ó Riada's recognition of implicit class divisions in musical traditions that were seen as more or less developed.[49] These divisions identified local traditions as a sign of poverty and internationally integrated art forms as more advanced. In turn, these hierarchies of art produced for the more educated middle and upper classes an idea of progress in which local folk traditions would be preserved in ideas of the past or developed through their incorporation into Western art, thereby using the same logic through which European economic integration would supposedly help the depressed Irish economy to develop into Western modernity.

In 1955, Ó Riada wrote a radio program under his anglicized name, John Reidy, called *The Armchair Time-Traveller* that implicitly asserts how the categories for "art" and "folk" music hinder recognition of innovation and cultural exchange in different types of music. The program described the influence (or lack thereof) of Russian folk music on the work of classical music composer Igor Stravinsky. Reidy implies that Stravinsky's social-class position would have put him at a far remove from folk traditions. This situation, Reidy notes, is analogous to the role of Irish folk music on Irish classical composers, presumably such as himself: "As Russia, in those days, was still largely uncivilized, there was little or no tradition of Russian art-music, outside that of the 'Five', who had not yet ceased to be prophets in their own country. A music student, therefore, would have had to rely mainly on the work of established foreign masters. The influence of folk-music as a factor to be reckoned with, is almost impossible to assess in Stravinsky's upper-middle-class circumstances. In short, the situation was not very different from that obtaining in Ireland today."[50] Reidy's description that "the influence of folk-music ... is almost impossible to assess in Stravinsky's upper-middle-class circumstances" demonstrates Reidy's recognition of class divisions between different kinds of music domestically and internationally. Indeed, his use of the phrase of "still largely uncivilized" to discuss Russia reveals an implicit awareness of hierarchies of music in which the Western classical tradition was perceived as more developed and associated with higher socioeconomic positions than were local folk traditions. Reidy's assertion that this situation is "not very different from that obtaining in Ireland today" reveals ongoing class divisions in art and folk music categories that apply to various parts of Europe, thereby positioning Ireland within European histories, even as he would later go on to distinguish Irish traditions from those elsewhere in Europe. Within the hierarchies of class and development that Reidy identifies in Europe and European classical music, the Irish language and Irish traditional music were associated with seemingly undeveloped and impoverished rural regions of Ireland. Reidy's program on Stravinsky shows how these implicit class divisions between folk and art-music traditions require "the music student ... to rely mainly on the work of established foreign masters," which was a situation that Reidy himself probably experienced just a few years prior when he was studying at UCC.[51] Yet Reidy would later go on to challenge these same hierarchies upon which he relied in this early radio program.

Almost a decade later, Ó Riada's *Our Musical Heritage* ruptures fixed categories of art and folk musical traditions that persisted along class lines by invoking contradictory and fluid conceptions of tradition and modernity and undeveloped and developed. The start of Ó Riada's 1962 *Our Musical Heritage* series demonstrates the inadequacy of contemporary music theory for defining or talking about Irish traditional music. The first of fourteen episodes defines Irish traditional music as "the untouched, un-arranged, undiluted, un-Europeanized, unwesternized, un-dressed-up, naked, orally transmitted music."[52] The repetition of "un" to list what Irish traditional music is not combines with the negative connotations of an implicitly "touched, arranged, diluted, ... dressed-up" European art or classical music. It also inverts the idea that Irish traditional music, or folk music generally, is less "civilized" or developed than the European classical tradition. Although Ó Riada's opening definition on *Our Musical Heritage* indicates that Irish traditional music is an authentic and developed form of music, it only defines Irish traditional music as not unauthentic. This definition exposes the inadequacy of Western frameworks for understanding Irish traditional music, and Ó Riada goes on in the program's episodes to advance theories and terms for analyzing and understanding the complexity of Irish traditional music and its long history as "orally transmitted music" within specific cultural contexts and conventions. By demonstrating the limitations of European classical music theory for even defining what Irish traditional music is, Ó Riada asserts the need for alternative ways to understand Gaeltacht traditions and communities that he saw as being actively undermined by persistent poverty and emigration in the 1950s and then by Lemassian modernization projects in the early 1960s.

The opening episode of *Our Musical Heritage* indicates ways in which oral traditions and newer media, like recording and radio, combine to challenge hierarchies that position both traditional music and broadcast media as less developed than Western classical music or stage productions. Ó Riada's use of national radio and musical recordings resists these hierarchies and revitalizes oral traditions in Irish culture, demonstrating what Cajetan Iheka theorizes as "imperfect media, which names media artefacts that make judicious use of limited resources and thereby lead us in the direction of more sustainable media."[53] Ó Riada's remediation of Irish traditional music and oral traditions on national radio "makes judicious use of limited resources" to reveal multiple temporalities across old and new media, natural and built infrastructure, and oral traditions, recordings, and radio. Radios, in Douglas Kahn's words, "resonated with energetic environments and received signals from terrestrial and extraterrestrial sources," thereby engaging with planetary systems that operate in geologic deep time.[54] The medium of radio thus contrasts with the temporality of sound recordings, which seek to preserve sounds from the past for the future. Since its inception, Jonathan Sterne explains, "sound recording was understood to have great possibilities as an archival medium. Its potential to preserve sound indefinitely into the future was immediately grasped by users and publicists alike."[55] In broadcasting sound recordings and theorizing Irish traditional music over national radio, Ó Riada reveals multiple temporalities that inform and innovate ongoing traditions. Rather than preserve a fixed understanding of the past, the repetition of certain recordings over radio alongside ongoing oral traditions establishes diachronic dialogues that rupture the linear temporality of progress narratives in Western forms of development.

Throughout the program, natural metaphors and material environments ground Ó Riada's theories of alternative forms of development for Ireland to adopt. Ó Riada draws on the aural ubiquity of national radio by the early 1960s to compare the "orally transmitted" Irish folk music with "rich and comparatively untouched pastures."[56] The assertion that

Irish traditional music is a "rich and comparatively untouched pasture" inserts an oxymoron of environmental and colonial history into the text. This oxymoron metaphorizes Irish traditional music as an "untouched pasture," which, in turn, connotes a longer history of gendered modern agriculture and pastoralism. Through this oxymoron, Ó Riada invokes a dynamic history of cultural and environmental change implicit in Irish traditional music. This history corresponds with epistemological shifts from the medieval era through the Renaissance, which build on pastoralism, as Caroline Merchant explains: "While the pastoral tradition symbolized nature as a benevolent female, it contained the implication that nature when plowed and cultivated could be used as a commodity and manipulated as a resource."[57] A feminized nature was a disorderly abundance requiring cultivation in a masculine modernity, a gendered trope upon which the CDB relied to justify the enclosure and drainage of wetlands, as I discuss in chapter 1.

Ó Riada draws on established gendered understandings of nature in modernization narratives in the medium of radio to undermine the implied linearity of progress narratives in which elements of nature and culture and precolonial and colonial pasts are entirely separate. The idea of a pastoral space in Ireland recalls the history of intense episodes of deforestation during the seventeenth century and the subsequent land reform policies that rendered land into pastures for an industrializing England in the eighteenth and nineteenth centuries.[58] The "untouched pasture" of Ó Riada's opening episode thus implicitly connects literary and musical representations of environments with the realities those environmental imaginings produce. The way in which understandings of the natural world help to shape human impacts on material and more-than-human spaces is a point Anna Pilz demonstrates in a literary analysis of colonial representations of Irish forests. Pilz shows how representations from figures like Edmund Spenser became realities through subsequent deforestation and the establishment of plantation systems, which "resulted in new ecologies and an entangled natural heritage."[59] Irish environments emerge out of literary and cultural understandings and depictions of place. Ó Riada's reference to Irish music as an "untouched pasture" exposes the impossibility of separating Irish traditional music in 1960s Ireland from the long histories of colonial occupation that led to the environmental impacts of empire.

Ó Riada's choice of words at the start of *Our Musical Heritage* implicitly inserts Irish traditional music as a cultural contributor to the imaginaries that have shaped Ireland's environmental history and people's connections to their material and more-than-human surroundings. Yet the idea of the "untouched pasture" acknowledges how oral traditions emerged alongside the highly cultivated pastures of colonial plantation systems and later cattle pasturage for English markets imposed on Irish forests and boglands through deforestation and enclosure. Through this entanglement of cultural, colonial, and environmental histories, Ó Riada's reference to the "rich and comparatively untouched pastures" of Irish traditional music obliquely connotes the Ulster Cycle in Irish mythology and Maebh's initiation of the cattle raid in *Táin Bó Cúailnge* to obtain as much wealth as her husband, Ailill, an act that complicates gendered constructions of pasturage emerging out of the Renaissance and intensifying forms of colonial expansion in certain European countries.[60] The "untouched pasture" in the opening of *Our Musical Heritage* thus paradoxically refers to both colonial and precolonial histories, a contradiction that destabilizes the idea of a fixed understanding of Irish traditions or an authentic Irish identity as arising from an imagined premodern and precolonial past. Instead, by using this term, Ó Riada positions Irish traditional music as part of ongoing and entangled histories of culture, place, and development.

Ó Riada goes on to reveal Irish traditional music as a dynamic historiographic archive comprising human and more-than-human histories that rework gendered constructions of development in material and cultural environments. In keeping with Merchant's descriptions of gendered divisions of a feminine natural space that is ordered through a masculine-inflected modernity, Leith Davis explains the ways in which music was gendered to establish Irish traditional music and the island of Ireland as feminine and antimodern. These gendered conceptions of Irish music and Irish space positioned Ireland as part of a feminized premodern past. The implicit understanding of Irish culture and land as undeveloped contrasts with the supposedly more masculine modernity in nation states like the United States, where many Irish people emigrated: "The image of tradition—in this case, a feminine Ireland—must be preserved because the articulation of the state of modernity depends upon the existence of a premodern state from which it has emerged."[61] Besides a feminized nature being tamed by an implicitly masculine pastoral idyll, supposedly premodern traditional practices were feminized while modernized nation states took on a masculine connotation. Historically, the way to pursue this teleology from a feminized past into a masculine modernity in Ireland was to emigrate, and intense emigration in the 1950s justified national shifts away from economic protectionism. Davis notes that "emigration as it is depicted in nostalgic songs becomes a process of reaching a more mature masculine and progressive state of modernity."[62] In turning away from protectionism and attempts to decolonize through agricultural land reforms, the early 1960s marked a shift in how the Irish government sought to envision its relationship to its colonial past. Instead of returning to a feminized precolonial idyll away from which many were forced to emigrate, the idea was that Ireland would transcend its history as a British colony by becoming a masculinized modern nation itself through Lemassian development projects and European economic integration.

Rather than gendering Irish traditional music on national radio as representative of a nostalgic and feminized past that national and neocolonial modernization projects sought to transcend, Ó Riada asserts a masculine-inflected and innovating modernity in the formal structures of Irish traditional music. Like Flann O'Brien's remediation of an Irish-language consciousness into a burgeoning postmodern aesthetic of *The Third Policeman,* as I discuss in chapter 2, these formal structures reveal multiple and more environmentally enduring modernities emerging alongside Western modernization schemes. Ó Riada strategically invokes gender metaphors to position the tradition of Irish music as already part of a masculine inflected modernity in a national and natural space—namely, the radio. Irish radio, as a historical assertion of national sovereignty, a twentieth-century technology, and a medium that relies on natural systems operating in deep time, implicitly and simultaneously invokes both masculine national modernities and feminized natures. This conflation of colonial gender binaries in time and space through the medium of radio destabilizes divisions in modernization narratives through which the feminized and seemingly more natural precolonial past transitions into a postcolonial masculine modernity, or, as Priya Satia describes, in which postcolonial nations "struggle to 'move on' from, even forget, the colonial past to 'catch up' and arrive at a long-deferred future marked by freedom and prosperity."[63] Through the medium of radio, Ó Riada tactically draws on gender metaphors to disrupt and rework implicit temporalities of progress that the Republic of Ireland embraced in its efforts to modernize after 1958.

Although analytical terms for both poetry and music employ gender metaphors, Ó Riada's regular use of gender metaphors to describe the stresses and style of music simultaneously and consistently inverts (rather than subverts) colonial gender hierarchies that persist in prevalent midcentury understandings of tradition and modernity. He notes the "virile rhythm" of flute players and laments attempts to revive the harping tradition, which, according to Ó Riada, have led the harp to become an accompaniment instrument with "feminine drooping musical figures" instead of the "vigorous masculine music" he attests traditional Irish harping must have once been.[64] Similarly, he describes the "strong masculine ending" to "Sliabh na mBan," a sean-nós, or old-style, song about a group of United Irishmen defeated in County Tipperary during the 1798 Rebellion near the "Women's Mountain."[65] Although these inverted gender hierarchies maintain patriarchal discourses undergirding rival notions of modernity, they combine with the medium of radio to rupture Lemassian understandings of modernization in Ireland in the early 1960s that would position both national radio and Irish traditional music as less modern and somewhat outdated.

Ó Riada's use of a masculine-inflected modernity in Irish traditional music implicitly critiques modernization projects occurring under the Lemass government through the song "Sliabh na mBan." Besides broadcasting "Sliabh na mBan" to demonstrate forms of sean-nós singing, Ó Riada replays the recording of sean-nós singer Nioclás Tóibín performing the song at the end of the final episode in the series, thereby giving the final word on *Our Musical Heritage* to a dynamic and multimodal demonstration of the sean-nós tradition. The continuous changes in ornamentation of sean-nós singing demonstrates the fluid and socially negotiated practices through which Irish traditional music and culture continuously modernize. The multiple modernities comprising Irish traditional music recall the paradoxical oxymoron of an "untouched pasture" that relationally emerges over time, space, and complex interactions with diverse forms of power and social hierarchies. Ó Riada resisted the gendered hierarchies of a masculine modernity and feminized premodern traditions by using his position at Raidió Teilifís Éireann (RTÉ) to materially support contemporary artists. Letters from Tóibín and Comhar Cultúra Éireann to Ó Riada in 1962 indicate that Ó Riada commissioned the recordings of Tóibín for the program for which RTÉ seems to have paid.[66] This commercial transaction indicates that Ó Riada used his work with RTÉ to financially value Irish traditional music and musicians, as well as provide a prominent position for a recent recording of an ongoing and still innovating traditional practice. The economic and cultural value that Ó Riada gives to Tóibín's performance of "Sliabh na mBan" on national radio in 1962 undermines conceptions of Irish traditional music as premodern or part of the colonial trope of a vanishing past. Through financially valuing cultural practices like Ó Riada did of Tóibín's sean-nós singing on national radio, Ó Riada asserts a material shift in the focus of modernization in Ireland. The way Ó Riada values oral traditions on radio reframes modernity and specifically Irish forms of progress as ongoing innovations in cultural practice on the periphery of national and international notions of development. In contrast to a modernity moving away from attempts to preserve or revive a seemingly natural and authentic feminized past within a supposedly more developed and masculine-inflected modern nation, Ó Riada indicates Ireland already is modern or has the potential to modernize through traditions that continue to innovate and develop potentially more enduring relationships to material environments rather than through Western forms of development. The idea of modernizing Irish traditional music reveals multiple modernities obscured by an embrace of mid-century conceptions of linear time and modernization promoted by an increasingly hegemonic US-led petro-economy after World War II.

Ó Riada highlights these multiple modernities in his use of "Sliabh na mBan" in the final episode to critique a reliance on singular forms of development coming out of colonial and neocolonial conceptions of modernity. Ó Riada recites the final stanza of the poem associated with "Sliabh na mBan" before broadcasting Tóibín's version of the song. This stanza critiques the United Irishmen's alliance with the French in the 1798 Rebellion. The French allies are prevented by a storm from landing their ships with the leader of the rebellion, Wolfe Tone. The speaker calls into question the United Irishmen's dependence on the French. The verse indicates that the speaker would be happy if the French were indeed coming to help restore the rights of the "Gaeil bhocht" or "poor Irish." Yet they note that "sé an síorscéal go bhfuil a dtriall ar Éirinn [it is the eternal story that they are bound for Ireland]."[67] To question the veracity of this "eternal story" of hope in the French intent to help Irish people, the speaker goes on to use the conditional tense: "Dá mba dhóigh liom féineach go mb'fhíor an scéal úd/Bheadh mo chroí héadrom le lon an sneach [If I thought that story were true/My heart would be light as a blackbird in a hawthorn bush]." The speaker does not, however, believe that the French alliance with the United Irishmen will help Irish-speaking communities.

The promise of help from abroad remains a hypothetical narrative that even the speaker can no longer believe to be true. Although the 1798 Rebellion failed to establish the forms of free trade and independence the United Irishmen sought to achieve, the speaker's doubt does not extend to the success or failure of the revolutionaries' actions. Rather, it calls into question a subordinating reliance on foreign aid, both in the dependence of the United Irishmen on the French in 1798 and the dependence of Lemassian modernization on conceptions of Western modernity rooted in FDI and European economic integration. Ó Riada states before reciting the last stanza of "Sliabh na mBan" that "we have too long been looking for help from elsewhere."[68] This final word from Ó Riada and the song's critique of a futile and denigrating dependence on foreign aid, models, or development indicates that Irish people should look to Irish cultural traditions for alternative and potentially more socially and environmentally enduring forms of development. In particular, Ó Riada's emphasis on the final lines of the song questions the story of Lemassian modernization to help the "Gaeil bhocht," thereby demonstrating an alternative Irish modernity in the lived experience of Gaeltacht communities and their ongoing and already highly developed practice of sean-nós singing. Ó Riada's implicit notion of an alternative modernity recognizes indigenous Irish technologies that prove resilient, even in histories that marginalize them within Western modernity's conceptions of a seemingly premodern and precolonial past.

The multiple modernities Ó Riada's examination of Irish traditional music highlights thus reframe the aural ubiquity of Irish national radio as a space of resistance to international forms of development that seemed to overwhelm local traditions and traditional communities' relationships to their material environments. These connections among environment, medium, and modernization emerge in Ó Riada's examples of land agitation. While Ó Riada implicitly criticizes alliances with foreign powers at the expense of Gaeltacht communities in the early 1960s through his historical references, he also demonstrates through the medium of national radio how oral traditions can innovate alongside and perhaps even in competition with neocolonial development projects. At this time, modernization projects were altering rural life, culture, and environments through FDI in Ireland's state resources, including in agriculture, the fisheries, mining, and fossil fuel extraction. Changes to people's relationships to land and their expectations for land acquisition in the 1960s implicitly emerge in several of Ó Riada's references to land agitation in the eighteenth century. Ó Riada offers translations of some songs that refer to the eighteenth-century agrarian social movement, the Whiteboys (na Buachaillí Bána), to protest oppressive rents and evictions imposed on tenant populations. Relatedly, in one of the episodes on piping, Ó Riada offers a recording of Tomás Reck playing a slow air on the pipes, "Lament of Stalker Wallace," a Whiteboy who was caught and hanged for his land agitation activities.[69] Columns that Ó Riada wrote for *The Irish Times* also critique economic integration with Europe, most notably, the satire of Ireland joining the Common Market, "F-F-F-Foreigners." This piece was written by Ó Riada in January, 1962, and it uses the motif of a pub conversation to respond to "Aon scéal agat?" or "Do you have a story?"[70] These examples, as well as Ó Riada's use of "Sliabh na mBan" after his final words on the program that "we have too long been looking for help from elsewhere," resist "foreign" models of development, whether they come from Europe or from state-led efforts that have internalized the logics of colonialism.[71] Such logics promote the national modernization of Irish-speaking communities based on European and Western models of development, which, in turn, contribute to the ongoing erasure of multiple modernities that offer potentially more enduring cultural and environmental futures.

Reframing Progress on Radio: Alternative Modernities in Irish Traditional Music

After disrupting the frameworks for understanding Western developmental forms that devalue oral and folk traditions and replace local practices with supposedly more advanced systems from elsewhere, Ó Riada calls listeners' attention to the multiple modernities implicit in Irish traditions that *Our Musical Heritage* actively remediates on national radio and consequently into the ephemeral auralities reverberating out into the air. In doing so, he theorizes modes of analysis for understanding alternative and multiple forms of modernization and modernity implicitly already developing in Gaeltacht traditions. Through establishing theoretical frameworks for understanding and articulating these innovating traditions, *Our Musical Heritage* indicates how the state should heed the multiple modernities across Ireland rather than privilege constructions of modernity defined largely by imperial-era logics and geopolitical hierarchies coming out of World War II. These logics persist in projects that fetishize notions of Irish tradition, culture, language, and landscape. At the time Ó Riada produced *Our Musical Heritage*, oral traditions in Ireland were seen as in danger of being overwhelmed by international economic modernization projects, including new media, cultural tourism, and resource development in the early 1960s. Such projects, Luke Gibbons shows, idealize Irish environments for industrial development and romanticize Irish cultural traditions into a static symbol of a lost civilization. Gibbons explains that romanticized images of Ireland as an empty rural landscape have been promoted by both the Irish Development Authority (IDA) and the tourist board, Bord Fáilte, to advance economic development: "The implication here is that the dynamic image of Ireland as a high-tech paradise projected by the IDA is somehow incompatible with the image of Ireland as an unspoiled romantic paradise promoted by Bord Fáilte. . . . The most striking feature of IDA promotional material is that it does not simply acknowledge but actively perpetuates the myth of romantic Ireland, incorporating both modernity and tradition within its frame of reference."[72] These romanticized representations of Irish rural space established the material environment as both a container of a premodern cultural past and an empty region ripe for development. These representations consequently justified national modernization projects and forms of development that Ó Riada critiques and materially pushed back against through the medium of radio in *Our Musical Heritage*.

Ó Riada associates certain forms of development with European art and environments that historically facilitated colonial occupation and in the early 1960s worked to privatize more-than-human communities and material agencies into natural resources through an increasingly hegemonic neocolonial global economy. Ó Riada emphasizes that "traditional Irish art never adopted the Greco-Roman forms spawned by the Renaissance, which have indeed become the basis of European art. I refer specifically to the European notion of 'development,' a development which moves in a rising crescendo of tension with its end being a crisis, the resolution of which produces catharsis."[73] The space and time of what Ó Riada calls "the European notion of 'development'" implies a series of steps going from "tension" through "crisis" and ending in "catharsis." The linearity implied by these phases of development signifies a teleology that outlines a singular path for progress, and this progress implicitly leads to a singular (neo)colonial notion of modernity. Indeed, the developmental structure Ó Riada outlines in Western European art elides alternative routes for modernization to take. It also devalues and obfuscates the potential to recognize existent multiple or alternative modernities developing alongside or even in contentious and resilient relationships against extraction economies. Ó Riada goes on to explain this "European notion of 'development'" through describing a diagram that he asserts maps the shape of Beethoven symphonies, Verde's operas, Greek plays like Sophocles's *Oedipus Rex*, Shakespearean drama, and Hollywood cinema: "It is the basis of European art, and it is quite foreign to traditional Irish art."[74] These European forms of development contrast with Ó Riada's earlier comment that Irish traditional music "is, indeed, much closer to some forms of Oriental music than to European music."[75] Ó Riada's reference to "Greco-Roman forms" implicitly points to longer literary and intellectual histories that positioned Ireland on the edge of the habitable world and as developmentally behind.[76] Joseph Lennon shows how colonial writers and thinkers, such as Edmund Spenser, continued to use this idea of Ireland as a peripheral borderland outside the supposedly civilized world as a justification of eradicating indigenous peoples and ways of life and replacing them with plantation systems.[77] Imperial understandings of development consequently spatially and temporally map Irish cultural and environmental histories in narratives of progress, from a kind of premodern barbarity to European conceptions of civilization.

Reclaiming the elements that make Irish traditional art and music "foreign" to European developmental forms, Ó Riada shows Irish traditional music to offer alternative forms of progress in the logic and structure of the tunes and practices of ornamentation. In contrast to linear, European forms of art and development, Ó Riada describes Irish traditional music as a circular form of progress that is "fundamentally more realistic" because it "corresponds with *real* life."[78] Ó Riada asserts that this shape of Irish traditional music is analogous in shape to planetary systems, such as the rotations of Earth: "Every day the sun rises, every day it sets. Every day possesses the same basic characteristics, follows the same fundamental pattern, while at the same time each day differs from the next in its ornamentation of *events*. The particular events of each day are, to the basic pattern of days, as the particular ornamentation of each verse of a song is to the basic pattern of *all* the verses of that song."[79] A single ornament in a song or tune contributes to an ongoing and dynamic tradition of Irish music that corresponds with "*real* life," as Ó Riada vocally stresses on the radio program. This "*real* life" indicates material conditions in which communities have enduring relationships with their natural environments that the shape of Irish traditional tunes reflects and records. The repetition of "fundamental pattern[s]" positions elements of Irish traditional music as part of a larger set of relations analogous to planetary systems that enable but also constrain human and more-than-human innovations. These fundamental patterns are based on three types of practice: "the variation principle," "internal logic," and "direct expression." The variation principle implies that no two verses of a song can be sung the same way.[80] Internal or interior logic, Ó Riada explains, is implicit in the form of Munster songs, where a select set of intervals create the tune and can be varied using melismatic, intervallic, or rhythmic variation.[81] Finally, Ó Riada details a concept called "direct expression," which relies on the performer's personal style within the aesthetic conventions of ornamentation in Irish traditional music.[82]

These three elements of Irish traditional music, according to Ó Riada, allow performers and the audience to draw on the tunes to socially negotiate cultural histories, practices, and conventions through ongoing innovations of ornamentation practices. The emphasis on the articulation of events through ornamentation in Ó Riada's analogy reworks understandings of history as a linear sequence of events to a circularity that organically builds on each repetition over time. Ó Riada's theories and the music he plays on national radio combine cultural, environmental, and political elements to demonstrate "fundamental patterns" existent in oral traditions and alternative forms of development that "correspon[d] with *real* life." That is, the multiple modernities Ó Riada theorizes through Irish traditional music on *Our Musical Heritage* continually emerge in and through interactions between human and more-than-human worlds. These interactions evolve across the ongoing innovation of oral traditions and the ephemeral but very physical electromagnetic pulses of Earth's atmosphere that enable Irish national radio. *Our Musical Heritage* implicitly engages the often overlooked and obscured cultural and environmental modernities through which Irish traditional music transmits over the landscapes and into homes across Ireland.

In contrast to the "European notion of development" in which events might fall into categories of "tension," "crisis," or "catharsis," Ó Riada's description of the role of ornamentation in the more circular structure of Irish traditional music situates events as part of ongoing interactions that have no beginning or end. Instead of leading to the product of "catharsis," they draw on the resources of a given historical moment and the material surroundings to articulate their existence and assert agency within the material conditions that enable life on Earth. Ó Riada describes this process of articulating events through the practice of ornamentation as "the progress of tradition in Ireland," and he compares the ongoing practice of ornamentation to a river: "You might compare the progress of tradition in Ireland to the flow of a river. Various foreign bodies may fall in, or be dropped in, or indeed thrown in, but they do not divert the course of the river, nor do they stop it flowing; it absorbs them, carrying them with it as it flows onwards."[83] The "progress of tradition in Ireland" is a seemingly never-ending flow that pushes back on teleological constructions of linear time through incorporating elements from surrounding material and cultural environments, "carrying them with it as it flows onwards." The current implied by the river in Ó Riada's metaphor indicates environmental conditions that shape Irish traditional forms of progress. Rather than pushing the boundaries of a seemingly limitless growth or controlling and extracting material surroundings, the "progress of tradition in Ireland" points to more enduring forms of development that interact with instead of dominate or control environments and natural systems.

While Ó Riada's metaphor indicates a kind of assimilation of ideas and influences, the "progress of tradition in Ireland" also demonstrates a dynamic and ongoing change implicit in Ó Riada's understanding of tradition that pushes back on conceptions of fixed cultural practices vanishing into an imagined past. Tradition as ongoing and socially negotiated cultural conventions are implicit in the music itself and demonstrate alternative forms of progress. Ó Riada draws on recordings, like the Irish Folklore recordings of the Traveller (Mincéir/Pavee) uilleann piper Johnny Doran, to offer "a continuous stream of every-varying music" that exemplifies a form of progress for the oral tradition of Irish music.[84] Doran's performance of the tune develops the tradition through innovations within shared cultural practices that, like natural environments, provide an enduring structure through which traditions grow, change, and modernize. Ó Riada articulated these environmental conditions as the variation principle, internal logic, and direct expression. The interaction among the performer, audience, and sociohistorical and environmental contexts asserts a resilient form of music that develops in and through material or cultural constraints because it heeds them and interacts with these constraints rather than trying to resolve them, as Western developmental structures attempt to do. By playing one of the few recordings of Doran's music on national radio in the early 1960s, Ó Riada embraces the multiple modernities emanating from the preservation, proliferation, and the ongoing production of Irish traditional music. Ó Riada's discussion and depictions of ornamentation in Irish traditional music reveal "a continuous stream of ever-varying music" that demonstrates an alternative modernity in the music itself through its constant innovations within the material conditions of a specific historical context.

The distinctions Ó Riada draws between "the progress of tradition in Ireland" and "European notions of development" on *Our Musical Heritage* thus indicate tensions between valuing process over product. These values inflect understandings of tradition and modernity on material environments and communities' relationships with natural systems that enable life, what Hannah Arendt, theorizes as the "the very quintessence of the human condition . . . providing human beings with a habitat in which they can move and breathe without effort and without artifice."[85] The history of colonial extraction economies, expansion of global capitalism, and mid-twentieth-century national shifts toward European economic integration operated on a colonial logic of development to produce prosperity through linear conceptions of growth, time, and progress. However, the complex and contradictory history of modernizing land and culture in Ireland implicit in Ó Riada's examples of Irish traditional music splinter conceptions of development in favor of a more multivalent and cyclical notion of "the progress of tradition" that not only values "the very quintessence of the human condition" but also embraces ongoing interactions between human and more-than-human worlds to advance and innovate. The ornamentation of Irish traditional music draws on a shared set of aesthetic practices that operate through alternative modernities of circular progress and ongoing interactions with material environments, both of which challenge Western modernity's implicit linear and singular trajectory of development.

The ornamentation practices Ó Riada theorizes collectively innovate across a spectrum of cyclical exchange, from individual expression to wider regional and historical contexts and back again to individual expression. The music itself becomes what Guy Beiner termed a "social memory," or "a process by which members of a community negotiate the identity of the society with which they are affiliated in relation to its past."[86] For instance, some of the piping and fiddle examples that Ó Riada offers mimic sounds of animals during hunting. In an example from the famous piper Seamus Ennis playing part of a longer tune, "The Fox Chase," known as "The Lament for the Fox," Ó Riada notes that "you hear some very peculiar to piping effects in it [the tune], such as the imitation of the sound of the hounds yelping, the sound of the hounds barking, and so on."[87] Similar examples are given with the fiddle, where Johnny Doherty plays "The Fox Chase" and Patrick Kelly plays "The Foxhunter's Reel." Ó Riada describes "The Fox Chase" as "that virtuoso piece in which the instrument, whether pipes or fiddle, imitates all the sounds of the chase," going on to note that the piece can last "over twenty minutes, highly elaborate and sophisticated."[88] Like the oxymoron of the "untouched pasture," these imitations of the more-than-human sounds in the hunt indicate longer contradictory histories in which traditional practices of ornamentation modernize alongside and through complex histories of class, imperialism, and environmental management.

The "highly elaborate and sophisticated" tune of "The Fox Chase" indicates the continually rearticulated entanglement of colonialism and multispecies environments. Irish traditional music documents these entangled histories and materialities, offering alternative historiographic methods for understanding and communicating the past's relationship to the present and future. The example of fox hunting, which is largely associated with the Anglo-Irish Ascendancy of the eighteenth century, refers to a type of sport hunting in which killing the fox simply asserts dominance over the land as the fox is not eaten. The fox, to use Maureen O'Connor's words, "is hunted, and often caught, by man—and woman—not for food or survival, but for the *pleasure* of killing."[89] This violent assertion of dominance over the more-than-human world conjures up a complex history of class identities and gender hierarchies in Ireland that are closely associated with colonial projects. Although Cromwell encouraged the eradication of wolves and foxes from Ireland in the seventeenth century, fox hunting most often recalls eighteenth-century Ascendancy opulence that relied on the extraction of human labor and more-than-human environments.[90] As Kathryn Kirkpatrick explains, "Just as the rise of fox-hunting coincides with the enclosure of land by the landed gentry, including the newly monied gentry, in England, so too its importation into Ireland becomes an emblem of exclusive right to land in the face of human and nonhuman Others."[91] The Ascendancy historically arose alongside and out of the oppressive effects of the penal laws, which were a series of acts that systematically dispossessed Catholic and native Irish populations of wealth, community, land, and language. This colonial history of dispossession overlaps with the masculinized practice of fox hunting and the feminized subordination of Irish people, environments, and traditions.[92] Irish-language texts challenge these colonial gender hierarchies by symbolically associating, in Donna Potts's words, "the 'little red fox' (An Maidrín Rua) [which] is the only fox indigenous to Ireland, . . . [with] the Irish peasant, and more generally, [with] Irish resourcefulness under colonization."[93] While red foxes are now nearly extinct in Ireland, the decline of fox populations in the eighteenth century led to the import of various fox species to supply the hunt, a fact that contradicts, as Kirkpatrick points out, the different reasons hunters used to justify killing foxes: "Protection of the human community's chickens is regularly invoked as the altruistic charge of the hunt. . . . However, fowl funds were in fact used to reimburse tenants for their losses so they would *not* kill foxes but leave them to the sport of the gentlemen."[94] Foxes were considered a threat to fowl, but they were, in fact, far more endangered. Ó Riada's description and use of "The Fox Chase" on *Our Musical Heritage* raises questions about what Irish traditional music teaches about this colonial history of land, people, and animals.

Through Ó Riada's discussion of "The Fox Chase," Irish traditional music emerges as a historiographic method for documenting human and more-than-human interactions with social and environmental systems. The incorporation of the sounds of the fox hunt in Irish traditional tunes demonstrates this oral tradition to contain human and animal histories. Drawing on Edmund Burke, Edith Somerville, and Violet Martin (Martin Ross), O'Connor notes that "the communicative potential of the inarticulate animal enables a disarticulation of the colonial subject."[95] In contrast to the erasure or "disarticulation of the colonial subject," the potential of the animal sounds in "The Fox Chase" on *Our Musical Heritage* opens possibilities for acknowledging several alternative histories remediated across multiple media and modernities. While Irish traditional music innovates within systems of ornamentation and oral transference, it also interacts with new media. Traditional music was, as Davis explains, "involved in a dynamic relationship that began well before the eighteenth century. This relationship was transformed, however, by two interrelated phenomena that occurred during the eighteenth century: an increasing interest in the consumption of leisure and the growth of the printed music industry."[96] The history of Irish music in print media defined and divided music along class lines that have persisted in various iterations of folk and art music. Davis describes how "critics have tended to encourage the division of music of Ireland before the eighteenth century into two entirely separate traditions, setting up rigid boundaries between the 'hidden Ireland' of the Gaelic world and the Anglo-Irish world."[97] Ó Riada's examples of fox hunting tunes undermine the idea of "two entirely separate traditions" by showing Irish traditional tunes to replicate the sounds of an Ascendancy sport to dominate the landscape and more-than-human communities.

Through "The Fox Chase" and "The Foxhunter's Reel," Ó Riada exposes multiple perspectives across the Irish landscape and in Irish music that undermine fixed categories dividing "the Gaelic world and the Anglo-Irish world." The music and discussion Ó Riada offers draw listeners' attention to the sounds of the fox hunt that fracture an emphasis on a single anthropocentric sound into multiple auralities, perspectives, and histories. The tunes include "the hounds yelping, the sound of the hounds barking" to "imitat[e] all the sounds of the chase."[98] By encompassing the aurality of the hunting dogs, Irish traditional music emphasizes an aural experience of the entire context rather than focusing on a particular sound or sight associated with prestige, class, or gender. Ó Riada's examples indicate that existing frameworks for discussing and understanding music historically categorize Irish traditional music in reductive and incomplete ways. *Our Musical Heritage* engages with Irish traditional tunes as a historiographic method across multiple remediations, from interactions with print to Ó Riada's theoretical frameworks for taking Irish traditional music seriously on national radio. Employing the music as a historiographic method and archive reveals rich multispecies histories and modernities archived in the form, content, and traditional practices of performing and expanding the tunes and songs themselves.

Indeed, Ó Riada also drew on traditional music to write a brief history of fox hunting. Around the same time as *Our Musical Heritage* aired, Ó Riada wrote a column for *The Irish Times* entitled "Fox and Hounds," in which he examined Irish-language songs to trace the history of hunting in Ireland. Ó Riada contends that Gaelic hunting ended with the surrender of John O'Dwyer in March 1652 at the end of the anti-Cromwellian war: "The boar-hunt, the wolf-hunt, the stag-hunt—all gone, all finished, 'with O'Leary in the grave.' All that remains is foxhunting."[99] Ó Riada inverts literary representations of music by drawing on W. B. Yeats's poem, "September 1913" to describe that "Romantic Ireland's [been] dead and gone" for longer than revivalists had previously envisioned; indeed, such an Ireland may never have existed as the nostalgic and vanished representation of a precolonial past. A history derived from musical sources reveals not a vanishing or dying culture as understandings of literary representations would suggest. Rather, using music and sound as historiography reveals a rich history that continues to innovate and archive events as it changes and emerges in multiple iterations over time. Representations of Irish traditional music that fetishize and stabilize an imagined past overlooks the dynamic histories and cultures the music contains and continues to innovate.

Ó Riada's article goes on to show sound to be a form in which historical memory persists. This use of music and sound as a historiographic method recalls Corkery's notion of a "hidden Ireland," or histories that often go unheeded due to their medium or form.[100] By drawing on songs and tunes as historical evidence, the imitation of the sounds of the hunt demonstrates the "progress of tradition in Ireland."[101] Heeding the various aural components of tunes and songs, such as in the "The Fox Chase," "The Foxhunter's Reel," and "Sliabh na mBan," ruptures an understanding of history and development as linear and teleological or visual and textual. Instead of a framework for understanding music that recognizes "a development which moves in a rising crescendo of tension with its end being a crisis, the resolution of which produces catharsis," Ó Riada implicitly calls for a more comprehensive aural experience that recognizes rival historical perspectives among humans and more-than-humans reverberating over soundwaves across the island.[102] These multiple and multispecies perspectives all participate in the ongoing negotiation of the tune through continuous ornamentation and variation.

Ó Riada's *Our Musical Heritage* thus demonstrates Irish traditional music to have innovated as a cultural practice for centuries, and that continues to modernize through the ubiquitous but still relatively new medium of radio. The program formally and semantically pushes back on Lemassian forms of modernization that draw on binaries of the premodern and modern. Such binaries indicate a turning away from a feminized premodern past to inhabit a masculine modernity. This process alters people's relationships to material environments in the name of progress.

Such progress narratives mirror the developmental forms of Western classical music Ó Riada described. Ó Riada's intentionally fluid and contemporary articulations of Irish traditional music assert "the progress of tradition in Ireland" as an alternative modernity that emerges through multiple and alternative forms of modernization.[103] The "progress of tradition in Ireland" challenges understandings of national identity on national radio that would relegate traditional practices to a premodern or precolonial past. Even when framed within anticolonial forms of cultural nationalism, the idea of precolonial traditions as separate from colonial histories depend on an implicitly imperial binary logic. These imperial logics, so often internalized in postcolonial efforts to emulate the industrialization and development of colonial oppressors, implicitly promote particular forms of economic modernization that fix traditions in the past and render material environments into extractable natural resources. Such logics entrench Western notions of modernity and obscure the multiple modernities documented in innovating oral traditions across an array of media.

New Media and Modernities: The Legacy of *Our Musical Heritage*

Subsequent iterations of *Our Musical Heritage* revised and reframed the complex theorization of Irish traditional music and its dynamism that Ó Riada offered, thereby demonstrating shifting understandings of the role music and broadcast media play in defining place and identity during the Troubles and after the Celtic Tiger, the era of unprecedented economic growth in Ireland between 1995 and 2008. In 1982, Dolmen Press worked with Thomas Kinsella and Tomás Ó Canainn to produce *Our Musical Heritage* as a printed but abridged book of Ó Riada's original script with a selection of the recordings on accompanying LPs. Dolmen Press grew out of the ongoing cultural negotiations of modernity and tradition after World War II. Beginning in 1951, a time when most Irish writers had to look abroad for publishers in England or the United States due to a dearth of Irish presses, the Dolmen Press founder, Liam Miller, was dedicated to fostering a specifically Irish literary scene emerging from the 1950s onward. The press published the early work of poets, such as Kinsella and John Montague, and cultivated lasting relationships with them.[104] Dolmen Press's shift from its literary focus to music in the revised version of *Our Musical Heritage* in print and LPs reveals the influence that Ó Riada had on many Irish writers, including Kinsella. Yet this version of Ó Riada's program also exposes the ways in which Ó Riada was memorialized were sometimes at odds with the historical dynamism he saw and promoted in Irish traditional music.

The dynamism and political engagement Ó Riada recognized in Irish traditional music was embraced by many musicians and activists in the 1970s. Albums like the 1978 *H Block*, produced by Christy Moore and Donal Lunny, indicate specific ways in which the Irish traditional music revival was aligning itself with forms of anticolonial cultural formations in Irish history and antiauthoritarian politics associated with folk music internationally, particularly coming out of the 1960s in the United States.[105] *H Block* asserts a solidarity between performers of Irish traditional music and republican political prisoners held in the Maze Prison in County Down, Northern Ireland. On this album, various Irish musicians (all men) perform traditional tunes and original songs that protest the treatment and criminalization of political prisoners. Tunes on the album, such as "Repeal the Union" or "The Rights of Man," indicate the longer history of traditional tunes referring to moments of struggle, such as the Act of Union in 1801 and the cultural role of the French Revolution in Irish independence movements, respectively. These tunes were both performed on the album by flute player Matt Molloy, who was asked the following year to join the Chieftains in 1979.[106] The presence of these tunes on *H Block* demonstrates the cultural relevance of Irish traditional music in contemporary struggles and alliances during the Troubles' violent contestations of entrenched colonial hierarchies in anti-Catholic forms of discrimination in Northern Ireland.

This cultural relevance of Irish traditional music during the Troubles echoes examples, like the story of foxhunting, that Ó Riada invoked on the *Our Musical Heritage* radio program to show Irish traditional music as both a model for historical change and a source of historiography. The album includes original songs that describe protests by prisoners that led to the hunger strikes, resulting notably in the death of Bobby Sands in 1981. For example, Mick Hanly's song "On the Blanket" depicts the cruel treatment of prisoners in the Maze when they demanded to be treated like political prisoners and wear civilian clothes instead of prison uniforms. Prison uniforms visibly marked them as perpetrators of criminal offences rather than anticolonial political protesters, however violent. This use of

Irish traditional music during the Troubles to support republican movements demonstrates a complex, dynamic, and multifaceted cultural role for Irish traditional music in the late 1970s and early 1980s. Such a dynamism would have been in keeping with Ó Riada's understanding of Irish traditional music as a resource for documenting and understanding historical events through ongoing cultural practice. The album also draws on the ways in which Ó Riada inverted gendered narratives of a masculine-inflected modernity through its all-male performers, a move that exposes the double marginalization of Irish women while recognizing the emasculation of colonized identities and anticolonial assertions of masculinity.[107] *H Block* implicitly draws on elements in Ó Riada's own understanding of the cultural relevance and active engagement of Irish traditional music with specific historical responses. This musical response to intensifying violence, surveillance, and crisis in Northern Ireland in the late 1970s reveals Irish traditional music to innovate cultural practices to politically participate in, as well as record specific events, occurring during the Troubles.

In contrast, literary responses to the Troubles implicitly invoke Western classical traditions and drew on an increasingly static legacy of Ó Riada after his death. The 1979 Dolmen Press publication *Fifteen Dead*, by Kinsella, includes elegies to Ó Riada that appear after Kinsella's "The Butcher's Dozen," which decries the injustice of Lord Widgery's report on the Bloody Sunday killings in Derry. The report discriminatorily legitimates the murder of thirteen civil rights activists when British soldiers opened fire during a peaceful demonstration in Derry on January 30, 1972, or "Bloody Sunday," shooting twenty-six people.[108] Kinsella had "finished, printed, and published ["The Butcher's Dozen"] within a week of the publication of the Widgery Report."[109] The poem expresses the acute anger at the injustice of the report, and, at moments, speaks directly to England: "England, the way to your respect/Is via murderous force, it seems;/ You push us to your own extremes."[110] The poem's rhyming AABB sequence is out of sync with the syntax of the sentences. The uneven syntax and even rhyme pattern formally assert a tension between competing systems of power and justice. The injustice of the Widgery report outlined in Kinsella's poem draws into sharp relief competing cultural conceptions of Irish identity that were challenged by the national borders drawn across the island of Ireland. The Troubles tested the Republic of Ireland's assertion of a thirty-two-county nation, because, as

Conor McCarthy explains, "while the Republic may assert its right to represent the entire nation, it also, in the exercise of that right, is compelled to recognise the Border, militarily, diplomatically, legally, in defence of its own sovereignty."[111] The Republic had to recognize the legitimacy of colonial strategies of partition that created the Northern Irish state. It also had to recognize Northern Ireland as separate from the Republic to respond as a modern European nation to the violence of the Troubles. The Troubles in Northern Ireland thus altered the Republic's assertions of territorial sovereignty and its associated cultural identity through forms of violence that required international negotiations on security between Britain and the Republic of Ireland.

The raw outrage in "The Butcher's Dozen" contrasts sharply with the elegies Kinsella wrote for Ó Riada that subsequently appear in *Fifteen Dead*. The two poetic sequences that Kinsella wrote about Ó Riada after his death are "A Selected Life" (1972) and "Vertical Man" (1973). These elegies offer brief, single-stanza snapshots of Ó Riada playing a bodhran in 1962 and present more extensive contemplations of his memory. The second and third poems in "A Selected Life" describe Ó Riada's wake and burial. "Vertical Man" was conceptualized during a kind of solitary second wake for Ó Riada that Kinsella had in his home in Philadelphia on the anniversary of Ó Riada's death on October 3, 1972.[112] Tidying up after a day working on an elegy for John F. Kennedy called "The Good Fight" (1973), Kinsella describes how he unexpectedly set a photograph of Ó Riada on the album *Vertical Man* next to Ó Riada's death mask and a cast of his left hand, which Kinsella had in his possession, thereby "making a little altar."[113] Drinking bourbon and listening to Gustav Mahler's *Das Lied von der Erde*, Kinsella explains how he came up with this elegy for Ó Riada, which became the poem "Vertical Man."[114] Kinsella's poem is named after Ó Riada's album *Vertical Man*, which itself draws on W. H. Auden's poem for Christopher Isherwood for its title.[115] The *Vertical Man* album, released in 1969, reveals the importance of Ó Riada to prominent Irish writers like Kinsella, Seamus Heaney, and John Montague. The album comprises poems from writers including Kinsella, Heaney, and Montague set to "a number of [Ó Riada's] songs and the orchestral *Hercules Dux Ferrariae*," which was Ó Riada's composition based on Schoenberg's tonal system.[116] While the "genesis" of the "Vertical Man" poem is, as Kinsella puts it, "one of the strangest of any poem [he had] written," the poem's form draws "on the poem [by Hans Bethge] used by

Mahler in the opening movement of *Das Lied von der Erde*, or 'the song of the Earth.'"[117] These intertextual references between Western classical music and European poetic traditions demonstrate Kinsella's association of Ó Riada's work with Western classical forms rather than with the traditional music for which Ó Riada developed theoretical frameworks in the early 1960s.

The republication of Kinsella's four poetic sequences together in the *Fifteen Dead* Dolmen Press collection in 1979 demonstrates the entanglement of cultural, political, and social crisis. Positioning "The Butcher's Dozen" alongside poems commemorating Ó Riada and John F. Kennedy in 1979 situates Ó Riada as a historical figure whose death is indicative of the start of a crisis of modernity. While this crisis indicates the contestations of power, identity, and belonging characteristic of civil rights movements in both the United States and Northern Ireland, as well as anticolonial struggles globally, it also suggests European forms of development that climax and resolve without challenging the underlying structures of geopolitical hierarchies or nation-state systems. Civil rights movements were indicative of the geographical constraints of anticolonial struggle and sovereignty, as Adrian Guelke writes: "Northern Ireland was one of a number of places within the First World of Western states where conflict erupted in the late 1960s and early 1970s that challenged attempts to limit the geographical scope of decolonisation."[118] Although many regions in the British Empire gained national independence in the mid-twentieth century, oppressed groups in settler-colonial and colonial states in the West had to appeal to the state to protect their rights as equal citizens. This paradoxically forced those experiencing discrimination to seek protections from state institutions which were often the source of oppression. The crisis of modernity in Ireland exposes the island's unique history within European colonialism as it also was absorbed into structural understandings of neocolonial and European development, in which the crisis climaxes and resolves in legal protections that reinforce state power.

In positioning the poems about Ó Riada's death as implicitly indicative of a crisis of modernity, Kinsella's collection ultimately elegizes a past with which Kinsella's poems associate Ó Riada's life and work. Yet, as my analysis of *Our Musical Heritage* argues, Ó Riada's work pushed against structures of crisis and resolution. While Ó Riada formally associated developmental structures of rising action, climax, and resolution with the shape of Western classical music, the Dolmen Press production of Kinsella's collection implicitly reflects this developmental form. Ó Riada asserted alternative models of progress in Irish cultural traditions. These traditions promote forms of modernization that are cyclical and that honor all the elements that "may fall in, or be dropped in, or indeed thrown in, but they do not divert the course of the river, nor do they stop it flowing; it absorbs them, carrying them with it as it flows onwards."[119] In contrast to Kinsella's poetry collection in which implicit forms of crisis associated with modernization and modernity work toward resolutions, laws, and consensus, Ó Riada's metaphor of the river demonstrates a more dynamic and potentially messy negotiation of material and cultural conditions and constraints in which borders are dissolved rather than reified in colonial understandings of territorial sovereignty. Inserting these elegies to Ó Riada in the middle of *Fifteen Dead* centers Ó Riada between Irish and international struggles. The elegies of Ó Riada appear between poems documenting Kinsella's anger at the murder of the nonviolent activists in Derry and those commemorating Kennedy after his assassination. Kinsella's focus on the ways in which the memory of Ó Riada was taken up in the unstable decades after his death and during the Troubles thus reveals the splintering of possible ways to interpret Ó Riada's life and work while fixing his legacy in the words on the page. This splintering of possible interpretations of Ó Riada's life and work with both Western classical and Irish traditional music ironically memorializes Ó Riada's promotion of alternative forms of modernization in Irish cultural traditions in a seemingly distant past. Kinsella's *Fifteen Dead* reveals tensions between fixed understandings of supposedly premodern traditions and innovations in modernity that were increasingly debated in the 1980s and 90s.

The Dolmen Press publication of Kinsella's poems consequently indicates ways in which the 1982 Dolmen Press edition of *Our Musical Heritage* responds to this period of social, political, and cultural upheaval by fixing Ó Riada's radio program in print and on LPs. While the publication of *Our Musical Heritage* by Dolmen Press was certainly a recognition of Ó Riada's lasting influence on Irish writers and Irish music, the altered text, order, and selected recordings attest to changing conceptions of Irish identity, place, and modernity. These changing understandings of identity and place in the modern world are most notable in the elision of numerous historical references. The Dolmen Press version of *Our Musical Heritage* omits references to historical events pertaining to land agitation or revolution. For example, Ó Riada translates the song "Donnchadh Bán," sung by Connemara singer Darach Ó Catháin. The song, as Ó Riada explains, is a "sad, bitter comment" ostensibly by Donnchadh's sister on his capture and subsequent hanging for his participation in the eighteenth-century agrarian protest movement, the Whiteboys, *na Buachaillí Bána*.[120] The song is on the LPs accompanying the printed version of the Dolmen Press edition, but only a brief introduction to the song exists, noting its title and that it "exemplifies the best features of the Connemara style."[121] Later in one of the episodes on piping, Ó Riada offers a recording of Tomás Reck playing an air on the pipes, "Lament of Stalker Wallace," who was also one of the Whiteboys, *na Buachaillí Bána*.[122] This recording and Ó Riada's description of the story of Stalker Wallace are completely absent from the Dolmen Press publication.

Perhaps most notably, however, is the complete absence of "Sliabh na mBan," the song that Ó Riada describes as "probably the most popular song to come from this region [the Déise Gaeltacht]," because "this song of the 1798 rising would move a stone to tears."[123] Ó Riada played this song twice on the radio program, including to end the entire series, thereby indicating its importance to the overall meaning of the program. The Dolmen Press publication implicitly asserts the relevance of this song by including a recording of Johnny Doran playing the melody on the pipes on the second LP and briefly mentioning the sean-nós song in the book to highlight differences between Doran and Tóibín's technical executions.[124] The publication of *Our Musical Heritage* as a book with accompanying LPs recognizes the significant role Irish traditional music played in cultural shifts occurring alongside the Troubles as it also memorializes Ó Riada's original program and its understanding of a dynamic and modernizing Irish traditional music as part of a fixed cultural practice and previous era. This contradictory cultural role of Ó Riada as representative of both innovating and preserving Irish traditional music indicates a temporal tension in understandings of Irish cultural history as a dynamic present dependent on fixed understandings of the past.

The 1982 *Our Musical Heritage* adaptation by Dolmen Press was produced at a moment when Irish traditional music was becoming increasingly recognized as a form of ethnic music internationally, a market trend that would lead to the creation of categories like Celtic and World music by the late 1980s and early 1990s. In contrast to Ó Riada's conception of Irish traditional music as a dynamic practice, representations of

Irish traditions as fixed cultural practices of a bygone era ironically legitimated economic modernization and natural resource development projects even as they implicitly deliberated how to preserve or revive musical traditions in the 1990s onwards. Seeming to carry on Ó Riada's original project of "the progress of tradition in Ireland" at the start of the Celtic Tiger, Ó Súilleabháin founded the Irish World Music Academy at the University of Limerick in 1994 and produced the debated BBC television program *A River of Sound* in 1995, which was about how music is always changing and exchanging with other cultural traditions.[125] These assertions of cultural exchange and practice in debates about how much Irish traditional music can and should change emerge out of the Irish music revival, which Ó Riada's innovation and valuation of Irish traditional music greatly influenced. Yet tensions between innovation and tradition intensified, as ethnomusicologist Scott Reiss explains, during the social changes brought about by the Celtic Tiger.[126] Such cultural trends and debates have arguably informed musical forms and industries that are now global in scope, with Irish music concerts, sessions, and festivals occurring around the world.

Musicians and cultural studies scholars often trace the Irish music revival back to Ó Riada's work with Ceoltóirí Chualann and on national radio. In 2011 and 2012, RTÉ's *The Rolling Wave*, hosted by Peter Browne, rebroadcast the entire series of *Our Musical Heritage*. The rebroadcast attests to particular understandings of Ó Riada's influence on Irish traditional music and radio from the Irish music revival of the 1970s until today. During *The Rolling Wave*, Ó Riada's original broadcasts are framed by conversations between Browne and renowned Irish musicians, including Ó Riada's son Peadar Ó Riada, Martin Hayes, Emer Mayock, Muireann Nic Amhlaoibh, and Mícheál Ó Súilleabháin. As fiddle player and former director and board member of the Irish Traditional Music Archives, Dermot McLaughlin, notes, Ó Riada established a "critical vocabulary" for talking about Irish music at a time when it was not, as other musicians on the program point out, considered as advanced or artistic as jazz or classical: "Even in 2012, we're still some way away from a critical vocabulary for talking about Irish traditional music. So in 1963, he's ahead of his time."[127] Ó Súilleabháin points out how Irish traditional music was not considered an art form worthy of consideration for arts council funding in the 1960s.[128] The interviews reveal that while representations of Ó Riada and his work often draw on prevalent conceptions of fixed traditions that seemingly cannot change, these representations are countered by analyzing the examples of the dynamic and ongoing innovations of traditions that Ó Riada demonstrates in his compositions and radio programs.[129]

Tracing the legacy of Ó Riada's influence on Irish traditional music and Irish writers through the Dolmen Press adaptation and the rebroadcast of *Our Musical Heritage* thus exposes some of the contrasting ways in which Irish poets like Kinsella and Heaney, whose work featured on *Vertical Man*, and Irish traditional musicians, such as those recorded on Moore and Lunny's *H Block* album, engaged with national and international political events. It also foregrounds the important influence of Ó Riada's life, work, and legacy on Irish cultural production in the second half of the twentieth century. Such an examination shows how later versions of *Our Musical Heritage* implicitly reflect colonial conceptions of modernization in binary understandings of past and present, undeveloped and developed, and colonial and postcolonial. While later versions of *Our Musical Heritage* inflect binary understandings of modernity, the poets and writers Ó Riada influenced also went on to use poetry and music in environmental protests that reflect the dynamic innovation of oral traditions that Ó Riada broadcast over national radio in the early 1960s.

Many artists and writers who engaged in protesting the conditions in Northern Ireland used similar forms of poetry and music to contest neocolonial forms of environmental development.[130] Notably, Moore and Lunny's production of *H Block* in 1978 coincided with the "Get to the Point" concert protesting the proposed Carnsore Point Nuclear Power Plant.[131] Like on *H Block*, musicians innovated traditional ballad forms and tunes to challenge environmental injustices emerging from neocolonial development projects.[132] Irish traditional music also played a role in the Burren Action Group's opposition to the building of a large interpretive center and parking lot on the ecologically and culturally significant location of the Burren. The group released *The Sound of Stone: Artists for Mullaghmore* in 1993.[133] New ballads and songs also played a prominent role in the Shell-to-Sea protests against the building of a natural gas pipeline through an Irish-speaking region, or Gaeltacht, in the early twenty-first century, in northwest County Mayo, which I discuss in chapter 5.[134] The local environmental justice movement opposing the pipeline also produced *Glór Na hAoise: Songs of Solidarity and Resistance* in 2015.[135] These albums feature renowned Irish musicians, including Luka Bloom,

Sharon Shannon, Kevin Crawford, and John Spillane. *Glór Na hAoise* also includes a track of Owens Wiwa reciting "Ogoni! Ogoni!" a poem by his brother, Ken Saro-Wiwa, in solidarity with the Shell-to-Sea protesters.[136] These dynamic uses of Irish traditional music in environmental protest continue the kind of innovation Ó Riada's *Our Musical Heritage* portrayed in the early 1960s.

The multiple and alternative modernities that the music of environmental protest both imagines and embodies extends many of the same concerns Ó Riada expressed on *Our Musical Heritage* and in his writing about neocolonial forms of development that were erasing material and cultural landscapes in 1960s Ireland. In an article Ó Riada wrote for *The Irish Times* in 1963, Ó Riada creates a satiric almanac for the year, noting that, in February, "Bord na Móna begins secret series of atomic tests in the Bog of Allen. Widespread fallout," and, in March, "President John F. Kennedy crowned king of the United Kingdom of Ireland and U.S.A."[137] The idea that the largest bogland in Ireland, the Bog of Allen, would become a testing ground for nuclear technologies foreshadows broader concerns about geopolitical hierarchies and sacrifice zones that Éilís Ní Dhuibhne critically satirizes in *The Bray House*, which I analyze in chapter 4. Ó Riada's notion that a colonizing nation will once more incorporate Ireland in an Act of Union expresses concerns about neocolonialism echoed by musicians and activists like Moore and Tommy Sands at the Carnsore Point protest concert.[138] Concerns about neocolonialism and environmental injustices in Ireland occur as human and geologic histories increasingly coincide during, in Dipesh Chakrabarty's words, "the period of great decolonization in countries that had been dominated by European imperial powers and that made a move toward modernization (the damming of rivers, for instance) over the ensuing decades."[139] As postcolonial modernization projects build on and rearticulate the foundational relationships between colonialism and environment, Ó Riada's dynamic innovation of Irish traditional music on the 1962 version of *Our Musical Heritage* and the musical environmental protest that builds on his work assert alternative forms of development to counter extractive neocolonial power structures and visions of modernity that oppress humans, more-than-humans, and environments.

Understanding Modernity Through Music: Seán Ó Riada's Overlooked Intervention

Ó Riada's original broadcast of *Our Musical Heritage* articulates alternative understandings of tradition and modernity that complicate scholarly understandings of Ó Riada's life and work, as well as the role of Irish traditional music in shaping social relations with material environments and cultural histories. In contrast to conceptions of Lemassian modernization during the Troubles, examples across Ó Riada's oeuvre indicate forms of modernization in the 1960s with which Irish people listening to Irish national radio might engage. The original broadcast of *Our Musical Heritage* presented a specifically Irish conception of progress through the dynamic practices implicit in "the progress of tradition in Ireland" and the multiple modernities it remediated onto national radio. Ó Riada's conceptions of Irish traditional music arose alongside complex histories of colonialism, postcolonial identity formations, modernizing recording and broadcast technologies, and oppositional or fixed understandings of Irish cultural traditions. These formations both invoke and push back on imperial logics of essentialism to assert ephemeral environments of "orally transmitted music" that recognized the ways in which Irish traditional music destabilized complex social and material interactions and relations across history. Through intersections of music and radio in the 1960s, alternative paths for Irish modernity emerge in *Our Musical Heritage* that continue to inform the ongoing innovation of Irish traditional music across media and social and environmental protest movements today.

Ongoing negotiations of cultural identity during European integration and the Troubles drew on understandings of the past and the present. The negotiations of tradition and modernity in national identity formations have been widely studied in literary writers like Kinsella and Friel. Although Friel and Ó Riada never finished their opera, *Grania*, Friel did write a play about Hugh O'Neill, a character who would have played a formative role in Grace O'Malley's transformation in the unfinished opera. Friel's later play on O'Neill, *Making History*, was first performed in 1988, and it exposes the way in which the past is crafted to speak explicitly to current events and understandings of identity. Like Ó Riada's reframing of Irish traditional music, Friel's *Making History* engages the idea of traditional cultural practices as continuing to innovate and as being internationally recognized. Yet these cultural practices are selectively curated to reveal more about the present than the past. For example, the character of Archbishop Lombard in *Making History* writes the history of Hugh O'Neill, but Lombard's version of O'Neill is as a national hero rather than the complex and deeply human character the play depicts him as.[140] While the character of O'Neill appeals to Lombard to tell the truth about him and give his "New English," Anglo, and Protestant wife, Mabel, a more prominent role in the history, Lombard dismisses O'Neill's requests as not being what future Irish people will want from their national history: "All those ladies you chose as your wives— . . . well, they didn't contribute significantly to—what was it Mabel herself used to call it?—to the overall thing—wasn't that it? . . . But in the overall thing, Hugh . . . How many heroes can one history accommodate?"[141] Lombard ironically reveals in his erasure of women as agents of Irish history how Mabel contributed to Lombard's own way of thinking about "the overall thing" and consequently to the writing of the history of Ireland, even as she supposedly stood for a settler-colonial population beginning to move to Ireland. Moreover, the character of Mabel explicitly tells O'Neill not to ally himself with the Spanish, saying, "Spain is using you."[142] This warning implies that a different history would have taken place if O'Neill had listened to Mabel and not allied himself with foreign powers, something Ó Riada critiqued, for instance, in columns for *The Irish Times* and through the song "Sliabh na mBan" in *Our Musical Heritage*. Friel's *Making History* thus reveals a shift in Friel's thinking that aligns him more with similar arguments Ó Riada made in the early 1960s to embrace the dynamic changes and negotiations characteristic of Irish cultural traditions and the multiple modernities to which such innovative and cyclical traditions gave rise.

In 1968, it is hard to tell if Friel recognized the complex exchanges and influences shaping the history and culture in the same way that Ó Riada did, despite his "intuition that our attitudes to the country that made us are very close."[143] Friel describes the complicated tensions arising in national identity formations in the late 1960s in one of his last letters to Ó Riada about their unfinished collaboration on *Grania:* "We should *implicitly* encourage the analogy with any modern emerging state—a tribal country on the verge of discovering its national identity, fighting for its material and spiritual life against a powerful country that is convinced it is God-directed. And against this large backdrop, small groping lives are lived in wonder and misery and joy and dedication and meanness."[144]

Friel assumes the "discover[y]" of "national identity" in the "tribal country's" struggle "for its material and spiritual life" in a way that indicates the progressive construction of an identity within colonial understandings of territorial sovereignty and geopolitically recognizable nation states. Such identities often rely on implicit understandings of racial and cultural homogeneity that valorize seemingly fixed traditions of an imagined past. This assumption is at odds with Ó Riada's understanding of Irish traditional music as a cultural practice that emerges relationally with material and multispecies environments and their historical contexts. Friel seems to later recognize the marginalization of such interactive and dynamic multiple modernities through the character of Lombard in *Making History*. In the leadup to the Battle of Kinsale in the play, Lombard tells O'Neill that the pope supports the Irish resistance to the English, asserting how this means "that we are no longer a casual grouping of tribes but a nation state united under the Papal colours."[145] Lombard's character ironically exposes precisely the formations of national identity that Friel initially foregrounded in discussions of *Grania*. In contrast, *Making History* uses Lombard's character to critique formations of cultural essentialism. Mabel and her apt warning to O'Neill complicate essentialist understandings of an authentic Irish identity by showing her, as a woman and Anglo-Irish settler, as having the potential to sustain and contribute to dynamic and modernizing Irish traditions rather than simply being an agent of colonialism. By using Lombard to explicitly write Mabel out of history because of her different ethnoreligious background and gender, Friel critiques the essentialist thinking that aligns him with the nuanced arguments Ó Riada made decades earlier on *Our Musical Heritage*.

Both Friel and Ó Riada ultimately seem to have seen the formation of an Irish nation to be less about "discovering . . . national identity" than about a long history of cultural interaction and competition in and through multispecies material environments. This apparent shift in Friel's thinking about formations of Irish national identity supports some of the ideas he might have been forming in the late 1960s. Such ideas suggest why he may have wanted to collaborate with Ó Riada, whose work ruptures frameworks that would essentialize Irish cultural practices and national identity, fixing them in time. Some of the examples Ó Riada offered on *Our Musical Heritage* explicitly demonstrate the interrelated cultural and environmental histories through which Irish traditional music dynamically emerged and continues to innovate. For instance, Ó Riada credits Carl Hardebeck for helping to preserve Irish music even as he critiques Hardebeck's arrangement for imposing European developmental forms onto Irish traditional music: "Hardebeck, though a German, brought to Irish music an understanding and a musicality which were conspicuous at a time when the academic study of Irish music was practically unknown.... While we might find fault with their arrangements of Irish music, they have preserved for us the skeletons of many tunes that might otherwise have been lost, and they stimulated interest in the study of Irish music at a time when such an interest was badly needed."[146] Ó Riada's clause "though a German" complicates predominant conceptions of Germany's relationship to Ireland in the early 1960s. By the late 1950s and early 1960s, Ireland's depressed economy enabled foreign nationals to purchase land that Irish people could not afford, which led to the 1965 Land Act.[147] In the years leading up to the 1965 Land Act, there were, to use Mervyn O'Driscoll's words, "countless questions about land sales to 'foreigners', chiefly identified (and frequently incorrectly) as 'Germans', put by backbenchers and Opposition TDs in Dáil Éireann during the 1960s."[148] Although most land purchases by foreign nationals were by English and US buyers, popular concerns about Germans in Ireland in the 1950s and 1960s arose through international critique from US and British governments, which indicated fears about Ireland's moral allegiances in their neutrality during World War II.[149] This example articulates that Irish traditional music was historically recognized and internationally valued in the eighteenth century. Ó Riada's assertion on national radio pushes back upon revivalist understandings of, in Davis's words, "the Gaelic world" as premodern. It also indicates ongoing cultural interactions that continue to shape Irish cultural traditions.

Ó Riada's thinking on these interrelated cultural histories emerges also in an unpublished manuscript from 1969 where Ó Riada articulates some of his concerns at recent events in Northern Ireland. Ó Riada describes his idea of Ireland as thirty-two counties, but he asserts that the Troubles are not about ethnoreligious divisions, noting that "the Protestants of the North are not our enemy; they, too, are Irishmen. Any group of people living in this country for over three hundred years is surely to be regarded as Irish."[150] Ó Riada's implicit assertion of multiple Irish ethnicities, or groups with shared cultural practices, across the island of Ireland reframes fixed constructions of tradition and the characterization of ethnic difference as atavism. Rather, dynamic producers of rival narratives of place, territory, and history comprise multiple modernities that shape and reshape understandings of identity and relationships to land. This idea is in keeping with Ó Riada's assertions about the Irish language on *Our Musical Heritage* in 1962: "Such foreign influences as were felt were quickly absorbed and Gaelicized. . . . Norman, Latin and English loanwords were absorbed into the Irish language, and henceforth treated as though they had always been Gaelic words, submitting to Gaelic declension, conjugation, etc."[151] Ó Riada indicates that cultural formation is a form of exchange and assimilation over time that does not erase cultural differences between groups, even as they form one language or even a nation. Such tensions among rival conceptions of tradition, national identity, and ethnicity thus existed simultaneously in the fragmented aural practice and performance of Irish traditional music on national radio. The medium and content of the original *Our Musical Heritage* series demonstrates the ongoing cultural negotiation of Irishness that refused definitions of fixed tradition or identity even as it seemed to assert them in the 1960s. The more popular rather than artistic venues where Ó Riada chose to produce his work reveal complex and developed artistic forms within Irish traditional music and broadcast media, both of which were seen as less important than more internationally recognized and established forms of art. Ó Riada drew on the ubiquitous but ephemeral aural medium of radio to assert alternative forms of progress in the practice of Irish traditional music. Such traditional practices emphasize the mundanities of everyday life rather than the grand narratives of national struggle, something Friel would do with *Making History* but sought to avoid in *Grania*. Ó Riada's work thus revises the definitions of nation and tradition in a postcolonial context that scholars still invoke to conceptualize formations of self-determination in Ireland today.

Studying Ó Riada's life and work consequently helps scholars to better understand the ongoing interactions among material environments, music, national media, constructions of Europeanness and cultural identity, and natural resource extraction amid decolonization and globalization in the latter half of the twentieth century. These dynamic formations of place and identity recall Ó Riada's words that "the particular events of each day are, to the basic pattern of days, as the particular ornamentation of each verse of a song is to the basic pattern of *all* the verses of that song."[152] The "fundamental pattern[s]" of cultural survival emerge in their ongoing relationships with place and innovation of traditions rather than in the transcendent moment of "discovery" of a national identity or in the "catharsis" moment of a piece of Western classical music. Ó Riada's alternative understandings of the role of Irish traditional music in the organic emergence of cultural identity and material environments reframe scholarly understandings of essentialist notions of Irish cultural identity. Moreover, they offer important insights into how environmental and cultural histories coconstruct each other in interactions across multiple media, especially older media that are often relegated to an outdated or even premodern past. Such media emerge as potential sites of resilience in the face of apocalyptic environmental change, as I will show in the following chapter.

4
1970–1995
ECOMEDIA EMBEDDED IN EARTH'S ARCHIVE IN ÉILÍS NÍ
DHUIBHNE'S *THE BRAY HOUSE*

IN CONTRAST to alternative forms of development that seemed possible in the decades after independence, Irish modernization projects of the late twentieth century built on colonial and neocolonial technologies and military advancements made during and globalized after World War II. These technologies gave rise to what has become known as the Great Acceleration and sparked debates about a potentially new geologic epoch, the Anthropocene.[1] By the 1980s, planetary changes to the atmosphere took on a new level of urgency, leading to international agreements and collaborations to manage the depletion of the ozone layer and intensifying effects of greenhouse gas emissions. The 1987 Montreal Protocol and the establishment of the Intergovernmental Panel on Climate Change in 1988 sought to address planetary problems through collaboration among autonomous nations.[2] Such efforts arose as former colonies around the world gained independence, and individual nations became equally culpable, thereby introducing the idea of, in Patrick Brodie's words, "oneworldism," which is based on "an ethic of 'personal responsibility' . . . [that] ignor[es] existing imbalances of global systems."[3] Rather, Brodie asserts that "there is no 'one world,' no planetary politics on equal footing, if we take seriously structural and spatial imbalances maintained by supply chain capitalism" emerging out of the era of colonialism.[4] The environmental impacts of empire come into sharp relief on a planetary scale as geopolitical hierarchies individualize and equalize responsibility across colonial and postcolonial regions, including in a globalizing Ireland.

These shifts in international relations and planetary systems informed the rise of Irish environmental movements alongside the ongoing violence of the Troubles, which collectively establish the context for the nuclear disaster in Éilís Ní Dhuibhne's ecoapocalypse novel, *The Bray House* (1990). The story extends political, social, and environmental conflicts of

1980s Ireland into a future twenty-first century. Amid early discussions of the climate crisis, proliferating nuclear technologies and protests, and the Troubles, Ní Dhuibhne's text calls attention to how the history of colonialism has transformed into a neocolonial modernity through geopolitical hierarchies of an integrating Europe. *The Bray House* begins after nuclear disaster has killed nearly everyone in Ireland and covered the island with a layer of radioactive dust. Adding a discursive layer to the nuclear fallout is Ní Dhuibhne's unreliable, megalomaniac narrator, Robin Lagerlof, a Swedish expert in "archaeo-anthropology," which is an amalgamation of archaeology training from her ironically named mentor, Per Bishop, and her own notion of anthropology, which she describes as a "pseudoscience that any intelligent person can learn in a week."[5] Using her own pseudoscientific framework, Robin seeks to become the leading authority over the memory of Ireland and Irish culture, a position that highlights ongoing subject-object hierarchies and colonial binary logics in authoritative systems of Western knowledge production amid the neocolonial geopolitics of an economically integrated Europe.

The nuclear explosion and subsequent obliteration of Ireland emerge in the novel as structurally dependent on the continuation of colonial histories of uneven development, displacement, and material and cultural dispossession in a neocolonial modernity. Robin's overbearing presence in the text depicts a neocolonial worldview that relies on reductive stereotypes of Ireland's relationship to its colonial past and the violent contestations of colonial occupation during the Troubles. Through Robin's narration and the nuclear fallout blanketing the entire island of Ireland, *The Bray House* demonstrates a neocolonial discourse that masks and facilitates ongoing colonial power relations. Neocolonial discourse refers to understandings of territorial sovereignty, technological expertise, and the implied progress of technological advancements. These technologies and authoritative forms of knowledge appear to advance values of equality, but they actually entrench colonial hierarchies in a seemingly postcolonial Europe, that is, a Europe that performatively bears witness to histories of colonialism it positions squarely in the past. Yet implicit divisions between the past and present (and future, in the case of Ní Dhuibhne's novel), rely on colonial conceptions of development as progress, as I demonstrate in previous chapters. The temporalities of European forms of development contribute to a neocolonial discourse that benefits from and insidiously promotes geopolitical hierarchies that build on the persistent environmental impacts of empire. *The Bray House* satirically represents colonialism's material and cultural fallout in a dystopian future to critique the Republic of Ireland's focus on foreign direct investment (FDI) after the 1960s as actively entrenching the environmental impacts of empire, which, in turn, ushered in a neocolonial modernity in 1980s Ireland. Beneath the layers of toxic ash and Robin's neocolonial discourse, however, Ní Dhuibhne reveals dynamic cultural relationships with the material environment that indicate the possibility of more just futures.

Despite the explicit references in *The Bray House* to environmental degradation and threats to sovereignty posed by nuclear power and climate change, scholars have yet to explore these elements in Ní Dhuibhne's novel through postcolonial ecocritical or ecomedia studies lenses.[6] Analyzing *The Bray House* through postcolonial ecocriticism and ecomedia studies theory builds on postcolonial readings like those of Derek Hand and Beth Wightman, the multispecies and gender studies approach of Maureen O'Connor, and the energy humanities perspective of Sharae Deckard, to reveal Ní Dhuibhne's critique of neocolonial economic regimes in 1980s Ireland. While postcolonial ecocriticism facilitates an analysis of uneven development and obscured alternatives to such development in *The Bray House*, ecomedia theory attends to the materiality of media and discourse in the novel that challenge extended histories of extraction remediated into supposedly more advanced but certainly changing technologies. Through alternative forms of development and tensions between new and ancient media in the novel, *The Bray House* reveals more enduring ways of knowing embedded in material environments, just below the surface of the seemingly obliterated landscape and Robin's flawed logic.

Indigenous feminist scholarship helpfully elucidates the novel's critique of ongoing colonial and neocolonial hierarchies that obscure an underlying cultural consciousness embedded in the land itself. As my analysis will explain, Ní Dhuibhne points to colonial contexts in Ireland in which indigenous Gaelic peoples were forcibly removed from their homelands. These contexts bring into sharp relief alternative and oppressed ways of knowing that reverberate in Irish understandings of place and history in the 1980s. While colonialism in Ireland and ongoing forms of settler-colonialism in the Americas are not commensurate, I draw on Indigenous scholarship in keeping with Maile Arvin, Eve Tuck, and Angie Morrill's assertion that Indigenous theories offer important forms of knowledge for studying non-Indigenous historical and cultural contexts. In referencing Qwo-Li Driskill, Arvin, Tuck, and Morrill write "that those who are generally supportive of Indigenous causes but feel that their research has nothing whatsoever to do with Indigenous issues may need to reassess what Indigenous theories are actually concerned with. . . . Such theories are much more expansive than many non-Indigenous peoples have been led to think."[7] In this vein of valuing the important forms of knowledge that Indigenous theories offer to critique colonial and neocolonial understandings of land as property and sovereignty as territory, I use Indigenous feminist theories and the work of Indigenous scholars in this chapter.

Reading Ní Dhuibhne's text through postcolonial ecocriticism, ecomedia studies, and Indigenous feminist theories reveals an underlying cultural consciousness embedded in the land. This cultural consciousness in the land guides readers to see the multiple media that the material environment comprises. The ongoing interactions among humans, more-than-humans, and material environments in *The Bray House*, exposes how, to use the words of Jussi Parikka, "humans leave their mark, and the Earth carries it forth as an archive."[8] The Earth archive in Ní Dhuibhne's novel shows connections between the material environment and media of ancient civilizations that persist even in nuclear apocalypse. These ancient media demonstrate alternative and multiple modernities emerging alongside histories of colonialism and neocolonial modernization projects that continue through seemingly progressive economic integration efforts across Europe. Ultimately, *The Bray House* evokes dimensions of a specifically Irish cultural consciousness enduring in material environments and in ongoing human and more-than-human interactions. By examining these long and material histories of power in *The Bray House*, my analysis shows how Ní Dhuibhne imagines more just futures in the protective spaces that the land and its memory offer in the wake of neocolonial modernity's horrific collapse in the novel.

"Wastelanding" Peoples and Places: Competing Histories of Neocolonial Modernity

The nuclear disaster in *The Bray House* engages with fears Irish people had about nuclear energy facilities in Britain that intensified in the 1980s. Combined with heightened awareness of the destruction nuclear facilities could cause after the Chernobyl disaster on April 26, 1986, nine different accidents at the nuclear processing plants Sellafield (originally called Windscale) and Calder Hall in Cumbria, UK, occurred in 1986, which, to quote Veronica McDermott, "included a series of radioactive leaks that contaminated Sellafield workers, the discharge of unmonitored effluent to the Irish Sea and incorrect labelling of materials sent to Dounreay."[9] These apparently unrelated incidents built on a history of skepticism in Ireland about the safety of Sellafield (Windscale) since its creation in the early 1950s, about which the Republic of Ireland had little say during Anglo-US relations after World War II. British Nuclear Fuels Ltd. (BNFL) researched acceptable levels of nuclear contamination on public health before Sellafield (Windscale) began depositing radioactive material into the Irish Sea in June of 1952 via a two-mile double pipeline, a practice that continued through the late twentieth century despite numerous protests.[10] The Windscale fire of 1957 established early concerns about the risk of nuclear energy as nuclear technology began to play a surprisingly prominent role in Anglo-Irish politics pertaining to modernization projects and potential economic integration with Northern Ireland before the Troubles.

The politics around nuclear technology and energy in Ireland inflect debates about how the Republic of Ireland should position itself as an independent nation in emerging geopolitical hierarchies during the Cold War, European economic integration, and anticolonial and civil rights movements occurring in Northern Ireland and globally. Nuclear proliferation began as the Cold War commenced, and proposals were put forth in the 1950s to include Ireland in alliances with France or the United States.[11] Despite pressure from opposition parties, Éamon de Valera ultimately ended the possibility of Irish participation in nuclear proliferation in 1959.[12] In the 1960s, Seán Lemass initiated economic modernization projects that indicate conceptions of political autonomy shifting from territorial boundaries and domestic industrialization to international flows of finance capital largely overseen by a US-dominated global economy.[13] After nearly fifty years of political impasse over partition, which established Northern Ireland in the six northeastern counties of the island and the Republic of Ireland in the remaining twenty-six counties, Northern Irish prime minister Terence O'Neill and Taoiseach of the Republic of Ireland Seán Lemass met in January 1965. At this historic meeting between the two heads of state, O'Neill and Lemass discussed a joint nuclear power station near Lough Neagh.[14] This echoes sentiments that Lemass had expressed in an early speech as Taoiseach to the Dáil in July of 1959, where he suggested the possibility of a joint nuclear power facility between the Republic and Northern Ireland as a way of furthering economic collaboration between the two countries.[15] It also expanded collaborations with Northern Ireland on energy production projects that Lemass had done as minister for industry and commerce in the 1940s and 1950s to facilitate the building of two hydroelectric power stations on the River Erne.[16] Nuclear power in Irish politics was seen in the 1960s as a way of meeting increasing energy demands, which arose when various industries and associated technologies heightened electricity consumption.[17] In addition to expressing Lemass's views on nuclear energy, his meeting with O'Neill also politically recognized Northern Ireland as a separate state, something de Valera had not done even while various departments in Northern Ireland and the Free State (or, after 1948, the Republic of Ireland) collaborated on the Erne scheme.[18] The 1965 meeting thus indicates a significant shift in conceptions of national autonomy in the Republic of Ireland. By recognizing partition, the Republic of Ireland implicitly reworked Ireland's relationship to its colonial past and embraced a subordinate position in neocolonial economic regimes.

While mid-twentieth-century forms of anticolonialism, civil rights, and national independence movements occurred throughout European and US colonies and settler-colonies, including Northern Ireland, the globalizing economy and decentralized networks of capital established neocolonial geopolitical hierarchies and energy regimes that continued to unevenly distribute the benefits and burdens of extraction economies across colonial and postcolonial regions. In 1968, the Fianna Fáil government under Taoiseach Jack Lynch proposed a nuclear power station at Carnsore Point in County Wexford. The plan for a nuclear facility in Wexford was promoted by the conservative Fine Gael party politician, Liam Cosgrave, during the oil crises of the 1970s.[19] The proposed Carnsore Point project echoes politics of Liam Cosgrave's father William T. Cosgrave, whose elite pro-Treaty Cumann na nGaedheal party governed Ireland in the first decade after independence, and in McDermott's words, "directed [its relations with Britain] towards portraying Ireland as a responsible dominion within the imperial fold."[20] William T. Cosgrave's government subscribed to forms of land management and taxation that reinforced socioeconomic class structures and maintained strong economic ties with Britain.²¹ His government also oversaw the Shannon Scheme and the building of the hydroelectric power station at Ardnacrusha, which laid the groundwork for a national electrical grid and energy extraction in the postcolonial nation. The push for more energy after World War II led to an intensification of industrial bog extraction projects as well as to the building of additional hydroelectric power stations, first at Poulaphouca on the River Liffey and later at Ballyshannon and Cathleen's Fall on the River Erne and Carrigadrohid and Inniscarra on the River Lee.²²

By the 1970s and 1980s, atomic energy had become a topic of intense political debate and social and environmental activism in Ireland, which was in ongoing conversation with the civil rights and social justice movements in both Northern Ireland and the Republic. The nuclear power station at Carnsore Point was never realized due to protests, including resistance from prominent Irish musicians and activists like Christy Moore.²³ The response from activists transitioned and combined forms of activism on the conditions in Northern Ireland to protest the nuclear power station and effectively launch the modern environmental movement in Ireland. International environmentalist organizations like Greenpeace also became increasingly active in Ireland in the 1980s as fears about nuclear contamination from Sellafield potentially causing leukemia or Down syndrome pervaded the Irish cultural imaginary, though not enough scientific data existed to confirm these fears.²⁴ General opposition meant that no nuclear power station was ever built on the island of Ireland.²⁵ This has had unintended consequences for Ireland, as Donna Potts explains: "The price of energy is higher than almost anywhere else in Europe, because most of it has to be imported, and because getting imported energy in Ireland is expensive due to its geographical isolation."²⁶ This dependence on importing energy from elsewhere extends to nuclear power, as Deckard shows: "Since 2012, the Republic's grid has become increasingly connected with Britain's electric grid and therefore is partly powered by overseas nuclear fission stations."²⁷ While resistance to nuclear proliferation on the island of Ireland was ultimately successful, energy extraction continued to rely on models of postcolonial dependence and neocolonial development that continues to exploit and endanger human and more-than-human worlds while it also economically subordinates Ireland's economy within British, US, and European economic integration.

Ní Dhuibhne's representation of an ultimately disastrous nuclear project in Northern Ireland raises questions about whether economic integration with Britain, the United States, or Europe would exacerbate existing social inequalities and colonial mindsets in Ireland that arise from its history as a British colony and its position within neocolonial extractivist and energy production projects in the late twentieth century. *The Bray House* exposes ongoing colonial hierarchies that persisted in 1980s Ireland despite the apparent social and technological advancements that economic modernization promised. Notwithstanding the gravity of nuclear systems destroying all of Ireland, the media coverage of the Ballylumford "Incident," as the media calls the nuclear explosion in the novel, tries to "scapegoat" the accident on the IRA, which Robin assesses "to be too obvious a choice."[28] Although Robin's narration is generally unreliable and biased, her critique of the media in this instance is ironically correct. Through this irony, Ní Dhuibhne satirizes how euphemistic terminology conceals complex constellations of colonial power hidden beneath mainstream media representations of the Irish state's relationships with Britain and the United States. The reference to the IRA indicates the Troubles, which itself is a euphemism for the armed conflict between Irish nationalist groups, including the Provisional IRA and the Official IRA, and pro-British Loyalist paramilitary organizations, such as the Ulster Volunteer Force, with which British state forces like the Police Service of Northern Ireland are known to have regularly colluded, most famously perhaps in the murder of human rights lawyer Pat Finucane.[29]

While the IRA had remained active in Ireland since partition and partial independence in 1922, their armed resistance intensified in the late 1960s in response to the police violence against Northern Irish civil rights activists. The civil rights movement called for an end to anti-Catholic discrimination, for example, in housing, education, health care, and employment, but peaceful demonstrations were brutally oppressed, notably on Bloody Sunday in 1972, when thirteen people were killed by British forces, which I discuss in chapter 3 through an analysis of Thomas Kinsella's poem "The Butcher's Dozen." Given the social and environmental discrimination against Catholic populations in Northern Ireland, distrust of BNFL data and British assurances of the safety of Sellafield and Calder Hall existed alongside the complex and violent contestations of power in the Troubles. Robin's ironic correction of mainstream media for inaccurately blaming the IRA for the nuclear disaster obliquely points to how euphemisms, like "the Incident" and "the Troubles," mask multiple layers of colonial and neocolonial power, social justice activism, and anticolonial conflict that come into sharp relief through the nuclear explosion in the novel.

Ní Dhuibhne's novel implicitly draws out the complexity of colonial power relations persisting in both the Troubles and the neocolonial modernity of 1980s Ireland through the location of the nuclear explosion in the text. The disaster in the novel emanates from Northern Ireland, beginning at the fictional nuclear power plant in Ballylumford and spreading across the Irish Sea to the actual nuclear energy and processing plants of Calder Hall and Sellafield. The location of the fictional nuclear explosion in Ballylumford, Northern Ireland, demonstrates an implicit cultural expectation of spectacular displays of violence emanating from the Troubles.[30] By giving the reader an enormous nuclear explosion, Ní Dhuibhne, to use the words of Rob Nixon, "help[s] us apprehend threats imaginatively that remain imperceptible to the senses, either because they are geographically remote, too vast or too minute in scale, or are played out across a time span that exceeds the instance of observation or even the physiological life of the human observer."[31] Through the geography of the explosion, Ní Dhuibhne calls the reader's attention to less visible forms of power and pollution implicit in neocolonial modernity, which builds on colonial power relations and the ongoing environmental impacts of empire. The nuclear disaster in *The Bray House* occurred, like that of Three Mile Island, through a series of human errors in which "experts" were "unable to cope with a technology which was rapidly becoming almighty."[32] Like colonial hierarchies and their afterlife in Ireland's neocolonial modernity, the seemingly invisible nuclear technologies attain an agency to act within systems that are out of the control of even the supposed authorities. Ní Dhuibhne points to how such systems structurally marginalize Irish interests and environments in late twentieth-century Anglo-Irish-US relations.

The Bray House reveals the interrelated and ongoing histories of colonial occupation and neocolonial modernization through the silence of the Irish Taoiseach in the story. Even after the entire island and its people are destroyed by the nuclear explosion, the nameless Taoiseach remains silent. Rather, the Thatcher-like British prime minister, Ms. Elizabeth Bennett, fills this silence with her statement from California, "where she was at a meeting with the President of the United States and the Irish premier, to discuss, ironically enough, the question of a new Anglo-Irish-American agreement."[33] The geopolitical marriage of Britain and the United States echoes Seán Ó Riada's satirizing of the intensifying economic power of the United States in Ireland through the "United Kingdom of Ireland and U.S.A." from his 1963 article in *The Irish Times*, which I discuss in chapter 3.[34] It also echoes longer histories of the institution of marriage to control the reproduction and distribution of wealth and property, as I examine through the position of women in modernization schemes in chapters 1 and 2. Moreover, this union uncannily foreshadows the Good Friday Agreement, which ended the Troubles in 1998 and was facilitated by the United States through the Clinton administration. The silence of the Irish prime minister in the novel registers the infantilizing and subordinate role into which the young postcolonial nation is forced in a postnuclear world, marginalizing its interests even when diplomatic discussions are directly about Ireland. Unable to represent his people's interests or even their memory after they have been killed in a coerced neocolonial nuclear modernity, the Irish premier stands silently next to the paternalistic leaders of a wedded United States and Britain.

The fictional Irish premier's silence in *The Bray House* reveals a crisis of national representation. Ongoing forms of colonialism combine with emerging neocolonial modernities in the 1970s and 1980s. The news media represent these shifting constructions of geopolitical and planetary-scale power relations in ways that marginalize the premier and, by extension, Ireland. The silent premier in the novel implicitly critiques Taoiseach FitzGerald's own silence on the issue of Sellafield during the negotiations and signing of the 1985 Anglo-Irish Treaty, even when the majority of Irish people historically opposed nuclear technology in the 1980s.[35] Indeed, the premier's silence indicates prevalent concerns that many environmental and social activists had about the Republic's entry into the European Economic Community (EEC) and the forms of modernization that would entail.[36] Ní Dhuibhne's novel exposes how forms of economic integration entailed selling off natural and cultural resources, including the physical and intellectual labor of Irish people, to Britain and the United States. It also involved capitulating to international media representations that implicitly promote extraction and modernization projects. These projects impose constraints on national autonomy to reinforce Ireland's subordinate position in geopolitical hierarchies and actively perpetuate colonial power relations that exploit human and more-than-human communities and erase forms of self-determination in postcolonial Ireland.

Drawing on flawed colonial representational tropes parading as authoritative forms of knowledge, like her made-up field of archaeo-anthropology, Robin asserts the right to write Ireland's history in the Taoiseach's silence. Despite the Taoiseach being an actual Irish person who could articulate what Robin feigns to research, Robin's narration dominates the novel and openly ignores anything Irish people might have to say about Ireland before the nuclear disaster. Robin points out that the Irish premier was in California at the time of the "Incident," indicating that there is at least one Irish person who could "tel[l] the story" of Ireland, but the Irish premier's silence in the novel gives Robin the opportunity to tell whatever story she wants: "It's only when there's nobody telling the story, nobody writing it, indeed, when nobody has ever written it, that archaeologists need to step in."[37] The material evidence Robin finds to support her narrative of Ireland sustains her authority (and the power relations that put her in a position of authority in the first place). The Taoiseach's silence further supports this narrative through its implied consent.

The "Anglo-Irish-American agreement" and the silent Taoiseach after the destruction of the entire island of Ireland by nuclear disaster expose how international economic and security alliances privilege certain places and communities in geopolitical hierarchies while making others disposable, even within sovereign territorial boundaries. Traci Brynne Voyles describes this process as "wastelanding," which "renders an environment and the bodies that inhabit it pollutable."[38] *The Bray House* critiques how economic reforms in the Republic of Ireland since the 1960s establish alliances between the postcolonial state and neocolonial power structures that guarantee the national security of those who control nuclear technologies. The Republic of Ireland's subordinate position in relations between Britain and the United States exposes how security alliances "wasteland" the entire island of Ireland. During the Cold War, nuclear technology in Anglo-US politics played a prominent role, and Ireland's overwhelming opposition to nuclear power and the ongoing contamination of the Irish Sea by the 1980s was largely ignored internationally. The national boundaries that international alliances supposedly protect actually work to unevenly distribute the benefits and burdens of this postnuclear neocolonial modernity across postcolonial nations like the Republic of Ireland, and subordinated populations in settler colonies, including Northern Ireland.

Although many former colonies obtained national independence or partial forms of territorial sovereignty in the latter decades of the twentieth century, Ní Dhuibhne's novel reveals the ongoing subordination of postcolonial regions by showing Ireland's intellectual, physical, and natural resources to benefit a globalizing economy dominated by colonial and neocolonial nations. By depicting the Taoiseach's curtailed autonomy to even speak for the memory of Irish people after the fictional nuclear disaster, *The Bray House* points to the Republic of Ireland and Northern Ireland's marginalization in negotiations that directly impacted people and environments in Ireland. Ní Dhuibhne connects the dystopian future in the novel with the longer history of British colonialism in Ireland and neocolonial forms of occupation through FDI and environmental degradation in Lemassian modernization since the 1960s.

The Bray House draws on the politics of nuclear energy in the 1980s to expose how such forms of modernization reinforce neocolonial hierarchies that perpetuate colonial-era social inequalities, both economically and in terms of environmental risk, despite perceived or attempted gains by anticolonial and civil rights movements. Through this connection between postcolonial independence, partition, and a neocolonial modernity, the text emphasizes persistent colonial power relations, including the anti-Catholic discrimination in the North, as well as the Republic's economic relations with Britain, an integrating Europe, and the United States, which cumulatively exacerbate the disastrous environmental impacts of empire in the novel. The novel's obliterated Ireland signifies how colonial hierarchies reach far deeper into neocolonial social and geopolitical relations than understandings of territorial sovereignty or state autonomy, upon which international environmental agreements, protocols, and management rely. Both within national boundaries dividing the island of Ireland and across geopolitical economic relations, *The Bray House* shows Ireland's neocolonial modernity to be the toxic fallout of centuries of colonization that, though beginning in Ireland, has rippled out across the world as the environmental impacts of empire take on planetary proportions.

Managing Time and Space: The Personal and Professional Logics of Empire

The neocolonial modernity and economic modernization that permit the destruction of the entire island of Ireland and all its life-forms show how the history of colonialism is not part of an unfortunate past. Rather, imperial logics perpetuate through material, discursive, and interpersonal relations into an apocalyptic future. By drawing broader connections among the history of colonialism, the Troubles, economic modernization, energy extraction, and a neocolonial modernity in Ireland in the late twentieth century, *The Bray House* critiques the systems of Western scientific knowledge and technological advancements that allow Robin to assert her megalomaniac authority over vast expanses of time and territory. After the nuclear explosion, Robin sails to Ireland on the ironically named *Saint Patrick* with her colleague, Karen, and two junior archaeologists, Karl and Jenny, to "discover exactly what, if any, fragments had survived the disaster."[39] Yet, rather than a voyage of discovery, Robin only asks questions for which she already has answers, however flawed. Robin revises and reorders materials and information to assert scholarly advancements that privilege her individual success, even destroying evidence that might challenge her position.

Robin uses the prestige of archaeology and its studies of ancient civilizations to legitimate her own narrative of Ireland. The use of material evidence in archaeology helped construct a cultural identity in Ireland before and after independence, as Patrick Carroll explains: "The study of archaeological material culture played an important role in the development of colonial nationalism and patriotism and later also republican nationalism, and therefore the Irish state-idea."[40] The material and cultural elements that support state formation in an independent Ireland draw on the idea of an ancient civilization to value modern Irish culture. Robin strategically manipulates this valuation of the past by describing Ireland after the nuclear disaster as a place and time "more different from the world in which we now live than that itself was from, say, the Middle Ages."[41] Robin implicitly positions Ireland before the nuclear disaster as relatively close to a medieval past. She also asserts that "what is archaic is entirely subjective," thereby undermining the implied objectivity of her academic discipline to study an ancient past.[42] Consequently, Robin inserts a false temporal distance between an ancient past and the apocalyptic present in the novel to justify her work.

Collapsing a hypothetical Middle Ages and postcolonial Ireland into the postnuclear disaster exposes how Robin's archaeo-anthropology relies on imperial logics that impose understandings of time as linear and space as territory to promote development.[43] Robin's attempt to divide a very recent past from the apocalyptic present calls the reader's attention to how imperial-era conceptions of linear time and territorial space persist in the neocolonial modernity emerging through political contestations and economic development in 1980s Ireland. Strategically, Robin uses imperial logics of time and space to retell Ireland's history, filling the multivalent political silences of an apocalyptic future with outdated colonial, patriarchal, and eugenics tropes. Robin's colonial discourse explicitly reduces the social inequities that gave rise to civil rights movements and the Troubles in the late twentieth century to atavistic stereotypes.[44]

Robin falls back on stereotypes of Irishness to explain why the family of her late husband, Michael Madden, moved to Dunquin (Dún Chaoin), County Kerry, from Portadown, Northern Ireland. Robin says that Michael's family moved "as far south" and "as far west" as they could to find an idea of authentic Ireland: "Catholic and of the strong old-fashioned nationalist streak endemic to the class in that place, at that time, they had never felt truly at home in Portadown, although their ancestors had lived in its vicinity for several hundred years. Not enough, it seemed, to get used to their Presbyterian neighbours."[45] Robin trivializes the social inequalities giving rise to the Troubles to equate the Maddens' move with misplaced notions of Irishness. Her insistence on cardinal directions of "as far south" and "as far west" impose ahistorical understandings of authenticity and identity on southwestern regions of Ireland, particularly on the Dingle Peninsula and its historical relevance to preserving Irish culture. Although Dunquin (Dún Chaoin) caters substantially to a tourist industry, it is officially a national park in the dystopian future of *The Bray House*. The Blasket Islands have historically connoted forms of authentic Irishness associated with the Irish language both before and after independence, as I show Flann O'Brien to satirize in revivalist uptakes of Blasket Island writings in chapter 2.[46] Through Robin's obtuse narration, Ní Dhuibhne critiques the commodification and reduction of the Irish language and of Irish cultural traditions to fixed practices marketed for tourists. Robin's view of the Maddens obscures the valuable forms of knowledge in the Gaeltacht and consequently perpetuates a neocolonial modernity.

The Bray House shows how entrenched colonial logics permeate personal and political relationships to sustain social and geopolitical hierarchies in an integrating economic European block in the 1980s. Intellectual and natural resources of economically subordinate nations like Ireland support more affluent nations like Sweden, a power dynamic that is mirrored in Robin's marriage to Michael.[47] In fact, the Swedish Robin exploits her Irish husband's intellectual and physical labor. For example, Robin's narration undermines Michael's agency, obscuring what Michael actually said or wanted. By subordinating Michael's interests, Robin is able to use Michael's labor to support her own interests: "Indeed, he became a housewife."[48] Although Robin can see that Michael is unhappy, she asserts that the situation "suited me admirably, although it was disconcerting to have a companion who was so clearly discontented with life. This, however, seemed a small price to pay for having a full-time unpaid servant, who took all domestic responsibility in return for some food and a roof over his head."[49] She blatantly ignores Michael's interests to benefit her own personal well-being and professional advancements, justifying her actions by conceding "that he always gave in."[50] Robin does not consider the "price" Michael pays to be in a union with her. Instead, she strategically draws on the gender roles implicit in heteronormative marriages and the normative exploitation of the private sphere to justify Michael's role as "a housewife" and legitimate her ongoing exploitation of him, including plagiarizing his master's thesis research, which becomes her best-known work. The use of gendered labor indicates, to quote Chandra Talpade Mohanty, "how capitalist production relations are built upon the backs of women workers defined as housewives."[51] Robin's strategic use of gender hierarchies is all the more pronounced since she herself is a woman. Her embrace of a masculine-inflected neocolonial modernity capitalizes on her strategic use of feminized cultural traditions in formerly colonized nations. Ní Dhuibhne's satiric critique of these underlying and pervasive structures of power demonstrates how decolonization cannot occur in isolation but must address the extensive geographic, historical, and epistemic spread of imperial logics.

Just as Robin's career can "soar" because her "ordinary living" was done "for" her by Michael, the uneven relations emerging across an integrating Europe allow some countries to benefit from the subordination of others.[52] In contrast to the communal way of life Michael and his parents had in Dunquin, Robin describes the "free[dom]" of independent living arrangements in Sweden: "He [Michael] could not get it into his head that in Sweden no one depended on another individual for basic needs.

The state guaranteed all citizens, even foreign ones like Michael, a decent lifestyle. For an Irishman, this was incredible, and I don't think he ever realised what it meant (that Swedes were free, as most people of other nations were not, to choose their way of life)."[53] Sweden "guaranteed" that everyone within the boundaries of the nation could "choose their own way of life," thus emphasizing a neoliberal individualism rather than the communal collectivism Michael's family embraced in Dunquin. Yet Michael is constrained by his relationship with Robin, a relationship that is reflected in the uneven relations between Ireland and more economically and geopolitically privileged nations in the novel, including the United States, Britain, and Sweden.[54]

Michael and Robin's marriage becomes analogous to Ireland's constrained autonomy within integrating European nations, in which countries like Sweden could make decisions about territorial boundaries while still benefiting from technological advancements and economic integration. Indeed, Sweden passed a referendum in 1980 to eventually eradicate nuclear power from within its borders while Ireland made very little progress in its campaign against the Sellafield processing plant.[55] *The Bray House* exposes how uneven power relations at local and global levels preclude the possibility of free choice for independent nations in a globalized economy or equal agency for the individuals within those nations. In an analysis of *The Bray House*, Deckard notes that "the key difference between Ireland's historical opposition to nuclearization and the novel's portrayal of Sweden's fictional refusal of nuclear power is that Swedish denuclearization is accompanied by a refusal of petro-dependency and a turn towards renewables."[56] Despite the representation of Swedish energy in the novel, wherein Sweden shifted more toward hydroelectricity and away from oil, Sweden in fact remained dependent on nuclear energy. Ireland's refusal of nuclear energy combined with the construction of dams on many of Ireland's rivers, but this did not reverse the postcolonial nation's dependency on fossil fuels, which intensified after World War II as it sought to modernize through FDI and Western forms of development.[57] In showing that "other nations," like Ireland, "were not [free] to choose their own way of life," *The Bray House* emphasizes the irony of Sweden's freedom being structurally dependent upon the exploitation of "foreign" people and places. Robin asserts "that in Sweden no one depended on another individual for basic needs," but she fails to mention how the needs of the Swedish people were met by technological advancements for environmental and social sustainability, which, in turn, to use Voyles's term, "wasteland[ed]" the entire island of Ireland and everyone who lived there. These networked forms of colonial and neocolonial power relations expose the impossibility of decolonizing anywhere if decolonization does not happen everywhere, thereby raising questions about how scholars frame colonial divisions across geographic categories of the Global North and South and indicating the need to reconsider the connections between power hierarchies, ongoing structural dependencies, and the continuous environmental impacts of empire globally. Such questions become particularly relevant as international agreements and governing agencies build on these logics of individualism and equal responsibility to counter planetary pollution and the climate crisis.

Through the absurdity of Robin's obtuse embrace of hierarchy under the pretense of equal footing and meritocracy, *The Bray House* challenges the cultural separations among individuals, nations, and environments in Ireland's neocolonial modernity of the 1980s. Institutions like marriage, the news media, and Western science sustain how such separations divide people from their material surroundings and into social hierarchies that materially impact different groups' abilities to survive. The novel critiques how such separations unevenly distribute environmental benefits and burdens in the name of progress, which ultimately advances a neocolonial modernity. In doing so, Ní Dhuibhne's text implicitly engages with what Kate Brown calls "plutopia" and "zones of immunity," or "the segregation of territory into nuclear and non-nuclear zones."[58] Such zones benefit some while sacrificing others: "Before Chernobyl and Fukushima came Hanford and Maiak, and with them the practices of plutopia: partitioning territory into 'nuclear' and 'clean' zones, skimping on safety and waste management to prioritize production, repressing information about accidents, forging safety records, deploying temporary 'jumpers' to do dirty work, and glossing over sick workers and radioactive territories, all while treating select citizens to generous government subsidies and soothing public relations programs."[59] *The Bray House* implicitly extends this logic of "clean" and "nuclear" zones through a Manichaean moral value system in Ireland's neocolonial modernity. The text parodies "the good" and "virtue" of technological progress by depicting Robin's scientific objectivity to reflect a subjective, religious devotion to the Western systems of knowledge production that her mentor Per Bishop represents. Per Bishop's name points to Ireland's complex relationship with Catholicism as both a marker of national identity after colonial oppression and the dispossession of Irish Catholic people, as well as a colonial institution that sustained Ireland's so-called Catholic empire of missions.⁶⁰ The teachings of Per Bishop encourage Robin to situate Sweden's "innocence" in the Swedish government's decision to foster a "friendship with nature."⁶¹ Although renewable sources of energy saved the Swedish people and nation from nuclear apocalypse in the novel, and their northern location allowed them to exist sustainably despite the effects of climate change, they "harness nature" to technology in a subordinating hierarchy.⁶² This nation-nature hierarchy reveals the underlying logic that also informs Ireland's subordinate relationship to other nations in economic globalization, including Sweden, the United States, and Britain, as well as Robin's marriage to Michael. These uneven personal and political relations are supposedly justified by how, as Robin asserts, the "virtue" of this "reasonably peaceful union" "was rewarded" since those in Sweden survived.⁶³

Yet the text exposes how this moral-value system comes at a cost, one that potentially destroys even those it ostensibly benefits. The superficial guilt Robin feels about stealing Michael's research before sending him to Ireland just ahead of the nuclear disaster is analogous to how the Swedish "suffer" "the psychic pain" of being "ridden with guilt."⁶⁴ The technological progress that implies Swedish "innocence" is only possible through resource extraction and risky technologies, like nuclear energy, being located outside the boundaries of their own "saved" nation.⁶⁵ Robin describes Swedish people as unable to "face the fact of their innocence" in "the heaven we made for ourselves" while she frames the fate of the Irish people who were killed in the Incident in terms of "radioactive burns" and "hellfire."⁶⁶ The novel satirically situates technological and scientific advancement within moral value systems that require sacrifices of the many for the greater "good" of a few. While Swedish people may regret the loss of most of the world, they do nothing to alter the material impacts of empire. Rather, Robin and the Swedish people she represents in the novel subscribe to dichotomous value systems that depend on conceptions of redemption. Robin maps this value system onto Europe to position Sweden within a space of "the good" and "the saved" while Ireland is depicted as seemingly inevitably damned.

While Robin considers Sweden as "free" and clean, she posits Ireland by contrast as heavily polluted even before the Incident in ways that justify the uneven distributions of environmental benefits and burdens within geopolitical hierarchies among nations and between nations and the natural world.[67] The latent Manichaean moral-value systems implicit in Robin's supposedly cutting-edge scientific knowledge reveal imperial logics of colonial institutional hierarchies. These hierarchies legitimate themselves in moral-value systems that perpetuate neocolonial power relations through modernization projects. Imperial logics attempt to justify neocolonial modernization projects as peoples and places are sacrificed in the name of progress. In this way, *The Bray House* exposes a continuity of the environmental impacts of empire in neocolonial structures of power that permeate the past, present, and imagined (and disastrous) future modernities.

Reinterpreting "the Writing on the Wall": Sites of Environmental and Cultural Resilience

As dominant as Robin is in the novel, *The Bray House* consistently reveals cracks in her unreliable and megalomaniac narration to indicate cultural resources upon which Irish people might draw to resist the imperial logics of economic modernization in the 1980s while honoring Irish cultural relationships to the material environment in an anthropogenically altered epoch. Offering glimpses past Robin's obtuse framing, the text reveals persisting forms of material and cultural meaning embedded in the environment. Natural and cultural elements gesture toward dimensions of Irish culture and history developing alongside histories of colonialism and the economic and environmental modernization in a neocolonial modernity. Such dimensions recognize what Eve Tuck theorizes as "an assemblage of experiences, ideas, and ideologies, both subversive and dominant, [that] necessarily complicates our understanding of human agency, complicity, and resistance."[68] Such an assemblage disrupts, as Tuck puts it, "the binary of reproduction versus resistance."[69] Tuck's theory of "desire-based research" for "communities ... that have troubled relations with research and researchers" like Robin in *The Bray House* helps to uncover multiple modernities in Ní Dhuibhne's novel that imagine alternatives to extraction economies inherent in neocolonial constructions of the nation state and binary resistance to those extraction economies.[70] Rather than a logic of "reproduction versus resistance" or colonial versus precolonial, *The Bray House* shows ongoing relations between communities and material agencies in Irish landscapes, language, and cultural traditions to establish alternative modernities. These multiple modernities prove more respectful of a community's place in environmental systems than the understandings of national territory, globalization, and technological advancements brought to Ireland under neocolonialism. In the name of progress, neocolonial understandings of economic modernization, natural resource extraction, and Western forms of knowledge disrupt more environmentally enduring relationships among people, place, and history.

The Maddens conceptualize their relationships with material environments and more-than-human agencies in different ways than Robin's neocolonial worldview. Michael's mother and father move to Dingle to live in mutually constitutive relationships with their surroundings.[71] They spend their time "growing vegetables organically, milking prize goats, freezing yoghurt."[72] On a fishing trip, John Madden accidentally catches a baby seal, which "were very rare at that point anywhere in Europe."[73] John describes the seal: "'He'd nearly talk to you!' Michael's father said, gently removing his hook from the animal's fin. The seal was in fact crying, quietly and persistently, like a truly miserable child. 'There!' said he, throwing him back into the churning black water, none too gently. 'He'll recover before he's twice married, and no harm done!'"[74] While John's words are filtered through Robin's sardonic narration, she quotes him as addressing the seal as an agent who acts with intention. Although John inadvertently harmed the seal with his fishing hook and dismisses the seal's pain, as O'Connor points out in her reading of this scene, John does address the seal as a fellow being, calling the seal "he" and considering the seal's ability to thrive after John "gently remov[es] his hook" and, however flippantly, determines that there's "no harm done!"[75] While what happens to the seal ultimately remains a mystery, this interaction demonstrates what Amitav Ghosh theorizes as "recognition" or "a renewed reckoning" with "something we had turned away from: that is to say, the presence and proximity of nonhuman interlocutors."[76] This scene shows that John has retained a sense of community with "nonhuman interlocutors" and continues to recognize the agency of the seal.

The awareness of interdependence with the material environment and more-than-human others that John exhibits contrasts sharply with Robin's understandings of freedom and independence as moral virtues in Sweden. Rather, John's ideas seem more informed by Irish folklore. Myths of selkies, or seals who can inhabit a human or seal form and who intermarry with humans, spending part of their time at sea and part on land, are implicitly invoked when John suggests the seal will "recover before he's twice married."[77] Environmental and cultural knowledge evolve in collaboration with specific places to establish interdependence with other creatures like seals. These interdependent relations within a region over time offer an alternative spatiotemporal logic to those implicit in the legacy of colonialism. Rather than the imperial logics of space as territory and time as linear, John's interactions with the seal demonstrate communal interactions with a place and its human and more-than-human inhabitants that offer alternative ways of being and knowing. These alternative modernities destabilize colonial and neocolonial hierarchies persisting across the island of Ireland during economic and environmental developments since the 1960s, hierarchies that Robin actively seeks to preserve and promote in the dystopian future in the novel.

The environmental and cultural knowledge inflected in the Maddens' way of life in Dingle affects Michael's marriage to Robin and his short career as an anthropologist in the Faroe Islands. Brought up with a sense of familial connections to other creatures, Michael's inability to cultivate a detached view of the *grindadráp* whaling tradition as part of his research on the Faroe Islands highlights complex understandings of mutually constructed environmental and cultural relations and competing notions of sovereignty, both of a geographic region but also of the body as bounded and autonomous.[78] In referring to Faroese whaling, *The Bray House* illuminates tensions between sovereignty as bounded territory and sovereignty as relationships among humans, more-than-humans, and material environments. Understandings of sovereignty as reciprocal relationships with material environments rather than forms of territorial boundaries and ownership are theorized in Indigenous feminist scholarship. As Maile Arvin, Eve Tuck, and Angie Morrill explain, "Within Indigenous contexts land is not property, as in settler colonialism, but rather land is knowing and knowledge."[79] Arvin, Tuck, and Morrill's definition of land in the context of Indigenous understandings of sovereignty helpfully elucidates how Ní Dhuibhne critically positions Robin's rigid views of modern authorities, the novel's depiction of fixed traditions in the Faroe Islands, and Michael's alternative forms of embodied knowledge. *The Bray House* shows Michael to embody relationships among the land, the Irish language, and cultural relations that continually adapt and work within the constraints of changing environments as Robin and the text's representation of the Faroese grindadráp indicate staunch attachments to neocolonial modern authorities and precolonial traditional practices, respectively.

The text juxtaposes possible postcolonial responses to multinational corporatism through the different relationships to cultural traditions and material environments that Michael and the Faroese grindadráp each demonstrate. Since the 1880s, Faroese nationalists have drawn on the grindadráp tradition as a way of asserting cultural difference from Denmark. Yet anti-whaling environmentalist campaigns in the 1970s and Denmark's simultaneous entry into the EEC together with Ireland and the UK led to strong critiques of Faroese pilot whaling, particularly by activist groups in the 1980s.[80] Under a Home Rule Act of 1948, the Faroese government has strategically asserted sovereignty both in relation to Denmark and the EU, as Rebecca Alder-Nissen explains, on issues of fishing rights generally and whaling traditions in particular.[81] Faroese nationalists have also asserted that "Denmark saved money by making the Faroe Islands a target for an atomic bomb" due to a discount the Danish government received from NATO for allowing NATO military bases to be placed in Greenland and on the Faroe Islands.[82] The Faroese critique of unequal nuclear threats placed on their sovereign territory occurred alongside their defense of the pilot-whaling tradition. The novel's representation of grindadráp indicates a conception of tradition that remains fixed despite changing environments, thereby showing the practice to assert domination over the pilot whales and embrace the idea of a fixed, precolonial tradition. Yet evidence emerged that whale consumption was leading to significant health problems in Faroese people due to heavy metals and persistent organic pollutants like mercury and polychlorinated biphenyls (PCBs) in pilot whale meat.[83] The permeability of contaminants into the body challenges the idea of fixed borders associated with territorial sovereignty. This bodily contamination through staunch attachments to fixed traditions highlights competing understandings of sovereignty, either as territorial or as reciprocal. The conception of sovereignty as territorial is implicit in how *The Bray House* represents the Faroese grindadráp. The novel critically depicts the grindadráp to expose colonial binaries of modern and premodern practices attached to the idea of sovereignty as territory. While Robin embraces the position of a modern researcher, the Faroese appear unwaveringly committed to a premodern tradition based on territorial rights rather than dynamic and adaptive relationships to the land and environment.

This modern-premodern binary contrasts with the text's representations of continually changing Irish cultural traditions that relationally adjust to shifting environmental conditions. By critically representing Robin and the grindadráp, Ní Dhuibhne shows binary logics to structurally impede the ability to recognize the alternative modernity that Michael embodies and inhabits. *The Bray House* reveals the colonial binaries of an authoritative subject and object of study, as well as modern and premodern cultural practices, in how Robin is "revolted" at Michael's failure to watch the pilot whaling. Robin asserts: "It struck me as perfectly natural, to enjoy a whale slaughter. It's the sort of thing all peoples have always enjoyed doing."[84] By generalizing what constitutes "natural" human feeling, Robin universalizes her experience of a subjective sense of distance from the objectified whales. She has internalized a clear divide between an implied modern human subject and premodern dehumanized objects of study. This spatiotemporal divide legitimates her role as a detached voyeur of the whale killing as well as the dehumanization of her material and sentient surroundings. Robin's attachment to understandings of fixed traditions and modern science sustains her neocolonial worldview because of, rather than despite, the Faroese assertion of territorial and bodily sovereignty through a tradition that represents a precolonial, premodern era. The novel's depiction of the Faroese pilot whaling thus exposes colonial logics to dictate what is traditional or modern, for both the Faroese and for Robin. This representation consequently shows that even those who are colonized can internalize imperial logics in efforts to revive cultural traditions or preserve conceptions of a precolonial past. Ní Dhuibhne thus uses the grindadráp to assert an analogous critique of revivalist ideology that Flann O'Brien (Myles na gCopaleen) satirizes through his critique of the picturesque in *The Third Policeman* and of rural poverty in *An Béal Bocht*, as I discuss in chapter 2. Attachments to ideas that something is a certain way because it has always been so appeals to conceptions of the natural that fail to recognize underlying logics and power hierarchies that have evolved and been normalized historically through colonial divisions of space and time into developed and undeveloped, modern and premodern, and colonial and precolonial. Robin's conception of what is "natural" is the ability to dissect the material world into subject authorities of modern science who view objectified premodern practices without emotion or attachment. By positioning both Robin and the Faroese in the text to embrace modern-premodern colonial binaries, Ní Dhuibhne points to the alternative both-and logic in Michael's ways of knowing.

The Bray House shows Michael to recognize more-than-humans as actors like himself, who have varying degrees of agency and intention. This worldview suggests a sense of shared responsibility that is in keeping with the myth of seal people, which exists in variations around the North Atlantic, including in the Faroe Islands, where the slaughter of entire groups of seals will bring unexpected vengeance upon the killers.[85] Unlike Robin's attachment to subject-object hierarchies and the novel's representation of the Faroese people's seemingly unwavering attachment to territorial sovereignty and fixed (rather than dynamic) precolonial practices, Michael engages in a nonbinary modernity in which his understanding of place is relational. He cohabits the world of more-than-humans in which eating certain creatures, like seals, "was considered a form of cannibalism."[86] Robin disdains Michael's sensitivity to environmental conditions and human and more-than-human communities as a failing, describing as negative the fact "that he was a chameleon, borrowing his colours from the surroundings, always ready to accommodate other points of view, to compromise, to back off, always ready to say 'yes', unless he suspected that the correct answer was 'no.'"[87] Rather than a lack of initiative, as Robin would deem it, the text shows Michael to continually learn from his surroundings and to demonstrate more relational ways of being and of embodying his environment. This relational inhabitation of the land and Irish cultural relationships to the land contrasts with the understandings of individual autonomy and boundaries that led to the "wastelanding" of Ireland. Instead of imposing a hierarchical subject-object order on the material environment, Michael "borrow[s]" from his surroundings and adapts within the constraints that his surroundings assert, being "always ready to accommodate other points of view, to compromise." In doing so, Michael demonstrates collaborations with material and multispecies agencies in his immediate surroundings that reveal, in the words of Arvin, Tuck, and Morrill, "land is knowing and knowledge."[88] Michael heeds the knowledge embedded in his material environments and acts and adapts according to that knowledge.

Despite Robin's ridicule, her narration registers Michael's embodied forms of knowing. It implicitly reveals how Michael's ability to "accommodate" and "compromise" allows him to emerge within and through practices of listening to and learning from the land to ensure more just relationships with those around him. Michael's engagement with existing environmental relations among humans, more-than-humans, and material agencies makes it impossible for him to watch the grindadráp as a detached subject authority who observes the slaughter of dehumanized objects. This failure to detach, to use Leanne Betasamosake Simpson's words, "produces knowledge because engagement in the process changes the actors embedded in process and aligns bodies with the implicate order. The only thing that doesn't produce knowledge is thinking in and of itself, because it is data created in dislocation and isolation and without movement."[89] Michael's ways of knowing and producing knowledge reveal him to be "embedded in process" even though he fails to finish his master's project.

Michael's experiences and ways of knowing consequently lead him to remove himself from higher educational institutions that would perpetuate the detached study of traditional practices, including his own Irish cultural knowledge as well as the grindadráp tradition. Instead, Michael dedicates himself to his relationship with Robin, a situation she exploits. Robin uses Michael's communal way of being in the world to further her own individual career, and she justifies her actions by pretending that her "thinking in and of itself" was for some greater good besides her own self interests. Yet Michael's self-removal from the institutions that produce authorities like Robin demonstrates his refusal, even within his constrained assertions of agency, to directly participate in the exploitative forms of knowledge that Robin values.

While Robin is appalled by Michael's failure to be an unemotional spectator of the whale slaughter, she conflates his expertise and success as an Irish folklore scholar with the commodification of Irish culture for tourism. Her reduction of Michael's knowledge to fetishizing stereotypes of Irish culture formally distracts from the more situated and traditional systems of knowledge that Michael's work and understanding of the Irish language indicate.[90] Michael attended *éigses,* or an "(assembly of) learned men, sages, poets," as a child and developed an understanding of the linguistic and cultural landscapes of his surroundings.[91] Michael's embrace of the Irish language resists the erasure of the worldview that the Irish language implicitly brings to material environments. The culturally specific understanding of place that the Irish language enabled for Michael had been steadily eroded away since the early modern period by the advent of the printing press and colonial occupation, both of which fostered specifically Anglo-Saxon ways of knowing through the English language.[92] These textual projects of modernization become a point of satiric speculation in Flann O'Brien's *The Third Policeman*, which I examine in chapter 2, and establish an early precursor to the broadcast media modernization that I discuss in chapter 3. Through representing Robin's inability to apprehend, let alone learn from, Michael's embodied forms of knowledge, *The Bray House* critiques how colonial ways of knowing and neocolonial modernization projects, including the advent of the printing press and subsequent media technologies promoting Anglo-Saxon and colonial worldviews, obscure alternative possibilities for modernity and modernizing.

The oppression of the Irish language through the colonial histories in which the printing press privileged English-language texts reveals Michael's knowledge of the Irish language and ways of knowing to be unique in their scarcity. The forms of knowledge Michael embodies indicate multiple modernities that offer more mutually constructive ways of dwelling in the world. While Robin cannot recognize the value in such ways of knowing (or deliberately ignores them), Michael and his family inhabit relationships among cultural practices, material surroundings, and more-than-human agencies built over longer periods of time and through an ongoing engagement with a particular region. These relational and regional forms of knowledge challenge colonial and neocolonial worldviews of time as developmental and space as territorial. Such ways of knowing continually emerge in ongoing interaction with changing environments. Consequently, these Irish traditional ways of knowing exceed Robin's ability to master the expertise Michael embodied. Although Robin tried to obtain authority over Michael's knowledge through stealing his research, she fails to see how Michael participated in relational ways of knowing that made him better able to adapt to shifting material and cultural conditions, something Robin sees as a flaw. Robin's theft of Michael's research and his subsequent death in the nuclear explosion expose how neocolonial logics foster extraction, exploitation, and an inability to observe, understand, or articulate situated relationships with the material environment that Michael embodies through traditional forms of knowledge. The neocolonial worldview Robin represents through international media and Western forms of knowledge reveals the hegemonic discourse the novel invites readers to look past.

Despite Michael's death, his embodied and situated forms of knowledge persist in Ní Dhuibhne's text and the material environments to which the story points. After Robin excludes Karl and Jenny from participating in the excavation once they have finished removing the fallout dust covering of the excavation site, they walk off into the Wicklow Mountains and meet the only known survivor of the nuclear disaster, Maggie Byrne, whom they bring back to the ship.[93] The text makes Irish cultural relationships to the environment explicit in descriptions of the tumulus that protected Maggie through the obliteration of Ireland. Maggie's husband, Eddie, made the shelter following "the old Civil Defence booklet," which suggests the collaborative effort between Northern Ireland and the Republic in the 1960s to integrate safety measures across the entire island.[94] By invoking a shared environmental risk across the island of Ireland, *The Bray House*, to quote Jennifer Wenzel, offers ways of "reading across those geographic and experiential divides, working against foreclosures of unimagining: the impossible necessity of *reading for the planet*."[95] Ní Dhuibhne's novel "read[s] across those geographic and experiential divides" to "unimagin[e]" the ways in which postcolonial national independence asserts forms of territorial sovereignty and fixed traditional practices that are ensnared in imperial logics. Rather, Ní Dhuibhne points the reader to how Irish cultural and natural environments reimagine relations to place through a cultural consciousness embedded in the land itself, even in the rubble of nuclear disaster and longer material histories of cultural oppression.

One way the text points to this underlying cultural consciousness is by showing natural and cultural elements to sustain Maggie in a fallout shelter that bears striking resemblance to the neolithic passage tomb Newgrange. In its similarities to Newgrange and through interior stones inscribed with Ogham, an early Irish-language writing, Maggie and Eddie's fallout shelter indicates ancient civilizations that remain embedded in the material landscape. Where established authorities failed to save Eddie, the ongoing relationships between cultural and natural elements in the tumulus ensured Maggie's survival even in nuclear disaster. As Robin's junior colleagues Jenny and Karl explain, Maggie survived the nuclear disaster because the tumulus that sheltered her had "its own spring, deep in a rock, and obviously that water never got contaminated."[96] Despite the nuclear explosion destroying all lifeforms on the island of Ireland, it failed to "contaminat[e]" the "spring, deep in a rock." The idea that geologic formations and water systems persist untouched by the nuclear disaster indicates planetary forces that exceed the technologies Robin deemed were "rapidly becoming almighty."[97] These planetary forces and systems indicate forms of natural resilience even in the devastation of an apocalyptic nuclear explosion.

Like the spring "deep in the rock" in Maggie's tumulus, a spring "deep in a rock" was also found at Newgrange during the excavations between 1962 and 1975.[98] Originally thought to be a winter stream, excavators and conservationists realized it was "a spring which welled up from the socket of R8."[99] The taxonomized location of the stream in the Newgrange excavation was subsequently outfitted with a pipe to drain off the water as the tumulus was prepared for visitors.[100] While this pipe and the excavation at Newgrange tie into Irish natural and cultural resources being reworked for industry and tourism in the 1970s and 1980s, it also attests to natural and cultural elements that persist outside national and geopolitical boundaries and relationships. Subterranean springs in the Irish landscape have often obtained religious or spiritual meanings as holy wells.[101] These geologic and sacred elements interrupt and slow down modernization efforts as they indicate alternative modernities persisting alongside Ireland's headlong rush into modernization in the late twentieth century and the neocolonial modernity to which Irish modernization projects capitulate. These material and cultural artifacts imagine alternative possibilities for development and relations to the environment that exceed Robin's authority and neocolonial worldview, and consequently also possibilities of narration in the novel and of 1980s Ireland.

Through the interwoven material and cultural histories of land and environment, Ní Dhuibhne presents an Irish cultural consciousness that relationally dwells in and with the material environments across the island of Ireland before, during, and after the nuclear disaster. Jenny and Karl describe how they "emerged from the passage into the chamber. Don't ask me why, but it was eerie enough, between the skeleton and the rubbish and the stones carved with old runes."[102] Unlike the printing press that sought to obscure and oppress non-Anglo-Saxon ways of thinking, the Ogham on "the stones carved with old runes" points to an ancient media that has persisted in the earth since 4 AD. Although "the skeleton" in the tumulus likely belongs to Eddie, it also signifies the persistence of the embodied forms of knowledge that comprise longer histories buried in the material environment and people's relationships to those environments.

When read as Eddie's remains, the skeleton indicates the failure of the authorities in which he put his faith. Maggie explains that "Eddie, however, was a believer in the cause. He maintained that they would be saved. The literature he read had encouraged this credence: it had convinced him that after a reasonable period, which he assessed as a month, things would be getting back to some sort of normality, and 'help' would be available."[103] Eddie's work to prepare the tumulus as an evacuation shelter attests to his confidence in the authorities he anticipated would eventually rescue them. Yet these authorities are experts like Robin who inhabit a modern colonial, authoritative position that produces and reproduces the systems of knowledge maintaining neocolonial hierarchies. Within these hierarchies, Eddie was always already positioned in a sacrificial role for the greater good, a greater good justified by Robin's moral-value judgements of Sweden and Ireland and the forms of knowledge she builds on these judgements. Indeed, such systems are structurally built to fail the "wastelanded" peoples and places upon which they rely.[104] Additionally, these uneven systems obscure vital relationships among humans, more-than-humans, histories, and material environments in alternative modernities, like the one in which Maggie lives. Within this alternative modernity, the skeleton and Ogham "runes" also register what Mohanty calls the "temporality of struggle," which "suggests an insistent, simultaneous, nonsynchronous process characterized by multiple locations, rather than a search for origins or endings."[105] Elements in an underlying and ongoing cultural consciousness emerge in the text through "insistent, simultaneous, nonsynchronous process[es]" among Irish cultural and material relationships with the land.

"Temporalit[ies] of struggle" across "multiple locations" emerge in Maggie Byrne's story, name, and survival, as well as in the McHugh family name and the material artifacts of the Bray house that Robin and the other Swedish archaeologists unearth in their excavation. These names intertextually invoke Feagh Mac Hugh O'Byrne, who is a symbol of resistance in his alliance with Hugh O'Neill during the final years of the Irish Chiefs' attempts to maintain autonomy and power in the midst of material and cultural colonialization under Elizabeth I.[106] Like Maggie, Feagh was also found hiding in a cave in the Wicklow Mountains at Glenmalure, from which he was taken and executed on May 7, 1597.[107] The skeleton in the tumulus thus also refers to longer histories of colonialism, which indigenous Irish civilizations resisted for generations, including through O'Neill's strategic diplomacy, military force, and use of indigenous Irish culture to oppose colonial occupation. Maggie's name also resembles that of Feagh's sister, Margaret Maol O'Byrne, who was murdered by colonial forces in August of 1580 after the Battle of Glenmalure.[108] These implicit intertextual references connect the history of the Irish Chiefdoms before the Flight of the Earls in 1607 to the Newgrange-like tumulus in a postapocalyptic neocolonial modernity. The text situates Maggie's experiences with nuclear disaster alongside imperial wars against indigenous Gaelic populations. During these wars, O'Neill adapted the chieftain system to protect the survival of his people and culture amid an encroaching imperial order, thus constructing an alternative modernity of which the text shows Maggie to also be a part. Ní Dhuibhne's text reveals interconnections among people, place, and history that ultimately demonstrate a "temporality of struggle" in which competing relationships to time, space, and environment emerge in parallel.

Through these references to ancient, early modern, and even recent pasts, the novel exposes multiple temporalities emerging alongside and in ongoing interaction with histories of colonialism in Ireland and in other parts of the British Empire. The skeletal remains and Ogham in Maggie's cave also make oblique references to eighteenth- and nineteenth-century Anglo-French Orientalist discourses in which Ireland was on the periphery of a perceived Eurocentric civilization and consequently was discursively associated with Asian and African traditions around the world that were also seen as outside civilization. As Joseph Lennon explains, Orientalist writers like John Whittley Boswell and later Sir Samuel Ferguson characterized subterranean caves and the skeletal remains in burial grounds of the Iron Age in County Roscommon as of Egyptian origin, even postulating that Egyptian skeletons last longer than the bones of other humans and translating Ogham inscriptions as references to Egyptian histories.[109] These literary histories of Orientalist discourse implicitly emerge in descriptions of Maggie's tumulus in *The Bray House* and indicate cross-colonial temporalities of struggle arising alongside colonial logics of development and civilization dating back to Roman texts about the borderlands of the habitable world.[110] Like understandings of linear time and space as territory, these discursive understandings of the world as having central and peripheral cultures resonate across multiple temporalities in the environmental impacts of empire that Ní Dhuibhne's novel highlights and contests.

The multiple temporalities of Maggie, the McHughs, and Ireland's material landscape reveal memories that endure literally and figuratively in the land to challenge colonial logics of development. The land's memory challenges the exploitation and extraction of material environments and bodies in the neoliberal economic modernization of 1980s Ireland. This embedded consciousness recalls what Parikka theorizes as "psychogeophysics," which "aims for planetary scales of aesthetics" and in which "geology transforms into media and media reveals their geological conditions" across senses that extend beyond visual observations.[111] The Ogham-inscribed stones materially substantiate media that directly embody the relationship between geology and modern writing and communication systems. Like the "spring, deep in a rock," the "old runes" in Maggie's tumulus express the entanglement of deep time and human history in ancient media that continue to make meaning across a range of human and more-than-human civilizations. These multiple media across multiple temporalities reconfigure and ultimately overwhelm the colonial constructions of time, space, and the bounded, embodied individuality to which Robin clings.

Indeed, these multiple temporalities embedded in the alternative modernity of which O'Neill, Feagh, Margaret, and Maggie are all part indicate a shared cultural consciousness that resists colonial historiography and Robin's imperial understandings of linear time. Robin tries to position Maggie in an ancient past by obtusely overwriting Maggie's own account of her husband's death as part of a "saga" through which Robin can conclude that "obviously what happened was that his spirit and health had broken."[112] By situating Maggie's experience in a saga, Robin attempts to relegate Maggie's story into a past over which she can assert authority. Yet the text shows Maggie's experiences to exceed an imagined developmental structure of past, present, and future through the multiple temporalities that the skeleton, Ogham, and tumulus-like fallout shelter collectively embody. Rather, a multiple and relational present emerges diachronically through an ongoing "temporality of struggle." This "temporality of struggle" in Ní Dhuibhne's novel situates the Troubles and the fictional nuclear disaster within larger cultural and environmental histories preserved in human and more-than-human media.

The text calls on the reader to attend to the geological and cultural media archived in the earth. In doing so, *The Bray House* reveals an underlying cultural consciousness that offers alternatives to persistent colonial and neocolonial power relations and visions of the future. The implicit shared cultural consciousness that *The Bray House* evokes challenges fixed understandings of sovereignty as national territory and controlled boundaries. Instead, it indicates relational understandings of people, material environments, and cultural histories that are more in keeping with definitions of sovereignty as reciprocity theorized by Indigenous scholars. The text registers the legacy of empire in geopolitical hierarchies and how the environmental impacts of empire are being written into geologic histories through nuclear technology and climate change. Yet it also reveals multiple modernities that persist in the land as knowledge, history, and ways of life.

The Bray House shows even the obtuse Robin to sense something in the land and her surroundings that her neocolonial lens for producing knowledge cannot situate or explain. During the few days Jenny and Karl appear to be lost, Robin waits while contemplating the devastated landscape: "Home. Home, which I have never had. Mother, mother! I cried, as I watched the specks. Mother, take me home! Mother, say it, Mother, just once. Say, say you love me!"[113] This distinctly out-of-character and emotional exclamation suggests elements of relational affect embedded in the land that Robin perceives. Robin apprehends the "psychogeophysics" that are necessary, in Parikka's words, "to talk about erasure of place—space—terrain, and how direct or indirect geoengineering has produced terrains through eradication."[114] The land, even after everything seems to be destroyed, continues to embody the cultural and geological media and multimodal meaning-making processes that endure in the face of utter devastation. Through Robin's overwhelmed emotions, Ní Dhuibhne's novel points to formations of cultural and environmental meaning in the utter "erasure of place." These formations of meaning persevere even in an apocalyptic landscape to reveal alternative relations to material environments and cultural histories in which, to once more quote Arvin, Tuck, and Morrill, "land is knowing and knowledge."[115] Although Robin implicitly falls back on entrenched gendered frameworks of Mother Ireland and Irish martyrdom for articulating the feelings she fails to understand, this outburst registers persistent forms of knowledge even in the wholly devastated environment around her.

The text shows Robin to quickly dismiss her feelings and to look for ways of bending her affective senses into neocolonial structural relations she knows, thereby indicating how entrenched and habitual such ways of knowing have become. She manipulates her perceptions into histories that develop linearly from understandings of the past to imagined modern futures. Rather than recognize the relational forms of knowledge both Michael and the island of Ireland embody, Robin views the empty landscape as the climax of a progress narrative toward an ultimate efficiency: "The shape of the earth, plain at last. Uncluttered by the frippery of flora and fauna which masquerades under the name of nature. Unfussed by the work of human hands, which always tend to overdo things, to leave the parts of the world they touch as gaudy and messy as a Victorian drawing room. So had Bray been before. . . . But now, this had grown on me, and I saw that it was right. I saw its perfection. The pure and simple perfection of form and light. There was nothing else. Nothing else that I want."[116] The empty "form[s]" and the repetition of "nothing else. Nothing else" emphasizes Robin's overt reliance on and desire for forms of knowledge that seek, in Mohanty's words, "origins and endings."[117] The clarity of "origins and endings" in linear progress narratives must climax in the erasure of life itself.

The ultimate endings that Robin desires lead her narration to result in multiple deaths. Robin murders Karl when she suspects his transcription of the Ogham in Maggie's tumulus might undermine her research report.[118] Then she asserts that Maggie, who is brought from the tumulus to Sweden is "killed by systematic institutional care at its most perfect."[119] Cut off from the natural and cultural elements that ensured her survival, Maggie suffers an institutional death. While this institutional death critiques how the Free State and later the Republic of Ireland embraced colonial-era institutions after independence, it also shows such forms of incarceration to rely on neocolonial notions of individualism, containment, and control that Robin lauds as good and morally better than the more communal and relational ways of living embodied by Michael and his family. Indeed, Robin also falls victim to the systems she promotes. Robin's logics of "origins and endings," of sacrifice and redemption, lead her to ultimately die by suicide at the end of the novel.

The endings of Ireland, Karl, Maggie, Michael, and Robin in *The Bray House* expose how Western institutions of knowledge, nation, territory, and autonomy tyrannically master and control even those who appear to benefit from them. The text thus critiques ongoing histories of colonialism and neocolonialism that violently erase multiple ways of knowing and being, logically ending at the extinction of all life and thus foreclosing the possibility of more just futures. Ní Dhuibhne's novel anticipates the intensification of the climate crisis and sixth mass extinction event, both of which are increasingly discussed in the twenty-first century.[120]

Despite the seemingly complete conclusions of history and the story in the novel, the text evinces through the narrative of Maggie and Michael, as well as Michael's family, the endurance of existent but multiple forms of knowledge and embodied environmental relationships embedded in the land. Even amid total destruction, the land holds an Irish cultural consciousness that relates more lasting ways of knowing and being and that offers alternative possible modernities to the most apocalyptic moments of erasure imaginable.

After History: Narrating More Just Futures in the Inevitable Collapse of Neocolonial Modernity

Through exposing hegemonic and counterhegemonic frameworks, *The Bray House* demonstrates how the modernization of the economy and natural resources in the late twentieth century reframed social and political relations in Ireland, drawing on the legacy of colonialism to revise colonial hierarchies into questions of individual or national success in a neocolonial modernity. The text registers the neocolonial modernity perpetuated by Anglo-Irish-US politics amid the Troubles and in the intensification of FDI in the Republic of Ireland in the 1970s and 1980s. Economic globalization, technologies like atomic energy, and the effects of climate change reinforce social and geopolitical hierarchies even as modernization projects promise national and postcolonial territorial sovereignty and independence. *The Bray House* uses representations of nuclear power and the effects of greenhouse gases from Ireland's intensifying dependence upon fossil fuels by the 1970s to expose shifting conceptions of land, identity, and sovereignty. Ní Dhuibhne critiques how territorial boundaries in a neocolonial modernity ultimately work to unevenly distribute forms of economic and natural resource development across populations within Ireland as well as geopolitical hierarchies of an economically integrating Europe in ongoing colonial power relations.

Although *The Bray House* reveals complex continuities between colonial histories and neocolonial economies, it also demonstrates an underlying cultural consciousness that resists erasure despite the seemingly utter destruction caused by the nuclear disaster and the neocolonial power relations that facilitated the disaster's impact on Ireland. Both Maggie's and Michael's understandings of their environments emerge from within situations rather than being studied from without, and they remain embodied in the land itself, even if under a layer of toxic nuclear fallout. This enduring cultural consciousness emerges in Michael and his family's interactions with more-than-human actors, such as the goats, seals, or whales. Similarly, Maggie's subsistence on "uncontaminated water" springing up from the Irish ground and cohabitation with the material and discursive knowledge systems and multiple temporalities of the skeleton and Ogham-inscribed walls demonstrate ways of knowing and being that remain embedded in the materiality of the ground itself after everything seems to be destroyed. The communal forms of knowledge and lived experience that Michael and Maggie embody in Irish environments contrast with the artificially separated individual freedoms in Sweden or the "zones of immunity" and "plutopia," to use Brown's terms, that rationalize geopolitical regions of Europe and the distribution of risk and degradation in processes Voyles calls "wastelanding."[121] The text foregrounds the multiple and alternative modernities in Michael's and Maggie's ways of knowing to reveal alternative environmental relations in an Irish cultural consciousness. These alternative environmental relations contrast with the social and geopolitical hierarchies emerging from histories of colonialism and the environmental impacts of empire through which a hegemonic neocolonial modernity comes to dominate.

Ní Dhuibhne's novel thus shows readers how to look through the cracks of hegemonic colonial binaries and their oppositions in counterhegemonic frameworks, like Robin's narration or assertions of territorial sovereignty and fixed precolonial traditions. Such colonial logics expose how, in Tuck's words, "the binary of reproduction versus resistance" obscures how to think or engage otherwise with material pasts, presents, and futures.[122] Ní Dhuibhne's text offers ways to reimagine and revitalize relationships to seemingly dead material and cultural environmental relationships in modern Ireland. It demonstrates ways of reading across media and time to apprehend the "psychogeophysical" messages held deep within the land, resilient even through apocalyptic scenarios to show alternative and potentially more enduring futures.[123] The Irish cultural consciousness *The Bray House* depicts offers alternative relationships with the material environment in which peoples and places coconstitute each other in ongoing relations. Like Mohanty's concept of the "temporality of struggle," the multiple modernities that arise through alternative and culturally informed relationships to the environment emerge across multiple locations and through diachronic interactions between past and present. By exposing the cracks in Robin's narration and the neocolonial worldview her narration reveals, *The Bray House* remediates geologic forms and ancient media into an apocalyptic future. In doing so, it presents multiple modernities emerging through the material agencies and environmental relations of embodied forms of knowledge and experience that Michael and Maggie each demonstrate. The material environment thus emerges in ongoing interactions across histories, cultures, and media to speak, make meaning, and assert agency through multiple temporalities of human historical and deep time. Attending to the environmental and cultural consciousness embedded in the land, even the devastated Irish landscape, points to practices of relationally reading and inhabiting a changing world.

Twenty-first-century economic developments in the Republic of Ireland build on and expand the environmental impacts of empire, as the Celtic Tiger economic boom embraced imperial logics of progress and development about which *The Bray House* warns. This more recent context to which I will now turn critically draws on the established aesthetics of fixed past traditions to oppose the façade of dynamism implied by neocolonial modernization and understandings of progress. In remediating these colonial conceptions of time and modernity in digital depictions of land, development, and struggle, my final chapter demonstrates how multispecies modernities emerge from the cultural remediations of multiple modernities across the twentieth century that I have discussed in this book thus far. These multispecies modernities revise understandings of place, belonging, and indigeneity in Ireland and point to alternative possibilities for more socially just and enduring environmental futures, in Ireland and globally.

5
1995–2010
READING MULTISPECIES MODERNITIES IN
POSTCOLONIAL CINEMA THROUGH RISTEARD
Ó DOMHNAILL'S *THE PIPE*

IN 1996, Enterprise Energy Ireland (EEI) found a natural gas field seventy kilometers off the west coast of County Mayo, Ireland.¹ Despite concerns about safety, EEI got permission to build a liquified natural gas (LNG) pipeline and refinery at Ballinaboy, in what became known as the Corrib Pipeline Project.² Nine kilometers of the pipe would run through the local Gaeltacht, or Irish-speaking community, in Rossport, in some cases less than a hundred meters from family homes and farms.³ Local opposition to the project began in the early 2000s as the Minister for the Marine and Natural Resources, Frank Fahey, created Compulsory Acquisition Orders (CAOs) that required local property owners to cede land to Shell E&P Ireland (Royal Dutch Shell acquired EEI in 2002).⁴ The resistance movement grew in 2003 as "twenty serious bogslides" around the area of the proposed pipeline made residents concerned about their safety.⁵ Additionally, the pipe was to transport raw natural gas at unprecedented pressures of 345 bars, though recommended pressures were only 144 bars.⁶ By 2005, the local community had formed the Shell-to-Sea environmental justice group to protest the Corrib Pipeline Project.

In February 2005, a group of local landowners refused to comply with the CAOs and blocked the road Shell workers used. Shell took legal action, and on June 29, 2005, Willie Corduff, Micheál Ó Seighin, Philip McGrath, Brendan Philbin, and Vincent McGrath were imprisoned in the Cloverhill Prison for ninety-four days.⁷ The arrest and incarceration of these five men, who became known as the Rossport Five, drew national and international attention. Resistance to the pipeline escalated while the Rossport Five were in jail. Despite slowing down construction, Shell started work again in 2006 and eventually completed the project amid ongoing protests from Shell-to-Sea and its splinter groups Pobal Chill

Chomáin and Pobal Le Chéile, as well as the environmental activists from across Ireland and Europe who founded the Rossport Solidarity Camp.[8] Risteard Ó Domhnaill's 2010 documentary film, *The Pipe*, follows this environmental justice movement from the time the five protesters were jailed in 2005 until Shell got the planning permission to complete the Corrib gas pipeline in 2011. While Ó Domhnaill's second film, *Atlantic* (2016), had more funding and design from the start, Ó Domhnaill's first film, *The Pipe*, emerged from within his community as the Shell-to-Sea environmental justice movement intensified. Ó Domhnaill was taking an evening class on filmmaking while living with his uncle, a prominent community member who contributed to the making of the film.[9] Ó Domhnaill began to film protests and sell footage to the national media. Upon seeing his recordings used to tell a different story from the one he was witnessing in his community, Ó Domhnaill decided to make a documentary.

The relatively small scale and local focus on a Gaeltacht region in *The Pipe* evinces what Nadia Bozak describes in terms of Fourth-World cinema as "the logical extension of orality," in which video is "digitally rendered and disseminated, democratically organized, tapping into local infrastructure and resources, and likewise giving back to the community rather than extracting from it."[10] *The Pipe* offers an "extension of orality" through the montage of aerial landscape views, social conflict, multispecies relationships, material agencies, and depictions of women's activism. These filmic strategies expose persisting colonial and neocolonial power relations embedded in tensions between regional relationships with land and the postcolonial nation's development goals. *The Pipe* depicts existent relationships with material environments that I am calling multispecies modernities, which, in turn, challenge colonial understandings of tradition, development, and modernity promoted in postcolonial national development projects.

Multispecies modernities refer to the relations among humans, more-than-humans, and material agencies and environments that emerge alongside and in ongoing interaction with cultural traditions and the environmental impacts of empire. The filmic strategies in *The Pipe* critically invoke and rework tropes for visualizing rural Ireland to resist the erasure of multispecies encounters in which ecological systems like the bog demonstrate "a technology of [their] own."[11] Examining depictions of multispecies relationships in *The Pipe* through representations of the environmental justice conflict, women's activism, and interspecies encounters demonstrates what Isabelle Carbonell calls "multispecies cinema," which "opens the imagination to relearn different ways to see, to hear, to know, to feel and to understand the long-now of our ecological crises."[12] *The Pipe* calls attention to material and more-than-human agencies that revise what the viewer observes upon encountering, in Harvey O'Brien's words, "extraordinarily beautiful sweeping image[s] of the West Coast of Ireland."[13] Through changing what such images of rural Irish landscapes signify in film, *The Pipe* offers multispecies cinema that "opens the imagination to relearn different ways to" perceive and interpret multispecies modernities.

My interdisciplinary theoretical framework for analyzing multispecies modernities in *The Pipe* revises how ecomedia studies scholars and postcolonial ecocritics analyze colonial-indebted imagery in postcolonial films. Drawing on the work of Bozak, Cajetan Iheka, Jennifer Wenzel, and Rob Nixon, my analysis elucidates how the film's production and content register tensions between the national government's embrace of neocolonial extraction economies and a marginalized Gaeltacht community. My examination also uses the work of Stacy Alaimo, Sandra Harding, and Chandra Talpade Mohanty to show how Ó Domhnaill's filmic strategies expose imperial-era gender hierarchies that obscure women's activism and multispecies modernities. Ultimately, analyzing *The Pipe* through postcolonial ecocritical, ecomedia studies, and feminist lenses expands and nuances the methods we have in ecocinema studies to examine filmic depictions of postcolonial landscapes and resource extraction.

Although few scholars have analyzed *The Pipe*, existing scholarship reflects recent turns away from postcolonial studies in ecocritical and ecocinema studies of Irish film. O'Brien, Pat Brereton, Danielle Barrios-O'Neill, and Michael Paye each use *The Pipe* as a case study to make broader claims about representations of activism, resource extraction, and Irish energy landscapes. Scholars critique *The Pipe* for reproducing visual tropes of a romanticized, primitive, and feminized rural Ireland, with Brereton and Barrios-O'Neill concluding that *The Pipe* is a "David-and-Goliath narrative" that depicts "an observable tension between old and new, or between a more traditional view of land (and sea) ownership and resistance and a more modern view."[14] By using postcolonial ecocritical, ecomedia studies, and feminist lenses to reevaluate the tensions between tradition and modernity that Brereton and Barrios-O'Neill identify, my analysis shows how *The Pipe* challenges filmic conventions from imperial-era documentary photography and promotional films after independence to reveal flourishing multispecies modernities.

Visual representations of people and places in imperial-era documentary photography and postcolonial promotional Irish films position traditional ways of life as ostensibly more authentic, precolonial, and vanishing. Such visual representations of modern and premodern landscapes extend back, as Luke Gibbons shows, to the era of romanticism when the Irish landscape "came to embody, along with other similar regions on the European periphery, all the attributes of a vanished pre-industrial era—if not a society entirely beyond the pale of civilisation."[15] To be "beyond the pale of civilisation" was to be developmentally behind other nations. The idea that Ireland should transition from premodern cultural relations into a modern nation after independence indicates how, as Priya Satia explains, "the development goal is a legacy of liberal empire so deeply embedded in political and institutional structures and practices that it is difficult for postcolonial societies to shake off; indeed, it is what makes postcolonial societies *postcolonial*."[16] The implied need to modernize was an idea promoted by late Victorian land-reform projects, such as those of the Congested Districts Board (CDB). As I discuss in chapter 1, the CDB attempted to remedy and visually document seemingly undeveloped regions in the west of Ireland. In the photos, the lush expanse of enclosed and modernized grass farms contrasts sharply with crowded and impoverished conditions in the CDB's photographs of traditional ways of life.[17]

Depictions of Gaeltacht communities as developmentally behind persists in films such as Robert Flaherty's 1934 *Man of Aran*, which, like *Nanook of the North* (1922), in Brereton's words, "remained preoccupied with showing primitive societies embodying a universal human trait of endurance and survival against all the odds."[18] Primitivist depictions of supposedly premodern traditions persist in mid-twentieth-century promotional films in which traditional ways of life transition into a future modernity promised by a globalized economy. A film such as *Gold in the Grass* (1964), in O'Brien's words, "was an unusually scientific argument in favour of the modernisation of Irish agriculture."[19] Other films, like *Life for the Soil* (1966) and *The Harvest of the Rich* (1966), were about peat and fisheries extraction, respectively.[20] The docudrama *The Promise of Barty O'Brien* (1951), a film written by Seán Ó Faoláin but partially funded by the Marshall Aid Program's Economic Co-Operation Administration (ECA), promotes gendered depictions of feminized underdevelopment transitioning into a more civilized, masculine modernity. Mid-century promotional films, in O'Brien's words, "encapsulat[e] the paradoxes of Lemass's [post 1958] Ireland, where modernisation remained subject to a lingering traditionalism modified to meet the demands of the expanding economy."[21] Heeding the nuanced critiques of colonial-inflected cinema histories in *The Pipe* reveals how Ó Domhnaill disrupts imperial-era aesthetic conventions and gender tropes embedded in progress narratives while visually honoring multispecies modernities.

By first analyzing representations of the complex relationships among the Gardaí (Irish police), activists, and Shell, I show how Ó Domhnaill subversively invokes and revises colonial-inflected romanticizations of Ireland's underdevelopment and gendered petromodernities. These representations highlight underacknowledged histories of gender in visual representations of colonial and neocolonial development projects that I subsequently explore in instances of women's agency in the film. Women's activism in *The Pipe* offers insight into the gendered politics of immigration, nation, and modernity as Ireland experienced unprecedented economic growth during the so-called Celtic Tiger between 1995 and 2008. *The Pipe*'s depiction of women's relationships to environmental justice elucidates multispecies modernities among the people, animals, bog, and coastal waters around Rossport that challenge state-sanctioned views of modernization. In the final section of this chapter, I demonstrate how Ó Domhnaill depicts multispecies modernities as permeating filmic histories, global economic integration, and environmental justice struggles connected with ongoing colonial and neocolonial histories.

Modernity Montage: The National Rights of Modernizing Industries

Through the montage and framing of Irish rural landscapes, protesters, the Gardaí, and specters of neocolonial capital haunting rural Ireland, *The Pipe* reveals imperial logics of territory and development to persist in the Republic of Ireland. These imperial logics facilitate the privatization of national resources at the expense of the rights of marginalized, rural Irish communities that national institutions ostensibly protect. Such imperial logics established forms of extraction, including fisheries and farming, that are subsequently rendered as anachronistic traditions even though many had been developed during imperial-era modernization projects a century before. Positioning local fisheries and agriculture as part of a traditional way of life in a supposedly undeveloped region makes way for the postcolonial national government and fossil fuel industry to develop the region in the early twenty-first century. In contrast to anticolonial forms of nationalism in Ireland, *The Pipe* emphasizes the postcolonial state's role in neocolonial projects through depictions of the Gardaí, roads, and several scenes of faded or frayed Irish flags flapping in the wind.[22] By reworking progress narratives and the binaries upon which colonial mindsets of development rely, Ó Domhnaill's film challenges established visual representations of rural Ireland and reveals multispecies modernities embedded in the Gaeltacht community's ongoing struggle against coerced forms of national and multinational modernization.

In its opening sequence, *The Pipe* destabilizes longer representational histories of rural Irish regions used to promote development in supposedly empty spaces. Panning, aerial long shots of vast and sparsely populated landscapes (see fig. 14)[23] switch back and forth three times with jarring handheld shots of the local Gardaí violently pushing protesters off the road.[24] O'Brien interprets the aerial shots in the film as setting up a "romantic story space" that fails to inspire action from the audience about the urgent issues it conveys.[25] While these scenes certainly recall colonial-era picturesque views of a seemingly undeveloped Ireland, they do so in a way that remediates romanticized views from colonial photography of Ireland into a newer digital form and critical montage. Ó Domhnaill, to quote Jay David Bolter and Richard Grusin, "refashion[s] older media ... to answer the challenges of new media" by tapping into the dual logic of remediation, in which the immediacy of content comes into tension with the hypermediacy of advancing media technologies.[26] The scenic views and close-up shots of the police and protesters each emphasize different aspects of the immediacy of modernization and its impact on the community. By contrast, the montage highlights the hypermediacy of representations of rural Ireland. The opening sequence in *The Pipe* consequently brings into sharp relief how visual technologies and picturesque aesthetics render rural Ireland into a space ripe for development, as I discuss in earlier chapters. These representations justify modernization projects while erasing multiple modernities left out of the camera's frame. Ó Domhnaill's opening sequence remediates abrasively different shots from morning to evening to critique recalcitrant aesthetic conventions that historically sought to naturalize certain forms of development

194　IRISH ECOMEDIA

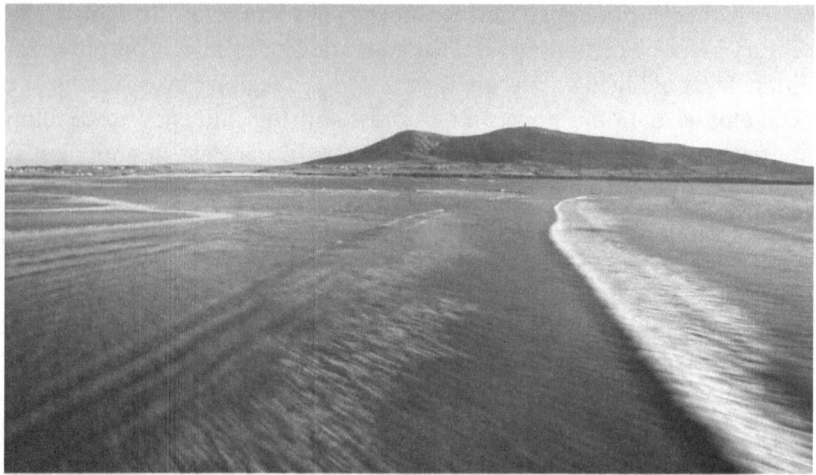

FIG. 14. Aerial shots of the rural landscape in *The Pipe*. (Courtesy of Risteard Ó Domhnaill)

as inevitable. These forms of development persist in the idealized understandings of development in the Corrib Pipeline Project.

The mediated aspect of rural representations and forms of development emerge in the production of these opening scenes. To produce the visual material for this opening montage, Ó Domhnaill drew on and gave back to the community. After receiving funding from the Irish Film Board at the editing stage of *The Pipe* in 2009, Ó Domhnaill borrowed a friend's camera, which they strapped it to the side of a helicopter they rented for a couple of hours from Knock Airport.[27] The aerial shots evince how Ó Domhnaill strategically reclaims representational strategies that justified changes to his community across multiple colonial and neocolonial modernization projects. The montage of aerial coastal shots with handheld close-ups of social conflict critically depicts the imposed divisions between tradition and modernity, undeveloped and developed, and viewer and viewed. By invoking colonial-era romanticizations of Irish landscapes in a montage with jostling close-ups of social protest against the Shell LNG pipeline, Ó Domhnaill's film techniques make use of the limited resources upon which the community could draw for representation. Like Ó Riada, whose work I discuss in chapter 3, Ó Domhnaill draws on existing media, technologies, and material conditions in rural Ireland to rework and remediate multiple modernities. In doing so, *The*

Pipe demonstrates what Iheka theorizes as "imperfect media," which are "low-carbon media practices and the infrastructures of finitude that are critical for ameliorating ecological precarity in the future."[28] While flying a helicopter is not a low-carbon activity, the fact that all the aerial shots in the film were done in a few hours on borrowed equipment and through community connections indicates production practices that "are critical for ameliorating ecological precarity in the future." The handheld aerial shots in *The Pipe*'s opening sequence register the creation of "imperfect media" as the montage of these shots exposes the spatial and temporal ruptures in the community and the specter of colonialism upon which national modernization projects in the postcolonial state strategically rely. The opening montage of *The Pipe* shows how Ó Domhnaill subversively invokes romanticized images of Irish rural regions to interrupt divisive narratives of development. Instead of underwriting development projects, *The Pipe*'s opening scenes expose picturesque images to construct binaries of developed modernity or preserved traditional lifestyles. These binaries obscure and disrupt existent postcolonial rural modernities, thereby showing Ó Domhnaill to implicitly build on the critique Flann O'Brien makes in *The Third Policeman*, as I discuss in chapter 2.

The contrastingly harsh scenes of social protest in the opening montage interrupt the colonial and neocolonial gaze overseeing seemingly picturesque views of a supposedly undeveloped rural Irish community. By turning the camera on the authorities who protect and promote development in the close-up shots of the opening sequence, the protesters become the viewers of the Gardaí, who use their batons and physical force to suppress resistance against the pipeline and refinery. These handheld shots indicate the camera's implicitly disciplinary purpose to conceal struggle and position the entire community in ongoing processes of modernization, thus reflecting how, in the words of Helen Hughes, "film is a medium that is imbricated in the modernity that it critiques."[29] At times the Gardaí wield a camera, and Shell's private security forces use cameras to surveil the protestors' homes and interactions.[30] Positioning the protesters behind the camera in these opening scenes registers spatial and temporal ruptures in the community upon which modernization projects strategically rely.

The montage of aerial coastal shots with handheld close-ups of social conflict critically depicts the imposed divisions between tradition and modernity, undeveloped and developed, and viewed and viewer. The handheld shots show the viewer and viewed to oscillate ambiguously across multiple rural modernities that the Gardaí and protesters in the community collectively inhabit. Indeed, the film shows many Gardaí to continue their work at the expense of severing friendships they previously held with local community members who participate in the protest. These rifts have, as activist Willie Corduff articulates, "a mark left in the community that'll never be healed."[31] This depiction of the Gardaí demonstrates the fractured social and environmental relations to region, nation, and globalized extraction economies in rural communities in the Republic of Ireland in the early twenty-first century. By foregrounding the role of the Gardaí as both community members undergoing modernization processes and as agents of modernization, *The Pipe* refuses binary oppositions that would divide people and places into tidy understandings of before and after, traditional or modern, undeveloped or developed. *The Pipe*'s representation of the Gardaí exposes the region to already inhabit an unexpected modernity outside the sanctioned view of development. The Gardaí demonstrate the fractured social and environmental relations to region, nation, and globalized extraction economies in rural communities in the Republic of Ireland in the early twenty-first century.

While the Gardaí represent the state and Shell's interests in developing fossil-fuel economies, they are also locals in Rossport who, like the protesters, seek to carry out their livelihoods in the community. The scenes of the Gardaí indicate the overlapping interests across local, national, and multinational contestations that raise the question, in Wenzel's words, "To whom do natural resources belong?"[32] The Gardaí ostensibly protect the resources that national sovereignty in postcolonial Ireland would grant to the local community. Yet the film shows the Gardaí to protect the state's interests in developing natural resources for a globalizing economy rooted in extraction and consumption. These competing interests reveal conflicts caused by modernization projects historically in the region and elsewhere in Ireland. These conflicts splinter progress into multiple modernities in which ongoing social and environmental relations interact with the unexpected effects of power.

Through the representation of the Gardaí in these persisting and multiplying ruptures in the community, *The Pipe* critiques the postcolonial Irish state's embrace of multinational interests in fossil fuel extraction that presumably would bring progress to the region. The film shows this embrace to challenge anew the multigenerational farming and fishing in rural Ireland that helped define Irish identity and territorial and natural resource sovereignty since imperial-era land and fisheries reform projects in the late-nineteenth and early twentieth centuries. *The Pipe*'s critique emerges in depictions of how the Gardaí use the road to protect ongoing forms of modernization that actively erase alternative modernities. Roads are an indicator of modernization in imperial-era land reform photographs in Ireland, as I argue in chapter 1, and they play an important role in framing the rural Irish landscape, as I show in chapter 2. The road embodies both a material marker of modernization and a modern view of surrounding natural and built environments. Like many of the CDB photographs of roads, as well as the narrator's descriptions from the road in Flann O'Brien's *The Third Policeman*, the road guides the gaze. To quote Bozak on railroads, "Nineteenth-century photographers tended to focus the camera's point of view into the direction the iron tracks were heading—that is, into an implied course of progress."[33] In contrast to "an implied course of progress," Ó Domhnaill's handheld shots show what is on and surrounding the road. The Gardaí throw protesters from the road in a violent imposition of order that puts the rural community back into the landscape and frees the road to facilitate further forms of development, of which the Gardaí and the road are both part (see fig. 15).[34] *The Pipe*'s opening sequence exposes how colonial, national, and

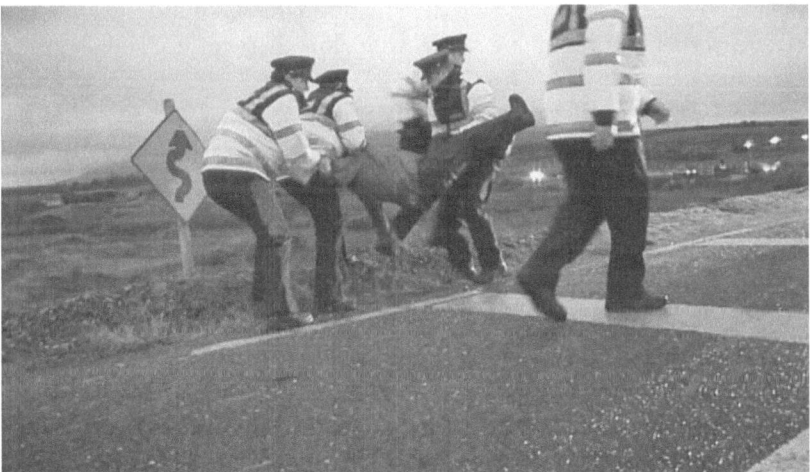

FIG. 15. The Gardaí throw protesters off the road in *The Pipe*. (Courtesy of Risteard Ó Domhnaill)

multinational interests rely on divisions between premodern and modern and undeveloped and developed to justify the changes they enact in the communities they alter. By critically drawing on visual representational conventions, *The Pipe* demonstrates how progress narratives obscure and erase existent alternative modernities that have emerged through ongoing interactions between traditional relations to the land and multiple modernization projects.

Like the Gardaí's complex relationship to local and national development projects, *The Pipe* narrates the struggles of individual protesters, their collective action, and their relationships to the region as entangled with their dependence on both their material environments and the industries they oppose. *The Pipe* introduces local farmers and fishermen who protest Shell and become the main voices in the documentary's narrative. Pat O'Donnell, who has been a fisherman of Broadhaven Bay since he was fourteen, states that he had two choices in life, either to fish the waters around the place where he was born or to emigrate.[35] Two farmers then describe their relationship to the land. Monica Müller explains her dependence, both personal and professional, on the commonage of the region, which is shared "undivided" by sixty-two people.[36] Willie Corduff demonstrates how to dig for shellfish on the local beach, a practice that has been passed down in his family for generations, saying these shellfish "were a great source of food in the old days."[37] These cameos highlight the individuals of Rossport who depend upon the surrounding lands and waters in their region to live, work, and allow their culture and language to thrive.

The Pipe's depiction of community members bears witness to longer histories of modernization through which the protesters have become dependent upon the fossil fuel economies their struggle seeks to resist. As the conflict escalates, the film shows local fishermen protesting on their diesel-powered fishing boats, and Maura Harrington, a local schoolteacher and one of the most vocal protesters in the Shell-to-Sea campaign, blocks the road to the development site with her car.[38] When the Gardaí impound O'Donnell's boat during a protest, the camera shows O'Donnell drinking Coca-Cola out of a plastic bottle as he walks to the police van, thus revealing multinational forms of fossil fuel extraction and consumption to permeate the bodies of people in the community.[39] The cars, roads, and motorized fishing vessels demonstrate the many forms of modernization that are already part of the everyday lives of the community. These scenes show that O'Donnell is aware of how the pipeline and refinery "destroy one industry to set up another," an observation he makes in the film over the whirring sounds of his boat's diesel engine.[40] O'Donnell recognizes that the extraction of fish is as much an "industry" as natural gas extraction by Shell, even as he frames his livelihood as a multigenerational tradition he has maintained across multiple forms of fisheries modernization.

The Pipe challenges myths of progress implicit in modernization narratives in its depiction of Shell as a specter of a neocolonial, multinational modernity. The agents and infrastructure of Shell emerge out of nowhere to privatize the public commons for its own profits. This detached representation is, in part, because Shell refused to participate in the film. Yet formal aspects of the cinematography enhance this spectral depiction, thereby indicating a decentralized form of power that occupies the territorial space of the Gaeltacht under the aegis of national development. The low-angle shots of the ship *Solitaire*, which sails into Broadhaven Bay to lay the undersea section of the pipeline, make the ship appear larger than life, as well as larger than the law. This framing of Shell offers a haunting specter of the colonial forms of development and forced land acquisitions during multiple imperial land reforms that intensified during and after the Tudor conquests of the sixteenth century. Indeed, community members recognize a sense of belonging in Rossport through a shared history of having been displaced during the expansion of the Ulster plantation and Protestant settlement in the seventeenth century, as Vincent McGrath describes in *Our Story*: "Indeed most families around here have their origins in the north of Ireland and are descendants of people who were forced to leave their homes in Ulster because of the Transplantation of Cromwell in 1650. That's when they were given the choice of To Hell or to Connaught."[41] This centuries-old narrative of modernization legitimates the contemporary cooptation of national resources with the postcolonial state's protection.

The film foregrounds this specter of colonialism through visual representations in which the *Solitaire*, security fencing, private security forces, and construction equipment are increasingly everywhere in the cinematography but have no identifiable point of origin or center (see fig. 16).[42] Fences around construction sites or the arm of an excavator emerge out of nowhere to take over and crowd the frame; handheld shots capture individual security workers through the bars of a fence.[43] The numerous

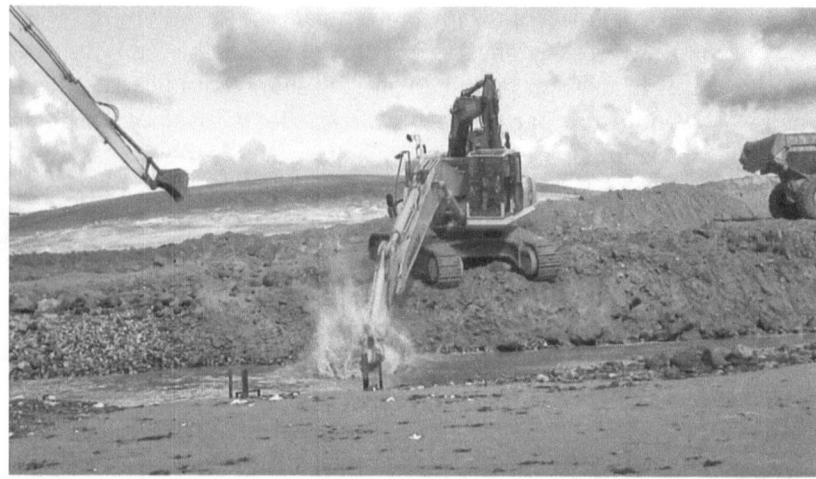

FIG. 16. Partial views foreground the spectral presence of Shell in *The Pipe*. (Courtesy of Risteard Ó Domhnaill)

scenes of fences, security cameras, construction equipment, private security officers, and the *Solitaire* serve as indexes for the corporation. Shell's spectral presence haunts the community with its colonized past, which shaped both the land in Rossport and the community's identity. The film emphasizes the expansiveness of this specter of neocolonial power as Shell is excused by the High Court in 2010 for the same conviction of contempt of court that put the Rossport Five in jail for ninety-four days.[44] As local resident and Shell-to-Sea activist John Monaghan puts it, it is now "Shell's law."[45] *The Pipe* exposes how "Shell's law" is part of a longer history of colonial and neocolonial modernization projects in Ireland that continue to dominate the community's relationships with its surroundings, ideas of nation and identity, and the legal and political institutions and histories through which rights are framed.

In contrast to anticolonial forms of nationalism in Ireland, *The Pipe* emphasizes the postcolonial state's role in neocolonial projects through its soundscape and depictions of the Gardaí, roads, and several scenes of faded or frayed Irish flags flapping in the wind.[46] O'Donnell receives sterile responses from the *Solitaire* over the VHF radio as the crew of *Solitaire* ignore O'Donnell's inquiries about his crab pots: "Please immediately take action to stay well clear of *Solitaire*."[47] The canned answer of the voice over the radio emphasizes how detached Shell and its outsourcing are from the community. Yet the anonymous voice also comes to occupy O'Donnell's boat, asserting a command over the radio to which O'Donnell and viewers of *The Pipe* must listen. The voice enters and dominates the frames and soundscapes of the film, as well as the lives, legal rights, and fishing and farming commons of the residents of Rossport. This aural occupation of O'Donnell's boat occurs under the protection of the Irish state.

When the Gardaí and Navy protect the interests of Shell and impound O'Donnell's fishing boat during a protest, the camera shows the *Solitaire* off the stern of O'Donnell's boat. The pitching of the waves and the distance between the boats position the Irish flag under the *Solitaire* in the two-dimensional screen.[48] This frame indicates that the Irish nation is subordinate to the multinational interests it promotes during the period of unparalleled economic growth from the mid-1990s to 2008. The subsequent scene shows O'Donnell rolling up the Irish flag he once flew off the stern of his boat. This action registers O'Donnell's allegiance to a conception of the Irish nation that would protect his interests over those of Shell.[49] In rolling up the flag, O'Donnell shows how the national institutions from which he seeks protection have become part of a larger neocolonial and multinational system. O'Donnell is coerced into a subordinate role with limited agency that he protests through his refusal to fly the Irish flag despite his inability to protect the fishing waters upon which he relies for his livelihood.

The scenes of the Gardaí, protesters, and Shell indicate how contestations of resource ownership subtend colonial indebted modernization narratives in state-supported extraction projects. Consistencies across colonial modernization narratives in postcolonial contexts gave rise to solidarities between the environmental justice movement in Rossport and the Movement for the Survival of the Ogoni People (MOSOP) in the Niger Delta.[50] Indeed, Dr. Owens Wiwa, the brother of Ken Saro-Wiwa, even marched to the Dáil in Dublin to protest the imprisonment of the Rossport Five, and numerous references to the MOSOP struggle exist in Rossport and the Shell-to-Sea campaign.[51] While *The Pipe* does not emphasize these international alliances, it critically depicts overarching colonial narratives that justify the marginalization of regional communities as an inevitable part of postcolonial national progress, in Ireland and elsewhere.

Splintered Communities: Gendered Conflicts and Ruptures in a Modern Society

The Pipe challenges modernization narratives by subverting gendered divisions between public and private spaces. The breadth of women's experiences and the forms of agency they assert challenge tensions between feminized private spaces in supposedly premodern traditions and masculine-inflected modern public forums where an implied petromodernity promises a supposedly better future for human communities. Maura Harrington's loud demonstrations against the pipeline in public spaces refuse the terms of reasonability dictated by Shell's masculine-inflected neocolonial modernity. The film reworks expectations of gendered public and private spaces by making the domestic labor of Mary Corduff's kitchen more public than the European Parliament. Ó Domhnaill thus critically reframes gendered spaces in progress narratives across a spectrum of competing modern experiences that come into sharp relief in representations of Monica Müller. Müller's trajectories over the bog reveal narrative spaces for visualizing the complex constellations of social systems and multispecies modernities that materially sculpt rural landscapes.

The modernization projects that *The Pipe* depicts rely on gendered understandings of progress and rationalized material environments. Harding asserts that "modernity narratives obsessively recuperate feminized tradition in order to define their own different, manly, and Western progressive features. In this way, tradition, exemplified within modern societies by women and women's worlds, becomes conceptually internal to modernity."[52] A feminized traditional past in the private, domestic sphere supposedly progresses into a masculine-inflected public good in a modernized future.[53] Such gendered modernization narratives are evident in the history of Irish documentary films about modernization.

Gendered modernization narratives emerge in mid-century promotional films to encourage postcolonial Ireland to integrate into an increasing US-led petroeconomy. The docudrama *The Promise of Barty O'Brien* (1951), for example, presents a feminized past tradition hindering the masculine modernity of technological advancements for extracting the bog for industrial energy production.[54] The traditional farmer's son, Barty, goes to the United States to become an electrician and returns to Ireland to work on the Rural Electrification Project, which began in 1946 and expanded the industrial extraction of peat bogs for fuel.[55] In the meantime, Barty's sister marries a local farmer who will maintain the family farm. Barty's sister carries on the traditions attached to the land, even as her husband brings new technologies like a tractor to the farm. This film positions tradition as a feminized hindrance to rendering the seemingly useless bog into a more efficient fossil fuel in a masculine-inflected modernity.

Heeding the specific roles that women play in *The Pipe* and the diverse forms of agency they assert shows how Ó Domhnaill's cinematographic choices resist established gendered modernization narratives. Depictions of women in the film rework gendered understandings of public and private spaces implicit in modernization projects to foreground fluid and continually unfolding networks of environmental relations existent in Rossport, which, in turn, create strategies for visually representing multispecies modernities. *The Pipe*'s representations of community members and activists Harrington, Mary Corduff, and Müller, as well as a member of the European Parliament (MEP) Kathy Sinnott, chart diverse and sometimes conflicting spatial and temporal relationships across seemingly divided public and private spaces. Through depictions of women's relationships to land, law, and activism in the film, gendered relationships to modernity and fossil fuels in *The Pipe* expose how, as Sheena Wilson puts it, "empowered feminist identities outside those sanctioned by the mainstream neoliberal petro-discourses are depoliticized and renegotiated in the public sphere."[56] *The Pipe* reworks gendered petro-discourses of public and private spheres in rural Ireland to carve out a space through which multispecies modernities can emerge within the camera's frame.

The film traces what is considered reasonable in typically masculine-inflected public spaces like community meetings. *The Pipe* shows Father Michael Nallen reading a letter the parish priests wrote in 2007 to Green Party member and minister for communications, energy, and natural resources Eamon Ryan asking that Shell reroute the pipeline through the "uninhabited area" of Glinsk.[57] Community members convene at two separate Shell-to-Sea meetings to discuss the priests' plan.[58] *The Pipe* juxtaposes the seemingly unreasonable but impassioned protester Harrington with the apparently more reasonable men in the community. Harrington's outspoken opposition to the priests' solution recognizes the futility of an alternative route as the pollution of the land and sea would just occur further down the coast. Yet others in the community, like Monaghan, contend that they should accept it to "show that we are reasonable people."⁵⁹ These scenes indicate the intensifying differences of opinion among the protesters, but they also show the men as rational and seeking a solution for Shell that would also work for the community. Conversely, Harrington's approach staunchly refuses to work within the implicitly gendered frameworks that render local sociorelational environments into empty spaces ripe for privatized development.⁶⁰

Indeed, Shell and the national media relied on these gendered spatiotemporal frameworks of modernization narratives to divide the community along binaries of tradition and modernity, past and present. Shell primarily targeted men with the injunctions, thereby recognizing them as the property owners in the community even though women in Rossport continued to protest the pipeline and refinery.⁶¹ Indeed, Bríd McGarry, who legally was in the same position as the five jailed men, walked away from the hearing despite also having her name on Shell's injunction. McGarry pointed out that legal documentation sent to the defendants showed that, as Lorna Siggins summarizes, "it would not be good from a [Shell] PR point of view to have all the objecting landowners jailed—particularly if one was a woman."⁶² According to this interpretation, Shell sought to make an example of the five men. In keeping with this gendered approach, the media also extensively covered the women in Rossport while the men were in jail. The five women whose husbands comprise the Rossport Five appeared on the popular national television program *The Late Late Show*. McGarry was also present, but she "had been conveniently bypassed when it came to her turn to express her opinion on the show."⁶³ The host, Pat Kenny, introduced the controversy that led to their husbands being held in contempt of court for over two months at the time of the broadcast on September 2, 2005, noting that, "meanwhile, their families survive in Mayo without the man of the house doing what needs to be done."⁶⁴ Kenny's ensuing interview with Mary Corduff avoids the reasons why the families in Rossport are protesting the pipeline, focusing instead on family affairs, such as what birthdays the husbands have missed and how the women are coping "without the man of the house." The final question Kenny asks is "What would it take for the men to purge their contempt?" While Kenny's questions implicitly encourage Mary Corduff to offer some domestic reason why the men should give up their cause, Mary Corduff answers by bringing the conversation back to the protest: "It would be Shell that would have to take that step, to lift the injunction. Then they [the men] would purge their contempt."[65] Mary Corduff's responses show that the conflict is not caused by the men's refusal to cooperate with the acquisition orders and cede land to Shell, thereby pushing back on narratives of rural people resistant to change. Her answer also refuses a gendered separation of a feminized private home from a more masculine public protest and sphere of debate. Instead, Mary Corduff demonstrates that she and the other women are as much a part of the protest as their husbands.

Both the men and women are committed to resisting the larger threat Shell's development poses to their homes, families, and ways of life. As Ó Domhnaill points out, "When the men were jailed, there was a large blockade of the refinery and work was stopped. And every morning hundreds of people would gather outside the refinery."[66] Along with other locals, the women held the protest line when their husbands were in jail. Despite their ongoing activism, the appearance of the women on *The Late Late Show* and the topics about which Mary Corduff was interviewed demonstrate how mainstream media perpetuated representational conventions in which, to use Harding's words, a "functional separation of public and private spheres is one of the significant marks of modernity's social progress 'for humanity.'"[67] *The Late Late Show* segment sustains the "functional separation" between the feminized, private domestic spaces that the women supposedly represent and the public stance against development that their husbands ostensibly willfully maintain. Despite the gendered divisions Kenny's questions promote, Mary Corduff's answers subtly challenge national media representations of gendered modernization narratives by positioning Shell as the entity that stands in the way of progress. Rather than allow "modernity [to] defin[e] itself against whatever it defines as past," as Harding put it, Mary Corduff's inclusion of the women as leaders of the protest inverts gendered modernization narratives to show that the future of the community relied on existing relationships to the land and ecosystems instead of on gendered labor roles that ignore multispecies and material relations.[68]

Many of the larger news media stories on the struggle maintained gendered divisions between public-modern-masculine and private-traditional-feminine spaces. Maureen McGrath, who did not feature in *The Pipe*, explains in *Our Story* how this increasing media attention affected her: "The wives had to get on with it and deal with the media. . . . They might come taking photographs or filming and it could take an hour with you walking back the road until they got the shots right, walking the way they want you too. You just did what you had to do."⁶⁹ McGrath's statement attests to the way visual representations craft the object of their gaze to meet viewer expectations and uphold dominant narratives. While the imprisonment of the Rossport Five was undoubtedly very difficult for the families, representations of the women as somehow outside the conflict preserves the image of a community of wives in a domestic, private sphere who are supposedly adrift without their husbands. The husbands are then rendered as recklessly risking their families to protest development, thereby indicating a fractured community rather than a unified environmental justice struggle. To establish Rossport as a region advancing in natural gas extraction and energy production, the news media shows the protest to interrupt feminized traditions in private spaces by the stubborn refusal of the five men to promote masculinized modernization projects of public spaces and national resources.

The Pipe disrupts these gendered divisions of public-private spaces and traditional and modern temporalities in modernization narratives by showing how Harrington, MEP Sinnott, and Mary Corduff assert forms of agency that cumulatively refuse, in Chandra Talpade Mohanty's words, "the normative referent in such a binary analytic."⁷⁰ While Harrington loudly demonstrates in public spaces and the national media draws on gendered divisions of public-private spheres, Ó Domhnaill's film depicts the relatively private gaze of a public figure. MEP Sinnott represented Ireland in the European Parliament, where the Rossport group stated their case to the petitions committee on a visit she sponsored.⁷¹ In its depiction of this visit, *The Pipe* only shows MEP Sinnott waving the community members off after their testimony.⁷² MEP Sinnott's silence in the story is notable, as she had the authority to give the community members a platform to voice their concerns at the level of the European Union (EU). Paye interprets such silences in Ó Domhnaill's films to perpetuate gender hierarchies that "uncomfortably mirror" longer histories of "capitalism, abstraction, extraction, and violence against nature/women."⁷³ Yet a closer examination of visual elements in the representation of MEP Sinnott reveals the film's subtle refusal of binary divisions, which, in turn, structurally challenges gender hierarchies.

Although MEP Sinnott is not named or interviewed in the film, the camera foregrounds her perspective during her emphatic farewells to the group.⁷⁴ MEP Sinnott briefly glances at the camera, thus acknowledging its focus upon her and asserting her agency to look away even as she stands in the center of the frame. The camera then follows MEP Sinnott's gaze as the group leaves the European Parliament to return to Rossport.[75] The camera's gaze in this farewell scene briefly presents the community members as objects of MEP Sinnott's view rather than as the subjects of the story. This implicit and momentary inversion of subject and object emphasizes the public authority MEP Sinnott holds and through which she oversees the effects of modernization processes on her constituents. Rather than offering a masculine-inflected depiction of MEP Sinnott's authority over public space, *The Pipe* conflates public and private by preventing the viewer access to a clear articulation of her perspective. MEP Sinnott's public service gives the protesters a voice while her own voice is present only through the camera's view. By putting the Rossport delegates under the purview of MEP Sinnott's public-private gaze, the film refuses to work within the aesthetic conventions it subtly disrupts.

Ó Domhnaill's film also acknowledges and complicates public-private divisions that the national media promoted. These divisions tend to devalue feminine-gendered household work through the conflation of women with domestic spaces. In contrast to national media representations of Mary Corduff, *The Pipe* shows Mary Corduff quietly but diligently attending meetings and protests, and it interviews her in private domestic spaces. She accompanies community members to the European Parliament, but she appears as silently observing the protest actions she supports. In interviews, Mary Corduff is in her kitchen cooking or minding a baby, and she provides her approval when the community calls off protests as violence escalates, an act Harrington sums up as a "dreadful mistake" and "a failure of courage."[76] These scenes of private domestic space frame Mary Corduff's more moderate approach to the struggle within traditionally feminized labor roles. Yet *The Pipe* positions Mary Corduff in a prominent role in the film, thus refusing to erase or conceal the household labor she does or the forms of agency she asserts as an environmental justice protester. Mary Corduff's activism shows how, as Mohanty put it, "superficially similar situations may have radically different, historically specific explanations and cannot be treated as identical."[77] Through regularly inserting Mary Corduff's perspective into the film as she carries out her work in the home, *The Pipe* does not metaphorize women as houses, as did visual representations of modernization projects before and after independence, as I discuss in chapters 1 and 2.

Instead, it shows how Mary Corduff's household work, perspectives, and agency are an integral part of modernization projects and the community's resistance to them.

The specificity of women's diverse experiences in the film destabilizes normative referents and understandings of development implicit in gendered binaries dividing a masculine, public modernity from feminine, private traditional spaces. By disrupting visual signifiers of gendered modernization narratives, *The Pipe* visually carves out a narrative space through which the region's multiple modernities come into sharper relief in representations of farmer and activist Monica Müller. *The Pipe* introduces shifting relationships to place in early twenty-first-century Ireland by following Müller as she uses legal action to delay Shell from completing its LNG projects in Broadhaven Bay and Rossport. Like the scenes of Harrington as a rogue Shell-to-Sea activist, the film also shows Müller to act alone in her efforts to thwart Shell's developments.[78] This representation of Müller acting alone but rationally within existing legal systems formally isolates her from the community even as it indicates her commitment to protect the lands upon which she too relies.

The film's representation of Müller's isolation tangentially refers to xenophobic notions of who belonged in the community that arose during the protests. Micheál Ó Seighin explains that he and Müller were accused of being "outsiders" because Ó Seighin moved from Galway to be a schoolteacher and Müller had immigrated to the region from Germany.[79] While the xenophobia Müller experienced recalls fears after World War II through the 1980s of Germans acquiring land that Irish people could not afford to buy, as I discuss at the end of chapter 3, it also articulates tensions between immigration during the Celtic Tiger and Ireland's long history of coerced emigration resulting from colonialism and neocolonial economic subordination. Indeed, O'Donnell asserts at the start of the film that he would be forced to emigrate if he could not fish the coastal waters around Broadhaven Bay. O'Donnell's experience of the threat of emigration contrasts with Müller's decision to immigrate, in Siggins's words, "from the highly industrialized Ruhr valley" in modernized Germany to rural Ireland, which suggests geopolitical privileges of mobility.[80]

Pressures of emigration and opportunities of immigration indicate gendered geopolitical hierarchies in modernizing European countries in which Ireland has historically been feminized and economically subordinate. Tropes of the masculine British John Bull patronizing a feminized

Mother Ireland implicitly persist in the uneven development across European countries to foster geopolitical privileges, such as international mobility and the capacity for property ownership. Eóin Flannery explains that "while nations such as Britain, France and Germany . . . were engines of European modernisation, . . . the Irish experience of modernity was enforced and traumatic, and in these ways had much in common with the experiences of other colonised, and often non-European, societies."[81] Uneven development within Europe exposes gendered modernization narratives exported to other parts of the British Empire, but it also indicates ongoing geopolitical hierarchies rooted in colonial histories to persist within the EU and the possibilities for mobility therein. Depictions of Müller in *The Pipe* demonstrate intersections of masculine-inflected modernities and feminine inflected traditions across twenty-first-century geopolitical hierarchies emerging through Ireland's postcolonial status and position on the geographic and economic periphery of an integrating European economy. While Müller was not targeted by Shell in legal proceedings over property ownership as the men comprising the Rossport Five were, the film implicitly associates her more with a masculinized German modernization rather than with rural Ireland's historically feminized experience of modernity.

From inside her home, Müller describes how she strategically draws on legal frameworks to protect the land. These moments in the film demonstrate Müller's settlement in Rossport and embrace of a traditional rural lifestyle and modern property ownership. Müller explains her analytical approach to the law and definition of the commonage that materially and legally substantiate her attachment to and belonging in Rossport, as well as her claims in the district court. Müller explains that "Shell thinks buying a share in the commonage means they can enter the commonage as they like. I disagree with that."[82] Müller's insight into both the national legal system and local land relations disrupts gendered divisions between a masculine modernity and feminized premodern traditions. By filming Müller's masculine-inflected analytical approach to public lands from within the domestic space she owns, *The Pipe* shows Müller to inhabit multiple gendered spaces at once, thereby disrupting implied temporalities of progress that divide private and public, tradition and modernity, and undeveloped and developed.

Analyzing the cinematography and montage around Müller's movements across the commons maps out multispecies modernities in which the people of Rossport implicitly already live and work in ongoing relationships with more-than-human communities and material agencies. The film shows Müller walking with her dog along a road lined with turf at the start of the film (see fig. 17).[83] These scenes remind the viewer of how road building and turf cutting have a long cultural history in rural Ireland and both remain topics of intense environmental debates.[84] Debates contesting how to preserve bog ecosystems or cultural relationships to bogs simultaneously must contend with histories of industrial turf extraction and the building of roads that have been iconic forms of modernization since imperial-era land and fisheries reform projects. State policies protecting colonial-indebted understandings of economic progress are literally pounded into the bog when Willie Corduff posts signs announcing Müller's claim in the district court that delayed Shell's project.[85] Müller's actions demonstrate her ability to navigate traditional local knowledge amid multinational extractive economies as she confronts Shell in the courts and on the bog with their misunderstanding of how the commonage works.

The Pipe's depiction of Müller foregrounds how the landscape embeds understandings of tradition, modernity, identity, agency, and belonging in postcolonial rural Ireland, even as such understandings shift from those of territorial sovereignty to ephemeral flows of multinational

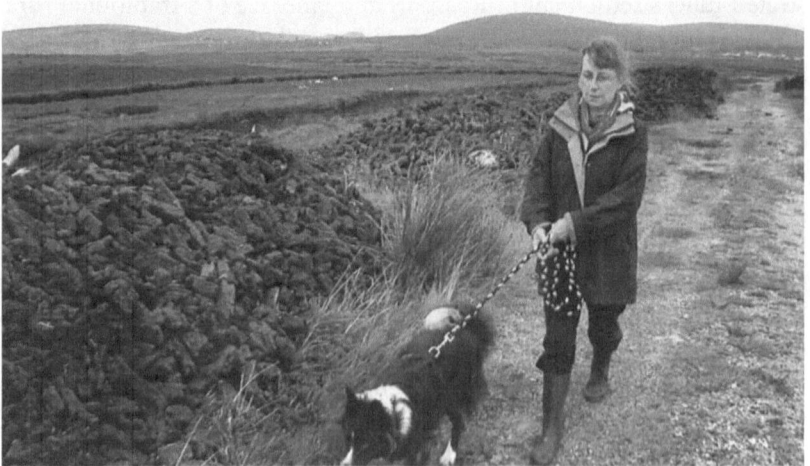

FIG. 17. Müller walks along a turf-lined road in *The Pipe*. (Courtesy of Risteard Ó Domhnaill)

capital associated with fossil-fuel extraction. Ó Domhnaill's cinematography of Müller complicates divisions between Europe and postcolonial regions that obscure uneven forms of development. The film thus challenges gendered modernization narratives that persist in divisions postcolonial ecocritics and ecomedia studies scholars often use to distinguish postcolonial from European film histories. Through representations of Müller, *The Pipe* implicitly reworks these divisions into a network of interrelated connections among histories of colonialism, neocolonial logics of development, gendered spatial relations, and material and multispecies environments in Ireland. The scenes of Müller's walks through the bog and commons bear witness to the environmental impacts of empire emerging through uneven forms of modernization within Europe and across the British Empire. The material impacts of these environmental and social histories of power continue to inform and alter everyday relations among humans, more-than-humans, and material environments. The scenes of Müller and the bog trace, conflate, and complicate the gendered territories and histories of modernization through which multispecies modernities emerge in ongoing interactions among human and more-than-human communities and material agencies in the surrounding environments.

"The Bog Is a Technology of Its Own": Multispecies Interactions in Postcolonial Modernities

By critically expanding the narrative spaces for visually representing postcolonial rural modernities in its opening scenes and depictions of women's activism, *The Pipe* shows collaborative multispecies relationships between natural and cultural systems. Such relationships refuse a bifurcation between nature and culture, either in the exploitation of nature by culture or the submergence of culture into nature. Land and landscapes are cultural actors in many Irish films, as Gibbons asserts: "Landscape has tended to play a leading role in Irish cinema, often upstaging both the main characters and narrative theme in the construction of Ireland on the screen."[86] Like Gibbons, O'Brien recognizes how documentary films present landscapes through the role they have played in social histories: "Less often observed is that the landscape itself is also constructed, a signifier of habitation replete with meanings of its own."[87] *The Pipe* highlights the processes through which landscapes produce meaning by foregrounding the possibilities and limitations of visually representing multispecies modernities.

The construction of landscapes takes opposing forms in the history of Irish documentary film. On the one hand, *The Promise of Barty O'Brien* shows the bog as a vast, empty space that could be used to create electricity if people would just let go of their traditional subsistence turf-cutting and enter the modern world of industrial extraction economies. In contrast, Peter Carey's documentary film *Oisín* (1970), made for the European Conservation Year, draws on the mythical Irish past of Fionn Mac Cumhaill to indicate interdependent relationships between indigenous societies and their more-than-human surroundings.[88] After briefly describing the story of Fionn Mac Cumhaill, *Oisín* offers a montage of close-ups and long shots from various angles that demonstrate ongoing and vibrant interactions among birds, insects, and plants in Irish ecosystems. By beginning with a traditional Irish story and then showing only ecological relationships among more-than-humans, *Oisín* contrasts an indigenous Irish culture with the Republic of Ireland as the state shifted toward foreign direct investments throughout the 1960s up until *Oisín* was produced in 1970. *The Pipe* implicitly builds on the opposing environmental perspectives evinced in these two historical films to refuse divisions between premodern or modern ways of life and to reveal multispecies modernities.

Multispecies modernities emerge in how *The Pipe* demonstrates material agencies to transgress the aims of both Shell and the Shell-to-Sea protesters. One such moment occurs after private security forces replace the Gardaí, demonstrating how, as Wenzel puts it, "In the oil complex, companies rival the state in a formal sense because they assume some of its functions."[89] The anonymity of the private security forces allows Shell to continue its work without causing further rifts between local police officers and protesters. The private security officers form a line across the beach to protect the building site as the tide comes in, and many of them laugh as they jump to avoid inevitably wet feet (see fig. 18).[90] Notably, their laughter here is the only time the officers reveal any emotion. Other scenes depict the robotic performance of their duty. Rather than subordinate the officers in hierarchies of humans over more-than-humans, these mechanisms of dehumanization reveal stoic bodies enforcing hierarchies through sterile and unfeeling surveillance programs on and around Shell's building site. The momentary interaction between the security forces and the tide destabilizes Shell's spectral and seemingly inhuman incursion

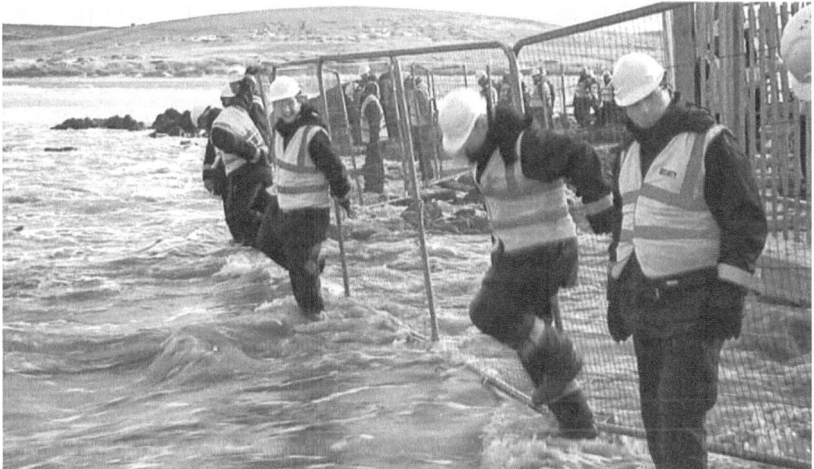

FIG. 18. Officers laugh as the tide permeates Shell's boundary in *The Pipe*. (Courtesy of Risteard Ó Domhnaill)

into the community to expose material agencies, making themselves affectively and viscerally known if only for a moment.

This affective moment in which the tidal waters permeate the line and countenances of security officers indicates how planetary processes like tides exceed the legal, social, and economic systems through which the activists protest and Shell carries out its development projects. Indeed, these planetary processes transcend the seemingly inhuman labor that the security officers do by making them laugh. Although the incoming tide shows that Shell workers are building below the high-water mark, which Monaghan explains is the limit of Shell's legal jurisdiction, the flow of the tide also reveals a physical force that exposes porous boundaries.[91] Shell may appear to be an impenetrable force imposing itself on the community and formally taking over the documentary's cinematic frames, but the film shows the material environment to transgress Shell's apparently impassable boundaries with ease, undermining even the severest expressions of Shell's hired security forces. By revealing environmental systems to transcend social barriers, *The Pipe* indicates material agencies that subtend and constrain local and global relations within the physical limits of planetary systems.

In honoring ongoing relationships to and oralities about land in the Gaeltacht, *The Pipe* shows certain community members to recognize the agencies of material environments. When Shell responds to the protests and letter from the parish priests by rerouting the pipe through the bog, Willie Corduff asserts that "the bog is a technology of its own.... If there's one thing about the bog, you can't trust the bog."[92] Like the tidal and coastal waters, bogs are complex multispecies environments. Colonial projects once associated these mucky and semi-aqueous bogland environments with dirt and wild lands and people supposedly in need of civilization.[93] The idea that the bog is a "technology" indicates rival modernities embedded in such material environments that coalesce around multispecies interactions. The "technology" of the bog has the agency to resist modernization projects by refusing to provide Shell's pipe with stable ground. Willie Corduff's statements also indicate cultural relationships with the bog that have emerged over multiple generations. The film emphasizes the cultural dimensions of these ongoing collaborations with multispecies environments through panning, aerial long shots of a vast bog landscape in which areas of turf have been cut out.[94] The ecological and cultural significance of the bog in Ireland reveals an ongoing history in which, as Derek Gladwin explains, "the micro-geography of bogs is constantly in flux, but the change is too slow for the human eye to observe the constant and intricate rearrangement of textures and colours over time and space."[95] This deep geologic time of the bog indicates spatiotemporalities that exceed visual representation and human historical social systems, even in the significant cultural value of cutting turf in rural Irish subsistence economies. The bog inserts an amorphous environmental agency into *The Pipe* that is both ecological and cultural, thus invoking a both-and rather than a binary logic that subverts gendered depictions of feminized, premodern landscapes. The viewer sees the bog while listening to Willie Corduff's description of it. This montage emphasizes complex interdependencies between bog ecosystems and local human communities, both in the film and in Rossport.

The cinematic emphasis in *The Pipe* on the bog, sea, estuary, and coastline reveals the liminal connections between human and more-than-human communities. An establishing shot of the estuary through which salmon travel to the Glenamoy River each year registers complex environmental systems in which many creatures, including humans, live and work.[96] *The Pipe* presents long shots of green hills and blue water coming in from the sea as Willie Corduff notes "a different type of shellfish."[97] A close-up of the shellfish appears before the film shows Willie Corduff digging through seaweed on the beach as he describes the movements of a crab: "Trying to get away there, see him? He's fast on the move. He knows the direction to go, out into the water, so he does."[98] Although the viewer cannot see where the crab is going during subsequent close-ups, they know from Willie Corduff's description that the crab scurrying between rocks and seaweed is moving toward the sea. Willie Corduff attributes agency and intention to the crab in ways that highlight, to use Colleen Taylor's words, "a complex ecosystem of material networks, relations, and, historically, creative co-survival" under colonial and now neocolonial developments transforming the land and people's relationships to it.[99] These scenes of multispecies environments represent the crab as an agent with intention who "knows" to go out to sea or to grab Willie Corduff's finger "if he gets the chance."[100] The montage of cameos and establishing, aerial, and close-up shots foregrounds liminal spaces in which human and more-than-human communities interact, sometimes unknowingly. Willie Corduff's recognition of the agency of the crab registers the myriad communities and individual actors that go unseen in visual representations. Through *The Pipe*'s montage, the establishing and aerial shots come to demonstrate interrelated multispecies communities across physical spaces of land, coast, and ocean. The close-ups of the shellfish and crab become indexes for all the living beings and the relationships among them in Rossport. *The Pipe* thus revises the viewer's perception and interpretation of picturesque images or romanticized views of rural Irish landscapes by showing such scenes to comprise infinite, unrepresentable multispecies relationships embedded in interconnected human and more-than-human environments.

These multispecies moments in the film expose how colonial and neocolonial representations of feminized premodern or masculinized modern landscapes elide complex interdependencies among humans, more-than-humans, and their material environments. Whether the security guards inadvertently interact with tides or the bog asserts "a technology of its own," *The Pipe* refuses to separate interspecies and agential material dependencies from the continuous interactions and geologic histories in which they dwell. Like *Oisín*, *The Pipe* captures material agencies and multispecies encounters, but it does so by gesturing toward these interactions in everyday human activities. Through the montage of material agencies and planetary forces, *The Pipe* reveals ongoing and inextricable relationships between local human and more-than-human communities in material environments that cannot always be visually represented for an implied, external viewer. While visual representations of modernization may attempt to contain and control material agencies through aesthetic markers of progress, *The Pipe* demonstrates the existence of material agencies and environments that escape visual representation. Scenes of Irish landscapes in the film thus become indexes for multispecies encounters that exceed the camera's frame.

By destabilizing the representational strategies for modernization in the film's initial juxtapositions and then disrupting gendered modernization narratives, *The Pipe* points to multispecies and agential material relations of which the human community is part. The film immerses the viewer in these multispecies modernities through scenes on O'Donnell's fishing boat. For example, the sound of the engine combines with the constant movement of the boat on the ocean's swell. Footage of fishing gear pulling up crabs and lobsters from a tumultuous sea indicates the ecosystems below. O'Donnell asserts that fishing is a relationship he and the men in his family have carried out for generations: "I have a right to be here. This is where I've been all my life."[101] Indeed, the film regularly shows O'Donnell's son working in the fisheries.[102] *The Pipe* reframes this relationship between fathers and sons to the sea by subordinating the masculine-inflected fishing industry to the interwoven fates of the human and more-than-human communities. Such a move builds on the work of previous documentary makers, as Ó Domhnaill implicitly, to use Erika Balsom's words on John Grierson's 1929 *Drifters*, "advances a structural understanding of fishing as a network of human and nonhuman agents within which any individual worker is just one small part."[103] Yet Ó Domhnaill shows how human and more-than-human relationships resist and undergo processes of modernization across colonial and neocolonial histories. The history of modernization in Ireland has strategically relied on the idea of relinquishing past traditional industries in favor of modern technologies that supposedly ensure more prosperous economic futures. Through refusing persistent colonial-era bifurcations of tradition and modernity in the numerous scenes on O'Donnell's boat, *The Pipe* reveals the human community's complex position within obscured ecosystems and extraction economies. In doing so, Ó Domhnaill's place-based filmmaking strategies reclaim oppositional premodern-modern visual representations to honor Gaeltacht oralities that are an integral part of modernizing traditions and multispecies modernities.

The Pipe foregrounds the interwoven fates of culture, language, and environment through the movement of the boat. The ocean swell constantly rolls the camera's gaze, thereby confronting the viewer with the physical forces of the ocean that refuse a stable position or complete view (see fig. 19).[104] Although such partial views are perhaps inevitable when the camera is situated on O'Donnell's boat, their prominence in the film demonstrates, to use Alaimo's words, how "oceanic depths, especially, resist the sort of flat mapping of the globe that assumes a 'God's-eye view.'"[105] The rolling scenes and ongoing sounds of the diesel engine destabilize understandings of a fixed place or time. The soundscape of the motor and camera's movement upon the waves reveal fluid and shifting waters that are metaphorically and literally, to quote Alaimo, "immersed in highly mediated environments that suggest the entanglements of knowledge, science, economics, and power."[106] By tracing the boat's motions and sounds, the film shows the human community's dependence upon the fossil fuel economies they protest and the material agencies and more-than-human interlocutors with whom they interact every day.

The Pipe thus refuses clear categories of complicity, culpability, and resistance in formations of citizens, consumers, and material and social surroundings. Such categories, as Wenzel puts it, "create the conditions for meaningful choice" in a "hydrocarbon modernity."[107] By rejecting and reworking these categories, The Pipe foregrounds otherwise obscured multispecies modernities. Like scenes of the bog, the scenes from O'Donnell's boat show material agencies and more-than-human communities to

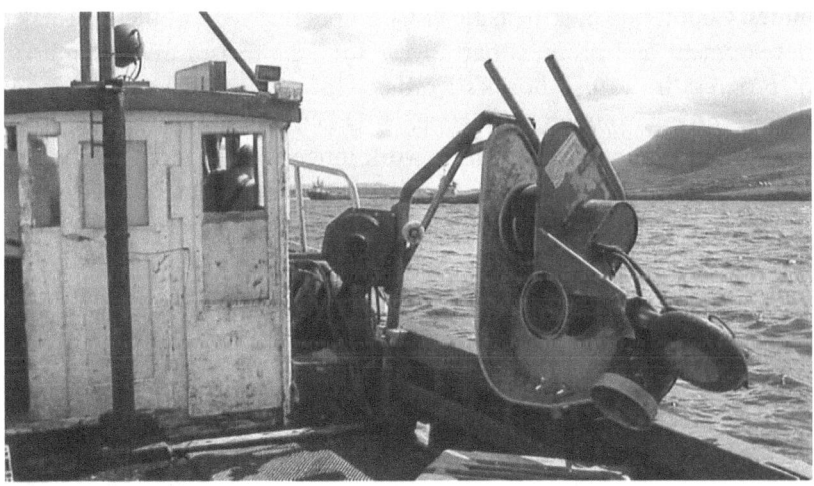

FIG. 19. Partial views register the limits of visual representations in The Pipe. (Courtesy of Risteard Ó Domhnaill)

surround and at times overwhelm the human community in Rossport and Shell's modernization projects. More-than-human actors in the film resist both erasure and visual representation to demonstrate the existence of dynamic multispecies modernities.

Conclusion: The Postcolonial Multispecies Modernities of Documentary Film

The Pipe concludes with another panning aerial shot of the bog, a space often invoked in Irish cultural and economic production and that plays an important role in Ireland's ecology and natural carbon sequestration. By the end of the film, the bog indicates rival narratives of modernity as they unfold across multispecies relationships among humans, more-than-humans, material environments, and the ongoing environmental impacts of empire. Through invoking and destabilizing visual representations of imperial-era development projects and romanticized Irish landscapes, *The Pipe* refuses gendered binaries in depictions of supposedly masculine, modernized regions and premodern, feminized empty spaces. Such binaries facilitated British colonial expansion into Ireland and continue to facilitate multinational neocolonial LNG development projects in the postcolonial nation.

Forms of modernization threaten to repeat and more deeply entrench colonial narratives of development through neocolonial economic regimes. Countering the cinematic visual tropes that support these forms of development and progress narratives, *The Pipe* revises understandings of progress in, to use Bozak's words, "video harnessed as a political, social, and environmental practice."[108] Ó Domhnaill's cinematography, sounds, and montage critically rework longer imperial cinematic histories to resist the erasure of women's activism and multispecies modernities. Heeding the multispecies modernities in *The Pipe* ultimately reveals continuously unfolding relationships through which humans and more-than-humans fluidly, collaboratively, and sometimes unknowingly interact to constitute our interwoven fates.

CONCLUSION
NEW DIRECTIONS FOR MULTIPLE MODERNITIES

IN RESPONSE to controversies about how to commemorate the centenaries of events leading to Ireland's partial independence and the partition of Northern Ireland in 1922, the Republic of Ireland's president, Michael D. Higgins, called in 2021 for a "journey of ethical remembering" that accounts for how "class, gender, religion, democracy, language, culture and violence all played important roles, and all were intertwined with British imperialist rule in Ireland."[1] Higgins asserts that Irish people should grapple with the complexity of ongoing histories of colonialism and the hierarchies of social difference to which such histories have given rise even as the Republic of Ireland consolidates its position in the European Union (EU) in the aftermath of Brexit. Yet such a reckoning with the colonial past and its impact on the present brings into sharp relief the environmental impacts of empire that persist in the Republic of Ireland's attempts to transcend its colonial past through development projects. Since the 1960s, the Republic has invited foreign direct investment (FDI) into the country, privatized national resources, offered multi-billion-dollar tax breaks to multinationals like Apple, Meta, Google, and Pfizer, and established immigration policies protecting those of Irish descent that mimic the British patrials acts, a series of laws that institutionalize antiblackness in immigration policy in the UK and that contributed to the Windrush scandal beginning in 2018. The Republic of Ireland strives politically to benefit from Western constructions of whiteness and media technologies that exacerbate the environmental impacts of empire and complicate its position as a postcolonial nation. These ambitions obscure potential solidarities and coalitions for resisting neocolonial extraction economies, especially as economic growth and surplus budgets resulting from corporate tax incentives fail to ameliorate the socioeconomic inequalities exacerbated during the Celtic Tiger.[2] Indeed, the austerity measures imposed by the Eurogroup, European Central Bank, and the

International Monetary Fund in 2008 make it unclear who benefits and who bears the burdens of the Republic's policies to modernize into a seemingly developed Western but subordinate postcolonial nation.

After more than a century of partition and postcolonial nationhood, Ireland's neocolonial modernity and the environmental impacts of empire on human and more-than-human communities and their relationships with material environments raise questions about how dominant progress narratives across a range of media in postcolonial contexts impede alternative forms of development. *Irish Ecomedia* explores these questions and highlights ongoing interactions among humans, more-than-humans, and their surroundings that attest to the existence and resilience of multiple modernities that promise more socially and environmentally just futures than those dictated by colonial and neocolonial power relations. The competing understandings of modernity and modernizing traditions represented in the visual, aural, and textual media I analyze in this book show an ongoing interplay among form, content, medium, and material and multispecies environments. Documentary photography and film, as well as the shifting role of print in Irish presses and oral traditions on radio and in recordings and protest movements, materially and semantically demonstrate the diverse ways people and places engage in multiple multispecies modernities every day. *Irish Ecomedia* consequently disrupts logics of development that persist in the Irish context and in postcolonial communities globally that emulate Ireland's forms of environmental and economic development. In doing so, this book shows the mechanisms and media that give rise to the uneven distribution of rights and resources across geopolitical hierarchies between and within nation states in a neocolonial modernity. My analyses foreground agencies and modes of resistance that imagine alternative and more just relationships among humans, more-than-humans, and material environments.

Colonial and neocolonial logics remain in understandings of progress and the transformation of supposedly premodern traditions into a rationalized future modernity. What looked decidedly modern in the CDB photographic archive was subsequently framed as traditional by the national media and policy makers during the Shell-to-Sea environmental justice struggle. Contradictions like this emerge in the mid-twentieth century as Seán Ó Riada describes innovative traditions on national radio that offer alternative forms of development to those rapidly expanding across Ireland in the 1960s. The economic policies before and after Ó Riada's *Our Musical Heritage* create social and cultural conditions to which Flann O'Brien's *The Third Policeman* and Éilís Ní Dhuibhne's *The Bray House* each respond. Free-State land reforms during the economic wars of the 1930s perpetuated imperial-era understandings of an extractive modernity in independent Ireland, as I show O'Brien's *The Third Policeman* to satirize. Extraction economies memorialize what they destroy and impose an idealized poverty on Irish-speaking communities through picturesque aesthetics, consequently encouraging emigration, often to settler-colonies around the world, thereby perpetuating empire. O'Brien's text points to alternative modernities embedded in Irish-language aesthetic and literary forms that assert more relational productions of meaning through ongoing interactions among the writer, reader, text, and material and cultural contexts. While these forms emerge as a postmodern disintegration between reality and representation, Ní Dhuibhne illustrates resilient cultural media and an Irish environmental consciousness continuing to exist and flourish in the land even in the face of nuclear apocalypse. Relational interactions and remediations among environment, media, and multiple modernities reveal the unfolding of dynamic Irish traditions that frame an Irish environmental consciousness and point to multiple overlooked modernities. This consciousness emerges in O'Brien, continues in Ó Riada's radio programs, and becomes a focal theme of *The Bray House*. In Ní Dhuibhne's dystopian future, late twentieth-century economic policies establish neocolonial regimes that perpetuate ideas of development that sacrifice particular peoples and places in the name of progress. The novel imagines the island of Ireland and Irish people as a sacrifice zone of European economic integration and energy development as it parodically critiques the reduction of the Troubles to colonial stereotypes of atavism. Yet the text demonstrates persisting cultural and material resources embedded in Irish folk traditions and the Irish landscape.

By reworking and refusing the gendered tradition-modern binary at distinct moments of modernization across the twentieth century, each of my chapters demonstrates multiple modernities that promise more just and lasting futures than those based on colonial forms of development. These multiple modernities emerge in and through old and new media and narrative forms across the twentieth century. For instance, the documentary photography that was relatively new to rural Ireland in the early twentieth century is echoed by Risteard Ó Domhnaill's in medias res grassroots documentary. While documentary film was not new to rural Ireland, the Irish film industry only expanded in the 1980s after the establishment of the Irish Film Board in 1981. Ó Domhnaill draws on this relatively new medium for self-representation in rural Ireland to demonstrate the historical limitations of gendered visual representations of modernization. This depiction contrasts with the portrayal by the national media and Shell PR crews of the struggle within the imperial logics of a seemingly traditional people resisting modernization. Instead, *The Pipe* offers montages that represent community struggle as well as the community's relationship to material agencies and more-than-human communities, thereby evincing the ongoing existence of multispecies modernities throughout multiple state-sanctioned modernization projects.

This use of relatively new media to rework imperial logics and assert the existence of multiple multispecies modernities challenges narrative forms and publishing and broadcast institutions in Ireland, as well as in the imperial centers of Britain and the United States, at different moments of the twentieth century. Ó Riada's description of oral traditions in Irish-speaking communities on national radio reminds the listener of the innovative potential of traditional forms of knowledge and oral cultures. Formal elements in traditional music and song contrast with more linear forms of development elsewhere in Europe. The publication of *The Bray House* by the feminist Attic Press indicates how marginalized groups like Irish women were organizing to rework understandings of Irish writing around the same time Dolmen Press published a revised version of *Our Musical Heritage*, which drew more on fixed understandings of tradition that Ó Riada's original program implicitly resisted. Although Dolmen Press historically sought to create a platform for Irish writers in an anglophone publishing world dominated by presses in the United States and Britain, the emergence of Attic Press in 1978 demonstrates the need for a broader conception of Irish writing and writers—namely, by recognizing and publishing more women writers. Such shifting understandings of Irish writing continue today with the establishment of Skein Press in 2017, which promotes the writing of marginalized groups in Ireland, including migrant and diaspora writers and indigenous ethnic minorities, such as Irish Travellers (Mincéirí/Pavee).

By tracing aesthetic trends across different media through different moments of modernization in Ireland, *Irish Ecomedia* demonstrates a multimodal practice of reading interconnections among media, history, and power that opens the possibilities for researching the ongoing environmental impacts of empire on expanding digital cultures as well as understandings of migration, belonging, and identity. *Irish Ecomedia* thus lays the foundation for further inquiries into how connections among media, colonialism, and the environment inform racial formations in Ireland after the Good Friday Agreement and the Celtic Tiger, as well as in Europe more generally. Uneven forms of colonial development sustain neocolonial economic modernity and continue to encourage migration to urban and imperial centers and emigration out of Ireland, even as immigration into Ireland increases. Tensions between immigration and emigration arise in Ireland to establish what Ronit Lentin theorizes as "the return of Ireland's repressed experience of e/migration."[3] Families severed by various forms of forced emigration historically must grapple with intergenerational trauma as neocolonial regimes and histories of colonial development encourage immigration into the Global North amid ongoing emigration out of Ireland. Uneven forms of development draw people from various postcolonial countries, including Ireland, to the British imperial center in what Doreen Massey describes as "a perverse subsidy, flowing from poor to rich" in neocolonial modernity.[4] These tensions and traumas around migration in Ireland rework constructions of Irishness within understandings of whiteness that emulate racial formations in Britain and the United States. As Steven Loyal explains: "National self-understanding, although an ambiguous and contested political process, no longer used Britain primarily as its negative foil of reference, especially after the Belfast Agreement. In the new socioeconomic context of the Celtic Tiger, black asylum-seekers became the negative markers of difference."[5] These black-white binaries come into sharp relief in the campaign leading up to, and in the overwhelming support of Irish voters for, the Citizenship Referendum of 2004.

Immigration reforms and racial formations in post-Celtic Tiger Ireland offer an uncomfortable echo of post-Windrush British racial formations, as well as broader understandings of belonging and indigeneity in Europe. Strategic understandings of British and European whiteness promote anti-Black immigration policies while continuing to discriminate against phenotypically white or white-presenting ethnicities in ways that lead to premature death.[6] Such racial formations construct whiteness to conceal difference through a "myth of homogeneity," but, as Bronwen Walter argues, "the failure to acknowledge difference does not mean that 'othering' has disappeared. Indeed there are strong continuities in reworked forms with denial of difference."[7] Twenty-first-century Irish national identity assumes whiteness among diverse and often oppressed populations to perpetuate broader Western forms of antiblackness, even among many white-presenting marginalized groups. Notably, eastern European workers, often from Poland or Romania, as well as the indigenous ethnic minority, the Irish Travellers (Mincéirí/Pavee), experience social and economic marginalization that mirrors "myth[s] of homogeneity." *Irish Ecomedia* establishes frameworks through which scholars can attend to these insidious environmental impacts of empire in modernization, conceptions of modernity, and changing media landscapes to better understand how power strategically adapts across competing histories and modernities to occlude assertions of agency and self-determination among gendered, classed, racialized, and ethnically marginalized populations.

The environmental impacts of empire exacerbate social inequalities as they expose the connections between colonial logics of development of the nineteenth and twentieth centuries and contemporary racial formations. Constructions of property ownership in understandings of civilization during the nineteenth century naturalized how, as Jim MacLaughlin puts it, "sedentary peoples, particularly those in the more powerful nation-states of Europe, had first claim on the world's resources because their approach to environmental management was superior to the environmental practices of nomadic peoples and pre-capitalist societies."[8] Colonial hierarchies were based on people's relationships to their material surroundings, and as Robert Young reminds us: "The culture of land has always been, in fact, the primary form of colonization; the focus on soil emphasizes the physicality of the territory that is coveted, occupied, cultivated, turned into plantations and made unsuitable for indigenous nomadic tribes."[9] This focus on land occupation and ownership compounds with the environmental impacts of empire in the twenty-first century as seemingly ephemeral but in fact very material digital infrastructures expand to rapaciously consume data, mined materials, water, and energy in a supposedly more interconnected world, giving rise to the conditions Zygmunt Bauman theorizes as "liquid modernity," which is characterized, in part, by "the compulsive and obsessive, continuous, unstoppable, forever incomplete *modernization*."[10] Although modernization narratives appear to work toward a future modernity, they never, in fact, resolve. As my analyses have shown, modernization narratives continually reframe space and time to maintain colonial and neocolonial hierarchies and build on the environmental impacts of empire.

As nations in the Global North attempt to sustain current lifestyles after crossing numerous planetary boundaries, expanding digital infrastructure and green-energy initiatives in Western nations rely on ongoing neocolonial extraction economies, as numerous scholars have shown (e.g., Siobhan Angus, Patrick Brodie, Jennifer Holt and Patrick Vonderau, Richard Maxwell and Toby Miller, Jussi Parikka, Nicole Starosielski, among others). To use the words of Brodie, "Environmentally just development goals will not be achieved equitably under the infrastructural regimes of datafied accumulation, and in some cases, communities are being turned into digital sacrifice zones through the expansion of extractive data infrastructure into new and already historically marginalized territories."[11] Colonial logics persist in the Republic of Ireland's push to be a center of big tech, which Denis O'Hearn traces back to the sixteenth century.[12] This push, Brodie shows, continues to marginalize rural Irish communities where local windfarms or other forms of energy are offered at a discount to multinationals in Dublin, who own and control the data centers and cabling in Ireland.[13] Indeed, the broader justifications for these expanding industries remain consistent across Ireland's colonial past and globalized neocolonial present, which Patrick Bresnihan and Patrick Brodie theorize as "Ireland's postcolonial ecological regime," writing: "This extractive logic is a decisive thread linking colonial and postcolonial relations to the rural, in Ireland, and elsewhere."[14] They go on to explain that "across its colonial and postcolonial histories, Ireland has acted as a sacrificial, experimental site for particular kinds of capitalist activity, in ways that arguably extend today through the forms of investment operating here [in Ireland]."[15] Consequently, the apparent newness of digital media and green energy industries builds on the environmental impacts of empire to exacerbate inequalities and environmental injustices within the Global North and between the Global North and South.

Understanding how people draw on the materiality of media and narrative forms to assert multiple multispecies modernities and resist the historical flattening of colonization into binary logics of before and after, undeveloped and developed, and premodern and modern is essential to analyses of how digitalization, the green energy transition, and citizenship laws increasingly perpetuate environmental injustices across the uneven distribution of wealth in the twenty-first century. Colonial conceptions of modernity continue to marginalize ongoing interactions among diverse peoples, ecosystems, and material agencies in varied environments. Uneven distributions of rights and resources stem from colonial development and endure in neocolonial regimes that fortify national borders throughout the West, often tapping into advancing digital technologies to surveil and control those borders.

In tracing multiple and multispecies modernities across the environmental impacts of empire in twentieth-century Ireland, *Irish Ecomedia* broadens theories of power and difference in postcolonial ecocriticism, ecomedia studies, and Irish studies to honor and amplify alternative forms of modernization that embody more just human, more-than-human, and material relationships. The processes through which the human and more-than-human relations in multiple modernities engage with dynamic cultural and material environments of Ireland offer new ways of thinking about environmental justice in Europe, expanding media landscapes, and postcolonial contexts. These processes situate current questions of migration and digital infrastructure in the EU as environmental justice issues, and they help to theorize the connections among resource extraction, development projects, and globalized migration patterns. The environmental and colonial history on the island of Ireland provides unique insight into how colonial logics of development persist and continue to shape what scholars perceive as nation, progress, migration, and identity today. Examining the multiple multispecies modernities and processes of remediation across the twentieth century in Ireland thus establishes an important case study of what Byron Caminero-Santangelo calls postcolonial regional particularism, which "emphasi[zes] regional alterity that cannot be subsumed by a more universal imperial or postcolonial condition . . . [while] still challeng[ing] imperial discourse's suppression of global entanglement in the representation of difference."[16] Cultural representations of modernization in twentieth-century Ireland demonstrate ongoing local and global relations across complex constellations of colonial and neocolonial power. *Irish Ecomedia* traces the aesthetics of modernity across media in narrative forms that seek to justify these flows in ongoing transimperial histories. In doing so, this book elucidates multiple modernities emerging alongside state-sanctioned views of progress and place. These multiple modernities demonstrate alternative forms of development that nuance how scholars theorize race, gender, and class in studies of environment across increasingly digitized expressions of place, belonging, migration, and indigeneity, which are foundational to many studies of literature, environment, postcolonial nation formation, and Irish history and culture.

By revising and expanding the geographical and historical methodologies in postcolonial ecocriticism, ecomedia studies, and Irish studies, *Irish Ecomedia* offers tools through which to examine the multiple modernities and remediations in an era of climate migration fractured across increasingly digital media networks. *Irish Ecomedia* thus implicitly responds to the question Elizabeth DeLoughrey poses: "What kinds of narratives help us navigate an ecological crisis that is understood as local and planetary, as historical and anticipatory?"[17] Irish cultural production across the twentieth and early twenty-first centuries demonstrates multiple narrative forms, media, experiences, and ways of life that people and communities remediated and reworked to resist coerced forms of development. These agencies and modes of resistance "help us navigate an ecological crisis that is understood as local and planetary, historical and anticipatory" by demonstrating the social and cultural formations through which multiple multispecies modernities emerge, innovate, and modernize in alternative ways of being. Drawing Ireland into broader postcolonial ecocritical and ecomedia studies conversations about environmental crisis and persisting constellations of colonial and neocolonial power deepens and expands scholarly understandings of modernity, agency, and difference in postcolonial nations and regional experiences. In expanding these understandings, *Irish Ecomedia* reframes histories of land, media, and environment to foreground multispecies relationships across interrelated pasts, presents, and futures. Ireland and the rest of Europe face uncertain futures as multiple planetary boundaries are transgressed and as the effects of the climate crisis intensify. By critically examining the ongoing environmental impacts of empire and their legacy in neocolonial economic regimes and environmental injustices across emerging media of the twentieth century, this book reveals multiple multispecies modernities embedded in the materialities of media, land, and human and more-than-human relationships. These multiple multispecies modernities invite scholars to reconsider the hegemonic forms of development that structure human and more-than-human relationships to each other and to the material world in a neocolonial modernity. Such reconsiderations offer more decolonial and environmentally just ways of envisioning and inhabiting multiple modernities in increasingly uncertain times.

NOTES

Acknowledgments

1. Katherine M. Huber, "The View from Mrs. Kelly's Window: Reframing Agency and Land in the Congested Districts Board Photographs," *Éire-Ireland* 55, nos. 3–4 (Fall–Winter 2020): 95–128; Katherine M. Huber, "'The bog is a technology of its own': Rupturing the Logic of Natural Resource Development in Risteard Ó Domhnaill's *The Pipe*," *ISLE: Interdisciplinary Studies in Literature and Environment* 31, no. 1 (Spring 2024): 176–99.

Introduction

1. I use the term "more-than-human" rather than "nonhuman" in an effort to resist the binary logics this book examines and critiques, as well as to avoid implicitly centering the human through its negation. The term "more-than-human" was coined by David Abram in the 1990s, and he notes that the term "is to remind us of our embedment in an earthly cosmos that we humans did not create, that we do not control, and that necessarily exceeds all our knowing." Madina Tlostanova notes that this concept also stems from Erin Manning's essay "Another Regard," in which, in Tlostanova's words, "the human is no longer the starting point for meaning formation or even any meaningful experience." Both scholars note that concepts of relational life and material agencies have existed in Indigenous cosmologies long before the term "more-than-human." By using the term, I seek to emphasize the embeddedness of humans within larger Earth systems and ongoing relations among agential beings that collectively enable human existence. See David Abram, "On the Origin of the Phrase 'More-than-Human,'" in *More than Human Rights: An Ecology of Law, Thought, and Narrative for Earthly Flourishing*, ed. César Rodríguez-Garavito (NYU Law, 2024), 347; and Madina Tlostanova, "Transcending the Human/Non-Human Divide: The Geo-politics and Body-politics of Being and Perception, and Decolonial Art," *Journal of Theoretical Humanities* 22, no. 2 (2017): 31.
2. Lorna Siggins, *Once upon a Time in the West: The Corrib Gas Controversy* (Transworld Ireland, 2010), 45, 65, 173.
3. Liam Leonard, *The Environmental Movement in Ireland* (Springer Science, 2008), 193.

4. This book's use of the term "indigenous" reflects how the meaning of this word has changed over time. I use a capital letter for peoples, political movements, and cultural practices officially recognized as Indigenous according to the UN Convention on the Rights of Indigenous Peoples, and a lowercase letter for traditions and cultural practices that are oppressed by colonial and neocolonial regimes. My use of the term "Indigenous" recognizes and seeks to honor the lifeways, histories, and political identities of First Nations, Native, Aboriginal, and other Indigenous peoples. In the context of Ireland, my use of the term "indigenous" acknowledges the dispossession, disenfranchisement, and dislocation of both itinerant and settled populations who called the island of Ireland home before 1169, when colonialism in Ireland began, and particularly before the Tudor era beginning in the late fifteenth century when colonialism intensified to oppress and attempted to eradicate Irish oral traditions, language, and cultural practices. In chapter 3, I discuss twentieth-century formations of indigeneity that did not come to include Irish populations. In chapter 4, I use Indigenous feminist theory to consider longer cultural and environmental practices in Ireland.
5. James Ferguson, *Global Shadows: Africa in the Neoliberal World Order* (Duke University Press, 2006), 37–38.
6. Shell-to-Sea activism shifted over time, leading to the splinter groups Pobal Chill Chomáin and Pobal Le Chéile, and environmentalists from across Europe also formed the Rossport Solidarity Camp. For a thorough overview of the campaign, see Siggins, *Once upon a Time*.
7. Joseph Lennon, *Irish Orientalism: A Literary and Intellectual History* (Syracuse University Press, 2004), 40, 50.
8. Graham Huggan and Helen Tiffin, *Postcolonial Ecocriticism: Literature, Animals, Environment* (Routledge, 2010), 27.
9. David Lambert and Alan Lester, "Introduction: Imperial Spaces, Imperial Subjects," in *Colonial Lives Across the British Empire: Imperial Careering in the Long Nineteenth Century*, ed. David Lambert and Alan Lester (Cambridge University Press, 2006), 13.
10. Lambert and Lester, "Introduction," 8.
11. For the rationale on why I capitalize "Black" and not "blackness," see Michael J. Dumas, "Against the Dark: Antiblackness in Education Policy and Discourse," *Theory into Practice* 55, no. 1 (2016): 12–13.
12. Elizabeth DeLoughrey, *Allegories of the Anthropocene* (Duke University Press, 2019), 7.
13. Rob Nixon, *Slow Violence and the Environmentalism of the Poor* (Harvard University Press, 2011), 15, 42, 279–80; Jennifer Wenzel, *The Disposition of Nature: Environmental Crisis and World Literature* (Fordham University Press, 2019), 12.

14. Wenzel, *Disposition of Nature*, 42, emphasis in original.
15. Byron Caminero-Santangelo, *Different Shades of Green: African Literature, Environmental Justice, and Political Ecology* (University of Virginia Press, 2014), 29–30.
16. Denis O'Hearn, *The Atlantic Economy: Britain, the US, and Ireland* (Manchester University Press, 2001), 112, 126–27, emphasis in original.
17. Robert Allen, *No Global: The People of Ireland Versus the Multinationals* (Pluto, 2004), 3–4.
18. Luke W. Cole and Sheila R. Foster, *From the Ground Up: Environmental Racism and the Rise of the Environmental Justice Movement* (New York University Press, 2001), 105.
19. Allen, *No Global*.
20. Julian Agyeman, Robert D. Bullard, and Bob Evans, "Introduction: Joined-up Thinking: Bringing Together Sustainability, Environmental Justice and Equity," in *Just Sustainabilities: Development in an Unequal World*, edited by Julian Agyeman, Robert D. Bullard, and Bob Evans (MIT Press, 2003), 10; Nerea Calvillo, *Aeropolis: Queering Air in Toxicpolluted Worlds* (Columbia Books, 2023), 127.
21. See, for example, the work of Sjerp de Vries, Florence Van Durme, Damilola S. Olawuyi, Richard Filčák, and Bianka Plüschke-Altof and Helen Sooväli-Sepping, among others.
22. Patrick Brodie, "Climate Extraction and Supply Chains of Data," *Media, Culture & Society* 42, nos. 7–8 (2020): 1099; Patrick Brodie, "Data Infrastructure Studies on an Unequal Planet," *Big Data & Society* 10, no. 1 (2023): 4–5.
23. Cajetan Iheka, *African Ecomedia: Network Forms, Planetary Politics* (Duke University Press, 2021), 28.
24. Iheka, *African Ecomedia*, 10, 225; Jussi Parikka, *A Geology of Media* (University of Minnesota Press, 2015), 61; Nadia Bozak, *The Cinematic Footprint: Light, Camera, Natural Resources* (Rutgers University Press, 2011), 199, 194.
25. DeLoughrey, *Allegories of the Anthropocene*, 105.
26. Sandra Harding, *Sciences from Below: Feminisms, Postcolonialities, and Modernities* (Duke University Press, 2008), 202–3.
27. Research on longer histories of Irish communities of color is expanding. See, for example, Conrad Koza Bryan and Chamion Caballero, *Irish People of Colour: A Social History of Mixed Race Irish in Britain and Ireland Between 1700 and 2000* (Association of Mixed Race Irish, 2024).
28. Clifford Siskin, "Textual Culture and the History of the Real," *Textual Cultures* 2, no. 2 (Autumn 2007): 125–26, emphasis in original.
29. Jay David Bolter and Richard Grusin, *Remediation: Understanding New Media* (MIT Press, 1999), 15.

30. Frederick H. A. Aalen, "Constructive Unionism and the Shaping of Rural Ireland, c. 1880–1921," *Rural History* 4, no. 2 (1993): 140–41; Thomas Bartlett, *Ireland, A History* (Cambridge University Press, 2010), 359.
31. Ciara Breathnach, *The Congested Districts Board of Ireland, 1891–1923: Poverty and Development in the West of Ireland* (Four Courts, 2005) 11, 16–17.
32. Bolter and Grusin, *Remediation*, 15.
33. For a definition of sacrifice zone, see Steve Lerner, *Sacrifice Zones: The Front Lines of Toxic Chemical Exposure in the United States* (MIT Press, 2010), 2.

1. 1891–1922

1. Robert John Welch, "View of Cappagh Village, Castlerea District, Co. Galway," ca. 1906–1914, CDB19, in Congested Districts Board Photograph Collection, National Library of Ireland, National Photographic Archive, Dublin (hereafter CDB and call number).
2. Mieke Bal, *Narratology: Introduction to the Theory of Narrative*, 2nd ed. (University of Toronto Press, 1997), 163.
3. Welch, "View of Cappagh Village," CDB19.
4. Jennifer Green-Lewis, *Framing the Victorians: Photography and the Culture of Realism* (Cornell University Press, 1996), 25, 223.
5. Green-Lewis, *Framing the Victorians*, 4.
6. Breathnach, *Congested Districts Board*, 11, 17, 45; Ciara Breathnach, "Smallholder Housing," 191–95.
7. Breathnach, *Congested Districts Board*, 11.
8. Green-Lewis, *Framing the Victorians*, 94.
9. Siobhan Angus, *Camera Geologica: An Elemental History of Photography* (Duke University Press, 2024), 77–78, 115, 153; Michael Langford, *The Story of Photography* (Focal, 1980), 50–51.
10. Sarah Rouse, *Into the Light: An Illustrated Guide to the Photographic Collections in the National Library of Ireland* (National Library of Ireland, 1998), 19.
11. Gail Baylis, "Technologies and Cultures: Robert J. Welch's Western Landscapes, 1895–1914," in *Framing the West: Images of Rural Ireland, 1891–1920*, ed. Ciara Breathnach (Irish Academic Press, 2007), 86.
12. Justin Carville, "Picturing Poverty: Colonial Photography and the Congested Districts Board," in *Framing the West: Images of Rural Ireland, 1891–1920*, ed. Ciara Breathnach (Irish Academic Press, 2007), 98–99, 107.
13. Bal, *Narratology*, 162.
14. Doreen Massey, *For Space* (Sage, 2005), 24.

15. Robert John Welch, "House on Cloonmore Grass Farm near Tuam, Co. Galway," CDB15, CDB16.
16. See, for example, Robert John Welch, "John Burke's Improved House in Levally, Co. Mayo," CDB40; and Robert John Welch, "New House of John Commons, farmer and tailor, Ryehill, Monivea, Co. Galway," CDB10. Women generally only appear in agricultural and housing photographs of regions that have yet to be modernized—for example, Robert John Welch, "Cottage of Martin Greavy, Ballintubber, Co. Mayo," CDB28; Congested Districts Board, "Members of the Congested Districts Board Receiving Directions from a Local Woman," CDB95; and Congested Districts Board, "Two Women Washing Clothes Outside a Stone Cottage, Bridge Visible in Background," CDB113.
17. Ciara Breathnach, "The Role of Women in the Economy of the West of Ireland, 1891–1923," *New Hibernia Review / Iris Éireannach Nua* 8, no. 1 (2004): 82; David M. Smith, "'I Thought I Was Landed!': The Congested Districts Board and the Women of Western Ireland." *Éire-Ireland* 31, nos. 3–4 (1996): 210.
18. Breathnach, "Role of Women," 80, 82, 85; Breathnach, *Congested Districts Board*, 49, 55, 72.
19. Colleen Taylor, *Irish Materialisms: The Nonhuman and the Making of Colonial Ireland, 1690–1830* (Oxford University Press, 2024), 75, 79.
20. Donna Potts, *Contemporary Irish Writing and Environmentalism: The Wearing of the Deep Green* (Palgrave Macmillan, 2018), xxxvi, 174.
21. Anne McClintock, *Imperial Leather: Race, Gender, and Sexuality in the Colonial Contest* (Routledge, 1995), 249.
22. Bliss Cua Lim, *Translating Time: Cinema, the Fantastic, and Temporal Critique* (Duke University Press, 2009), 181.
23. Breathnach, *Congested Districts Board*, 31; Aalen, "Constructive Unionism," 140–41; P. J. Mathews, *Revival: The Abbey Theatre, Sinn Féin, the Gaelic League, and the Co-operative Movement* (University of Notre Dame with Field Day, 2003), 7.
24. Smith, "'I Thought I Was Landed!,'" 222.
25. Ciara Breathnach, "Lady Dudley's District Nursing Scheme and the Congested Districts Board, 1903–1923," in *Gender and Medicine in Ireland, 1700–1950*, ed. Margaret Preston and Margaret Ó hÓgartaigh (Syracuse University Press, 2012), 143. Besides the nursing schemes, the CDB collaborated with other initiatives in the west of Ireland, including cooperative programs overseen by the Irish Agricultural Organizational Society (IAOS) and the Department of Agricultural and Technical Instruction (DATI). See Breathnach, *Congested Districts Board*, 142–43; and Patrick Doyle, *Civilising Rural Ireland: The Co-operative Movement, Development and Nation-State, 1889–1939* (Manchester University Press, 2019), 76, 110.

26. Breathnach, "Lady Dudley's District Nursing Scheme," 147.
27. Congested Districts Board, "Lord and Lady Aberdeen with Nurse, Outside House at Geesala, Ballina, Co. Mayo," CDB56. Several photographs in the CDB's collection show nurses presenting class and gender roles for women in rural Ireland. See, for example, Congested Districts Board, "Nurse Talking to Old Woman Holding Turf Basket, Outside Cottage," CDB88; and Congested Districts Board, "Nurse Visiting a Family, Arranmore, Co. Donegal," CDB55.
28. Margaret Ó Hógartaigh, "Nurses and Teachers in the West of Ireland in the Late Nineteenth and Early Twentieth Centuries," in *Framing the West: Images of Rural Ireland, 1891–1920,* ed. Ciara Breathnach (Irish Academic Press, 2007), 204.
29. Breathnach, "Lady Dudley's District Nursing Scheme," 147.
30. Breathnach, 148.
31. Val McLeish, "Sunshine and Sorrows: Canada, Ireland, and Lady Aberdeen," in *Colonial Lives Across the British Empire: Imperial Careering in the Long Nineteenth Century,* ed. David Lambert and Alan Lester (Cambridge University Press, 2006), 265.
32. McLeish, "Sunshine and Sorrows," 272–73, 275.
33. Breathnach, *Congested Districts Board,* 127.
34. For more information on the role of nurses in the congested districts, see Breathnach, "Lady Dudley's District Nursing Scheme."
35. Gregory Castle, *Modernism and the Celtic Revival* (Cambridge University Press, 2001), 6.
36. Huggan and Tiffin, *Postcolonial Ecocriticism,* 82.
37. Anthony Bradley, *Imagining Ireland in the Poems and Plays of W. B. Yeats: Nation, Class, and State* (Palgrave Macmillan, 2011), 69.
38. Robert John Welch, "Two New Holdings in Cloonkeen, Castlebar, Co. Mayo," CDB23.
39. Aalen, "Constructive Unionism," 147.
40. Sarah Smyth, "Tuke's Connemara Album," in *Framing the West: Images of Rural Ireland, 1891–1920,* ed. Ciara Breathnach (Irish Academic Press, 2007), 30, 34; Breathnach, *Congested Districts Board,* 129.
41. Breathnach, 22.
42. Breathnach, 168.
43. S. Smyth, "Tuke's Connemara Album," 29.
44. S. Smyth, 38–39.
45. S. Smyth, 38, 41–42; Breathnach, *Congested Districts Board,* 21–22.
46. Breathnach, 30–31, 138; S. Smyth, 44; Seán Beattie, *Donegal in Transition: The Impact of the Congested Districts Board,* (Merrion Press of the Irish Academic Press, 2013), 32.

NOTES TO PAGES 39-45   235

47. Breathnach, *Congested Districts Board*, 30-31.
48. Breathnach, 138.
49. David Lloyd, *Irish Times: Temporalities of Modernity* (Keough-Naughton Institute for Irish Studies, University of Notre Dame/Field Day, 2008), 40.
50. Jonathan Bell, "The Agricultural Work of the Congested Districts Board," in *Framing the West: Images of Rural Ireland, 1891-1920*, ed. Ciara Breathnach (Irish Academic Press, 2007), 177, 176.
51. Bell, "Agricultural Work of the Congested Districts Board," 177, emphasis in original.
52. Robert John Welch, "View of Flooded Areas in the Townlands of Clooneen and Knockatee East, Co. Galway," CDB17.
53. Given that this photo was also taken by Welch, it was probably taken in 1914. See Rouse, *Into the Light*, 18-19.
54. Lloyd, *Irish Times*, 41.
55. Frantz Fanon, *The Wretched of the Earth*, trans. Richard Philcox (Grove, 2004), 56.
56. Robert John Welch, "Extensive Marl Beds at Moorehall, North East Corner of Lough Cara, Co. Mayo," CDB39.
57. Jean Archer, "Geological Artistry: The Drawings and Watercolors of George Victor du Noyer in the Archives of the Geological Survey of Ireland," in *Visualizing Ireland: National Identity and the Pictorial Tradition*, ed. Adele M. Dalsimer (Faber & Faber, 1993), 141.
58. Parikka, *Geology of Media*, 69; S. Angus, *Camera Geologica*, 38.
59. S. Angus, 78.
60. S. Angus, 15.
61. Robert John Welch, "Frame for a New Concrete House on a Grass Farm in the Castlerea District, Co. Galway," CDB21.
62. Massey, *For Space*, 24; Ciara Breathnach "Smallholder Housing and People's Health, 1890-1915," in *Framing the West: Images of Rural Ireland, 1891-1920*, ed. Ciara Breathnach (Irish Academic Press, 2007), 186.
63. Robert John Welch, "View of Flooded Areas in the Townlands of Clooneen and Knockatee East, Co. Galway," CDB17.
64. Breathnach, *Congested Districts Board*, 168.
65. Robert John Welch, "View of Congested Village of Graigue, Co. Galway, from Where Migrants Were Taken to Holdings in Graigueachuillaire," CDB7.
66. Carville, "Picturing Poverty," 106.
67. Breathnach, *Congested Districts Board*, 44-45.
68. Sarah Jane Edge, "Photographic History and the Visual Appearance of an Irish Nationalist Discourse, 1840-1870," *Victorian Literature and Culture* 32, no. 1 (2004): 21.
69. Langford, *Story of Photography*, 31-32, 54, 72-74.

70. While this photograph best demonstrates narrative elements that invert gendered labor roles, it is one of many that depict women and children outside the home in areas yet to be modernized. See, for example, Congested Districts Board, "Children Playing on Rocks in Front of Stone Cottages," CDB97; Congested Districts Board, "Girl Carrying Child on Her Back," CDB96; Congested Districts Board, "Group of School Children with Teacher," CDB57; Congested Districts Board, "Man, Woman, and Children Outside a Thatched Cottage," CDB99; and Congested Districts Board, "Dunmore Castle, Co. Galway," CDB18.
71. Welch, "House on Cloonmore Grass Farm," CDB15, CDB16.
72. Welch, "A Grass Farm in Graigueachuillaire, Seven Miles North of Tuam, Co. Galway," CDB3.
73. Welch, "Grass Farm in Graigueachuillaire."
74. Breathnach, *Congested Districts Board*, 113, 116–17, 124.
75. Mathews, *Revival*, 128.
76. Castle, *Modernism and the Celtic Revival*, 101; Adele M. Dalsimer, "'The Irish Peasant Had All His Heart': J. M. Synge in *The Country Shop*," in *Visualizing Ireland: National Identity and the Pictorial Tradition*, ed. Adele M. Dalsimer (Faber & Faber, 1993), 215–17.
77. Justin Carville, "Visible Others: Photography and Romantic Ethnography in Ireland," in *Irish Modernism and the Global Primitive*, ed. Maria McGarrity and Claire A. Culleton (Palgrave Macmillan, 2009), 94; Giulia Bruna, *J. M. Synge and Travel Writing of the Irish Revival* (Syracuse University Press, 2017), 50.
78. Justin Carville, "With His 'Mind-Guided Camera': J. M. Synge, J. J. Clarke, and the Visual Politics of Edwardian Street Photography," in *Synge and Edwardian Ireland*, ed. Brian Cliff and Nicholas Grene (Oxford University Press, 2012), 197.
79. Carville, "With His 'Mind-Guided Camera,'" 197.
80. Justin Carville, *Photography and Ireland* (Reaktion, 2011), 33.
81. John M. Synge, *The Aran Islands* (John W. Luce, 1911), 156.
82. John M. Synge, *My Wallet of Photographs: The Collected Photographs of J. M. Synge* (Dolmen, 1971), 29.
83. Bruna, *J. M. Synge and Travel Writing*, 64.
84. Bruna, 60.
85. Bruna, 61.
86. Bruna, 83.
87. John M. Synge, *Travelling Ireland: Essays, 1898–1908*, ed. Nicholas Grene (Lilliput, 2009), 83.
88. Robert John Welch, "View from the New Dwelling House of Mrs Bridget Kelly, Lisvalley Vesey, near Tuam, Co. Galway," CDB2; Carville, "Picturing Poverty," 113.

NOTES TO PAGES 52-60   237

89. Robert John Welch, "House of Mrs Bridget Kelly, Lisvalley Vesey, near Tuam, Co. Galway," CDB1.
90. Carville, "Picturing Poverty," 113.
91. Breathnach, *Congested Districts Board*, 138. Besides the photographs of Mrs. Kelly's view and house, other photographs in the CDB collection indicate how, in Terence Brown's words, "Irish rural life was characterized . . . by a calculating sensitivity to the economic meaning of marriage and . . . a political will to achieve individual economic security." Terence Brown, *Ireland: A Social and Cultural History, 1922 to the Present* (Cornell University Press, 1985), 19. See, for example, Robert John Welch, "Mrs Philban's House and Farm, Ballymacragh, Co. Mayo, One of the First to Be Purchased by the Congested Districts Board in Mayo," CDB24.
92. Bal, *Narratology*, 163.
93. Breathnach, *Congested Districts Board*, 151–55.
94. Breathnach, 154.
95. Breathnach, 154.
96. Massey, *For Space*, 24.
97. Bal, *Narratology*, 163.
98. Welch, "House of Mrs Bridget Kelly," CDB1.
99. Smith, "'I Thought I Was Landed!,'" 226; Lim, *Translating Time*, 182; Breathnach "Role of Women," 90, 88, 90–91.
100. Massey, *For Space*, 24.
101. Breathnach, *Congested Districts Board*, 99.
102. Niamh Connolly, "Fisheries in the West," in *Framing the West: Images of Rural Ireland, 1891–1920*, ed. Ciara Breathnach (Irish Academic Press, 2007), 130.
103. Connolly, "Fisheries in the West," 130.
104. Beattie, *Donegal in Transition*, 109, 101.
105. William L. Micks, *An Account of the Constitution, Administration, and Dissolution of the Congested Districts Board for Ireland from 1891 to 1923* (Eason & Sons, 1925), 61, 60.
106. Connolly, "Fisheries in the West," 143–44; Rouse, *Into the Light*, 19.
107. Connolly, 143.
108. Breathnach, *Congested Districts Board*, 111, 117–18; Smith, "'I Thought I Was Landed!,'" 226–27.
109. Breathnach, 118.
110. Congested Districts Board, "Downings Pier, Co. Donegal," CDB73.
111. Mathews, *Revival*, 2–3.
112. Congested Districts Board, "Fishing Vessels at Sea," CDB60.
113. Congested Districts Board, "Group of Cottages Beside the Sea," CDB102.
114. Carville, "Picturing Poverty," 107.
115. For related photographs, see Congested Districts Board, "Stone Thatched Cottages with Currachs and a Cow Visible in the Foreground," CDB105;

Congested Districts Board, "Group of Cottages with Bridge Visible in Foreground," CDB101.
116. Connolly, "Fisheries in the West," 133; John De Courcy, *Ireland's Sea Fisheries: A History* (Glendale, 1981), 63.
117. Congested Districts Board, "Curing Fish, Downings Pier, Co. Donegal," CDB72, CDB49, CDB48, CDB50, CDB71.
118. Carville, "Picturing Poverty," 106.
119. Congested Districts Board, "Curing Fish," CDB72, CDB49, CDB48, CDB50.
120. Congested Districts Board, "Curing Fish," CDB71.
121. Michel Foucault, *The History of Sexuality: Volume 1*, trans. Robert Hurley (Pantheon, 1978), 45, 12.
122. Congested Districts Board, "Group Gathered on Downings Pier, Co. Donegal," CDB67; Congested Districts Board, "Downings Pier, Co. Donegal," CDB47.
123. Edge, "Photographic History," 21.
124. For the candid photographs of this pier, see Congested Districts Board, "Downings Pier, Co. Donegal," CDB45; "Downings Pier, Co. Donegal," CDB46; "Fishermen, Downings Pier, Co. Donegal," CDB51; "Fishermen, Downings Pier, Co. Donegal," CDB68; "Downings Pier, Co. Donegal," CDB69; and "Fishermen, Downings Pier, Co. Donegal," CDB70.
125. Luke Gibbons, "Mirrors and Memory: Ireland, Photography, and the Modern," in *The Moderns*, ed. Enrique Juncosa and Christina Kennedy (Irish Museum of Modern Art, 2011), 336.
126. Roland Barthes, *Camera Lucida* (Hill & Wang, 2010), 85.

2. 1922–1950

1. O'Hearn, *Atlantic Economy*, 114.
2. Terence Dooley, *The Land for the People: The Land Question in Independent Ireland* (University College Dublin, 2004), 59, 63; Lloyd, *Irish Times*, 41.
3. Maria Tymoczko, *Translation in a Postcolonial Context: Early Irish Literature in English Translation* (St. Jerome, 1999), 133.
4. Brian O'Nolan (Brian Ó Nualláin) wrote under several pseudonyms with various spellings, most notably Flann O'Brien for his English-language texts and Myles na gCopaleen for his Irish-language texts. Throughout this chapter, I will refer to O'Nolan by the name under which he published a particular work and use his anglicized name for unpublished material and biographical details.
5. Siskin, "Textual Culture," 125–26, emphasis in original.

6. Katherine Ebury, Paul Fagan, and John Greaney, "Editor's Introduction: Brian O'Nolan's Nonhuman Imaginary," in *Flann O'Brien and the Nonhuman: Environments, Animals, Machines*, ed. Katherine Ebury, Paul Fagan, and John Greaney (Cork University Press, 2024), 6–8.
7. Mikhail Bakhtin, *Rabelais and His World*, trans. Helene Iswolsky (Indiana University Press, 1984), 26.
8. Keith Hopper, *Flann O'Brien: A Portrait of the Artist as a Young Post-Modernist* (Cork University Press, 1995), 5–6.
9. Hopper, *Flann O'Brien*, 157.
10. Hopper, 264.
11. Michael Rubenstein, *Public Works: Infrastructure, Irish Modernism, and the Postcolonial* (University of Notre Dame Press, 2010), 14, 98–99.
12. Rubenstein, *Public Works*, 98, 14–15.
13. Siskin, "Textual Culture," 123, emphasis in original.
14. Carol Taaffe, *Ireland Through the Looking-Glass: Flann O'Brien, Myles na gCopaleen, and Irish Cultural Debate* (Cork University Press, 2008), 222n127; Louis de Paor, "'A scholar manqué'? Further Notes on Brian Ó Nualláin's Engagement with Early Irish Literature," in *Flann O'Brien: Problems with Authority*, ed. Ruben Borg, Paul Fagan, and John McCourt (Cork University Press, 2017), 197; Ebury, Fagan, and Greaney, "Editor's Introduction," 9; Jonathan Foster, "'The reassuring unmistakability of the abiding earth': Nature Writing, State Engineering, the Anthropocene in *The Third Policeman*," in *Flann O'Brien and the Nonhuman: Environments, Animals, Machines*, ed. Katherine Ebury, Paul Fagan, and John Greaney (Cork University Press, 2024), 76–77; Adrian Naughton, "'*Nádúir-fhilíocht na Gaedhilge*' and Flann O'Brien's Fiction," in *"Is It About a Bicycle?" Flann O'Brien in the Twenty-First Century*, ed. Jennika Baines (Four Courts, 2011), 90.
15. Anthony Cronin, *No Laughing Matter: The Life and Times of Flann O'Brien* (Fromm International, 1989), 5, 9; Taaffe, *Ireland Through the Looking Glass*, 222n127; de Paor, "'A scholar manqué?,'" 197.
16. Taaffe, 222n127.
17. de Paor, "'A scholar manqué?,'" 197.
18. Taaffe, *Ireland Through the Looking Glass*, 222n127.
19. Taaffe, 46.
20. Naughton, "'*Nádúir-fhilíocht na Gaedhilge*,'" 90.
21. In an analysis of Old and Medieval Irish writing, Amy C. Mulligan acknowledges religious, gendered, and allegorical representations of material environments while also, like O'Nolan, demonstrating interactions in which "literary practice is envisioned as environmental practice and back again" and the ways in which writers "develop the mode of the

environment as a creative and generative space." See Amy C. Mulligan, "Landscape and Literature in Medieval Ireland," in *A History of Irish Literature and the Environment*, ed. Malcolm Sen (Cambridge University Press, 2022), 37, 51.
22. Taaffe, 46.
23. Brian O'Nolan, "The Pathology of Revivalism," box 2, folder 43, Flann O'Brien Papers, MS.1997.027, John J. Burns Library, Boston College. Copyright © by Brian O'Nolan. Used by permission of Brandt & Hochman Literary Agents, Inc. Any copying or distribution of this text is expressly forbidden. All rights reserved; Taaffe, *Ireland Through the Looking Glass*, 119.
24. O'Nolan, "Pathology of Revivalism," 5–6, 4.
25. O'Nolan, 7.
26. O'Nolan, 2.
27. O'Nolan, 5; Taaffe, *Ireland Through the Looking Glass*, 119.
28. Dooley, *Land for the People*, 59–63.
29. McLeish, "Sunshine and Sorrows," 259.
30. McLeish, 259–60.
31. Lambert and Lester, "Introduction," 7, 25.
32. McLeish, "Sunshine and Sorrows," 271.
33. For an extensive analysis of how imperial powers strategically used and at times established divisions between native and settler populations in various colonies and settler-colonies, see Mahmood Mamdani, *Neither Settler nor Native: The Making and Unmaking of Permanent Minorities* (Harvard University Press, 2020).
34. Smith, "'I Thought I Was Landed!,'" 218, 224.
35. McLeish, "Sunshine and Sorrows," 271.
36. John M. Regan, *The Irish Counter-Revolution, 1921–1936: Treatyite Politics and Settlement in Independent Ireland* (St. Martin's, 1999), 378.
37. Regan, *Irish Counter-Revolution*, 377.
38. See, for example, the photography of Thomas Jackson, an Alsea photographer whose depictions of Native peoples differ markedly from those of settler-photographer Edward Curtis. Whereas Jackson captures the dynamism of Native peoples and their endurance under settler-colonial regimes, Curtis frames a way of life out of sync with an expanding modernity. I first encountered Jackson's work through the presentation Nick Viles gave to the SB13 Community of Practice professional development program while teaching in Oregon public schools. I am grateful to Viles and the Tribal History/Shared History Curriculum offered by the Confederated Tribes of Siletz Indians for this introduction, https://ctsi.nsn.us/sb-13-curriculum/.
39. Dooley, *Land for the People*, 99.
40. Donal Ó Drisceoil, *Peadar O'Donnell* (Cork University Press, 2001), 75.

41. Sarah E. McKibben, "An Béal Bocht: Mouthing Off at National Identity," Éire-Ireland 38, nos. 1–2 (2003): 44.
42. McKibben, "An Béal Bocht," 38, 47.
43. Tymoczko, Translation in a Postcolonial Context, 165.
44. Flann O'Brien, The Third Policeman (Dalkey Archive, 1999), 37.
45. O'Brien, Third Policeman, 38.
46. O'Brien, 38.
47. Bell, "Agricultural Work," 176–77; Dooley, Land for the People, 159.
48. Lloyd, Irish Culture, 62; Dooley, 159.
49. O'Brien, Third Policeman, 37.
50. O'Brien, 37.
51. O'Brien, 157.
52. O'Brien, 114.
53. Rubenstein, Public Works, 113; Foster, "'The reassuring unmistakability of the abiding earth,'" 82, 77.
54. O'Brien, Third Policeman, 158.
55. Potts, Contemporary Irish Writing and Environmentalism, xxviii; Rubenstein, Public Works, 113–15.
56. O'Nolan, 5.
57. Taaffe, Ireland Through the Looking Glass, 222n127; Foster, "'The reassuring unmistakability of the abiding earth,'" 82.
58. Daniel Shtob and Jordan Fox Besek, "Environmental Precedent: Foregrounding the Environmental Consequences of Law in Sociology," Sociological Forum 36, no. 3 (2021): 713.
59. O'Brien, Third Policeman, 37, 39.
60. O'Brien, 86.
61. Potts, Contemporary Irish Writing and Environmentalism, 71.
62. Potts, 72.
63. Derek Gladwin, Contentious Terrains: Boglands, Ireland, Postcolonial Gothic (Cork University Press, 2016), 34.
64. Potts, Contemporary Irish Writing and Environmentalism, 74.
65. Claire Wills, That Neutral Island: A Cultural History of Ireland During the Second World War (Belknap, 2007), 327; Potts, Contemporary Irish Writing and Environmentalism, xxx–xxxi.
66. Since the Land Commission documents are not yet available to most researchers, memoirs like that of Patrick Sammon, who worked for the Land Commission from 1933 to 1978, are sources of historical insight. Sammon noted that Bord na Móna "w[as] actively acquiring bogland throughout the midlands" by the late 1940s. This would lead, Sammon explains, to a government push, particularly by Seán Lemass, who worked for the Ministry of Industry and Commerce throughout the 1940s, to

create "turf-burning stations . . . constructed by the ESB, with the objective of producing electricity which would be fed into the national grid." O'Brien's description of the distorted landscape in which the bog figures as a commercial source of energy demonstrates trends that were already in motion by the early 1940s. O'Brien's novel perceptively depicts the bog as a form of specifically Irish energy, something that Bord na Móna would capitalize on after World War II as the Electricity Supply Board's Rural Electrification Project got underway in 1946. See Patrick J. Sammon, *In the Land Commission: A Memoir, 1933–1978* (Ashfield, 1997), 13, 40. For more on elements of air and atmosphere in *The Third Policeman*, see Julie Bates, "Writing with Air in *The Third Policeman*," in *Flann O'Brien and the Nonhuman: Environments, Animals, Machines*, ed. Katherine Ebury, Paul Fagan, and John Greaney (Cork University Press, 2024), 41–55.

67. Paul Henry, *Connemara Cottages*, ca. 1936–37, oil on canvas, 69x84 cm, bequeathed Mrs. M. Henry, 1974 National Gallery of Ireland Collection, NGI.4077, © Paul Henry, *Connemara Cottages*, 1936–1937 c/o Pictoright Amsterdam 2025.
68. O'Brien, *Third Policeman*, 38.
69. O'Brien, 86.
70. O'Brien, 86.
71. Hopper, *Flann O'Brien*, 31.
72. O'Brien, *Third Policeman*, 86.
73. Hopper, *Flann O'Brien*, 31.
74. Suzanne M. Pegley, *The Land Commission and the Making of Ráth Cairn: The First Gaeltacht Colony* (Four Courts, 2011), 33.
75. Taylor, *Irish Materialisms*, 75, 79.
76. Maebh Long, *Assembling Flann O'Brien* (Bloomsbury, 2014), 156, 161, 166, 185.
77. O'Brien, *Third Policeman*, 7.
78. O'Brien, 86.
79. Smith, "'I Thought I Was Landed!,'" 215; Joanna Bourke, "Women and Poultry in Ireland," *Irish Historical Studies* 25, no. 99 (1987): 293.
80. Smith, 215–16; Breathnach, "Role of Women," 85; Breathnach, *Congested Districts Board*, 48.
81. Maureen O'Connor, *The Female and the Species: The Animal in Irish Women's Writing* (Peter Lang AG, 2010), 145.
82. O'Connor, *Female and the Species*, 145.
83. O'Brien, *Third Policeman*, 86.
84. Bronwen Walter, *Outsiders Inside: Whiteness, Place, and Irish Women* (Routledge, 2001), 20.
85. Sarah Townsend, "Porcine Pasts and Bourgeois Pigs: Consumption and the Irish Counterculture," in *Animals in Irish Literature*, ed. Kathryn Kirkpatrick and Borbála Faragó (Palgrave Macmillan, 2015), 56.

86. Taaffe, *Ireland Through the Looking Glass*, 222 n. 127.
87. O'Brien, *Third Policeman*, 22.
88. O'Brien, 21.
89. Breathnach, "Smallholder Housing," 195.
90. O'Brien, *Third Policeman*, 21.
91. Breathnach, *Congested Districts Board*, 125; Breathnach, "Lady Dudley," 143; Breathnach, "Smallholder Housing," 191–95.
92. O'Brien, *Third Policeman*, 21.
93. Taylor, *Irish Materialisms*, 156.
94. Taylor, 152.
95. O'Brien, *Third Policeman*, 50.
96. O'Brien, 51.
97. O'Brien, 50.
98. Bolter and Grusin, *Remediation*, 4, 70.
99. Kevin Rockett, Luke Gibbons, and John Hill, *Cinema and Ireland* (Syracuse University Press, 1988), 6.
100. O'Brien, *Third Policeman*, 157.
101. O'Brien, 50.
102. Taaffe, *Ireland Through the Looking Glass*, 222 n. 127.
103. O'Brien, *Third Policeman*, 83–88.
104. Stacy Alaimo, *Bodily Natures: Science, Environment, and the Material Self* (Indiana University Press, 2010), 2.
105. Karen Barad, *Meeting the Universe Halfway: Quantum Physics and the Entanglement of Matter and Meaning* (Duke University Press, 2007), 161, emphasis in original.
106. O'Brien, *Third Policeman*, 90.
107. O'Brien, 88.
108. O'Brien, 88, emphasis in original.
109. McLeish, "Sunshine and Sorrows," 270.
110. O'Nolan, "Pathology of Revivalism," 6.
111. O'Brien, *Third Policeman*, 52–53, 198–99.
112. Long, *Assembling Flann O'Brien*, 77.
113. Satia, *Time's Monster*, 269.
114. O'Brien, *Third Policeman*, 188; Rubenstein, *Public Works*, 109.
115. O'Brien, 188.
116. O'Brien, 135.
117. O'Brien, 135.
118. Wills, *That Neutral Island*, 30.
119. Wills, 307.

3. 1950–1970

1. Besides the direct influence Ó Riada's group Ceoltóirí Chualann has had on groups such as the internationally known band the Chieftains and rise of the Irish music revival in the 1970s with groups like the Bothy Band and Planxty, Peadar Ó Riada, in correspondence with the author on June 12, 2019, pointed out that Van Morrison and U2 have also given credit to Seán Ó Riada as an influence on their music.
2. Damien Keane, "Poetry, Music, and Reproduced Sound," in *Oxford Handbook of Modern Irish Poetry*, ed. Fran Brearton and Alan A. Gillis (Oxford University Press, 2012), 270.
3. Keane, "Poetry, Music, and Reproduced Sound," 270.
4. Tomás Ó Canainn, *Seán Ó Riada: His Life and Work* (Collins, 2003), 9, 15, 17.
5. Ó Canainn, *Seán Ó Riada*, 63–64.
6. Ó Canainn, 32–40; *The Rolling Wave*, December 18, 2011, Prod. RTÉ, hosted by Peter Browne, RTÉ Archives; Thomas Kinsella, *Fifteen Dead, with Commentary* (Dolmen, 1979), 67.
7. Joe Cleary, *Outrageous Fortune: Capital and Culture in Modern Ireland* (Field Day, 2007), 296.
8. Richard Pine, *2RN and the Origins of Irish Radio* (Four Courts, 2002), 271; Harry White, *The Keeper's Recital: Music and Cultural History in Ireland, 1770–1970* (University of Notre Dame Press in association with Field Day, 1998), 136–37, 141.
9. Scholars' critique of *Our Musical Heritage* is perhaps analogous to Heather Laird's assertion that critiques of essentialism in the work of Daniel Corkery often indicate current theoretical approaches in postcolonial studies more than the historical and cultural moment in which they arose. Laird discusses why Corkery is perhaps not taken up as a postcolonial scholar himself despite some overlap with early postcolonialists, including Frantz Fanon: "Given the present-day dominance of a poststructuralist strand of postcolonial studies that is characterized by an undifferentiated disavowal of all forms of nationalism and a corresponding exaltation of liminality, hybridity, ambivalence and multiculturality that results from colonialism, it is perhaps not surprising that doubt might arise about Corkery's suitability to this scholarly field." See Heather Laird, ed., *Daniel Corkery's Cultural Criticism, Selected Writings* (Cork University Press, 2013), 13.
10. IE BL/PP/OR 185 (1), Seán Ó Riada Collection/Bailiúchán Sheáin Uí Riada, unnamed correspondence from Brian Friel to Seán Ó Riada, November 8, 1967, University College Cork Archives Service, Cork, Ireland.
11. IE BL/PP/OR 185 (1–2), Seán Ó Riada Collection/Bailiúchán Sheáin Uí Riada, unnamed correspondence from Brian Friel to Seán Ó Riada, November 8, 1967, University College Cork Archives Service, Cork, Ireland.

12. Michael Kennedy, "Northern Ireland and Cross-Border Co-operation," in *The Lemass Era: Politics and Society in the Ireland of Seán Lemass*, ed. Brian Girvin and Gary Murphy (University College Dublin Press, 2005), 118; O'Hearn, *Atlantic Economy*, 134.
13. IE BL/PP/OR 185 (19–23), Seán Ó Riada Collection/Bailiúchán Sheáin Uí Riada, unnamed correspondence from Brian Friel to Seán Ó Riada, May 2, 1968, University College Cork Archives Service, Cork, Ireland. Reasons why Friel and Ó Riada never finished the opera are not entirely known, though letters between Friel and Ó Riada, as well as Michael Emmerson, the founder of the Queens University Festival, indicate that the logistics of the production they envisioned were financially difficult. See IE BL/PP/OR 185 (16–18), Seán Ó Riada Collection/Bailiúchán Sheáin Uí Riada, unnamed correspondence from Brian Friel to Seán Ó Riada, April 2, 1968, University College Cork Archives Service, Cork, Ireland.
14. John Horgan, *Broadcasting and Public Life: RTÉ News and Current Affairs, 1926–1997* (Four Courts, 2004), 28.
15. John Horgan, *Irish Media: A Critical History Since 1922* (Routledge, 2001), 73; Pine, *2RN*, 176.
16. Early national radio under 2RN could not keep up with the BBC radio orchestra, which was a source of political tension around state-led radio policies and funding. Jazz was seen as immoral by the conservative state, which fostered conceptions of authentic Irish culture as rooted in moral value systems approved by key figures in the Irish Catholic hierarchy, most notably the Archbishop of Dublin, John Charles McQuaid. See Pine, 153, 165.
17. IE BL/PP/OR 185 (29), Seán Ó Riada Collection/Bailiúchán Sheáin Uí Riada, unnamed correspondence from Brian Friel to Seán Ó Riada, October 1, 1968, University College Cork Archives Service, Cork, Ireland.
18. Brian Girvin and Gary Murphy, "Chapter One: Whose Ireland? The Lemass Era," in *The Lemass Era: Politics and Society in the Ireland of Seán Lemass*, ed. Brian Girvin and Gary Murphy (University College Dublin Press, 2005), 8.
19. Éimear O'Connor, *Seán Keating: Art, Politics and Building the Irish Nation* (Irish Academic Press, 2013), 160.
20. Siemens Schuckert, "Power Station: General Description of the Electrical Part," *Progress on the Shannon*, no. 11 (August 1929), National Library of Ireland, Dublin, K30, 44; G. T. Bloomfield, "London: Electricity Hub of Britain," British Electricity History, University of Guelph, 2024, https://www.britelechist.uoguelph.ca/. I would like to thank Joachim Fischer and Jan Frohburg for bringing this to my attention on a tour of the Ardnacrusha power station at the 2022 IASIL conference at the University of Limerick.

21. Christopher Morash, *A History of Media in Ireland* (Cambridge University Press, 2010), 129; Michael J. Shiel, *The Quiet Revolution: The Electrification of Rural Ireland, 1946–1976* (O'Brien, 1984), 18, 29.
22. Sharae Deckard, "Energy Futures in Contemporary Irish Fiction," in *A History of Irish Literature and the Environment*, ed. Malcolm Sen (Cambridge University Press, 2022), 379–80; Sammon, *In the Land Commission*, 13.
23. Dooley, *Land for the People*, 194.
24. 2RN became Raidío (Radio) Éireann. National broadcasts were consolidated under Radio Teilifís Éireann (RTÉ) after the Broadcasting Authority Act of 1960.
25. Pine, *2RN*, 34.
26. Pine, 38–39, 42. Notably, the first radio broadcast in the world was during the 1916 Rising when Irish Volunteer Fergus O'Kelly took over the Irish School of Wireless Telegraphy and began announcing the Irish Republic via a transmitter without an operable receiver. Christopher Morash notes the ingenuity of this event: "While it might seem obvious to us today that seizing the local radio station is the first thing any self-respecting rebel should do, it took a considerable act of imagination to make use of the new medium of wireless telegraphy in 1916." Official radio stations began emerging in the UK and the US in the early 1920s, as Morash goes on to describe: "In the month that the Anglo-Irish Treaty was signed—December, 1921—a new radio station began broadcasting in the US almost every day. The following month, in January, 1922, the Marconi Company made the first English broadcast at Writtle, and by November of 1922, the BBC was on the air in England." See Morash, *History of Media in Ireland*, 125–31; and Pine, *2RN*, 11.
27. Pine, 40.
28. Horgan, *Irish Media*, 18, 15.
29. Horgan, *Broadcasting*, 14; Horgan, *Irish Media*, 18, 126; Morash, *History of Media in Ireland*, 186, 194, 206–7.
30. Horgan, *Irish Media*, 18.
31. Laird, *Daniel Corkery's Cultural Criticism*, 6.
32. Parikka, *Geology of Media*, 72; Douglas Kahn, *Earth Sound Earth Signal: Energies and Earth Magnitude in the Arts* (University of California Press, 2013), 1–2, 6–7.
33. Pine, *2RN*, 150, 153, 171–74; White, *Keeper's Recital*, 133; Alacoque Kealy and Radio Telefís Éireann, Audience Research Dept. *Irish Radio Data: 1926–1980* (Radio Telefís Éireann, 1981), 27–28.
34. Brian Boydell, "The Future of Music in Ireland," *Bell* 16, no. 4, January 1951, ed. Peadar O'Donnell, National Library of Ireland, Dublin, F397, 25.

35. Boydell, "Future of Music," 22.
36. Boydell, 23.
37. Boydell, 26, 25.
38. Ó Canainn, Seán Ó Riada, 24.
39. Mícheál Ó Súilleabháin, Ceol Na nUasal: Seán Ó Riada and the Search for a Native Irish Art Music, Léacht Chomórtha an Riadaigh 15 (Irish Traditional Music Archive and the Irish Traditional Music Society, University College Cork, 2004), 12.
40. Ó Súilleabháin, Ceol Na nUasal, 2.
41. Ó Súilleabháin, 5.
42. White, Keeper's Recital, 155.
43. Our Musical Heritage, "Episode 1: Sean-nós Singing," Prog. ID: AR0023049, RTÉ Archives, July 7, 1962, 29:50 mins, 3:38–3:44.
44. For a comprehensive examination of colonial and anticolonial iterations of Irish orientalisms, see Joseph Lennon's Irish Orientalism: A Literary and Intellectual History (2004).
45. Aileen Dillane and Matthew Noone, "Irish Music Orientalism," New Hibernia Review / Iris Éireannach Nua 20, no. 1 (Earrach/Spring 2016): 136.
46. Ó Súilleabháin, Ceol Na nUasal, 12.
47. Ó Súilleabháin, 12.
48. A history of comparisons between marginalized populations in Ireland and Indigenous groups in the United States exists. Most notably is the donation the Choctaw people gave to Irish people during the Famine and the Irish State's establishment of a third-level scholarship in 2018 specifically for Choctaw people to recognize their support during the Great Famine. Irish people also donated over two million euro to the Navajo Nation during the COVID 19 pandemic. Additionally, the Choctaw Nation recognized the struggle of the Shell-to-Sea protesters against the LNG pipeline being built in their community in northwest County Mayo, which I discuss in chapter 5. See Suzanne Lynch, "Choctaw Generosity to Famine Ireland Saluted by Varadkar," Irish Times, March 13, 2018; Ronan McGreevy, "Irish People Donate €2.5m to Native American Tribe Devastated by Coronavirus," Irish Times, November 20, 2020; Siggins, Once upon a Time, 249.
49. IE BL/PP/OR 185 (17 18), Seán Ó Riada Collection/Bailiúchán Sheáin Uí Riada, unnamed correspondence from Brian Friel to Seán Ó Riada, April 2, 1968, University College Cork Archives Service, Cork, Ireland.
50. IE BL/PP/OR554 (17), Seán Ó Riada Collection/Bailiúchán Sheáin Uí Riada, "The Armchair Time-Traveller" by John Reidy, August 13, 1955, University College Cork Archives Service, Cork, Ireland.
51. Ó Riada/Reidy wrote various programs for Raidió Éireann in the late 1950s, including reviews of books on jazz and classical music, as well as Bypaths in Music, a 1957 three-episode series with each broadcast

showcasing a different European musician in history from sixteenth-century Venosa, Serenissimo; eighteenth-century Germany; and late nineteenth-century France. See IE BL/PP/OR554 (97–118, 119, 125, 132), Seán Ó Riada Collection/Bailiúchán Sheáin Uí Riada, "Bypaths in Music" by John Reidy, November 10, 1955–September 8, 1972, University College Cork Archives Service, Cork, Ireland. He also wrote a children's program, "You'll Enjoy This Music," in 1956. See IE BL/PP/OR/ 554 (189–218), Seán Ó Riada Collection/Bailiúchán Sheáin Uí Riada, "You'll Enjoy This Music" by John Reidy, August 27–November 19, 1956, University College Cork Archives Service, Cork, Ireland.

52. *Our Musical Heritage,* "Episode 1: Sean-nós Singing," Prog. ID: AR0023049. RTÉ Archives. 7 July 1962. 29:50 mins, 0:34–0:48.
53. Iheka, *African Ecomedia,* 225.
54. Kahn, *Earth Sound Earth Signal,* 1.
55. Jonathan Sterne, *The Audible Past: Cultural Origins of Sound Reproduction* (Duke University Press, 2003), 288. In Ireland, the Irish Folklore Commission made thousands of recordings of stories and music in Irish-speaking communities in the late 1930s, thereby indicating the cultural role sound recordings were understood to have to capture seemingly vanishing traditions in an Irish postcolonial modernity. For more information on these recordings, see the National Folklore Collection and the Dúchas Project: https://www.duchas.ie/en/info/cbe.
56. *Our Musical Heritage,* "Episode 1: Sean-nós Singing," Prog. ID: AR0023049, RTÉ Archives, 7 July 1962, 0:08–0:18.
57. Carolyn Merchant, *The Death of Nature: Women, Ecology, and the Scientific Revolution* (HarperCollins, 1983), 8.
58. Potts, *Contemporary Irish Writing and Environmentalism,* xxi.
59. Anna Pilz, "Narratives of Arboreal Landscapes," in *A History of Irish Literature and the Environment,* ed. Malcolm Sen (Cambridge University Press, 2022), 102.
60. Robert Welch, ed., *The Oxford Companion to Irish Literature* (Clarendon, 1996), 551–52.
61. Leith Davis, *Music, Postcolonialism, and Gender: The Construction of Irish National Identity, 1724–1874* (University of Notre Dame, 2006), 26, 211.
62. Davis, *Music, Postcolonialism, and Gender,* 211.
63. Satia, *Time's Monster,* 264.
64. *Our Musical Heritage,* "Episode 13: Piano, Harp, Bodhran, Céilí Bands," Prog. ID: AR0023065, RTÉ Archives, 6 October 1962, 23:52–24:45.
65. *Our Musical Heritage.* "Episode 10: Flute," Prog. ID: AR0023062. RTÉ Archives. 15 September 1962, 19:00; *Our Musical Heritage,* "Episode 3: Sean-nós Singing," Prog. ID: AR0023051, RTÉ Archives, 28 July 1962, 23:20.

NOTES TO PAGES 123-129   249

Please note that this sean-nós song, "Sliabh na mBan," is based on the poem by the same name, and it is different from the possibly more popular song "Slievenamon."

66. IE BL/PP/OR554 (131, 138), Seán Ó Riada Collection/Bailiúchán Sheáin Uí Riada, letters to Seán Ó Riada from Nioclás Tóibín on July 4, 1962, and from Comhar Cultúra Éireann on August 23, 1962, University College Cork Archives Service, Cork, Ireland.
67. I would like to thank Irish-language instructor and Fulbright scholar Orla McCague for providing the translation of this stanza. For the full text, see "Sliabh na mBan," Cranford Publications, August 3, 2003, https://www.cranfordpub.com/langan/Sliabh_na_mBan.htm.
68. *Our Musical Heritage*, "Episode 14: Concluding Talk," Prog. ID: AR0023066, RTÉ Archives, 13 October 1962, 23:55-24:00.
69. *Our Musical Heritage*, "Episode 6: Piping Part Two," Prog. ID: AR0023054, RTÉ Archives, 18 August 1962, 19:00.
70. IE BL/PP/OR/645 (61-64), Seán Ó Riada Collection/Bailiúchán Sheáin Uí Riada, "F-F-F-Foreigners," January 1962, University College Cork Archives Service, Cork, Ireland.
71. *Our Musical Heritage*, "Episode 14: Concluding Talk," Prog. ID: AR0023066, RTÉ Archives, 13 October 1962, 23:55-24:00.
72. Luke Gibbons, *Transformations in Irish Culture* (University of Notre Dame Press, 1996), 86.
73. *Our Musical Heritage*, "Episode 2: Sean-nós Singing," Prog. ID: AR0023050, RTÉ Archives, July 21, 1962, 0:33-0:55.
74. *Our Musical Heritage*, "Episode 2: Sean-nós Singing," Prog. ID: AR0023050, RTÉ Archives, July 21, 1962, 1:00-2:23.
75. *Our Musical Heritage*, "Episode 1: Sean-nós Singing," Prog. ID: AR0023049, RTÉ Archives, July 7, 1962, 3:38-3:44.
76. Lennon, *Irish Orientalism*, 15.
77. Lennon, 48-53.
78. *Our Musical Heritage*, "Episode 2: Sean-nós Singing," Prog. ID: AR0023050, RTÉ Archives, July 21, 1962, 2:58-3:01.
79. *Our Musical Heritage*, "Episode 2: Sean-nós Singing," Prog. ID: AR0023050, RTÉ Archives, July 21, 1962, 3:05-3:33.
80. *Our Musical Heritage*, "Episode 1: Sean-nós Singing," Prog. ID: AR0023049, RTÉ Archives, July 7, 1962, 21:44-23:12.
81. *Our Musical Heritage*, "Episode 3: Sean-nós Singing," Prog. ID: AR0023051, RTÉ Archives, July 28, 1962, 5:57-7:15.
82. *Our Musical Heritage*, "Episode 12: Accordion and Concertina," Prog. ID: AR0023064, RTÉ Archives, September 29, 1962, 1:17-2:01, 2:30-2:40.

83. *Our Musical Heritage,* "Episode 1: Sean-nós Singing," Prog. ID: AR0023049, RTÉ Archives, July 7, 1962, 2:08–2:24.
84. *Our Musical Heritage,* "Episode 7: Piping Part Three," Prog. ID: AR0023056, RTÉ Archives, August 25, 1962, 26:30–26:33.
85. Hannah Arendt, *The Human Condition,* 2nd ed. (University of Chicago Press, [1958] 2018), 2.
86. Guy Beiner, *Remembering the Year of the French: Irish Folk History and Social Memory* (University of Wisconsin Press, 2007), 28.
87. *Our Musical Heritage,* "Episode 6: Piping Part Two," Prog. ID: AR0023054, RTÉ Archives, August 18, 1962, 27:22–27:49.
88. *Our Musical Heritage,* "Episode 8: Fiddle," Prog. ID: AR0023057, RTÉ Archives, September 1, 1962, 10:44–10:59.
89. O'Connor, *Female and the Species,* 117, emphasis in original.
90. Potts, *Contemporary Irish Writing and Environmentalism,* xxii, 6; Kathryn Kirkpatrick, "Quick Red Foxes: Irish Women Write the Hunt," in *Animals in Irish Literature,* ed. Kathryn Kirkpatrick and Borbála Faragó (Palgrave Macmillan, 2015), 31.
91. Kirkpatrick, "Quick Red Foxes," 31.
92. O'Connor, *Female and the Species,* 117–18; Kirkpatrick, "Quick Red Foxes," 31.
93. Potts, *Contemporary Irish Writing and Environmentalism,* 159.
94. Kirkpatrick, "Quick Red Foxes," 30, emphasis in original.
95. O'Connor, *Female and the Species,* 117.
96. Davis, *Music, Postcolonialism, and Gender,* 26.
97. Davis, 24.
98. *Our Musical Heritage,* "Episode 6: Piping Part Two," Prog. ID: AR0023054, RTÉ Archives, August 18, 1962, 27:22–27:49; *Our Musical Heritage,* "Episode 8: Fiddle," Prog. ID: AR0023057, RTÉ Archives, September 1, 1962, 10:50–10:54.
99. IE BL/PP/OR/645 (60), Seán Ó Riada Collection/Bailiúchán Sheáin Uí Riada, "Fox and Hounds," ca. January 1962–January 1964, University College Cork Archives Service, Cork, Ireland.
100. Laird, *Daniel Corkery's Cultural Criticism,* 5.
101. *Our Musical Heritage,* "Episode 1: Sean-nós Singing," Prog. ID: AR0023049, RTÉ Archives, July 7, 1962, 2:08–2:24.
102. *Our Musical Heritage,* "Episode 2: Sean-nós Singing," Prog. ID: AR0023050, RTÉ Archives, July 21, 1962, 0:33–0:55.
103. *Our Musical Heritage,* "Episode 1: Sean-nós Singing," Prog. ID: AR0023049, RTÉ Archives, July 7, 1962, 2:08–2:24.
104. Maurice Harmon, ed., *The Dolmen Press: A Celebration* (Lilliput, 2001), 11.

105. *H Block*, produced by Donal Lunny and Christy Moore, Mild Music, 1978, LP.
106. "Biography," on Matt Molloy's official website, http://www.mattmolloy.com/matt-molloy.
107. The Fair Plé movement is a positive reaction to the gender hierarchies in narratives of modernity and the history of Irish traditional music: https://www.fairple.com.
108. Kinsella, *Fifteen Dead*, 53–58.
109. Kinsella, 58.
110. Kinsella, 17.
111. Conor McCarthy, *Modernisation, Crisis and Culture in Ireland, 1969–1992* (Four Courts, 2000), 64.
112. Kinsella, *Fifteen Dead*, 72.
113. Kinsella, 72.
114. Kinsella, 72.
115. Kinsella, 73.
116. Kinsella, 73.
117. Kinsella, 72, 73.
118. Adrian Guelke, "Northern Ireland and the International System," in *Ireland on the World Stage*, ed. William Crotty and David E. Schmitt (Longman, 2002), 129.
119. *Our Musical Heritage*, "Episode 1: Sean-nós Singing," Prog. ID: AR0023049, RTÉ Archives, July 7, 1962, 2:08–2:24.
120. *Our Musical Heritage*, "Episode 2: Sean-nós Singing," Prog. ID: AR0023050, RTÉ Archives, July 21, 1962, 23:20–25:00.
121. Seán Ó Riada, *Our Musical Heritage*, ed. Thomas Kinsella, musical editor Tomás Ó Canainn (Dolmen, 1982), 34.
122. *Our Musical Heritage*, "Episode 6: Piping Part Two," Prog. ID: AR0023054, RTÉ Archives, August 18, 1962, 19:00.
123. *Our Musical Heritage*, "Episode 3: Sean-nós Singing," Prog. ID: AR0023051, RTÉ Archives, July 28, 1962, 23:05–23:31.
124. Ó Riada, *Our Musical Heritage*, 48.
125. *Our Musical Heritage*, "Episode 1: Sean-nós Singing," Prog. ID: AR0023049, RTÉ Archives, July 7, 1962, 2:08–2:24; Scott Reiss, "Tradition and Imaginary: Irish Traditional Music and the Celtic Phenomenon," in *Celtic Modern: Music at the Global Fringe*, ed. Martin Stokes and Philip V. Bohlman (Scarecrow, 2003), 154–55.
126. Reiss, "Tradition and Imaginary," 153.
127. *The Rolling Wave*, prod. RTÉ, hosted by Peter Browne, Prog. ID: AR0183524, RTÉ Archives, January 29, 2012.

128. *The Rolling Wave*, prod. RTÉ, hosted by Peter Browne, Prog. ID: AR0184703, RTÉ Archives, February 26, 2012.
129. In 2021, Doireann Ní Ghlacáin released a documentary on TG4, *Seán Ó Riada—Mo Sheanathair*, in which she films her journey to learn about her grandfather, Seán Ó Riada. While the documentary does not delve into *Our Musical Heritage*, it includes various interviews that, like *The Rolling Wave*, demonstrate the innovations Ó Riada's life and work made in the Irish language and to Irish traditional music. In documenting Ó Riada's legacy, it thereby reveals the dynamism of Ó Riada's 1962 version of *Our Musical Heritage*. See Doireann Ní Ghlacáin, *Seán Ó Riada—Mo Sheanathair*, produced by TG4, December 26, 2021, https://www.tg4.ie/en/player/categories/top-documentaries/?series=Se%C3%A1n%20%C3%93%20Riada%20-%20Mo%20Sheanathair&genre=Faisneis.
130. Celebrations for the Shell-to-Sea activist and Rossport Five member who became a Goldman Environmental Award recipient Willie Corduff were attended by writers Seamus Heaney, whose poetry appears on Ó Riada's *Vertical Man*, as well as Éilis Ní Dhuibhne, whose work I discuss in chapter 4. Heaney also played an active role in the early 2000s in efforts to stop the M3 motorway being built through the historic and sacred heritage landscape of Tara, and he used poetry alongside musicians in these protests. See Siggins, *Once upon a Time*, 234, 243; Potts, *Contemporary Irish Writing and Environmentalism*, 22, 29.
131. Potts, 97.
132. Potts, 99.
133. Potts, 55.
134. Siggins, *Once upon a Time*, 243, 250.
135. Potts, *Contemporary Irish Writing and Environmentalism*, 113.
136. Potts, 128.
137. IE BL/PP/OR/645 (65), Seán Ó Riada Collection/Bailiúchán Sheáin Uí Riada, "Young Moore's Almanac," January 1, 1963, University College Cork Archives Service, Cork, Ireland.
138. Potts, *Contemporary Irish Writing and Environmentalism*, 101–2.
139. Dipesh Chakrabarty, *The Climate of History in a Planetary Age* (University of Chicago Press, 2021), 61–62.
140. Friel's play implicitly refers to Peter Lombard's *De Regno Hiberniae Commentairus*, which was completed in 1600 and published in 1632 and, to quote Joseph Lennon, "lauded Hugh O'Neill as a champion of the Counter-Reformation and presented an anti-English view of the events in Ireland under Elizabeth's forces, stirring support for Gaelic Catholic Ireland on the Continent and refuting Strabo, Solinus, and Giraldus Cambrensis." See Lennon, *Irish Orientalism*, 58.

141. Brian Friel, "Making History," in *Collected Plays* (Gallery, 2016), 3:416–17.
142. Friel, "Making History," 381.
143. IE BL/PP/OR 185 (1), Seán Ó Riada Collection/Bailiúchán Sheáin Uí Riada, unnamed correspondence from Brian Friel to Seán Ó Riada, November 8, 1967, University College Cork Archives Service, Cork, Ireland.
144. IE BL/PP/OR 185 (23), Seán Ó Riada Collection/Bailiúchán Sheáin Uí Riada, unnamed correspondence from Brian Friel to Seán Ó Riada, May 1968, underline in original, University College Cork Archives Service, Cork, Ireland.
145. Friel, "Making History," 376.
146. *Our Musical Heritage*, "Episode 1: Sean-nós Singing," Prog. ID: AR0023049, RTÉ Archives, July 7, 1962, 6:30–7:17.
147. Dooley, *Land for the People*, 182.
148. Mervyn O'Driscoll, "A 'German Invasion'? Irish Rural Radicalism, European Integration, and Irish Modernisation, 1958–73," *International History Review* 38, no. 3 (2016): 529.
149. O'Driscoll, "'German Invasion,'?" 538, 529. This situation was complicated, as O'Driscoll explains, by a "flaw in Irish legislation which permitted foreign nationals to buy property in Ireland without having residence qualifications." This ended up being the case for some former Nazis who had been acquitted by the Nuremberg trials, for example, Otto Skorzeny. While the nationality of land purchases was not recorded, many Irish people believed individuals and companies from England and the Federal Republic of Germany (FRG) were buying up agricultural land, concerns that were addressed to a degree in the 1965 Land Act, which required residence of seven years prior to purchase. See O'Driscoll, 531, 533–34, 538.
150. IE BL/PP/OR/250 (2), Seán Ó Riada Collection/Bailiúchán Sheáin Uí Riada, unpublished manuscript, 1969, University College Cork Archives Service, Cork, Ireland.
151. *Our Musical Heritage*, "Episode 1: Sean-nós Singing," Prog. ID: AR0023049, RTÉ Archives, July 7, 1962, 1:33–1:38, 1:45–1:57. Given that the Northern Irish state reached an impasse about the Irish language in 2017, Ó Riada's assertion of Irish identity as a kind of melting pot of a Gaelic ethnic identity would not have been welcome by many Northern Irish unionists in the 1960s and 1970s, or even today, in many areas of Northern Ireland.
152. *Our Musical Heritage*, "Episode 2: Sean-nós Singing," Prog. ID: AR0023050, RTÉ Archives, July 21, 1962, 3:05–3:33.

4. 1970–1995

1. Ian Angus, *Facing the Anthropocene: Fossil Capitalism and the Crisis of the Earth System* (Monthly Review, 2016), 42–45.
2. Chakrabarty, *Climate of History*, 12–13.
3. Chakrabarty, 61–62.
4. Brodie, "Data Infrastructure," 3.
5. Éilís Ní Dhuibhne, *The Bray House* (Attic, 1990), 79.
6. Maureen O'Connor examines animalization and feminization in the novel while Val Nolan demonstrates connections between Old Irish narrative forms and nuclear anxiety. Sharae Deckard analyzes representations of energy industries and technologies in The Bray House alongside a range of contemporary Irish literature. Besides, O'Connor, Nolan, and Deckard, many other scholars have examined different elements of *The Bray House*. While scholars like Susan Cahill and Jesse Bordwin analyze elements of materiality in the novel, including the body and the objects Robin documents in her excavation report, others like Carol Morris, Elke D'Hoker, and Jacqueline Fulmer have focused on how formal elements like genre, narrative voice, and folkloric storytelling in *The Bray House* engage with feminist theory and perspectives to resist patriarchy. The overt intertextual references in the novel to *Robinson Crusoe* are examined in separate analyses by Derek Hand and Beth Wightman to critique discursive colonial structures that Constanza del Río draws out in her use of psychoanalysis to illuminate the imperialist agenda in the novel's critical representations of ethnography and anthropology. Although Gerry Smyth asserts that *The Bray House* develops ecocritical themes through its explicit references to environmental degradation, Smyth does not analyze these themes in his overview of contemporary novels.
7. Maile Arvin, Eve Tuck, and Angie Morrill, "Decolonizing Feminism: Challenging Connections Between Settler Colonialism and Heteropatriarchy," *Feminist Formations* 25, no. 1 (Spring 2013): 27.
8. Parikka, *Geology of Media*, x.
9. Veronica McDermott, *Going Nuclear: Ireland, Britain, and the Campaign to Close Sellafield* (Irish Academic Press, 2008), 191.
10. McDermott, *Going Nuclear*, 97, 181.
11. McDermott, 80–85.
12. McDermott, 85.
13. O'Hearn, *Atlantic Economy*, 111–13.
14. McDermott, *Going Nuclear*, 118.
15. Kennedy, "Northern Ireland and Cross-Border Co-operation," 105–6.
16. Michael Kennedy, "Prologue: Political Considerations 'Good Business for Both of Us': North-South Cooperation on the Erne Hydroelectric Scheme," *The Erne Hydroelectric Scheme* (Lilliput, 2013), xii, xiv.

17. Shiel, *Quiet Revolution*, 235.
18. Kennedy, "Prologue," xvii.
19. McDermott, *Going Nuclear*, 121; Diarmaid Ferriter, *Ambiguous Republic: Ireland in the 1970s* (Profile, 2013), 531; Eamonn Sweeney, *Down Down Deeper and Down: Ireland in the 70s and 80s* (Gill & Macmillan, 2010), 144–45, 151; Maurice Manning and Moore McDowell, *Electricity Supply in Ireland: The History of the ESB* (Gill and Macmillan, 1984), 207.
20. McDermott, 24.
21. Regan, *Irish Counter-Revolution*, 158, 207, 308.
22. Deckard "Energy Futures," 380; Potts, *Contemporary Irish Writing and Environmentalism*, 90; Robert Kiely, "World-Ecological Satire: Peat, Brian O'Nolan, and the Irish Free State's Energy Regime," *Irish University Review* 49, no. 1 (2019): 92–93, 95; Kennedy, "Prologue," xii.
23. Potts, *Contemporary Irish Writing and Environmentalism*, xxxiii. The ESB did create a wind farm at Carnsore Point in 2003. See Potts, 108.
24. Although research was being done on survivors of the atomic bombs dropped on Japan after World War II, long-term exposure to radiation was not as well documented, nor were the effects known about intergenerational exposure or exposure to multiple environmental contaminants, such as pesticides, alongside radioactive substances. See Kate Brown, *Plutopia: Nuclear Families, Atomic Cities, and the Great Soviet and American Plutonium Disasters* (Oxford University Press, 2013), 308, 310; and Colum Kenny, *Fearing Sellafield: What It Is and Why the Irish Want It Shut* (Gill & Macmillan, 2003), 32–33. The 1983 documentary film *Windscale: The Nuclear Laundries* attests to heightened concerns about the risk of nuclear contamination on people and environments, and such concerns persist, as programs like Frontier Film's 2006 docudrama, *Fallout*, demonstrate. See *Fallout*, episodes 1 and 2, produced by Frontier Films for RTÉ, aired April 23–24, 2006, RTÉ Archives, Prog. ID IP10000 and IP15680. Anglo-Irish debates about Sellafield culminated with Ireland bringing an unsuccessful international court case against Britain in 2002 through the OSPAR Commission and the UN Law of the Sea for the environmental damage caused by Sellafield. See McDermott, *Going Nuclear*, 258; and Paul Cullen, "Irish Debate on Sellafield 'Dishonest,'" *Irish Times*, May 29, 2003, https://www.irishtimes.com/news/irish-debate-on-sellafield-dishonest-1.360613. While the Republic of Ireland was unsuccessful in these legal challenges, Sellafield is set to close in the wake of the COVID-19 pandemic and outbreaks of COVID-19 among the facility employees. See Jillian Ambrose, "Sellafield Nuclear Waste Site to Close Due to Coronavirus," *Guardian*, March 18, 2020, https://www.theguardian.com/business/2020/mar/18/sellafield-nuclear-waste-plant-close-coronavirus-staff.
25. Deckard, "Energy Futures," 381.

26. Potts, *Contemporary Irish Writing and Environmentalism*, 108.
27. Deckard, "Energy Futures," 381.
28. Ní Dhuibhne, *Bray House*, 37, 62.
29. See Ronit Lentin and Robbie McVeigh, *After Optimism? Ireland, Racism, and Globalisation* (Metro Eireann, 2006), 156. The IRA splintered into the Official and the Provisional IRA in late 1969. See Brian Hanley and Scott Millar, *The Lost Revolution: The Story of the Official IRA and The Workers' Party* (Penguin, 2009), 145. The reference to "the IRA" in the novel is therefore necessarily ambiguous and reductive.
30. Ballylumford does have a natural gas power station.
31. Nixon, *Slow Violence*, 15.
32. Ní Dhuibhne, *Bray House*, 63.
33. Ní Dhuibhne, 64.
34. "Young Moore's Almanac," Seán Ó Riada Collection/Bailiúchán Sheáin Uí Riada, January 1, 1963, BL/PP/OR/645 65; O'Hearn, *Atlantic Economy*, 112–113, 126–127, 143, 156.
35. McDermott, *Going Nuclear*, 277–78; Ní Dhuibhne, *Bray House*, 64–65. During the coalition government of the mid-1980s, FitzGerald's concerns about rising support for Sinn Féin led him to make concessions about the possibility of a united Ireland that aligned Fine Gael more with their coalition partner, the Social Democratic and Labour Party (SDLP). See Sweeney, *Down Down Deeper and Down*, 348.
36. Hanley and Millar, *Lost Revolution*, 207, 242–43, 277.
37. Ní Dhuibhne, *Bray House*, 249.
38. Traci Brynne Voyles, *Wastelanding: Legacies of Uranium Mining in Navajo Country* (University of Minnesota Press, 2015), 9.
39. Ní Dhuibhne, *Bray House*, 109.
40. Patrick Carroll, *Science, Culture, and Modern State Formation* (University of California Press, 2006), 151.
41. Ní Dhuibhne, *Bray House*, 108.
42. Ní Dhuibhne, 108.
43. Chandra Talpade Mohanty, *Feminism Without Borders: Decolonizing Theory, Practicing Solidarity* (Duke University Press, 2003). 121.
44. Hanley and Millar, *Lost Revolution*, 54–55, 175, 200–203, 232–33, 84–85. Fishing and natural resources rights were areas of focus in the civil rights movements both Northern Ireland and the Republic in the 1960s and 1970s. For example, many rights on fishing continued to rely on colonial-era allocations. Brian Hanley and Scott Millar explain, for instance, how in 1966 the National Waters Restoration League pushed back on what was known as the "king's mile" at the mouth of the Corrib River: "The legal rights to fish this area owned by members of the British gentry, whose

families had been granted them during the Cromwellian settlement, and similar situations existed on many of Ireland's other rivers." See Hanley and Miller, 84–85. These colonial-era fishing allocations continued to restrict Irish people's ability to retain connections to traditional stories and practices, such as the importance of the salmon in the Fionn Mac Cumhaill folk story, let alone in allocations of fish as potential natural resources for sustaining one's family.

45. Ní Dhuibhne, *Bray House*, 55.
46. Nuala Ní Dhomhnaill's sequence of poems, entitled "Immram," in *The Astrakhan Cloak* (trans. Paul Muldoon, 1992) also draws attention to the commodification of Irish culture in western County Kerry, in particular the Dingle Peninsula and the Blasket Islands. The notion of commodifying conceptions of authentic Irishness resonates with Taoiseach Charles Haughey's An Blascaod Mór National Historic Park Act of 1989, which attempted to turn the Great Blasket into a national park. See "Court Rules Blasket Act Is Unconstitutional," *Irish Times*, February 28, 1998, https://www.irishtimes.com/news/court-rules-blasket-act-is-unconstitutional-1.137279. Under the act, the state would "acquire their lands by compulsorily purchase order" and preserve the Blasket Islands as a cultural resource for tourism, though this was later found unconstitutional in 1999. See "Haughey Sees Shattering of Dream in Court's Blasket Islands Judgement," *Irish Times*, July 28, 1999, https://www.irishtimes.com/news/haughey-sees-shattering-of-dream-in-court-s-blasket-islands-judgment-1.210999. For the entire act, see "An Blascaod Mór National Historic Park Act, 1989," *Irish Statute Book*, https://www.irishstatutebook.ie/eli/1989/act/11/enacted/en/print.html.
47. As William Crotty points out, EEC subsidies imposed "a special emphasis on the skills needed by multinationals in international trade and information services." These subsidies supposedly benefited Ireland but, in Crotty's quote of Richard Rapaport, "During one dismal year in the early '80s recruiters from Sweden poached an entire graduating IT [Information Technology] class from the University of Limerick for overseas jobs." Brigid Laffan explains that the willingness of Ireland to defer parts of its national sovereignty to emerging opportunities and restrictions in the European community contrasted with other member states, like Sweden and Denmark: "Size is not a good predictor of approaches to European integration. Some small states, notably the Benelux, have embraced a federalist view of the European project with zeal, whereas others, such as Denmark and Sweden, are among the most reticent about political integration." These differences between European countries vying for and benefiting from economic integration in various ways illuminates uneven

geopolitical hierarchies that demonstrate changes to conceptions of identity and sovereignty as attached to territorial boundaries. See William Crotty, "Introduction: The Irish Way in World Affairs," in *Ireland on the World Stage*, ed. William Crotty and David E. Schmitt (Longman, 2002), 4, 11, brackets in original; and Brigid Laffan, "Chapter 5: Ireland and the European Union," in *Ireland on the World Stage*, ed. William Crotty and David E. Schmitt (Longman, 2002), 90.

48. Ní Dhuibhne, *Bray House*, 78.
49. Ní Dhuibhne, 78.
50. Ní Dhuibhne, 59.
51. Mohanty, *Feminism Without Borders*, 149.
52. Ní Dhuibhne, *Bray House*, 79.
53. Ní Dhuibhne, 74.
54. O'Hearn, *Atlantic Economy*, 186–90.
55. This referendum to phase out nuclear power was reversed in 2009. See Johan Bergenäs, "Sweden Reverses Nuclear Phase-out Policy," Nuclear Threat Initiative, November 10, 2009, https://www.nti.org/analysis/articles/sweden-reverses-nuclear-phase-out/.
56. Deckard, "Energy Futures," 383.
57. Deckard, 379–80.
58. Brown, *Plutopia*, 6.
59. Brown, 9.
60. Denis Linehan, "Irish Empire: Assembling the Geographical Imagination of Irish Missionaries in Africa," *Cultural Geographies* 21, no. 3 (2014): 432–33.
61. Ní Dhuibhne, *Bray House*, 23.
62. Ní Dhuibhne, 22, 23.
63. Ní Dhuibhne, 23.
64. Ní Dhuibhne, 73, 23.
65. Ní Dhuibhne, 23.
66. Ní Dhuibhne, 23.
67. Ní Dhuibhne, 90.
68. Eve Tuck, "Suspending Damage: A Letter to Communities," in *Harvard Educational Review* 79, no. 3 (Fall 2009): 420.
69. Tuck, "Suspending Damage," 419.
70. Tuck, 411, 416.
71. Ní Dhuibhne, *Bray House*, 56, 57–58.
72. Ní Dhuibhne, 56.
73. Ní Dhuibhne, 57.
74. Ní Dhuibhne, 57.
75. Ní Dhuibhne, 57; O'Connor, *Female and the Species*, 153.
76. Amitav Ghosh, *The Great Derangement: Climate Change and the Unthinkable* (University of Chicago Press, 2016), 4, 30.

77. Ní Dhuibhne, *Bray House*, 57; Patricia Monaghan, *The Encyclopedia of Celtic Mythology and Folklore* (Facts on File, 2004), 411–12.
78. Ní Dhuibhne, 76.
79. Arvin, Tuck, and Morrill, "Decolonizing Feminism," 21.
80. Rebecca Alder-Nissen, "The Faroe Islands: Independence Dreams, Globalist Separatism, and the Europeanization of Postcolonial Home Rule," *Cooperation and Conflict* 49, no. 1 (2014): 56, 70; Karen Oslund, *Iceland Imagined: Nature, Culture, and Storytelling in the North Atlantic* (University of Washington Press, 2011), 163–67.
81. Alder-Nissen, "Faroe Islands," 59, 66.
82. Alder-Nissen, 60.
83. Alder-Nissen, 71.
84. Ní Dhuibhne, *Bray House*, 77.
85. John F. West, *Faroese Folk-Tales and Legends* (Shetland, 1980), 90–91.
86. Monaghan, *Encyclopedia of Celtic Mythology and Folklore*, 411.
87. Ní Dhuibhne, *Bray House*, 59.
88. Arvin, Tuck, and Morrill, "Decolonizing Feminism," 21.
89. Leanne Betasomasake Simpson, *As We Have Always Done: Indigenous Freedom Through Radical Resistance* (University of Minnesota Press, 2017), 20.
90. Ní Dhuibhne, *Bray House*, 56.
91. Ní Dhuibhne, 56; "éigse," Teanglann, accessed November 13, 2024, https://www.teanglann.ie/ga/fgb/%c3%a9igse.
92. Morash, *History of Media in Ireland*, 6, 14, 15, 22; Diarmait Mac Giolla Chríost, *The Irish Language in Ireland: From Goídel to Globalisation* (Routledge, 2005), 4, 96; Laura O'Connor, *Haunted English: The Celtic Fringe, the British Empire, and De-anglicization* (Johns Hopkins University Press, 2006), 1–2.
93. Ní Dhuibhne, *Bray House*, 175, 200–201.
94. Ní Dhuibhne, 245; Kennedy, "Northern Ireland and Cross-Border Co-operation," 119.
95. Wenzel, *Disposition of Nature*, 134, emphasis in original.
96. Ní Dhuibhne, *Bray House*, 224–25.
97. Ní Dhuibhne, 63
98. Ní Dhuibhne, 224; Michael J. O'Kelly, *Newgrange: Archaeology, Art, and Legend* (Thames & Hudson, 1982), 112–13. The tumulus at Newgrange was rediscovered by a Williamite settler, Charles Campbell, in 1699 and preserved under the Ancient Monuments Protection Act of 1882, but the extensive archaeological excavations that make Newgrange accessible to visitors today were carried out between 1962 and 1975. See O'Kelly, *Newgrange*, 24, 38, 9.
99. O'Kelly, 113.
100. O'Kelly, 113.
101. Potts, *Contemporary Irish Writing and Environmentalism*, 45.

260 NOTES TO PAGES 179-189

102. Ní Dhuibhne, *Bray House*, 224.
103. Ní Dhuibhne, 246-47.
104. Voyles, *Wastelanding*, 9.
105. Mohanty, *Feminism Without Borders*, 120.
106. Chris Lawlor, "From a Spark to a Firebrand: Feagh Mac Hugh O'Byrne," *History Ireland* 21, no. 5 (September-October 2013): 22-23; Christopher Maginn, *"Civilizing" Gaelic Leinster: The Extension of Tudor Rule in the O'Byrne and O'Toole Leaderships* (Four Courts, 2005), 2.
107. Lawlor, "From a Spark to a Firebrand," 23.
108. Lawlor, 23.
109. Lennon, *Irish Orientalism*, 104-5, 107.
110. Lennon, 16.
111. Parikka, *Geology of Media*, 67, 81.
112. Ní Dhuibhne, *Bray House*, 217.
113. Ní Dhuibhne, 216.
114. Parikka, *Geology of Media*, 79.
115. Arvin, Tuck, and Morrill, "Decolonizing Feminism," 21.
116. Ní Dhuibhne, *Bray House*, 215.
117. Ní Dhuibhne, 215; Mohanty, *Feminism Without Borders*, 120.
118. Ní Dhuibhne, 239.
119. Ní Dhuibhne, 252.
120. Dominic O'Key, "Extinction in Public: Thinking Through the Sixth Mass Extinction, Environmental Humanities, and Extinction Studies," *Environmental Humanities* 15, no. 1 (March 2023): 168.
121. Brown, *Plutopia*, 6; Voyles, *Wastelanding*, 9.
122. Tuck, "Suspending Damage," 419.
123. Parikka, *Geology of Media*, 61.

5. 1995-2010

1. Mark Garavan ed., *Our Story: The Rossport Five* (Small World Media, 2006), 134.
2. Garavan, *Our Story*, 142-46.
3. Garavan, 136, 101.
4. Garavan, 149.
5. Garavan, 8; Siggins, *Once upon a Time*, 120-31.
6. Garavan, 9, 135; Siggins, 153, 176-77.
7. Garavan, 9; Siggins, 149, 167.
8. Siggins, 155, 261, 279.
9. Risteard Ó Domhnaill, "Live Q&A Zoom Meeting About *The Pipe* and *Atlantic*," English 230: Introduction to Environmental Literature (class lecture at the University of Oregon, Eugene, May 20, 2020).

10. Bozak, *Cinematic Footprint*, 199, 194.
11. *The Pipe*, directed and filmed by Risteard Ó Domhnaill (Galway, Ireland: Scannáin Inbhear, 2010), DVD, 31:30.
12. Isabelle Carbonell, "Multispecies Cinema in Wretched Waters: The Slow Violence of the Rio Doce Disaster," in *The Routledge Companion to Contemporary Art, Visual Culture, and Climate Change*, ed. T. J. Demos, Emily Eliza Scott, and Subhankar Banerjee (Routledge, 2021), 139.
13. Harvey O'Brien, "Advocating Advocacy: The Protest Paradigm of Documentary Representation—*Meeting Room* (2010) and *The Pipe* (2010)," *Estudios Irlandeses* 6 (2011): 222–23.
14. Pat Brereton and Danielle Barrios-O'Neill, "Irish Energy Landscapes on Film," *Journal of Environmental Media* 2, no. 1 (2021): 108, 110.
15. Rockett, Gibbons, and Hill, *Cinema and Ireland*, 203–4.
16. Satia, *Time's Monster*, 264.
17. Carville, "Picturing Poverty," 98–99.
18. Pat Brereton, "Ecological Representations of Irish Films," in *Culture and Media: Ecocritical Explorations*, ed. Rayson K. Alex, S. Susan Deborah, and Sachindev P.S. (Cambridge Scholars, 2014), 119.
19. Harvey O'Brien, *The Real Ireland: The Evolution of Ireland in Documentary Film* (Manchester University Press, 2004), 151.
20. O'Brien, *Real Ireland*, 151.
21. O'Brien, 150.
22. *The Pipe*, Ó Domhnaill, 56:57, 58:56, 59:58, 1:04:40–50.
23. *The Pipe*, Ó Domhnaill, 1:06.
24. *The Pipe*, Ó Domhnaill, 1:00–2:30. The violence continued to escalate, with numerous protesters injured at various moments throughout the struggle. Willie Corduff, whose activism won him the Goldman Environmental Prize on behalf of the Rossport Five, sustained serious injuries after being severely beaten in April 2009 by several people wearing balaclavas as security guards prevented family members from coming to his aid. Pat O'Donnell's boat *Iona Isle* was boarded and sunk by armed men in wetsuits as O'Donnell and his crew escaped in a life raft on 11 June 2009. See Siggins, *Once upon a Time*, 3, 6, 208, 234, 303, 313–15, 336, 344; and Potts, *Contemporary Irish Writing and Environmentalism*, 132.
25. O'Brien, "Advocating Advocacy," 223.
26. Bolter and Grusin, *Remediation*, 15, 5, 70.
27. Ó Domhnaill, "Live Q&A," 12:58–13:48.
28. Iheka, *African Ecomedia*, 10.
29. Helen Hughes, *Green Documentary: Environmental Documentary in the 21st Century* (Intellect, 2014), 5.
30. *The Pipe*, Ó Domhnaill, 28:29; 41:15.
31. *The Pipe*, Ó Domhnaill, 49:38.

32. Wenzel, *Disposition of Nature*, 102.
33. Bozak, *Cinematic Footprint*, 91.
34. *The Pipe*, Ó Domhnaill, 2:14.
35. *The Pipe*, Ó Domhnaill, 2:50–2:53.
36. *The Pipe*, Ó Domhnaill, 31:50–32:00.
37. *The Pipe*, Ó Domhnaill, 6:10–6:12.
38. *The Pipe*, Ó Domhnaill, 16:30, 1:07:14.
39. *The Pipe*, Ó Domhnaill, 1:05:24.
40. *The Pipe*, Ó Domhnaill, 14:00–14:20.
41. Garavan, *Our Story*, 157.
42. *The Pipe*, Ó Domhnaill, 56:30.
43. *The Pipe*, Ó Domhnaill, 48:26, 56:15–56:45, 1:00:35–1:01:04.
44. *The Pipe*, Ó Domhnaill, 1:18:30, 9:00.
45. *The Pipe*, Ó Domhnaill, 44:25.
46. *The Pipe*, Ó Domhnaill, 56:57, 58:56, 59:58, 1:04:40–50; While "soundscape" is a widely used term, my use of it draws on Ari Y. Kelman's discussion of Murray Schafer's theorization of that term. Rather than simply an aural backdrop, a soundscape, like a landscape, is crafted by culture. Ó Domhnaill's curation of the soundscape in this scene emphasizes the aurality of neocolonial modernization in rural Ireland. See Ari Y. Kelman, "Rethinking the Soundscape: A Critical Genealogy of a Key Term in Sound Studies," *Senses & Society* 5, no. 2 (2010), 214.
47. *The Pipe*, Ó Domhnaill, 1:00:40–1:01:35.
48. *The Pipe*, Ó Domhnaill, 1:04:40.
49. *The Pipe*, Ó Domhnaill, 1:04:48.
50. Nixon, *Slow Violence*, 28.
51. Leonard, *Environmental Movement in Ireland*, 193; Nixon, *Slow Violence*, 28–29; Potts, *Contemporary Irish Writing and Environmentalism*,115, 117, 124, 128, 134–136; Siggins, *Once upon a Time*, 45, 65, 173.
52. Harding, *Sciences from Below*, 206.
53. Harding, 206; Nancy Fraser, "Rethinking the Public Sphere: A Contribution to the Critique of Actually Existing Democracy," *Social Text*, nos. 25–26 (1990): 59–60.
54. *The Promise of Barty O'Brien*, written by Seán Ó Faoláin (American National Archives, 1951), DVD.
55. Potts, *Contemporary Irish Writing and Environmentalism*, 76; Deckard, "Energy Futures," 380.
56. Sheena Wilson, "Gendering Oil: Tracing Western Petrosexual Relations," in *Energy Humanities: An Anthology*, ed. Imre Szeman and Dominic Boyer (Johns Hopkins University Press, 2017), 280.
57. *The Pipe*, Ó Domhnaill, 19:49.

58. *The Pipe*, Ó Domhnaill, 21:53–24:11, 24:55–26.48.
59. *The Pipe*, Ó Domhnaill, 22:20, 26:20.
60. *The Pipe*, Ó Domhnaill, 23:00.
61. Garavan, *Our Story*, 87, 201, 205, 207.
62. Siggins, *Once upon a Time*, 152.
63. Siggins, 219.
64. "Nightmare for the Rossport Five and Their Families," *The Late Late Show*, hosted by Pat Kenny, 2 September 2005, produced by RTÉ, prog. ID IH68662, RTÉ Archives, 0:37-:040.
65. "Nightmare for the Rossport Five."
66. Ó Domhnaill, "Live Q&A."
67. Harding, *Sciences from Below*, 198.
68. Harding, 206.
69. Garavan, *Our Story*, 201.
70. Mohanty, *Feminism Without Borders*, 22.
71. Siggins, *Once upon a Time*, 231.
72. *The Pipe*, Ó Domhnaill, 40:00–40:11.
73. Michael Paye, "Beyond a Capitalist Atlantic: Fish, Fuel, and the Collapse of Cheap Nature in Ireland, Newfoundland, and Nigeria," *Irish University Review* 49, no. 2 (2019): 124.
74. *The Pipe*, Ó Domhnaill, 39:49–40:07.
75. *The Pipe*, Ó Domhnaill, 40:07–40:12.
76. *The Pipe*, Ó Domhnaill, 18:45, 9:00, 27:15, 41:15.
77. Mohanty, *Feminism Without Borders*, 35.
78. *The Pipe*, Ó Domhnaill, 31:45–35:00; 56:30.
79. Garavan, *Our Story*, 75.
80. Siggins, *Once upon a Time*, 42.
81. Eóin Flannery, *Ireland and Postcolonial Studies: Theory, Discourse, Utopia* (Palgrave Macmillan, 2009), 226.
82. *The Pipe*, Ó Domhnaill, 34:40–35:00.
83. *The Pipe*, Ó Domhnaill, 4:26.
84. Brereton and Barrios-O'Neill, "Irish Energy Landscapes," 21; Potts, *Contemporary Irish Writing and Environmentalism*, xxvii-xxviii, 18, 20–21, 71.
85. *The Pipe*, Ó Domhnaill, 1:15:30–1:16:52, 1:18:40.
86. Rockett, Gibbons, and Hill, *Cinema and Ireland*, 198, 200, 203.
87. O'Brien, *Real Ireland*, 17.
88. *Oisín*, directed by Peter Carey, produced by Vivien and Patrick Carey (Irish Film Institute Player, 1970): https://ifiplayer.ie/oisin-son-of-fionn-mac-cumhaill/.
89. Wenzel, *Disposition of Nature*, 108.
90. *The Pipe*, Ó Domhnaill, 45:29.

91. *The Pipe*, Ó Domhnaill, 44:25–45:30. For more details about Shell's construction crossing the high-water mark, see Siggins, *Once upon a Time*, 272.
92. *The Pipe*, Ó Domhnaill, 31:30–31:43.
93. Potts, *Contemporary Irish Writing and Environmentalism*, 71; Taylor, *Irish Materialisms*, 97.
94. *The Pipe*, Ó Domhnaill, 31:45.
95. Gladwin, *Contentious Terrains*, 29.
96. *The Pipe*, Ó Domhnaill, 36:32.
97. *The Pipe*, Ó Domhnaill, 36:34.
98. *The Pipe*, Ó Domhnaill, 36:43–36:53.
99. Taylor, *Irish Materialisms*, 217.
100. *The Pipe*, Ó Domhnaill, 36:57.
101. *The Pipe*, Ó Domhnaill, 59:30.
102. *The Pipe*, Ó Domhnaill, 15:15; 1:17:50.
103. Erika Balsom, *An Oceanic Feeling: Cinema and the Sea* (Govett-Brewster Art Gallery, 2018), 41.
104. *The Pipe*, Ó Domhnaill, 59:02.
105. Stacy Alaimo, *Exposed: Environmental Politics and Pleasures in Posthuman Times* (University of Minnesota Press, 2016), 161.
106. Alaimo, *Exposed*, 161.
107. Wenzel, *Disposition of Nature*, 137.
108. Bozak, *Cinematic Footprint*, 193.

Conclusion

1. Michael D. Higgins, *Machnamh 100: President of Ireland Centenary Reflections*, vol. 1 (Department of Tourism, Culture, Arts, Gaeltacht, Sport, and Media, Dublin, 2021), 78.
2. Peadar Kirby, "Contested Pedigrees of the Celtic Tiger," in *Reinventing Ireland: Culture, Society and the Global Economy*, ed. Peadar Kirby, Luke Gibbons, and Michael Cronin (Pluto, 2002), 30; O'Hearn, *Atlantic Economy*, 188–89.
3. Ronit Lentin, "Asylum Seekers, Ireland, and the Return of the Repressed," *Irish Studies Review* 24, no. 1 (2016): 26.
4. Doreen Massey, *World City* (Polity, 2007), 175.
5. Steven Loyal, *Understanding Immigration in Ireland: State, Capital, and Labour in a Global Age* (Manchester University Press, 2011), 149.
6. I am drawing here on Ruth Wilson Gilmore's definition of racism. See Ruth Wilson Gilmore, *Golden Gulag: Prisons, Surplus, Crisis, and Opposition in Globalizing California* (University of California Press, 2007), 28.

See also Malcolm Sen and Julie McCormick Weng, eds., *Race in Irish Literature and Culture*, (Cambridge University Press, 2024); and, John Brannigan, *Race in Modern Irish Literature and Culture* (Edinburgh University Press, 2009).
7. Walter, *Outsiders Inside*, 107.
8. Jim Mac Laughlin, *Travellers and Ireland: Whose Country, Whose History?* (Cork University Press, 1995), 26.
9. Robert J. C. Young, *Colonial Desire: Hybridity in Theory, Culture and Race* (Routledge, 1995), 31; see also Mary Burke, "Irish Travellers, the Environment, and Literature," in *A History of Irish Literature and the Environment*, ed. Malcolm Sen (Cambridge University Press, 2022), 206–26.
10. Zygmunt Bauman, *Liquid Modernity* (Polity, 2000), 12–13, 28, emphasis in original.
11. Brodie, "Data Infrastructures," 6.
12. O'Hearn, *Atlantic Economy*, 7.
13. Brodie, "Data Infrastructures," 4–5.
14. Patrick Bresnihan and Patrick Brodie, "From Toxic Industries to Green Extractivism: Rural Environmental Struggles, Multinational Corporations, and Ireland's Postcolonial Ecological Regime," *Irish Studies Review* 32, no. 1 (2024): 94, 112.
15. Bresnihan and Brodie, "From Toxic Industries to Green Extractivism," 113.
16. Caminero-Santangelo, *Different Shades of Green*, 9.
17. DeLoughrey, *Allegories of the Anthropocene*, 3.

BIBLIOGRAPHY

Aalen, Frederick H. A. "Constructive Unionism and the Shaping of Rural Ireland, c. 1880–1921." *Rural History* 4, no. 2 (1993): 137–64.
Abram, David. "On the Origin of the Phrase 'More-than-Human.'" In *More than Human Rights: An Ecology of Law, Thought, and Narrative for Earthly Flourishing*, edited by César Rodríguez-Garavito, 341–47. NYU Law, 2024.
Agyeman, Julian, Robert D. Bullard, and Bob Evans. "Introduction: Joined-up Thinking: Bringing Together Sustainability, Environmental Justice and Equity." In *Just Sustainabilities: Development in an Unequal World*, edited by Julian Agyeman, Robert D. Bullard, and Bob Evans, 1–16. MIT Press, 2003.
Alaimo, Stacy. *Bodily Natures: Science, Environment, and the Material Self*. Indiana University Press, 2010.
Alaimo, Stacy. *Exposed: Environmental Politics and Pleasures in Posthuman Times*. University of Minnesota Press, 2016.
Alder-Nissen, Rebecca. "The Faroe Islands: Independence Dreams, Globalist Separatism, and the Europeanization of Postcolonial Home Rule." *Cooperation and Conflict* 49, no. 1 (2014): 55–79.
Allen, Robert. *No Global: The People of Ireland Versus the Multinationals*. Pluto, 2004.
Ambrose, Jillian. "Sellafield Nuclear Waste Site to Close Due to Coronavirus." *Guardian*, March 18, 2020. https://www.theguardian.com/business/2020/mar/18/sellafield-nuclear-waste-plant-close-coronavirus-staff.
"An Blascaod Mór National Historic Park Act, 1989." *Irish Statute Book*. Accessed April 8, 2025. https://www.irishstatutebook.ie/eli/1989/act/11/enacted/en/print.html.
Angus, Ian. *Facing the Anthropocene: Fossil Capitalism and the Crisis of the Earth System*. Monthly Review, 2016.
Angus, Siobhan. *Camera Geologica: An Elemental History of Photography*. Duke University Press, 2024.
Archer, Jean. "Geological Artistry: The Drawings and Watercolors of George Victor du Noyer in the Archives of the Geological Survey of Ireland." In *Visualizing Ireland: National Identity and the Pictorial Tradition*, edited by Adele M. Dalsimer, 133–44. Faber & Faber, 1993.
Arendt, Hannah. *The Human Condition*. 2nd ed. University of Chicago Press, [1958] 2018.

Arvin, Maile, Eve Tuck, and Angie Morrill. "Decolonizing Feminism: Challenging Connections Between Settler Colonialism and Heteropatriarchy." *Feminist Formations* 25, no. 1 (Spring 2013): 8–34.
Bakhtin, Mikhail. "Epic and Novel: Toward a Methodology for the Study of the Novel." In *The Dialogic Imagination: Four Essays*, edited by Michael Holquist and translated by Caryl Emerson and Michael Holquist, 3–40. University of Texas Press, 1981.
Bakhtin, Mikhail. *Rabelais and His World*. Translated by Helene Iswolsky. Indiana University Press, 1984.
Bal, Mieke. *Narratology: Introduction to the Theory of Narrative*. 2nd ed. University of Toronto Press, 1997.
Balsom, Erika. *An Oceanic Feeling: Cinema and the Sea*. Govett-Brewster Art Gallery, 2018.
Barad, Karen. *Meeting the Universe Halfway: Quantum Physics and the Entanglement of Matter and Meaning*. Duke University Press, 2007.
Barthes, Roland. *Camera Lucida*. Hill & Wang, [1980] 2010.
Bartlett, Thomas. *Ireland, A History*. Cambridge University Press, 2010.
Bates, Julie. "Writing with Air in *The Third Policeman*." In *Flann O'Brien and the Nonhuman: Environments, Animals, Machines*, edited by Katherine Ebury, Paul Fagan, and John Greaney, 41–55. Cork University Press, 2024.
Bauman, Zygmunt. *Liquid Modernity*. Polity, 2000.
Baylis, Gail. "Technologies and Cultures: Robert J. Welch's Western Landscapes, 1895–1914." In *Framing the West: Images of Rural Ireland, 1891–1920*, edited by Ciara Breathnach, 77–96. Irish Academic Press, 2007.
Beattie, Seán. *Donegal in Transition: The Impact of the Congested Districts Board*. Merrion Press of the Irish Academic Press, 2013.
Beiner, Guy. *Remembering the Year of the French: Irish Folk History and Social Memory*. University of Wisconsin Press, 2007.
Bell, Jonathan. "The Agricultural Work of the Congested Districts Board." In *Framing the West: Images of Rural Ireland, 1891–1920*, edited by Ciara Breathnach, 163–78. Irish Academic Press, 2007.
Bergenäs, Johan. "Sweden Reverses Nuclear Phase-out Policy." Nuclear Threat Initiative, November 10, 2009. https://www.nti.org/analysis/articles/sweden-reverses-nuclear-phase-out/.
Bloomfield, G. T. "London: Electricity Hub of Britain," British Electricity History, University of Guelph, 2024. https://www.britelechist.uoguelph.ca/.
Bolter, Jay David, and Richard Grusin. *Remediation: Understanding New Media*. MIT Press, 1999.
Booker, Keith. *Flann O'Brien, Bakhtin, and Menippean Satire*. Syracuse University Press, 1995.
Bordwin, Jesse. "Against Reference: On Reading Objects in Éilís Ní Dhuibhne's *The Bray House*." *New Hibernia Review / Iris Éireannach Nua* 21, no. 4 (2017): 70–88.

Bourke, Joanna. "Women and Poultry in Ireland, 1891–1914." *Irish Historical Studies* 25, no. 99 (1987): 293–310.
Boydell, Brian. "The Future of Music in Ireland." *Bell*, January 1951, edited by Peadar O'Donnell, 15–29. National Library of Ireland, Dublin, F397.
Bozak, Nadia. *The Cinematic Footprint: Light, Camera, Natural Resources*. Rutgers University Press, 2011.
Bradley, Anthony. *Imagining Ireland in the Poems and Plays of W. B. Yeats: Nation, Class, and State*. Palgrave Macmillan, 2011.
Brannigan, John. *Race in Modern Irish Literature and Culture*. Edinburgh University Press, 2009.
Breathnach, Ciara. "The Role of Women in the Economy of the West of Ireland, 1891–1923." *New Hibernia Review / Iris Éireannach Nua*. 8, no. 1 (2004): 80–92.
Breathnach, Ciara. *The Congested Districts Board of Ireland, 1891–1923: Poverty and Development in the West of Ireland*. Four Courts, 2005.
Breathnach, Ciara. "Lady Dudley's District Nursing Scheme and the Congested Districts Board, 1903–1923." In *Gender and Medicine in Ireland, 1700–1950*, edited by Margaret Preston and Margaret Ó hÓgartaigh, 138–53. Syracuse University Press, 2012.
Breathnach, Ciara. "Smallholder Housing and People's Health, 1890–1915." In *Framing the West: Images of Rural Ireland, 1891–1920*, edited by Ciara Breathnach, 179–96. Irish Academic Press, 2007.
Brereton, Pat. "Ecological Representations of Irish Films." In *Culture and Media: Ecocritical Explorations*, edited by Rayson K. Alex, S. Susan Deborah, and Sachindev P.S., 114–30. Cambridge Scholars, 2014.
Brereton, Pat, and Danielle Barrios-O'Neill. "Irish Energy Landscapes on Film." *Journal of Environmental Media* 2, no. 1 (2021): 105–15.
Bresnihan, Patrick, and Patrick Brodie, "From Toxic Industries to Green Ex tractivism: Rural Environmental Struggles, Multinational Corporations, and Ireland's Postcolonial Ecological Regime." *Irish Studies Review* 32, no. 1 (2024): 93–122.
"Broadcasting Authority Act, 1960." Irish Statute Book. Accessed August 20, 2025. https://www.irishstatutebook.ie/eli/1960/act/10/enacted/en/print.html.
Brodie, Patrick. "Climate Extraction and Supply Chains of Data." *Media, Culture & Society* 42, nos. 7–8 (2020): 1095–114.
Brodie, Patrick. "Data Infrastructure Studies on an Unequal Planet." *Big Data & Society* 10, no. 1 (2023): 1–14.
Brown, Kate. *Plutopia: Nuclear Families, Atomic Cities, and the Great Soviet and American Plutonium Disasters*. Oxford University Press, 2013.
Brown, Terence. *Ireland: A Social and Cultural History, 1922 to the Present*. Cornell University Press, 1985.
Bruna, Giulia. *J. M. Synge and Travel Writing of the Irish Revival*. Syracuse University Press, 2017.

Bryan, Conrad Koza, and Chamion Caballero. *Irish People of Colour: A Social History of Mixed Race Irish in Britain and Ireland Between 1700 and 2000.* Association of Mixed Race Irish, 2024.
Burke, Mary. "Irish Travellers, the Environment, and Literature." In *A History of Irish Literature and the Environment*, edited by Malcolm Sen, 206–26. Cambridge University Press, 2022.
Cahill, Susan. *Irish Literature in the Celtic Tiger Years, 1990 to 2008: Gender, Bodies, Memory.* Continuum, 2011.
Calvillo, Nerea. *Aeropolis: Queering Air in Toxicpolluted Worlds.* Columbia Books, 2023.
Caminero-Santangelo, Byron. *Different Shades of Green: African Literature, Environmental Justice, and Political Ecology.* University of Virginia Press, 2014.
Carbonell, Isabelle. "Multispecies Cinema in Wretched Waters: The Slow Violence of the Rio Doce Disaster." In *The Routledge Companion to Contemporary Art, Visual Culture, and Climate Change*, edited by T. J. Demos, Emily Eliza Scott, and Subhankar Banerjee, 139–48. Routledge, 2021.
Carey, Peter, dir. *Oisín.* Produced by Vivien and Patrick Carey. Irish Film Institute Player, 1970.
Carroll, Patrick. *Science, Culture, and Modern State Formation.* University of California Press, 2006.
Carville, Justin. "Picturing Poverty: Colonial Photography and the Congested Districts Board." In *Framing the West: Images of Rural Ireland, 1891–1920*, edited by Ciara Breathnach, 97–114. Irish Academic Press, 2007.
Carville, Justin. *Photography and Ireland.* Reaktion, 2011.
Carville, Justin. "Visible Others: Photography and Romantic Ethnography in Ireland." In *Irish Modernism and the Global Primitive*, edited by Maria McGarrity and Claire A. Culleton, 63–76. Palgrave Macmillan, 2009.
Carville, Justin. "With His 'Mind-Guided Camera': J. M. Synge, J. J. Clarke, and the Visual Politics of Edwardian Street Photography." In *Synge and Edwardian Ireland*, edited by Brian Cliff and Nicholas Grene, 186–207. Oxford University Press, 2012.
Castle, Gregory. *Modernism and the Celtic Revival.* Cambridge University Press, 2001.
Chakrabarty, Dipesh. *The Climate of History in a Planetary Age.* University of Chicago Press, 2021.
Cleary, Joe. *Outrageous Fortune: Capital and Culture in Modern Ireland.* Field Day, 2007.
Cole, Luke W., and Sheila R. Foster. *From the Ground Up: Environmental Racism and the Rise of the Environmental Justice Movement.* New York University Press, 2001.

Congested Districts Board Photograph Collection. Ca. 1906–14. National Library of Ireland, National Photographic Archive, and National Library of Ireland Online Catalogue, Dublin. http://catalogue.nli.ie/Collection/vtls000033747.

Connolly, Niamh. "Fisheries in the West." In *Framing the West: Images of Rural Ireland, 1891–1920*, edited by Ciara Breathnach, 129–44. Irish Academic Press, 2007.

"Court Rules Blasket Act Is Unconstitutional." *Irish Times*, February 28, 1998. https://www.irishtimes.com/news/court-rules-blasket-act-is-unconstitutional-1.137279.

Cronin, Anthony. *No Laughing Matter: The Life and Times of Flann O'Brien*. Fromm International, 1989.

Crotty, William. "Introduction: The Irish Way in World Affairs." In *Ireland on the World Stage*, edited by William Crotty and David E. Schmitt, 1–23. Longman, 2002.

Cullen, Paul. "Irish Debate on Sellafield 'Dishonest.'" *Irish Times*, May 29, 2003. https://www.irishtimes.com/news/irish-debate-on-sellafield-dishonest-1.360613.

Dalsimer, Adele M. "'The Irish Peasant Had All His Heart': J. M. Synge in *The Country Shop*." In *Visualizing Ireland: National Identity and the Pictorial Tradition*, edited by Adele M. Dalsimer, 201–30. Faber & Faber, 1993.

Davis, Leith. *Music, Postcolonialism, and Gender: The Construction of Irish National Identity, 1724–1874*. University of Notre Dame, 2006.

Deckard, Sharae. "World-Ecology and Ireland: The Neoliberal Ecological Regime." *Journal of World-Systems Research*. 22, no. 1 (2016): 145–76.

Deckard, Sharae. "Energy Futures in Contemporary Irish Fiction." In *A History of Irish Literature and the Environment*, edited by Malcolm Sen, 377–94. Cambridge University Press, 2022.

Deckard, Sharae. "Introduction: Reading Ireland's Food, Energy, and Climate." *Irish University Review* 49, No. 2 (2019): 1–12.

De Courcy, John. *Ireland's Sea Fisheries: A History*. Glendale, 1981.

Delaney, Enda. "Emigration, Political Cultures, and the Evolution of Post-war Irish Society." In *The Lemass Era: Politics and Society in the Ireland of Seán Lemass*, edited by Brian Girvin and Gary Murphy, 49–65. University College Dublin Press, 2005.

DeLoughrey, Elizabeth. *Allegories of the Anthropocene*. Duke University Press, 2019.

DeLoughrey, Elizabeth, and George B. Handley, eds. *Postcolonial Ecologies: Literatures of the Environment*. Oxford University Press, 2011.

Del Río, Constanza. "Excavating Ireland's Contemporary Heritage in Éilís Ní Dhuibhne's *The Bray House*." *Estudios Irlandeses*, no. 4 (2009): 1–8.

D'Hoker, Elke. "Powerful Voices: Female Narrators and Unreliability in Three Irish Novels." *Etudes Irlandaises* 32, no. 1 (2007): 21–31.
Dillane, Aileen, and Matthew Noone. "Irish Music Orientalism." *New Hibernia Review / Iris Éireannach Nua* 20, no. 1 (Earrach / Spring 2016): 121–37.
Dooley, Terence. *The Land for the People: The Land Question in Independent Ireland*. University College Dublin, 2004.
Doyle, Patrick. *Civilising Rural Ireland: The Co-operative Movement, Development and Nation-State, 1889–1939*. Manchester University Press, 2019.
Dumas, Michael J. "Against the Dark: Antiblackness in Education Policy and Discourse." *Theory into Practice* 55, no. 1 (2016): 11–19.
Ebury, Katherine, Paul Fagan, and John Greaney. "Editor's Introduction: Brian O'Nolan's Nonhuman Imaginary." In *Flann O'Brien and the Nonhuman: Environments, Animals, Machines*, edited by Katherine Ebury, Paul Fagan, and John Greaney, 1–21. Cork University Press, 2024.
Edge, Sarah Jane. "Photographic History and the Visual Appearance of an Irish Nationalist Discourse, 1840–1870." *Victorian Literature and Culture* 32, no. 1 (2004): 17–39.
"éigse." Teanglann. Accessed November 13, 2024. https://www.teanglann.ie/ga/fgb/%c3%a9igse.
Evans, E. Estyn, and Brian S. Turner, eds. *Ireland's Eye: The Photographs of Robert John Welch*. Blackstaff, 1977.
Fallout. Episodes 1 and 2, produced by Frontier Films for RTÉ, aired April 23–24, 2006. RTE Archives, Prog. ID IP10000 and IP15680.
Fanon, Frantz. *The Wretched of the Earth*. Translated by Richard Philcox. Grove, 2004.
Farrell, Michael. "Radio Debates in Ireland." *Bell*, January 1951, edited by Peadar O'Donnell, 53–59. National Library of Ireland, Dublin, F397.
Ferguson, James. *Global Shadows: Africa in the Neoliberal World Order*. Duke University Press, 2006.
Ferriter, Diarmaid. *Ambiguous Republic: Ireland in the 1970s*. Profile, 2013.
Flannery, Eóin. *Ireland and Ecocriticism: Literature, History, and Environmental Justice*. Routledge, 2016.
Flannery, Eóin. *Ireland and Postcolonial Studies: Theory, Discourse, Utopia*. Palgrave Macmillan, 2009.
Foster, Jonathan. "'The reassuring unmistakability of the abiding earth': Nature Writing, State Engineering, the Anthropocene in *The Third Policeman*." In *Flann O'Brien and the Nonhuman: Environments, Animals, Machines*, edited by Katherine Ebury, Paul Fagan, and John Greaney, 73–87. Cork University Press, 2024.
Foucault, Michel. *The History of Sexuality: Volume 1*. Translated from French by Robert Hurley. Pantheon, 1978.

Fraser, Nancy. "Rethinking the Public Sphere: A Contribution to the Critique of Actually Existing Democracy." *Social Text*, nos. 25–26 (1990): 56–80.
Friel, Brian. *The Enemy Within*. Gallery, 1975.
Friel, Brian. "Making History." In *Collected Plays*, Vol. 3. Gallery, 2016.
Fulmer, Jacqueline. *Folk Women and Indirection in Morrison, Ní Dhuibhne, Hurston, and Lavin*. Ashgate, 2007.
Garavan, Mark, ed. *Our Story: The Rossport Five*. Small World Media, 2006.
Ghosh, Amitav. *The Great Derangement: Climate Change and the Unthinkable*. University of Chicago Press, 2016.
Gibbons, Luke. "Mirrors and Memory: Ireland, Photography, and the Modern." In *The Moderns*, edited by Enrique Juncosa and Christina Kennedy, 331–39. Irish Museum of Modern Art, 2011.
Gibbons, Luke. *Transformations in Irish Culture*. University of Notre Dame Press, 1996.
Gilmore, Ruth Wilson. *Golden Gulag: Prisons, Surplus, Crisis, and Opposition in Globalizing California*. University of California Press, 2007.
Girvin, Brian, and Gary Murphy. "Chapter One: Whose Ireland? The Lemass Era." In *The Lemass Era: Politics and Society in the Ireland of Seán Lemass*, edited by Brian Girvin and Gary Murphy, 1–11. University College Dublin Press, 2005.
Gladwin, Derek. *Contentious Terrains: Boglands, Ireland, Postcolonial Gothic*. Cork University Press, 2016.
Green-Lewis, Jennifer. *Framing the Victorians: Photography and the Culture of Realism*. Cornell University Press, 1996.
Guelke, Adrian. "Northern Ireland and the International System." In *Ireland on the World Stage*, edited by William Crotty and David E. Schmitt, 127–39. Longman, 2002.
Hand, Derek. "Being Ordinary. Ireland from Elsewhere: A Reading of Éilís Ní Dhuibhne's *The Bray House*." *Irish University Review* 30, no. 1 (2000): 103–16.
Hanley, Brian, and Scott Millar. *The Lost Revolution: The Story of the Official IRA and The Workers' Party*. Penguin, 2009.
Harding, Sandra. *Sciences from Below: Feminisms, Postcolonialities, and Modernities*. Duke University Press, 2008.
Harmon, Maurice, ed. *The Dolmen Press: A Celebration*. Lilliput, 2001.
"Haughey Sees Shattering of Dream in Court's Blasket Islands Judgement." *Irish Times*, July 28, 1999. https://www.irishtimes.com/news/haughey-sees-shattering-of-dream-in-court-s-blasket-islands-judgment-1.210999.
H Block. Produced by Donal Lunny and Christy Moore. Mild Music, 1978. LP.
Heise, Ursula. *Sense of Place and Sense of Planet. The Environmental Imagination of the Global*. Oxford University Press, 2008.

Henry, Paul. *Connemara Cottages*. Ca. 1936–37. Oil on canvas, 69x84 cm. Bequeathed, Mrs. M. Henry, 1974. National Gallery of Ireland Collection, NGI.4077. © Paul Henry, *Connemara Cottages*, c/o Pictoright Amsterdam 2025.

Higgins, Michael D. *Machnamh 100: President of Ireland Centenary Reflections*. Vol. 1. Department of Tourism, Culture, Arts, Gaeltacht, Sport and Media, 2021.

"History of Forestry in Ireland." Teagasc: Agriculture and Food Development Authority, June 6, 2019. https://www.teagasc.ie/crops/forestry/advice/general-topics/history-of-forestry-in-ireland/.

Holt, Jennifer, and Patrick Vonderau. "'Where the Internet Lives': Data Centers as Cloud Infrastructure." In *Signal Traffic: Critical Studies of Media Infrastructures*, edited by Lisa Parks and Nicole Starosielski, 71–93. University of Illinois Press, 2015.

Hopper, Keith. *Flann O'Brien: A Portrait of the Artist as a Young Post-Modernist*. Cork University Press, 1995.

Horgan, John. *Irish Media: A Critical History Since 1922*. Routledge, 2001.

Horgan, John. *Broadcasting and Public Life: RTÉ News and Current Affairs, 1926–1997*. Four Courts, 2004.

Huber, Katherine M. "'The bog is a technology of its own': Rupturing the Logic of Natural Resource Development in Risteard Ó Domhnaill's *The Pipe*." *ISLE: Interdisciplinary Studies in Literature and Environment* 31, no. 1 (Spring 2024): 176–99.

Huber, Katherine M. "The View from Mrs. Kelly's Window: Reframing Agency and Land in the Congested Districts Board Photographs." *Éire-Ireland* 55, nos. 3–4 (Fall–Winter 2020): 95–128.

Huggan, Graham, and Helen Tiffin. *Postcolonial Ecocriticism: Literature, Animals, Environment*. Routledge, 2010.

Hughes, Helen. *Green Documentary: Environmental Documentary in the 21st Century*. Intellect, 2014.

Iheka, Cajetan. *African Ecomedia: Network Forms, Planetary Politics*. Duke University Press, 2021.

Kahn, Douglas. *Earth Sound Earth Signal: Energies and Earth Magnitude in the Arts*. University of California Press, 2013.

Kealy, Alacoque, and Radio Telefís Éireann. Audience Research Dept. *Irish Radio Data: 1926–1980*. Radio Telefís Éireann, 1981.

Keane, Damien. "Poetry, Music, and Reproduced Sound." In *Oxford Handbook of Modern Irish Poetry*, edited by Fran Brearton and Alan A. Gillis, 266–81. Oxford University Press, 2012.

Kelman, Ari Y. "Rethinking the Soundscape: A Critical Genealogy of a Key Term in Sound Studies." *Senses & Society* 5, no. 2 (2010): 212–34.

Kennedy, Michael. "Northern Ireland and Cross-Border Co-operation." In *The Lemass Era: Politics and Society in the Ireland of Seán Lemass*, edited by Brian Girvin and Gary Murphy, 99–121. University College Dublin Press, 2005.

Kennedy, Michael. "Prologue: Political Considerations 'Good Business for Both of Us': North-South Cooperation on the Erne Hydroelectric Scheme." In *The Erne Hydroelectric Scheme*, x–xx. Lilliput, 2013.

Kenny, Colum. *Fearing Sellafield: What It Is and Why the Irish Want It Shut*. Gill & Macmillan, 2003.

Kiely, Robert. "World-Ecological Satire: Peat, Brian O'Nolan, and the Irish Free State's Energy Regime." *Irish University Review* 49, no. 1 (2019): 90–104.

Kinsella, Thomas. *Fifteen Dead, with Commentary*. Dolmen, 1979.

Kirby, Peadar. "Contested Pedigrees of the Celtic Tiger." In *Reinventing Ireland: Culture, Society and the Global Economy*, edited by Peadar Kirby, Luke Gibbons, and Michael Cronin, 21–37. Pluto, 2002.

Kirkpatrick, Kathryn. "Quick Red Foxes: Irish Women Write the Hunt." In *Animals in Irish Literature*, edited by Kathryn Kirkpatrick and Borbála Faragó, 26–41. Palgrave Macmillan, 2015.

Laffan, Brigid. "Chapter 5: Ireland and the European Union." In *Ireland on the World Stage*, edited by William Crotty and David E. Schmitt, 83–94. Longman, 2002.

Laird, Heather, ed. *Daniel Corkery's Cultural Criticism, Selected Writings*. Cork University Press, 2013.

Lambert, David, and Alan Lester. "Introduction: Imperial Spaces, Imperial Subjects." In *Colonial Lives Across the British Empire: Imperial Careering in the Long Nineteenth Century*, edited by David Lambert and Alan Lester, 1–31. Cambridge University Press, 2006.

Langford, Michael. *The Story of Photography*. Focal, 1980.

Lawlor, Chris. "From a Spark to a Firebrand: Feagh Mac Hugh O'Byrne." *History Ireland* 21, no. 5 (2013): 20–23.

Leonard, Liam. *The Environmental Movement in Ireland*. Springer, 2008.

Lennon, Joseph. *Irish Orientalism: A Literary and Intellectual History*. Syracuse University Press, 2004.

Lentin, Ronit. "Asylum Seekers, Ireland, and the Return of the Repressed." *Irish Studies Review* 24, no. 1 (2016): 21–34.

Lentin, Ronit, and Robbie McVeigh. *After Optimism? Ireland, Racism, and Globalisation*. Metro Éireann, 2006.

Lerner, Steve. *Sacrifice Zones: The Front Lines of Toxic Chemical Exposure in the United States*. MIT Press, 2010.

Lim, Bliss Cua. *Translating Time: Cinema, the Fantastic, and Temporal Critique*. Duke University Press, 2009.

Linehan, Denis. "Irish Empire: Assembling the Geographical Imagination of Irish Missionaries in Africa." *Cultural Geographies* 21, no. 3 (2014): 429–47.

Lloyd, David. *Irish Times: Temporalities of Modernity*. Keough-Naughton Institute for Irish Studies, University of Notre Dame/Field Day, 2008.

Lloyd, David. *Irish Culture and Colonial Modernity, 1800–2000: The Transformation of Oral Space*. Cambridge University Press, 2011.

Long, Maebh. *Assembling Flann O'Brien*. Bloomsbury, 2014.

Loyal, Steven. *Understanding Immigration in Ireland: State, Capital, and Labour in a Global Age*. Manchester University Press, 2011.

Lynch, Suzanne. "Choctaw Generosity to Famine Ireland Saluted by Varadkar." *Irish Times*, March 13, 2018. https://www.irishtimes.com/news/ireland/irish-news/choctaw-generosity-to-famine-ireland-saluted-by-varadkar-1.3424542.

Mac Giolla Chríost, Diarmait. *The Irish Language in Ireland: From Goídel to Globalisation*. Routledge, 2005.

MacLaughlin, Jim. *Travellers and Ireland: Whose Country, Whose History?* Cork University Press, 1995.

Maginn, Christopher. *"Civilizing" Gaelic Leinster: The Extension of Tudor Rule in the O'Byrne and O'Toole Leaderships*. Four Courts, 2005.

Mamdani, Mahmood. *Neither Settler nor Native: The Making and Unmaking of Permanent Minorities*. Harvard University Press, 2020.

Manning, Maurice and Moore McDowell. *Electricity Supply in Ireland: The History of the ESB*. Gill and MacMillan, 1984.

Massey, Doreen. *For Space*. Sage, 2005.

Massey, Doreen. *World City*. Polity, 2007.

Mathews, P. J. *Revival: The Abbey Theatre, Sinn Féin, the Gaelic League, and the Co-operative Movement*. University of Notre Dame with Field Day, 2003.

Maxwell, Richard, and Toby Miller. *Greening the Media*. Oxford University Press, 2012.

McCarthy, Conor. *Modernisation, Crisis and Culture in Ireland, 1969–1992*. Four Courts, 2000.

McClintock, Anne. *Imperial Leather: Race, Gender, and Sexuality in the Colonial Contest*. Routledge, 1995.

McDermott, Veronica. *Going Nuclear: Ireland, Britain, and the Campaign to Close Sellafield*. Irish Academic Press, 2008.

McGreevy, Ronan. "Irish People Donate €2.5m to Native American Tribe Devastated by Coronavirus." *Irish Times*, November 20, 2020. https://www.irishtimes.com/news/ireland/irish-news/irish-people-donate-2-5m-to-native-american-tribe-devastated-by-coronavirus-1.4414963.

McKibben, Sarah E. "*An Béal Bocht*: Mouthing Off at National Identity." *Éire-Ireland* 38, nos. 1–2 (2003): 37–53.

McLeish, Val. "Sunshine and Sorrows: Canada, Ireland, and Lady Aberdeen." In *Colonial Lives Across the British Empire: Imperial Careering in the Long Nineteenth Century*, edited by David Lambert and Alan Lester, 257–84. Cambridge University Press, 2006.
Merchant, Carolyn. *The Death of Nature: Women, Ecology, and the Scientific Revolution*. HarperCollins, 1983.
Micks, William L. *An Account of the Constitution, Administration, and Dissolution of the Congested Districts Board for Ireland from 1891 to 1923*. Eason & Sons, 1925.
Mohanty, Chandra Talpade. *Feminism Without Borders: Decolonizing Theory, Practicing Solidarity*. Duke University Press, 2003.
Molloy, Matt. "Biography." Accessed May 23, 2025. http://www.mattmolloy.com/matt-molloy.
Monaghan, Patricia. *The Encyclopedia of Celtic Mythology and Folklore*. Facts on File, 2004.
Morash, Christopher. *A History of Media in Ireland*. Cambridge University Press, 2010.
Morris, Carol. "*The Bray House*: An Irish Critical Utopia," *Etudes Irlandaises* 21, no. 1 (1996), 127–40.
Mulligan, Amy C. "Landscape and Literature in Medieval Ireland." In *A History of Irish Literature and the Environment*, edited by Malcolm Sen, 33–51. Cambridge University Press, 2022.
Naughton, Adrian. "'Nádúir-fhilíocht na Gaedhilge' and Flann O'Brien's Fiction." In *"Is It About a Bicycle?" Flann O'Brien in the Twenty-First Century*, edited by Jennika Baines, 83–97. Four Courts, 2011.
Naughton, Adrian. "'More of your fancy kiss-my-hand': A Further Note on Brian O'Nolan's *Nádúir-fhilíocht na Gaedhilge.*" *The Parish Review: Journal of Flann O'Brien Studies* 1, no. 2 (2013): 11–23.
Ní Dhuibhne, Éilís. *The Bray House*. Attic, 1990.
Ní Ghlacáin, Doireann. *Seán Ó Riada—Mo Sheanathair*. Produced by TG4. December 26, 2021. https://www.tg4.ie/en/player/categories/top-documentaries/?series=Se%C3%A1n%20%C3%93%20Riada%20-%20Mo%20Sheanathair&genre=Faisneis.
"Nightmare for the Rossport Five and Their Families." *The Late Late Show*, hosted by Pat Kenny, September 2, 2005. Produced by RTÉ. Prog. ID IH68662. RTÉ Archives.
Nixon, Rob. *Slow Violence and the Environmentalism of the Poor*. Harvard University Press, 2011.
Nolan, Val. "'All of Ireland had been wiped out': Irish Nuclear Anxiety and Éilís Ní Dhuibhne's The Bray House." *Irish University Review* 51, no. 2 (2021): 247–62.

O'Brien, Flann. *The Third Policeman*. Dalkey Archive, [1967] 1999.
O'Brien, Harvey. "Advocating Advocacy: The Protest Paradigm of Documentary Representation—*Meeting Room* (2010) and *The Pipe* (2010)." *Estudios Irlandeses* 6 (2011): 221–24.
O'Brien, Harvey. *The Real Ireland: The Evolution of Ireland in Documentary Film*. Manchester University Press, 2004.
O'Brien, Sorcha. *Powering the Nation: Images of the Shannon Scheme and Electricity in Ireland*. Irish Academic Press, 2017.
Ó Canainn, Tomás. *Seán Ó Riada: His Life and Work*. Collins, 2003.
O'Connor, Éimear. *Seán Keating: Art, Politics and Building the Irish Nation*. Irish Academic Press, 2013.
O'Connor, Laura. *Haunted English: The Celtic Fringe, the British Empire, and De-anglicization*. Johns Hopkins University Press, 2006.
O'Connor, Maureen. *The Female and the Species: The Animal in Irish Women's Writing*. Peter Lang AG, 2010.
Ó Domhnaill, Risteard. Live Q&A Zoom meeting about *The Pipe* and *Atlantic*. English 230: Introduction to Environmental Literature. Class lecture at the University of Oregon, Eugene, OR, May 20, 2020.
Ó Domhnaill, Risteard, dir. *The Pipe*. Scannáin Inbhear, 2010. DVD.
Ó Drisceoil, Donal. *Peadar O'Donnell*. Cork University Press, 2001.
O'Driscoll, Mervyn. "A 'German Invasion'? Irish Rural Radicalism, European Integration, and Irish Modernisation, 1958–73." *International History Review* 38, no. 3 (2016): 527–50.
Ó Faoláin, Seán. *The Promise of Barty O'Brien*. American National Archives, 1951. DVD.
O'Hearn, Denis. *The Atlantic Economy: Britain, the US, and Ireland*. Manchester University Press, 2001.
Ohlmeyer, Jane. *Making Empire: Ireland, Imperialism, and the Early Modern World*. Oxford University Press, 2023.
Ó Hógartaigh, Margaret. "Nurses and Teachers in the West of Ireland in the Late Nineteenth and Early Twentieth Centuries." In *Framing the West: Images of Rural Ireland, 1891–1920*, edited by Ciara Breathnach, 198–214. Irish Academic Press, 2007.
O'Kelly, Michael J. *Newgrange: Archaeology, Art, and Legend*. Thames & Hudson, 1982.
O'Key, Dominic. "Extinction in Public: Thinking Through the Sixth Mass Extinction, Environmental Humanities, and Extinction Studies." *Environmental Humanities* 15, no. 1 (March 2023): 168–86.
O'Neil, Timothy. "Handing away the Trump Card? Peadar O'Donnell, Fianna Fáil, and the Non-Payment of Land Annuities Campaign, 1926–32." *New Hibernia Review / Iris Éireannach Nua* 12, no. 1 (2008): 19–40.

O'Nolan, Brian. "The Pathology of Revivalism." Flann O'Brien Papers, MS.1997.027, Box 2, Folder 43, John J. Burns Library, Boston College. Copyright © by Brian O'Nolan. Used by permission of Brandt & Hochman Literary Agents, Inc. Any copying or distribution of this text is expressly forbidden. All rights reserved.

Oslund, Karen. *Iceland Imagined: Nature, Culture, and Storytelling in the North Atlantic.* University of Washington Press, 2011.

Ó Riada, Peadar. "Re: research project on Our Musical Heritage radio program." Email received by author, June 12, 2019.

Ó Riada, Seán. *Our Musical Heritage*, edited by Thomas Kinsella; musical editor, Tomás Ó Canainn. Dolmen, 1982.

Ó Súilleabháin, Mícheál. *Ceol Na nUasal: Seán Ó Riada and the Search for a Native Irish Art Music.* Léacht Chomórtha an Riadaigh 15. The Traditional Music Archive and the Traditional Music Society, University College Cork, 2004. Irish Traditional Music Archives, 26508-BK.

Our Musical Heritage. "Episode 1: Sean-nós Singing." Prog. ID: AR0023049. RTÉ Archives. July 7, 1962. 29:50 mins.

Our Musical Heritage. "Episode 2: Sean-nós Singing." Prog. ID: AR0023050. RTÉ Archives. July 21, 1962. 28:50 mins.

Our Musical Heritage. "Episode 3: Sean-nós Singing." Prog. ID: AR0023051. RTÉ Archives. July 28, 1962. 29:05 mins.

Our Musical Heritage. "Episode 4: Sean-nós Singing." Prog. ID: AR0023052. RTÉ Archives. August 4, 1962. 28:00 mins.

Our Musical Heritage. "Episode 5: Piping Part One." Prog. ID: AR0023053. RTÉ Archives. August 11, 1962. 29:50 mins.

Our Musical Heritage. "Episode 6: Piping Part Two." Prog. ID: AR0023054. RTÉ Archives. August 18, 1962. 29:40 mins.

Our Musical Heritage. "Episode 7: Piping Part Three." Prog. ID: AR0023056. RTÉ Archives. August 25, 1962. 29:35 mins.

Our Musical Heritage. "Episode 8: Fiddle." Prog. ID: AR0023057. RTÉ Archives. 1 Sept. 1962. 29:50 mins.

Our Musical Heritage. "Episode 9: Fiddle—Regional Styles." Prog. ID: AR0023058. RTÉ Archives. September 8, 1962. 29:10 mins.

Our Musical Heritage. "Episode 10: Flute." Prog. ID: AR0023062. RTÉ Archives. September 15, 1962. 29:15 mins.

Our Musical Heritage. "Episode 11: Tin Whistle." Prog. ID: AR0023063. RTÉ Archives. September 22, 1962. 29:30 mins.

Our Musical Heritage. "Episode 12: Accordion and Concertina." Prog. ID: AR0023064. RTÉ Archives. September 29, 1962. 29:10 mins.

Our Musical Heritage. "Episode 13: Piano, Harp, Bodhran, Céilí Bands." Prog. ID: AR0023065. RTÉ Archives. October 6, 1962. 29:25 mins.

Our Musical Heritage. "Episode 14: Concluding Talk." Prog. ID: AR0023066. RTÉ Archives. October 13, 1962. 29:30 mins.

Paor, Louis de. "'A scholar manqué'? Further Notes on Brian Ó Nualláin's Engagement with Early Irish Literature." In *Flann O'Brien: Problems with Authority*, edited by Ruben Borg, Paul Fagan, and John McCourt, 189–203. Cork University Press, 2017.

"pasture, n." OED Online, Oxford University Press. Accessed May 23, 2025. www.oed.com/view/Entry/138655.

Paye, Michael. "Beyond a Capitalist Atlantic: Fish, Fuel, and the Collapse of Cheap Nature in Ireland, Newfoundland, and Nigeria." *Irish University Review* 49, no. 2 (2019): 117–34.

Parikka, Jussi. *A Geology of Media*. University of Minnesota Press, 2015.

Pegley, Suzanne M. *The Land Commission and the Making of Ráth Cairn: The First Gaeltacht Colony*. Four Courts, 2011.

Pilkington, Lionel. *Theatre and the State in Twentieth-Century Ireland: Cultivating the People*. Routledge, 2001.

Pilz, Anna. "Narratives of Arboreal Landscapes." In *A History of Irish Literature and the Environment*, edited by Malcolm Sen, 97–114. Cambridge University Press, 2022.

Pine, Richard. *2RN and the Origins of Irish Radio*. Four Courts, 2002.

Pine, Richard. *Music and Broadcasting in Ireland*. Four Courts, 2005.

Potts, Donna. *Contemporary Irish Writing and Environmentalism: The Wearing of the Deep Green*. Palgrave Macmillan, 2018.

Quigley, Mark. "Modernization's Lost Pasts: Sean O'Faolain, *The Bell*, and Irish Modernization Before Lemass." *New Hibernia Review / Iris Éireannach Nua* 18, no. 4 (2014): 44–67.

Regan, John M. *The Irish Counter-Revolution, 1921–1936: Treatyite Politics and Settlement in Independent Ireland*. St. Martin's, 1999.

Reiss, Scott "Tradition and Imaginary: Irish Traditional Music and the Celtic Phenomenon." In *Celtic Modern: Music at the Global Fringe*, edited by Martin Stokes and Philip V. Bohlman, 145–69. Scarecrow, 2003.

Rockett, Kevin, Luke Gibbons, and John Hill. *Cinema and Ireland*. Syracuse University Press, 1988.

The Rolling Wave. Produced by RTÉ. Hosted by Peter Browne. Prog. ID: AR0187624. RTÉ Archives. November 20, 2011. 00:45:03 mins.

The Rolling Wave. Produced by RTÉ. Hosted by Peter Browne. Prog. ID: AR0188345. RTÉ Archives. November 27, 2011. 00:45:00 mins.

The Rolling Wave. Produced by RTÉ. Hosted by Peter Browne. Prog. ID: AR0190248. RTÉ Archives. December 4, 2011. 00:46:53 mins.

The Rolling Wave. Produced by RTÉ. Hosted by Peter Browne. Prog. ID: AR0191808. RTÉ Archives. December 11, 2011. 00:45:21 mins.

The Rolling Wave. Produced by RTÉ. Hosted by Peter Browne. Prog. ID: AR0192122. RTÉ Archives. December 18, 2011. 00:47:55 mins.
The Rolling Wave. Produced by RTÉ. Hosted by Peter Browne. Prog. ID: AR0182660. RTÉ Archives. January 8, 2012. 00:46:36 mins.
The Rolling Wave. Produced by RTÉ. Hosted by Peter Browne. Prog. ID: AR0182905. RTÉ Archives. January 15, 2012. 00:45:39 mins.
The Rolling Wave. Produced by RTÉ. Hosted by Peter Browne. Prog. ID: AR0183177. RTÉ Archives. January 22, 2012. 00:46:23 mins.
The Rolling Wave. Produced by RTÉ. Hosted by Peter Browne. Prog. ID: AR0183524. RTÉ Archives. January 29, 2012. 00:45:56 mins.
The Rolling Wave. Produced by RTÉ. Hosted by Peter Browne. Prog. ID: AR0183651. RTÉ Archives. February 5, 2012. 00:47:07 mins.
The Rolling Wave. Produced by RTÉ. Hosted by Peter Browne. Prog. ID: AR0184131. RTÉ Archives. February 12, 2012. 00:45:36 mins.
The Rolling Wave. Produced by RTÉ. Hosted by Peter Browne. Prog. ID: AR0184425. RTÉ Archives. February 19, 2012. 00:46:28 mins.
The Rolling Wave. Produced by RTÉ. Hosted by Peter Browne. Prog. ID: AR0184703. RTÉ Archives. February 26, 2012. 00:48:48 mins.
Rouse, Sarah. *Into the Light: An Illustrated Guide to the Photographic Collections in the National Library of Ireland.* National Library of Ireland, 1998.
Rubenstein, Michael. *Public Works: Infrastructure, Irish Modernism, and the Postcolonial.* University of Notre Dame Press, 2010.
Said, Edward W. *Culture and Imperialism.* Vintage, 1991.
Said, Edward W. *Musical Elaborations.* Columbia University Press, 1991.
Sammon, Patrick J. *In the Land Commission: A Memoir, 1933–1978.* Ashfield, 1997.
Satia, Priya. *Time's Monster: How History Makes History.* Belknap, 2020.
Savage, Robert. "Introducing Television in the Age of Seán Lemass." In *The Lemass Era: Politics and Society in the Ireland of Seán Lemass,* edited by Brian Girvin and Gary Murphy, 191–214. University College Dublin Press, 2005.
Seán Ó Riada Collection/Bailiúchán Sheáin Uí Riada. Ca. 1913–81. University College Cork Archives, Cork.
Sen, Malcolm and Julie McCormick Weng, editors. *Race in Irish Literature and Culture.* Cambridge University Press, 2024.
Shiel, Michael J. *The Quiet Revolution: The Electrification of Rural Ireland, 1946–1976.* O'Brien, 1984.
Shiel, Michael J. "Electricity for Social Development in Ireland." In *The Challenge of Rural Electrification: Strategies for Developing Countries,* edited by Douglas F. Barnes, 293–312. Resources for the Future, 2007.
Shtob, Daniel, and Jordan Fox Besek. "Environmental Precedent: Foregrounding the Environmental Consequences of Law in Sociology." *Sociological Forum* 36, no. 3 (2021): 712–34.

Siemens Schuckert, "Power Station: General Description of the Electrical Part." *Progress on the Shannon*, no. 11 (August 1929). National Library of Ireland, Dublin, K30.
Siggins, Lorna. *Once upon a Time in the West: The Corrib Gas Controversy*. Transworld Ireland, 2010.
Simpson, Leanne Betasomasake. *As We Have Always Done: Indigenous Freedom Through Radical Resistance*. University of Minnesota Press, 2017.
Siskin, Clifford. "Textual Culture and the History of the Real." *Textual Cultures* 2, no. 2 (Autumn 2007): 118–30.
"Sliabh na mBan." Cranford Publications, August 3, 2003. https://www.cranfordpub.com/langan/Sliabh_na_mBan.htm.
Slominksi, Tes. *Trad Nation: Gender, Sexuality, and Race in Irish Traditional Music*. Wesleyan University Press, 2020.
Smith, David M. "'I Thought I Was Landed!': The Congested Districts Board and the Women of Western Ireland." *Éire-Ireland* 31, nos. 3–4 (1996): 209–27.
Smyth, Gerry. *The Novel and the Nation: Studies in the New Irish Fiction*. Pluto, 1997.
Smyth, Sara. "Tuke's Connemara Album." In *Framing the West: Images of Rural Ireland, 1891–1920*, edited by Ciara Breathnach, 29–47. Irish Academic Press, 2007.
Starosielski, Nicole. *The Undersea Network*. Duke University Press, 2015.
Sterne, Jonathan. *The Audible Past: Cultural Origins of Sound Reproduction*. Duke University Press, 2003.
Stokes, Martin. "Introduction: Ethnicity, Identity, and Music." In *Ethnicity Identity and Music. The Musical Construction of Place*, edited by Martin Stokes, 1–27. Berg, 1994.
Sweeney, Eamonn. *Down Down Deeper and Down: Ireland in the 70s and 80s*. Gill & Macmillan, 2010.
Synge, J. M. *The Aran Islands*. John W. Luce, [1907] 1911.
Synge, J. M. *My Wallet of Photographs: The Collected Photographs of J. M. Synge*. Dolmen, 1971.
Synge, J. M. *Travelling Ireland: Essays, 1898–1908*. Edited by Nicholas Grene. Lilliput, 2009.
Taaffe, Carol. *Ireland Through the Looking-Glass: Flann O'Brien, Myles na gCopaleen, and Irish Cultural Debate*. Cork University Press, 2008.
Taylor, Colleen. *Irish Materialisms: The Nonhuman and the Making of Colonial Ireland, 1690–1830*. Oxford University Press, 2024.
Townsend, Sarah. "Porcine Pasts and Bourgeois Pigs: Consumption and the Irish Counterculture." In *Animals in Irish Literature*, edited by Kathryn Kirkpatrick and Borbála Faragó, 55–74. Palgrave Macmillan, 2015.

Tlostanova, Madina. "Transcending the Human/Non-Human Divide: The Geo-politics and Body-politics of Being and Perception, and Decolonial Art." *Journal of Theoretical Humanities* 22, no. 2 (2017): 25–37.
Tuck, Eve. "Suspending Damage: A Letter to Communities." *Harvard Educational Review* 79, no. 3 (Fall 2009): 409–27.
Tymoczko, Maria. *Translation in a Postcolonial Context: Early Irish Literature in English Translation*. St. Jerome, 1999.
Voyles, Traci Brynne. *Wastelanding: Legacies of Uranium Mining in Navajo Country*. University of Minnesota Press, 2015.
Wall, Eamonn. *Writing the Irish West: Ecologies and Traditions*. University of Notre Dame Press, 2011.
Walsh, John. "The Politics of Educational Expansion." In *The Lemass Era: Politics and Society in the Ireland of Seán Lemass*, edited by Brian Girvin and Gary Murphy, 146–65. University College Dublin Press, 2005.
Walter, Bronwen. *Outsiders Inside: Whiteness, Place, and Irish Women*. Routledge, 2001.
Welch, Robert, ed. *The Oxford Companion to Irish Literature*. Clarendon, 1996.
West, John F. *Faroese Folk-Tales and Legends*. Shetland, 1980.
Wenzel, Jennifer. *The Disposition of Nature: Environmental Crisis and World Literature*. Fordham University Press, 2019.
White, Harry. *The Keeper's Recital: Music and Cultural History in Ireland, 1770–1970*. University of Notre Dame Press in association with Field Day, 1998.
Wightman, Beth. "Lost in Space: Geography, Architecture and Culture in Éilís Ní Dhuibhne's *The Bray House*." *Space and Culture* 13, no. 2 (2010): 164–77.
Wills, Clair. *That Neutral Island: A Cultural History of Ireland During the Second World War*. Belknap, 2007.
Wilson, Sheena. "Gendering Oil: Tracing Western Petrosexual Relations." In *Energy Humanities: An Anthology*, edited by Imre Szeman and Dominic Boyer, 269–84. Johns Hopkins University Press, 2017.
Young, Robert J. C. *Colonial Desire: Hybridity in Theory, Culture and Race*. Routledge, 1995.

INDEX

Note: Italicized page numbers refer to illustrations.

Aalen, Frederick H. A., 38
Aarhus Convention, 9–10
Aberdeen, Lady: *Lord and Lady Aberdeen with Nurse, Outside House at Geesala, Ballina, Co. Mayo* (CDB), *34*, 35–36; picturesque aesthetics and modernization projects, 73–74
Abram, David, 229n1
activists and activism: Moore, Christy, 137, 144, 145, 158; music and, 144–45; women and, 190, 192, 202–11. *See also* environmental justice movements; IRA (Irish Republican Army); *Pipe, The* (Ó Domhnaill); Shell-to-Sea activism
Act of Union of 1801, 58, 137, 145
aesthetic forms. *See Third Policeman, The* (O'Brien)
Alaimo, Stacy, 94, 98, 190, 217
Alder-Nissen, Rebecca, 173
Allegories of the Anthropocene (DeLoughrey), 7–8
Allen, Robert, 9
alternative modernities, 4, 6, 11, 221; *The Bray House* and, 170, 172, 174, 179–82, 186; Congested Districts Board photography and, 51, 55; *Our Musical Heritage* and, 125, 126–36, 145; *The Pipe* and, 197, 198; *The Third Policeman* and, 67, 80, 99
ancient Celtic people: conceptions of, 20–21; idealized poverty, 72, 78; influences of, 154, 155, 164, 178–79, 181–82, 187; modernization and, 37
Anglo-Irish Agreement of 1985, 161
Anglo-Irish Ascendancy, 37–38

Anglo-Irish Free Trade Agreement, 107
Anglo-Irish settler class, 36–37, 148
Anglo-Irish Trade War, 19, 75
Anglo-Irish Treaty of Independence (1921), 66, 111
Angus, Siobhan, 41, 225
Anthropocene, 7–8, 152
apocalyptic future. *See Bray House, The* (Ní Dhuibhne)
Aran Islands, 48–50, 72
Aran Islands, The (Synge), 48–50
archaeology. *See Bray House, The* (Ní Dhuibhne)
Ardnacrusha hydroelectric power station, 110, 158, 245n20
Arendt, Hannah, 131
Armchair Time-Traveller, The (Reidy), 117–18
Arrears of Rent Act of 1882, 38
arts. *See* film and cinema; literature; music; painters; photography; poetry and poets; stage productions
Arvin, Maile, 154–55, 172, 175, 183
assertion of agency. *See* activists and activism
assisted emigration, 38–39, 43
Atlantic (Ó Domhnaill), 189
atomic energy. *See* nuclear energy and technology
"Atomic Theory," from *The Third Policeman*, 94, 98
Attic Press, 222

baile (village), 40, 44. *See also* clachan system
Bakhtin, Mikhail, 68

285

Bal, Mieke, 25, 29
Balfour, Arthur, 18, 38–39
Ballina, Co. Mayo, 34, 35–36
Ballinaboy, Co. Mayo, 188. See also *Pipe, The* (Ó Domhnaill)
Balsom, Erika, 216
Barad, Karen, 98
Barrios-O'Neill, Danielle, 190
Barthes, Roland, 64
Bauman, Zygmunt, 15, 224
Baylis, Gail, 29
An Béal Bocht (na gCopaleen), 76
Beattie, Seán, 57
Beiner, Guy, 131
Belfast Agreement, 223
Bell, Jonathan, 40
Bell, The (music periodical), 112, 113
Benjamin, Walter, 8
Besek, Jordan Fox, 81
Biosemiotics, 11, 90
Bishop, Per (character). See *Bray House, The* (Ní Dhuibhne)
Blasket Islands: *The Bray House*, 165; commodification of Irish culture in, 257n46
Bloody Sunday, 138, 152
Bloom, Luka, 144
BNFL (British Nuclear Fuels Ltd.), 156, 159
boglands and peat, 82–85, 158, 203; extractable resource, bogland as, 86, 158; "technology of its own," 211–17. See also extraction of resources
Bog of Allen, 145
Bolter, Jay David, 16, 20, 92, 193
Booker, Keith, 68
Bord Fáilte Éireann (Tourist Board), 102, 127
Bordwin, Jesse, 254n6
Boswell, John Wittley, 181
Boydell, Brian, 112, 113
Bozak, Nadia, 11, 189, 190, 197, 218
Bradley, Anthony, 37

Bray House, The (Ní Dhuibhne), 20–21, 145, 152–87, 221, 254n6; collapse of neocolonial modernity, inevitable, 185–87; environmental impacts of empire, 152, 154, 160, 163, 168, 170, 181, 183, 186, 187; logics of empire, personal and professional, 164–70; narrating just futures in collapse of neocolonial modernity, 185–87; neocolonial modernity, competing histories of, 155–63; remediation, 20–21, 187; sites of environmental and cultural resilience, 170–85; wastelanding, 155–63; "writing on the wall," reinterpreting, 170–85
Breathnach, Ciara, 27–28, 31, 34–36, 38–39, 43, 52–54, 57, 87, 90
Brereton, Pat, 190, 191
Bresnihan, Patrick, 225
Britain's penal laws, Catholics and, 36–37, 133
British Nuclear Fuels Ltd. (BNFL), 156, 159
broadcasting. See radio; television
Broadcasting Authority Act of 1960, 19, 246n24
Brodie, Patrick, 10, 152, 225
Brown, Kate, 168, 255n24
Brown, Terence, 237n91
Browne, Peter, 143
Bruna, Giulia, 48, 50
Burke, Edmund, 133
"Butcher's Dozen, The" (Kinsella), 138–40, 159
Byrne, Maggie (character). See *Bray House, The* (Ní Dhuibhne)

Cage, John, 111, 113
Cahill, Susan, 254n6
calcium carbonate extraction, 41
Calder Hall (nuclear plant), 156, 159, 160
Caminero-Santangelo, Byron, 9, 226
Canada, 73–74

INDEX   287

Cappagh Village, Co. Galway, 25–28, 32–33, 45; *View of Cappagh Village, Castlerea District, Co. Galway,* 25, 26, 27–28
Carbonell, Isabelle, 190
Carey, Peter, 212
Carnsore Point Nuclear Power Plant, 144, 145, 157, 158
Carroll, Patrick, 164
Carville, Justin, 29, 44, 48, 49, 51–52, 59–62
Cassidy, J. D., 28
Castle, Gregory, 37
Castlebar, Co. Mayo, 38, 39
Castlerea District, Co. Galway: *Frame for a New Concrete House on a Grass Farm in the Castlerea District, Co. Galway* (CDB), 42, *42*; *View of Cappagh Village, Castlerea District, Co. Galway,* 25, 26, 27–28. See also Cappagh Village, Co. Galway
Catholic people and Catholicism: Britain's penal laws and, 36–37, 168–69; Northern Ireland, discrimination against, 159–60
CDB. *See* Congested Districts Board (CDB)
Celtic Tiger, 14, 187, 192, 208, 219, 223; *Our Musical Heritage* and, 105, 136, 143
Ceoltóirí Chualann (musicians), 103, 143
Chieftains (musicians), 103, 137
chieftain system, 180–81
Choctaw Nation, 247n48
Citizenship Referendum of 2004, 223
clachan system: Congested Districts Board's erasure of, 25–65; idealized poverty in *The Third Policeman,* 77–78
Cleary, Joe, 15, 104
climate change, 8, 20, 227; *The Bray House,* 20–21, 145, 152–87, 221, 254n6
Clooneen, Co. Galway, 40, 43

Cloverhill Prison, 188
coffin ships, 38
Cole, Luke W., 9
Comhar Cultúra Éireann, 123
commercial fisheries. *See* fishing industry
Compulsory Acquisition Orders (CAOs), 188
Congested Districts Board (CDB): 1897 Parish Committee Scheme, 34; Irish-speaking people and, 37–38, 64; modernization projects, 25–65; relocation schemes, 18, 37–39, 43, 45, 67, 85; sanitation and hygiene, 30, 34, 34–36, 73, 90–91. *See also* Congested Districts Board Photograph Collection; Irish Land Commission
Congested Districts Board Photograph Collection, 29; *Curing Fish, Downings Pier, Co. Donegal,* 61; *Downings Pier, Co. Donegal,* 57–58, 62, 62–64; *Extensive Marl Beds at Moorehall, North East Corner of Lough Cara, Co. Mayo,* 41; *Fishing Vessels at Sea,* 58, 59; *Frame for a New Concrete House on a Grass Farm in the Castlerea District, Co. Galway,* 42, *42*; *Group Gathered on Downings Pier, Co. Donegal,* 63–64; *Group of Cottages Beside the Sea,* 59, 59–60; *Lord and Lady Aberdeen with Nurse, Outside House at Geesala, Ballina, Co. Mayo,* 34, 35–36; *Two New Holdings in Cloonkeen, Castlebar, Co. Mayo,* 38, 39; *View of Flooded Areas in the Townlands of Clooneen and Knockatee East, Co. Galway,* 40, 43
Connemara: *Connemara Cottages,* 83–85, *84*; music, 142; Tuke Collection, National Photographic Archive, 38–39
Connemara Cottages (Henry), 83–85, *84*
Connolly, Niamh, 56–57
constructive unionism, 32, 36, 58

288 INDEX

Contemporary Irish Writing and Environmentalism: The Wearing of the Deep Green (Potts), 12
Contentious Terrains: Boglands, Ireland, Postcolonial Gothic (Gladwin), 12
Corduff, Mary, 202, 203, 204–5, 206, 207–8, 252n130
Corduff, Willie, 188, 196, 198, 210, 214–15, 252n130, 261n24
Corkery, Daniel, 111
Corrib Pipeline Project, 188–89, 194. See also *Pipe, The* (Ó Domhnaill)
Cosgrave, Liam, 157
Cosgrave, William T., 157
counties. See names of specific counties
Crawford, Kevin, 145
Cromwell, Transplantation of, 199
Crotty, William, 257n47
cultural consciousness: *The Bray House*, 154–55, 178–80, 182–83, 185–87; *The Third Policeman* and, 99
Cumann na nGaedheal party, 66, 67, 157
Curing Fish, Downings Pier, Co. Donegal (CDB), 60–62, 61

Dáil Éireann, 149
Davis, Leith, 121–22, 133–34
Deckard, Sharae, 154, 158, 167, 254n6
DeLoughrey, Elizabeth, 7–8, 227
Del Río, Constanza, 254n6
Denmark, 173, 257n47
Department of Agricultural and Technical Instruction, 87
de Selby (character in *The Third Policeman*), 78, 89–94, 98, 100
de Valera, Éamon, 66, 111, 114, 156, 157
development, 102–51. See also modernization projects
D'Hoker, Elke, 254n6
Dillane, Aileen, 115
Dingle Peninsula: *The Bray House*, 165, 171, 172; commodification of Irish culture in, 257n46; Ó Riada's time in Gaeltachtaí on, 113

displacement. See relocation and land redistribution schemes
Doherty, Johnny, 132
Dolmen Press, 136–37, 138, 140, 141–42, 144, 222
Donegal: commercial fisheries, 56–64; *Curing Fish, Downings Pier, Co. Donegal* (CDB), 60–62, 61; *Downings Pier, Co. Donegal* (CDB), 57–58, 62, 62–64; *Group Gathered on Downings Pier, Co. Donegal*, 63–64; O'Nolan's visits to Gaeltachtaí in, 70
"Donnchadh Bán" (song), 142
Doran, Johnny, 130–31, 142
Down, 137
Downings Pier, Co. Donegal: *Curing Fish, Downings Pier, Co. Donegal* (CDB), 60–62, 61; *Downings Pier, Co. Donegal* (CDB), 57–58, 62, 62–64; *Group Gathered on Downings Pier, Co. Donegal*, 63–64
Drifters (film), 216
Driskill, Qwo-Li, 155
Dún Chaoin (Dunquin), Co. Kerry, 104, 165, 166, 167

Eddie (character). See *Bray House, The* (Ní Dhuibhne)
Edge, Sarah Jane, 63–64
eggs and poultry, 86–87, 133
Egyptian histories, 181
electricity: Electricity Supply Board (ESB), 110, 241n66; hydroelectricity, 107, 110, 157–58, 167; Rural Electrification Project, 110, 202–3, 241n66
Electricity Supply Board (ESB), 110, 241n66
emigration: coerced, 208–9, 223; "coffin ships," 38; erasure of Indigenous Irish traditions and Irish language, 50; poverty, assisted emigration and, 38–39, 43; protectionist policies and, 109; racializing

INDEX 289

aesthetics as justification for, 74. See also assisted emigration
Emmerson, Michael, 117
Enemy Within, The (Friel), 106
energy: green energy industries, 225; hydroelectricity, 107, 110, 157–58, 167; imports, dependence on, 158; peat, 82–85, 158, 203. See also electricity; extraction of resources
Ennis, Seamus, 132
Enterprise Energy Ireland (EEI), 188
environmental consciousness, 12, 69, 70, 76–77, 99, 221, 225–26
environmental development, resisting, 109–16
environmental impacts of empire, 2–3, 5, 7–8, 10–11, 13–15, 17, 21–22, 219–27; *The Bray House* and, 152, 154, 160, 163, 168, 170, 181, 183, 186, 187; *Our Musical Heritage* and, 103, 106, 120; *The Pipe* and, 189, 211, 218; *The Third Policeman* and, 81, 83, 91
environmental justice movements, 8–10; Burren Action Group, 144; Carnsore Point Nuclear Power Plant, 144, 157, 158; Greenpeace, 158; Movement for the Survival of the Ogoni People (MOSOP), 1, 3, 201; music and, 103, 105, 144–45. See also *Pipe, The* (Ó Domhnaill); Shell-to-Sea activism
Erne scheme (hydroelectric power), 157–58
Eurogroup, 219–20
European Broadcasting Union, 110
European Central Bank, 219–20
European classical forms, 114, 115, 127–31, 140–41
European Economic Community (EEC), 107, 110, 161, 173, 257n47
European Union (EU), 4, 206, 219
Extensive Marl Beds at Moorehall, North East Corner of Lough Cara, Co. Mayo (CDB), 41

extraction of resources, 2, 3, 8, 13–14, 21, 219, 221, 225; *The Bray House* and, 157, 170; Congested Districts Board and, 31, 41–42; development rendering material environments into extractable and exploitable natural resources, 97–98; *Extensive Marl Beds at Moorehall, North East Corner of Lough Cara, Co. Mayo* (CDB), 41; Free State initiatives, 74–75, 82–83; gender and, 42–44; hydroelectricity, 107, 110, 157–58, 167; Lemassian modernization and, 106; *Our Musical Heritage* and, 102, 108, 125, 128, 131; peat, 82–85, 158, 203; Victorian era, 13. See also boglands and peat; *Pipe, The* (Ó Domhnaill)

Fahey, Frank, 188
Fáilte Ireland, 102, 127
fallout shelter, 178, 182, 184
famine. See Great Famine of 1845–1848
Fanon, Frantz, 41, 244n9
farming: eggs and poultry, 86–87; *Frame for a New Concrete House on a Grass Farm in the Castlerea District, Co. Galway* (CDB), 42, 42; *A Grass Farm in Graigueachuillaire, Seven Miles North of Tuam, Co. Galway*, 46, 46–48, 47; grass farms, 30–34, 32–33, 42, 42, 43, 46, 46–48, 47; *House on Cloonmore Grass Farm near Tuam, Co. Galway*, 30–34, 32–33, 43; livestock, 90
Faroe Islands, 172–75
FDI (foreign direct investment), 102, 103, 107, 125, 154, 163, 167, 185, 212, 219
Ferguson, James, 2–3
Ferguson, Samuel, 181
Fianna Fáil government, 66, 67, 75, 109, 110, 157
fiction. See *Bray House, The* (Ní Dhuibhne)
Fifteen Dead (Kinsella), 138–41

film and cinema: Irish Film Board, 194, 222; misunderstanding of logistics of, 92–93; *Oisín* (film), 212, 215; *The Pipe* and, 16, 21, 188–218, 194, 221–22, 262n46. See also specific films by title
Finucane, Pat, 159
Fionn Mac Cumhaill (mythical story), 212
fishing industry: *Curing Fish, Downings Pier, Co. Donegal* (CDB), 60–62, 61; Donegal, commercial fisheries, 56–64; *Downings Pier, Co. Donegal* (CDB), 57–58, 62, 62–64; *Fishing Vessels at Sea* (CDB), 58, 59; gendered labor of commercial fisheries, 56–64; *Group Gathered on Downings Pier, Co. Donegal*, 63–64; photography, power and progress in gendered labor, 56–64; *The Pipe* and, 214–17; shellfish, 214–15; whaling, 172–74, 176, 186
Fishing Vessels at Sea (CDB), 58, 59
FitzGerald, Garret, 161, 256n35
Flaherty, Robert, 191
Flannery, Eóin, 12, 209
Flight of the Earls, 181
focalizations in photographs: double focalization, 25–31, 33, 35–36, 52–56, 62; external, 26–28, 30–31, 35, 39, 42–43, 45–48, 50, 52–53, 55, 58–64; internal, 27, 28, 35, 45, 52–53, 55–56, 60, 62, 64
foreign aid, dependence on, 125
foreign direct investment (FDI), 102, 103, 107, 125, 154, 163, 167, 185, 212, 219
fossil fuels, dependence on, 167, 185. See also boglands and peat; extraction of resources; liquified natural gas (LNG) pipelines; *Pipe, The* (Ó Domhnaill); Shell E&P Ireland
Foster, Sheila R., 9
Foucault, Michel, 61, 62
Fourth-World cinema, 11, 189
"Fox and Hounds" (Ó Riada), 134

"Fox Chase, The," 132–35
"Foxhunter's Reel, The," 132, 134, 135
fox hunting, music about, 132–35
Frame for a New Concrete House on a Grass Farm in the Castlerea District, Co. Galway (CDB), 42, 42
Free State. See Irish Free State
French alliance with United Irishmen, 124–25, 137
French Revolution, influence of, 137
Friel, Brian, 103, 104, 106–8, 146–48, 150; *The Enemy Within* (play), 106; *Grania* (unrealized project with Ó Riada), 106–8, 146–48, 150

Gaelic League, 111
Gael Linn, 113
Gaeltachtaí (Irish-speaking communities). See Irish-speaking people and Gaeltachtaí (Irish-speaking communities)
Galway: *Frame for a New Concrete House on a Grass Farm in the Castlerea District, Co. Galway* (CDB), 42, 42; *A Grass Farm in Graigueachuillaire, Seven Miles North of Tuam, Co. Galway*, 46, 46–48, 47; *House of Mrs Bridget Kelly, Lisvalley Vesey, near Tuam, Co. Galway*, 54, 54–56; *House on Cloonmore Grass Farm near Tuam, Co. Galway*, 30–34, 32–33, 43; *View from the New Dwelling House of Mrs Bridget Kelly, Lisvalley Vesey, near Tuam, Co. Galway*, 51, 51–54; *View of Cappagh Village, Castlerea District, Co. Galway*, 25, 26, 27–28; *View of Congested Village of Graigue, Co. Galway, from Where Migrants Were Taken to Holdings in Graigueachuillaire*, 43–45, 44; *View of Flooded Areas in the Townlands of Clooneen and Knockatee East, Co. Galway* (CDB), 40, 43

INDEX   291

Gardaí (Irish police), 192–93, 195–98, 197, 200–201, 212
gender roles and hierarchies, 31–32, 60–61, 105, 116, 190, 206; *The Bray House* and, 154–55; commercial fisheries, power and progress in gendered labor of, 56–64; feminized traditions and masculinized modernity, 103, 105–6, 120–22; hierarchies of progress: developing gendered and classed views of modernity, 30–46; hunting metaphors, 132–33; inversion of gender and class roles, 43–45; metaphors, 119–23, 132–33, 166; modernization narratives, 203, 211; music and gender hierarchies/metaphors, 119–23; *The Pipe* and, 190, 192, 202–11, 215; representations of tradition, 14; subordinated gender roles of women, 86–87. See also women
"Get to the Point" (concert), 144
Ghosh, Amitav, 171
Gibbons, Luke, 64, 127, 191, 211
Girvin, Brian, 109
Gladwin, Derek, 12, 82, 214
Glenamoy River, 214
Glór Na hAoise: Songs of Solidarity and Resistance, 144–45
Gold in the Grass (film), 191
Good Friday Agreement, 161, 223
Graigue, Co. Galway, *View of Congested Village of Graigue, Co. Galway, from Where Migrants Were Taken to Holdings in Graigueachuillaire*, 43–45, 44
Graigueachuillaire, Co. Galway: *A Grass Farm in Graigueachuillaire, Seven Miles North of Tuam, Co. Galway*, 46, 46–48, 47; *View of Congested Village of Graigue, Co. Galway, from Where Migrants Were Taken to Holdings in Graigueachuillaire*, 43–45, 44
Grania (unrealized project by Friel and Ó Riada), 106–8, 146–48, 150

grass farms, 30–34, 32–33, 42, 42, 43, 46, 46–48, 47
Great Acceleration, 152
Great Famine of 1845–1848, 37, 38, 79, 247n48
green energy industries, 225
Green-Lewis, Jennifer, 27
Greenpeace, 158
Gregory, Lady, 37
Grierson, John, 216
grindadráp whaling tradition, 172–74, 176, 186
Group of Cottages Beside the Sea (CDB), 59, 59–60
Grusin, Richard, 16, 20, 92, 193
Guelke, Adrian, 140

Hand, Derek, 154, 254n6
Hanly, Mick, 137
Hardebeck, Carl, 149
Harding, Sandra, 15, 190, 202, 205
Harrington, Maura, 198, 203, 204, 206, 207, 208
Harvest of the Rich, The (film), 191
Hayes, Martin, 143
H Block (music album), 137, 138, 144
Heaney, Seamus, 103, 104, 139, 144, 252n130
Henry, Paul, 82–85; *Connemara Cottages*, 83–85, 84
hierarchies: inverting hierarchical imperial logics in postcolonial Ireland, 117–26; photography, hierarchies of progress, 30–46. See also gender roles and hierarchies
Higgins, Michael D., 219
Holt, Jennifer, 225
Home Rule Act of 1948, 173
Home Rule movement, 32, 58, 74
Hopper, Keith, 68, 69, 85
Horgan, John, 110–11
House of Mrs Bridget Kelly, Lisvalley Vesey, near Tuam, Co. Galway, 54, 54–56

292　INDEX

House on Cloonmore Grass Farm near Tuam, Co. Galway, 30–34, 32–33, 43
Huggan, Graham, 5, 37
Hughes, Helen, 195
hunting, music about, 132–35
Hutchinson, Pearse, 103
Hyde, Douglas, 111
hydroelectricity, 107, 110, 157–58, 167
hygiene and sanitation: description in *The Third Policeman*, 90–91; modernization and, 30, 34, 34–36, 73, 90–91. *See also* nurses and nursing programs

IDA (Irish Development Authority), 127
idealized representations. *See* romanticized representations
Iheka, Cajetan, 11, 119, 190, 195
immigration policies, anti-Black, 223
imperfect media, 11, 119, 195
Indigenous populations, 75, 113–14, 116; feminist scholarship, 172; Russian folk music, 117–18; sovereignty, understandings of, 172. *See also* Irish-speaking people and Gaeltachtaí (Irish-speaking communities)
industrialization projects, 66, 82
infrastructure. *See* roads and road building, symbolism of
Inishmaan, Aran Islands, 49–50
innovation, land reforms and, 72
Intergovernmental Panel on Climate Change, 152
international economic and security alliances. *See Bray House, The* (Ní Dhuibhne)
International Monetary Fund, 220
IRA (Irish Republican Army), 159–60
Ireland and Ecocriticism: Literature, History, and Environmental Justice (Flannery), 12
Irish Agricultural Organization Society, 87
Irish Chiefs, 180–81

Irish Development Authority (IDA), 127
Irish Film Board, 194, 222
Irish Free State: *The Bray House* and, 157, 184; establishment of, 66; land reforms, 71–72, 97, 221; modernization projects, 109–11; representations of idealized poverty, 66–101
Irish Industries Association (IIA), 36
Irish Land Commission, 71–73, 78, 93; effort to revive traditional ways, 110–12; relocation and land redistribution schemes, 66, 67, 71, 74, 85, 86, 110; roads and, 78
Irish Materialisms (Taylor), 11–12
Irish Parliamentary Party, 39
Irish Sea, nuclear plants and, 156, 160, 162
Irish-speaking people and Gaeltachtaí (Irish-speaking communities), 2, 16, 19, 20; *The Bray House* and, 176–77; Congested Districts Board (CDB) and, 37–38, 64; depictions as developmentally behind, 191–92; erasure of, 67, 97; Ogham writing, 178–82, 184, 186; oppression of, 177; *Our Musical Heritage* and, 16, 19–21, 102–51, 220–22, 244n1, 252nn129–30, 253n151; relocation of, 37–38; representations of, 66–101; "Tráchtas ar Nádúirfhilíocht na Gaedhilge," 70–71, 73, 76–77, 81, 88–89, 93, 98–99; 2RN and, 110–12. *See also* modernization projects; *Pipe, The* (Ó Domhnaill)
Irish Times, The, 126, 134, 145, 147, 161
Irish traditional music, 102, 112, 114, 118; alternative modernities in Irish traditional music, 126–36; definition, 118–19; fundamental elements and patterns of, 128–30, 150–51; pasture comparison, 119–21, 123, 132. *See also Our Musical Heritage* (Ó Riada)
Irish Travellers (Mincéirí/Pavee), 130–31, 222, 224
Irish World Music Academy, University of Limerick, 143

INDEX   293

John Bull, 95, 208–9
Joyce, James, 68

Karen (character). See *Bray House, The* (Ní Dhuibhne)
Karl (character). See *Bray House, The* (Ní Dhuibhne)
Keane, Damien, 103
Kelly, Bridget: *House of Mrs Bridget Kelly, Lisvalley Vesey, near Tuam, Co. Galway,* 54, 54–56; *View from the New Dwelling House of Mrs Bridget Kelly, Lisvalley Vesey, near Tuam, Co. Galway,* 51, 51–54
Kelly, Patrick, 132
Kennedy, John F., 139, 140, 141, 145
Kenny, Pat, 204
Kerry: commodification of Irish culture in, 257n46; Dún Chaoin (Dunquin), 104, 165, 166, 167
Kinsella, Thomas, 103, 104, 136–39, 144, 146
Kirkpatrick, Kathryn, 11, 132, 133
Knockatee East, Co. Galway, *View of Flooded Areas in the Townlands of Clooneen and Knockatee East, Co. Galway* (CDB), 40, 43
knowledge and understanding: communal forms of knowledge and lived experience, 186; embodied knowledge, forms of, 172, 174; environmental and cultural, 171–72, 174–76, 179; music, understanding modernity through, 146–51; overdependence on colonial ways of knowing, 89–96; traditional ways of knowing, 176–77. See also cultural consciousness; scientific knowledge

Lady Dudley District Nursing Scheme, 34
Laffan, Brigid, 257n47
Lagerlof, Robin (character). See *Bray House, The* (Ní Dhuibhne)

Laird, Heather, 244n9
Lambert, David, 6, 73
"Lament of Stalker Wallace" (song), 126, 142
Land Act of 1891, 38
Land Act of 1923, 73
Land Act of 1933, 75, 86
Land Act of 1965, 149, 253n149
Land League, 39
landlords and landholders, 37, 40, 98
Land Purchase Act of 1891, 18, 38, 39. See also Congested Districts Board (CDB)
land reform projects: Irish Free State, 71–72, 77, 97, 221; Victorian, 191. See also Congested Districts Board (CDB); Irish Land Commission; specific projects and locations
landscapes: *Connemara Cottages,* 83–85, *84;* as cultural actors in Irish films, 211–12; *Frame for a New Concrete House on a Grass Farm in the Castlerea District, Co. Galway* (CDB), 42, *42; House of Mrs Bridget Kelly, Lisvalley Vesey, near Tuam, Co. Galway,* 54, 54–56; *House on Cloonmore Grass Farm near Tuam, Co. Galway,* 30–34, *32–33, 43; Lord and Lady Aberdeen with Nurse, Outside House at Geesala, Ballina, Co. Mayo* (CDB), 34, 35–36; in *The Pipe,* 210, 210–11, 215–16, 218; *View from the New Dwelling House of Mrs Bridget Kelly, Lisvalley Vesey, near Tuam, Co. Galway,* 51, 51–54; *View of Congested Village of Graigue, Co. Galway, from Where Migrants Were Taken to Holdings in Graigucachuillaire,* 43–45, *44; View of Flooded Areas in the Townlands of Clooneen and Knockatee East, Co. Galway* (CDB), 40, 43. See also boglands and peat; roads and road building, symbolism of
Land Wars, 37, 58, 74, 100

294 INDEX

Late Late Show, The (television program), 204, 205
League of Nations, 110
Lemass, Seán, 20, 102, 123, 156–57, 241n66; media in Lemassian modernity, 106–9; modernization projects, 106–9, 115, 119, 122, 125, 135, 146, 163
Lennon, Joseph, 5, 128, 181
Lentin, Ronit, 223
Lester, Alan, 6, 73
Life for the Soil (film), 191
Lim, Bliss Cua, 31–32, 56
Limerick, University of, 143, 257n47
liquified natural gas (LNG) pipelines, 1, 188. See also *Pipe, The* (Ó Domhnaill)
literature: *The Bray House*, 20–21, 145, 152–87, 221, 254n6; the Troubles and, 138–41. See also poetry and poets
livestock, 90; eggs and poultry, 86–87
Lloyd, David, 39, 40, 66
LNG (liquified natural gas) pipelines, 1, 188. See also *Pipe, The* (Ó Domhnaill)
local resistance movements, 9. See also activists and activism; Shell-to-Sea activism
Lombard, Archbishop (Friel's character), 147–48
Long, Maebh, 86–87, 97
Lord and Lady Aberdeen with Nurse, Outside House at Geesala, Ballina, Co. Mayo (CDB), 34, 35–36
Lough Cara, Co. Mayo, *Extensive Marl Beds at Moorehall, North East Corner of Lough Cara, Co. Mayo* (CDB), 41
Lough Neagh, 156–57
Loyal, Steven, 223
Lucy, Seán, 103
Lynch, Jack, 157
Lynch, Suzanne, 247n48

Mabel (Friel's character), 147–48
MacGonigal, Maurice, 82

MacLaughlin, Jim, 224
Madden, Michael (character). See *Bray House, The* (Ní Dhuibhne)
Making History (play), 146–48, 150
Manchester Guardian, The, 48, 50
Man of Aran (Flaherty), 191
marl beds, 41–42
Marshall Aid Program's Economic Co-Operation Administration (ECA), 192
Marshall Plan, 9
Martin Ross, Violet, 133
Massey, Doreen, 30, 43, 56, 223
Mathews, P. J., 48
Maxwell, Richard, 225
Mayo: *Extensive Marl Beds at Moorehall, North East Corner of Lough Cara, Co. Mayo* (CDB), 41; *Lord and Lady Aberdeen with Nurse, Outside House at Geesala, Ballina, Co. Mayo* (CDB), 34, 35–36; *Two New Holdings in Cloonkeen, Castlebar, Co. Mayo*, 38, 39. See also *Pipe, The* (Ó Domhnaill)
Mayock, Emer, 143
Maze Prison, Co. Down, 137
McCarthy, Conor, 15, 139
McClintock, Anne, 31, 32
McDermott, Veronica, 156
McGarry, Bríd, 204
McGrath, Maureen, 205–6
McGrath, Philip, 188
McGrath, Vincent, 188, 199
McGreevy, Ronan, 247n48
McHughs (characters). See *Bray House, The* (Ní Dhuibhne)
McLaughlin, Dermot, 143
McLeish, Val, 36, 73–74
Meath, relocation of people to, 86
media. See film and cinema; literature; music; painters; photography; poetry and poets; publishers and publishing; stage productions
Menippean satire, *The Third Policeman* as, 66–101

Merchant, Carolyn, 120
Micks, William L., 57
migration within Ireland: commercial fishing labor, 57; 1891 Land Purchase Act, 39; *View from the New Dwelling House of Mrs Bridget Kelly, Lisvalley Vesey, near Tuam, Co. Galway*, 51, 51–54. *See also* relocation and land redistribution schemes
Miller, Liam, 136
Miller, Toby, 225
Mincéirí/Pavee (Irish Travellers), 130, 222, 224
minorities, 223–24, 231n27. *See also* Catholic people and Catholicism; Irish-speaking people and Gaeltachtaí (Irish-speaking communities); Irish Travellers (Mincéirí/Pavee); women
modernization projects: *The Bray House* and, 185; Congested Districts Board, 25–65; hierarchies between modernizing subjects and modernized objects, 96–97; Irish Free State, 109–10; Irish traditional music and, 105; Lady Aberdeen's, 73–74; Lemassian, 115, 119, 122, 125, 135, 146, 163; *The Pipe* and, 193; representations of Irish-speaking communities and, 66–101
Mohanty, Chandra Talpade, 166, 180, 190, 207
Molloy, Matt, 137
Monaghan, John, 200, 204, 213
Montague, John, 103, 136, 139
Montreal Protocol of 1987, 152
Moore, Christy, 137, 144, 145, 158
Morash, Christopher, 246n26
"more-than-human" relationships, 1–2, 6–14, 17, 18, 21, 220, 222, 226, 227, 229n1; bogland's "technology of its own," 211–17; *The Bray House*, 155, 158, 162, 171–72, 175–76, 177, 180, 182, 186, 190; defined, 229n1; *Our Musical Heritage*, 120, 121, 127, 129, 131–35, 145;

The Pipe and, 190, 210–18; *The Third Policeman*, 67, 69–70, 76–77, 82, 85, 88–89, 100
Morrill, Angie, 154–55, 172, 175, 183
Movement for the Survival of the Ogoni People (MOSOP), 1, 3, 201
movies. *See* film and cinema
mud cabins, 90–91
Müller, Monica, 198, 202, 203, 208–10, 210, 211
Mulligan, Amy C., 239n21
multiple modernities, 3, 6–7, 18, 22–23; *The Bray House* and, 21, 155, 170–71, 177, 183, 186, 187; Congested Districts Board and, 18, 29–30, 50, 55, 56, 64–65; defined, 14–15; developing theories of, 13–17; new directions for, 219–27; *Our Musical Heritage* and, 105, 114, 123–27, 129, 131, 136–51; photography, power and agency across multiple modernities, 64–65; *The Pipe* and, 21, 193, 194, 196, 198, 208; power and agency across, 64–65; *The Third Policeman* and, 69–70, 72, 73, 88, 89, 98
multispecies modernities, 12–14, 220, 225–27; *The Bray House* and, 187, 222; defined, 14, 189–90; *The Pipe* and, 16, 21–22, 188–218, 222
Murphy, Gary, 109
music: activism and, 144–45; *The Bell* (periodical), 112, 113; Connemara style, 142; "Donnchadh Bán" (song), 142; European classical, 114, 115; folk music, influence of, 117–18; gender hierarchies/metaphors and, 119–23; harp music, 123; Irish art music, 112; "Lament of Stalker Wallace" (song), 126, 142; "On the Blanket" (song), 137; "Oriental" music, 115–16, 128; printed music industry, 134; Russian folk music, 117–18; "Sliabh na mBan" (song), 123–26, 135, 142, 147; theory, 117–19. *See also* Irish traditional music

na Buachaillí Bána (Whiteboys), 126, 142
na gCopaleen, Myles, 76, 174; *An Béal Bocht*, 76. See also O'Brien, Flann; O'Nolan, Brian (Brian Ó Nualláin)
Nallen, Michael, 203
NATO military bases, 173
natural resources: development rendering material environments into extractable and exploitable natural resources, 97–98; omnium (mythical), 98–100; privatization of, 102, 192; women as, 86–89. See also boglands and peat; extraction of resources; liquified natural gas (LNG) pipelines; *Pipe, The* (Ó Domhnaill)
Naughton, Adrian, 71
neocolonial discourse, 153. See also *Bray House, The* (Ní Dhuibhne)
Newgrange, 178–79, 181, 259n98
new materialism, 11–12
news media coverage of Shell-to-Sea activism, 205–6
Nic Amhlaoibh, Muireann, 143
Ní Dhuibhne, Éilís, 20–21, 145, 152–87, 221
Nixon, Rob, 7, 8, 160, 190
nonhuman interlocutors, 171
Noone, Matthew, 115
Northern Ireland: joint nuclear power station near Lough Neagh, 156–57; Maze Prison, Co. Down, 137; "wastelanding," 155–63, 168, 175, 180, 186. See also Troubles, the
nuclear energy and technology: *The Bray House* and, 20–21, 145, 152–87, 221, 254n6; British Nuclear Fuels Ltd. (BNFL), 156, 159; Calder Hall plant, 156, 159, 160; Carnsore Point Nuclear Power Plant, 144, 157, 158; Irish Sea and, 156, 160, 162; Lough Neagh, joint nuclear power station near, 156–57; Sellafield plant, 156, 158–61, 167, 255n24; threats from, 173;

"wastelanding," 155–63, 168, 175, 180, 186
nurses and nursing programs, 34–36, 73; *Lord and Lady Aberdeen with Nurse, Outside House at Geesala, Ballina, Co. Mayo* (CDB), 34, 35–36

O'Brien, Flann, 193, 238n4. See also na gCopaleen, Myles; O'Nolan, Brian (Brian Ó Nualláin); *Third Policeman, The* (O'Brien)
O'Brien, Harvey, 190–93
O'Brien, Sorcha, 15
O'Byrne, Feagh Mac Hugh, 180
O'Byrne, Margaret Maol, 180–81
Ó Canainn, Tomás, 136
Ó Catháin, Darach, 142
ocean and tides: Aran Islands, 48–50, 72; Atlantic, 189; Faroe Islands, 172–75; *Fishing Vessels at Sea* (CDB), 58, 59; *Group of Cottages Beside the Sea* (CDB), 59, 59–60; Irish Sea, 156, 160, 162; Shell private security guards, 213; *Solitaire* (ship), 199, 200–201. See also Blasket Islands; *Pipe, The* (Ó Domhnaill); Shell-to-Sea activism
O'Connor, Maureen, 11, 87, 132, 133, 154, 171, 254n6
Ó Criomhthain, Tomás, *An tOileánach*, 76
Ó Domhnaill, Risteard: *Atlantic*, 189; *The Pipe*, 16, 21, 188–218, 194, 221–22, 262n46
O'Donnell, Pat, 198–201, 208, 216–18
Ó Drisceoil, Donal, 75
O'Driscoll, Mervyn, 149, 253n149
O'Dwyer, John, 134
Ó Faoláin, Seán, *The Promise of Barty O'Brien* (film), 191–92, 202–3, 212
O'Feersa brothers (characters in *The Third Policeman*), 94–96
Ogham writing, 178–82, 184, 186
Ogoni People, 1, 3, 201

O'Hearn, Denis, 9, 225
Ohlmeyer, Jane, 5
Oisín (film), 212, 215
O'Kelly, Fergus, 246n26
omnium (mythical), 98–100
O'Neil, Terence, 106–7, 156, 157
O'Neill, Hugh (Friel's character), 146–48, 180, 181, 182, 252n140
O'Nolan, Brian (Brian Ó Nualláin), 238n4; master's thesis, 70–71, 73, 76–77, 81, 88, 93, 98–99. *See also* na gCopaleen, Myles; O'Brien, Flann
"On the Blanket" (song), 137
oral traditions. See *Our Musical Heritage* (Ó Riada)
Ordinance Surveys, 41
Ó Riada, Peadar, 143, 244n1
Ó Riada, Seán, 247n51; death of, 138–40; *Grania* (unrealized project with Friel), 106–8, 146–48, 150; *The Irish Times* articles, 126, 134, 145, 147, 161; *Our Musical Heritage*, 16, 19–21, 102–51, 220–22, 244n1, 252nn129–30, 253n151. *See also* Reidy, John
Orientalism, 181; music and, 115–16, 128
Ó Seighin, Micheál, 188, 208
Ó Súilleabháin, Mícheál, 113, 116, 143
Our Musical Heritage (Ó Riada), 16, 19–21, 102–51, 220–22, 244n1, 252nn129–30, 253n151; alternative modernities in Irish traditional music, 126–36; background, 102–6; destabilizing decolonization, 117–26; environmental impacts of empire, 103, 106, 120; inverting hierarchical imperial logics in postcolonial Ireland, 117–26; legacy of, 136–45; Lemassian modernity, media in, 106–9; negotiating place and identity on stage, radio, television, and film, 106–9; new media and modernities, 136–45; onslaught of Western culture, resisting, 109–16; reframing

progress on radio, 126–36; remediation, 20, 103–5, 109, 119, 122, 134; resisting neocolonial environmental development, 109–16; understanding modernity through music, 146–51
Our Story: The Rossport Five, 199, 205–6

painters, 82–85
Paor, Louis de, 70
Parikka, Jussi, 11, 155, 182, 183, 225
Parnell, Charles Stewart, 32, 39
pastoralism, 119–21
Paye, Michael, 190, 206
peat. *See* boglands and peat
Pegley, Suzanne M., 86
perspective. See focalizations in photographs
Philbin, Brendan, 188
photography: *The Aran Islands*, 48–50; commercial fisheries, power and progress in gendered labor of, 56–64; contrasting views of modernized landscape, 46–56; gendered and classed views of modernity, 30–46; hierarchies of progress, 30–46; multiple modernities, power and agency across, 64–65; narrative realities, 27–30; National Photographic Archive, 38–39; rival experiences of modernization, 27–30; Major Ruttledge-Fair, 38–39; smiling in, 64; splintered modernities, 46–56; Tuke Collection, 38–39; Valentine and Sons (photographers), 28; vision for modernized relationships to land, 25–65. *See also* focalizations in photographs
picturesque aesthetics. See *Third Policeman, The* (O'Brien)
pilot whaling, 172–74, 176, 186
Pilz, Anna, 120
Pine, Richard, 104

Pipe, The (Ó Domhnaill), 16, 21, 188–218, *194*, 221–22, 262n46; aerial shots of rural landscape, *194*; documentary film, postcolonial multispecies modernities of, 218; environmental impacts of empire, 189, 211, 218; Gardaí throw protesters off the road, *197*; gendered conflicts and ruptures in a modern society, 202–11; modernity montage, 192–201; Monica Müller walks along turf-lined road, *210*; multispecies interactions in postcolonial modernities, 211–17; national rights of modernizing industries, 192–201; officers laugh as tide permeates Shell's boundary, *213*; opening montage, 195–98; partial views foreground spectral presence of Shell, *200*; partial views register limits of visual representations, *217*; remediation, 19, 193; screenshots from, *194*, *197*, *200*, *210*, *213*, *217*; splintered communities, 202–11
planetary forces, 178–79, 213
Pluck, Sgt. (character in *The Third Policeman*), 94–96
Plunkett, Horace, 36, 39, 54, 74
"plutopia," 168, 186, 255n24
Pobal Chill Chomáin, 188–89, 230n6
Pobal Le Chéile, 189, 230n6
poetry and poets: Irish music in, 103; Kinsella, Thomas, 103, 104, 136–39, 144, 146; Montague, John, 103, 136, 139; "Tráchtas ar Nádúir-fhilíocht na Gaedhilge," 70–71, 73, 76–77, 81, 88–89, 93, 98–99; Yeats, W. B., 37–38, 135
Pogues (musicians), 104
Potts, Donna, 12, 31, 82, 133, 158
poverty: assisted emigration and, 38–39, 43; Congested Districts Board and, 25–65; policing idealized poverty in *The Third Policeman*, 66–101. See also modernization projects
primitive Ireland, *The Aran Islands*, 48–50. See also romanticized representations
printed music industry, 134
progress, myths of, 91, 199. See also modernization projects
Promise of Barty O'Brien, The (film), 191–92, 202–3, 212
"psychogeophysics," 11, 182, 183
publishers and publishing: Attic Press, 222; Dolmen Press, 136–37, 138, 140, 141–42, 144, 222; printed music industry, 134; Skein Press, 222

Quigley, Mark, 15

radio, 14, 17, 19–20, 103; *The Armchair Time-Traveller*, 117–18; Lemassian modernity, media in, 106–9; *Our Musical Heritage* and, 16, 19–21, 102–51, 220–22, 244n1, 252nn129–30, 253n151; *The Rolling Wave* (radio program), 143, 252n129
Raidió Éireann/Radio Telefís Éireann (RTÉ), 110, 113, 123, 246n24, 247n51. See also 2RN (national radio station)
Rebellion of 1798, 125
Reck, Tomás, 126, 142
redemption, conceptions of, 169–70
redistribution of land. See relocation and land redistribution schemes
Regan, John M., 74
Reidy, John, 247n51; *The Armchair Time-Traveller*, 117–18
Reiss, Scott, 143
relocation and land redistribution schemes, 2, 18; CDB and, 37–39, 43, 45; Irish Land Commission, 66, 67, 71, 74, 85, 86, 110. See also assisted emigration
remediation, 22, 221, 226, 227; *The Bray House* and, 20–21, 187; definition, 15–16, 19, 69; developing theories of, 13–17; environmental development,

INDEX   299

100–101; *Our Musical Heritage* and, 20, 103–5, 109, 119, 122, 134; paradoxical dual logic of, 92–93; *The Pipe* and, 19, 193; *The Third Policeman* and, 67, 69, 82, 85, 86, 89, 92–93, 97, 100–101 resources, natural. *See* extraction of resources; fishing industry
revivalist ideology, 20, 174; CDB modernization schemes, 29, 36, 37, 48, 50; idealized poverty as progress, 75–76, 79, 80, 93; oral traditions, 114, 115, 135, 149
River Erne, 157–58
River of Sound, A (BBC television program), 143
roads and road building, symbolism of: modernization, as symbols of, 197; *The Pipe* and, 197–98, 210; *The Third Policeman* and, 77–89. *See also* Congested Districts Board Photograph Collection
Rolling Wave, The (radio program), 143, 252n129
romanticized representations: idealized poverty as progress, 75–76, 79, 80, 93; Irish Development Authority and, 127; policing idealized poverty in *The Third Policeman*, 66–101; used in *The Pipe*, 194
Rossport, Co. Mayo. *See Pipe, The* (Ó Domhnaill)
Rossport Five, 188, 200, 201, 204, 206, 209, 252n130, 261n24
Rossport Solidarity Camp, 189
Royal Commission on Congestion for Ireland (RCCI), 53–54. *See also* Congested Districts Board (CDB)
Royal Dutch Shell, 188
Rubenstein, Michael, 15, 68, 69, 79
Rural Electrification Project, 110, 202–3, 241n66
Ruskin, John, 70
Ruttledge-Fair, Major, 38–39
Ryan, Eamon, 203

Said, Edward W., 5
Sammon, Patrick J., 241n66
Sands, Bobby, 137
Sands, Tommy, 145
Saro-Wiwa, Ken, 1, 145, 201
Satia, Priya, 1, 97, 122, 191
Schoenberg, Arnold, 104, 113, 139
scientific knowledge, 94–95, 98. *See also* hygiene and sanitation; technology
Scott, Walter, 70
seals and seal people myth, 171–72, 175, 186
"Selected Life, A" (Kinsella), 139
Sellafield (nuclear plant), 156, 158–61, 167, 255n24
separatist movement, 32, 58
"September 1913" (Yeats), 135
Shannon, Sharon, 145
Shannon Scheme, 110, 158. *See also* Ardnacrusha hydroelectric power station
Shell E&P Ireland, 5, 188; private security force, 195, 212–13, 213; public relations, 204, 222; *Solitaire* (ship), 199, 200–201; spectral presence of, 198–201. *See also Pipe, The* (Ó Domhnaill)
shellfish, 214–15
Shell-to-Sea activism, 1, 3–4; music and recordings, 144, 145; Rossport Five, 188, 200, 201, 204, 206, 209, 252n130, 261n24. *See also Pipe, The* (Ó Domhnaill)
Shtob, Daniel, 81
Siemens Schuckert, 110
Siggins, Lorna, 204, 208
Simpson, Leanne Betasamosake, 176
Sinnott, Kathy, 203, 206–7
Siskin, Clifford, 16, 19, 67, 69
Skein Press, 222
"Sliabh na mBan" (song), 123–26, 135, 142, 147
Smith, David M., 74, 87

300 INDEX

Smyth, Gerry, 254n6
social class: Anglo-Irish settlers, 37; class and gender expectations, 30–46; inversion of gender and class roles, 43–45; photography, hierarchies of progress, 30–46; promise of social mobility, 35–36, 43, 51, 51–53
Solitaire (ship), 199, 200–201
Somerville, Edith, 133
Sound of Stone: Artists for Mullaghmore, The, 144
Spenser, Edmund, 5, 120, 128
Spillane, John, 145
springs, subterranean, 20, 178–79, 182, 186
stage productions, 108; *The Enemy Within*, 106; *Grania* (unrealized project by Friel and Ó Riada), 106–8, 146–48, 150; *Making History* (play), 146–48, 150
Starosielski, Nicole, 225
stereotypes of Irishness, 165. *See also* romanticized representations
Sterne, Jonathan, 119
Stockhausen, Karlheinz, 113, 114
Stravinsky, Igor, 117–18
Sweden, 257n47; in *The Bray House*, 166–67, 169, 171, 180, 184, 186
Synge, J. M., 48–51, 72, 106

Taaffe, Carol, 70–71
Taylor, Colleen, 11–12, 90, 215
technology: "big tech" and data centers, 225; bogland is a "technology of its own," 211–17; commercial fisheries, 57; extraction of resources, 82; media technologies, 219; tax incentives and, 10. *See also* nuclear energy and technology; *specific topics*
television, 14, 17, 19–20, 103; *The Late Late Show* (television program), 204, 205; Lemassian modernity, media in, 106–9; national television, 107;

A River of Sound (BBC television program), 143
temporalities of struggle, 180–82, 186
Third Policeman, The (O'Brien), 16, 19, 66–101, 108, 122, 165, 174, 177, 195, 197, 211, 221; colonial mindset, perpetuating poverty, 70–77; environmental development, remediating postmodern relations into, 100–101; environmental impacts of empire, 81, 83, 91; infrastructure and picturesque scene of progress from the road, 77–89; limits of decolonization, enacting divisions in two-dimensional spacetime, 96–100; overdependence on colonial ways of knowing, 89–96; poverty, perpetuation as progress, 70–77; remediating postmodern relations into environmental development, 100–101; remediation, 67, 69, 82, 85, 86, 89, 92–93, 97, 100–101
Tiffin, Helen, 5, 37
Tlostanova, Madina, 229n1
Tóibín, Nioclás, 123–24, 142
An tOileánach (Ó Criomhthain), 76
Tone, Wolfe, 124
Topographia Hibernica (Wales), 5
tourism, 49, 104, 165, 176, 257n46; Bord Fáilte Éireann (Tourist Board), 102, 127; Newgrange, 179
Townsend, Sarah, 88
"Tráchtas ar Nádúir-fhilíocht na Gaedhilge" (O'Nolan/O'Brien), 70–71, 73, 76–77, 81, 88, 93, 98–99
Transplantation of Cromwell in 1650, 199
Troubles, the, 20, 221; *The Bray House* and, 152–53, 156, 159–61, 164–65, 182, 185; Irish Republican Army (IRA), 159–60; literary responses to, 138–41; *Our Musical Heritage* and, 104–7, 136–39, 141, 142, 144, 146, 149
Tuam, Galway: *A Grass Farm in Graigueachuillaire, Seven Miles North of*

INDEX 301

Tuam, Co. Galway, 46, 46–48, 47; House of Mrs Bridget Kelly, Lisvalley Vesey, near Tuam, Co. Galway, 54, 54–56; House on Cloonmore Grass Farm near Tuam, Co. Galway, 30–34, 32–33, 43; View from the New Dwelling House of Mrs Bridget Kelly, Lisvalley Vesey, near Tuam, Co. Galway, 51, 51–54
Tuck, Eve, 154–55, 170, 172, 175, 183, 186
Tuke, James Hack, 38–39
Tuke Collection, National Photographic Archive, 38–39
turf cutting, 82–85, 210. See also boglands and peat
Two New Holdings in Cloonkeen, Castlebar, Co. Mayo, 38, 39
2RN (national radio station), 110–11, 245n16. See also Raidió Éireann/Radio Telefís Éireann (RTÉ)
Tymoczko, Maria, 66, 76

Ulysses (Joyce), comparison of The Third Policeman, 68
United Irishmen, 123–25
United Irishwomen, 36
United States, Britain's connections with, 156, 159–63, 167, 169, 185
University of Limerick, 143, 257n47

Valentine and Sons (photographers), 28
"Vertical Man" (Kinsella), 139–40, 144
Victorian Order of Nurses, 36
Victorian society: class and gender expectations, 30–46; hierarchies of progress, 30–46; visual expectations, 18, 27, 30, 48, 53, 56, 65. See also Congested Districts Board (CDB); hygiene and sanitation
View from the New Dwelling House of Mrs Bridget Kelly, Lisvalley Vesey, near Tuam, Co. Galway, 51, 51–54
View of Cappagh Village, Castlerea District, Co. Galway, 25, 26, 27–28

View of Congested Village of Graigue, Co. Galway, from Where Migrants Were Taken to Holdings in Graigueachuillaire, 43–45, 44
View of Flooded Areas in the Townlands of Clooneen and Knockatee East, Co. Galway (CDB), 40, 43
View of the Present State of Irelande, A (Spenser), 5
visual representations. See film and cinema; painters; photography
Vonderau, Patrick, 225
Voyles, Traci Brynne, 162, 168, 186

Wales, Gerald of, 5
Walter, Bronwen, 88, 223–24
wastelanding, 155–63, 168, 175, 180, 186
Welch, Robert John (photographer), 28, 29, 54; A Grass Farm in Graigueachuillaire, Seven Miles North of Tuam, Co. Galway, 46, 46–48, 47; House of Mrs Bridget Kelly, Lisvalley Vesey, near Tuam, Co. Galway, 54, 54–56; House on Cloonmore Grass Farm near Tuam, Co. Galway, 30–34, 32–33, 43; Two New Holdings in Cloonkeen, Castlebar, Co. Mayo, 38, 39; View from the New Dwelling House of Mrs Bridget Kelly, Lisvalley Vesey, near Tuam, Co. Galway, 51, 51–54; View of Cappagh Village, Castlerea District, Co. Galway, 25, 26, 27–28; View of Congested Village of Graigue, Co. Galway, from Where Migrants Were Taken to Holdings in Graigueachuillaire, 43–45, 44
Wenzel, Jennifer, 7, 8, 178, 190, 212, 217
Wexford, 144, 157, 158
whaling tradition, 172–74, 176, 186
Whitaker, T. K., 109
White, Harry, 104, 114
Whiteboys (na Buachaillí Bána), 126, 142
Widgery Report, 138

Wightman, Beth, 154, 254n6
Wills, Clair, 101
Wilson, Sheena, 203
Windrush scandal, 219, 223
Windscale nuclear plant. *See* Sellafield (nuclear plant)
Wiwa, Owens, 1, 145, 201
women, 34; activists, 190, 192, 202–11; Attic Press, 222; commercial fisheries, gendered labor of, 56–64; commercial fisheries, power and progress in gendered labor of, 56–64; dehumanization of feminized labor, 86–88; erasure of women's labor from scenes, 86; *House of Mrs Bridget Kelly, Lisvalley Vesey, near Tuam, Co. Galway*, 54, 54–56; houses as metaphors for, 86, 87–88; Indigenous feminist scholarship, 172; *Lord and Lady Aberdeen with Nurse, Outside House at Geesala, Ballina, Co. Mayo* (CDB), 34, 35–36; metaphors, 86, 87–88, 202; Monica Müller walks along turf-lined road, screenshot from *The Pipe*, 210; music and gender hierarchies/metaphors, 119–23; as natural resources, 86–89; nurses and nursing, 34, 34–36; photography and, 30–46, 34, 35–36, 38–39, 51, 51–64, 54, 86, 210, 233n16; physical hardships of, 87; progress, developing gendered and classed views of modernity, 30–46; promise of social mobility, 35–36, 43, 51, 51–53; Tuke Collection, National Photographic Archive, 38–39; *View from the New Dwelling House of Mrs Bridget Kelly, Lisvalley Vesey, near Tuam, Co. Galway*, 51, 51–54. *See also* gender roles and hierarchies

Women's National Health Association (WNHA) of Ireland, 34, 36

Yeats, Jack B., 48
Yeats, W. B., 37–38, 135
Young, Robert J. C., 224

zones of immunity, 168, 186

RECENT BOOKS IN THE SERIES
Under the Sign of Nature: Explorations in Environmental Humanities

The Ecological Plot: How Stories Gave Rise to a Science
John Macneill Miller

Cli-Fi and Class: Socioeconomic Justice in Contemporary American Climate Fiction
Debra J. Rosenthal and Jason de Lara Molesky, editors

Thoreau's Botany: Thinking and Writing with Plants
James Perrin Warren

Climate Change and Original Sin: The Moral Ecology of John Milton's Poetry
Katherine Cox

The Queerness of Water: Troubled Ecologies in the Eighteenth Century
Jeremy Chow

Toxic Matters: Narrating Italy's Dioxin
Monica Seger

Unsettling Nature: Ecology, Phenomenology, and the Settler Colonial Imagination
Taylor A. Eggan

Basura: Cultures of Waste in Contemporary Spain
Samuel Amago

Narrating the Mesh: Form and Story in the Anthropocene
Marco Caracciolo

Magnificent Decay: Melville and Ecology
Tom Nurmi

Eden's Endemics: Narratives of Biodiversity on Earth and Beyond
Elizabeth Callaway

New Woman Ecologies: From Arts and Crafts to the Great War and Beyond
Alicia Carroll

Of Land, Bones, and Money: Toward a South African Ecopoetics
Emily McGiffin

Novel Cultivations: Plants in British Literature of the Global Nineteenth Century
Elizabeth Hope Chang

Evergreen Ash: Ecology and Catastrophe in Old Norse Myth and Literature
Christopher Abram

Italy and the Environmental Humanities: Landscapes, Natures, Ecologies
Serenella Iovino, Enrico Cesaretti, and Elena Past, editors

Building Natures: Modern American Poetry, Landscape Architecture, and City Planning
Julia E. Daniel

Recomposing Ecopoetics: North American Poetry of the Self-Conscious Anthropocene
Lynn Keller

"The Best Read Naturalist": Nature Writings of Ralph Waldo Emerson
Michael P. Branch and Clinton Mohs, editors

The Sky of Our Manufacture: The London Fog in British Fiction from Dickens to Woolf
Jesse Oak Taylor

Ossianic Unconformities: Bardic Poetry in the Industrial Age
Eric Gidal

Anthropocene Fictions: The Novel in a Time of Climate Change
Adam Trexler

Dancing with Disaster: Environmental Histories, Narratives, and Ethics for Perilous Times
Kate Rigby

Different Shades of Green: African Literature, Environmental Justice, and Political Ecology
Byron Caminero-Santangelo

Reclaiming Nostalgia: Longing for Nature in American Literature
Jennifer K. Ladino

Shakespeare's Ocean: An Ecocritical Exploration
Dan Brayton

William Wordsworth and the Ecology of Authorship: The Roots of Environmentalism in Nineteenth-Century Culture
Scott Hess

www.ingramcontent.com/pod-product-compliance
Lightning Source LLC
Chambersburg PA
CBHW021337230426
43666CB00006B/321